introduction to teaching

consulting editor **Paul Nash** Boston University

introduction to teaching

John F. Ohles Kent State University

random house new york

First Printing

Published in the United States by Random House, Inc., New York, and simultaneously in Canada by Random House of Canada Limited, Toronto.
Library of Congress Catalog Card Number: 72-82045
Manufactured in the United States of America by H. Wolff Book Mfg. Co. Inc.
Typography by Leon Bolognese

to
Shirley M. Ohles

to the teacher

Introduction to Teaching is the result of one instructor's inability to find a satisfactory text for an introductory course in education. Some texts were found wanting because they attempted to present all sides to every argument: they discussed with equal concern all philosophies and all theories. Some joint authorships have been bland presentations that seem to represent an excessive effort to evolve a consensus.

Introduction to Teaching is intended to be used as a textbook in education courses. It is believed that others interested in the schools, the occupation of teaching, the roles of the learner and the expectations placed on youngsters, theories of learning and curriculum, and methods of teaching will find this book informative and interesting.

Introduction to Teaching has been written for students but with the needs and the role of instructors clearly in mind. Teaching is conceived as a manifold and complex process. The task of an introductory text is perceived as providing a philosophical, theoretical, and practical contact with aspects across the breadth of the topic. When a text is concerned with introductory exercises, the instructor is then free to enlarge on the topics; he may emphasize his own strengths in philosophy, theory, or practical experience.

A subject may be organized in many different sequences; those who have examined several texts will have noticed variations on organization, each of which claims unique advantages. The rationale behind the organization of **Introduction to Teaching** is that an advisable approach for a study of teaching is to exploit the teacher's inherent interest in himself as a person and as a professional in the first two chapters with an emphasis on teaching as a function and on the teacher as a person and a functionary. Chapter 3 discusses youngsters, the object of the teaching role. The sequence then moves to a description of the school as a social institution, a historical phenomenon, and a current reality. Chapter 5 centers on the relationships within the school between teachers and administrators, pupils, and other teachers as well as the relationships among the pupil population. The progression moves on from teacher, pupil, and school to the school curriculum, the learning process, and the organizing and execution of the teaching process. The last five chapters are concerned with the crucial matters of a teacher's noninstructional duties, individuals or groups who facilitate instruction, the role of philosophy and theory in teaching, teaching as a profession, and what the future holds for the prospective teacher and education in general.

Instructors may prefer another sequence of topics and should feel free to propose an alternative reading pattern. Chapters are not dependent for understanding on previous chapters; that is one benefit derived from an introductory overview. It should be noted, on the other hand, that certain themes run through the chapters—concepts such as an emphasis on learning outcomes, the complexities of educating others, and a concern for reality and practical information as well as for philosophy and theory. Aspects of teaching overlap as they are related to differing emphases of teaching or to different roles of the teacher; the topics recur in the chapters to meet these requirements for a complete discussion of teaching.

Instructors are encouraged to make use of the "On Your Own" sections. The sections seek to respond to student interests and needs. Students who make use of these sections will have experienced a short course in library techniques and an introduction to educational literature. They will have expressed their beliefs about the social responsibilities of the schools, the nature of children, appropriate concerns of the curriculum, the processes of learning and teaching, and the roles of the teacher; they will have reexamined these beliefs in an exposure to additional information. Instructors may select activities from "On Your Own" to be assigned to their classes.

A book of readings, *Principles and Practice of Teaching: Selected Readings,* is available as a source of supplementary information to enlarge on the philosophical, theoretical, and practical aspects of teaching. An *Instructor's Manual* is available as a source of teaching and evaluation suggestions and resources for instruction.

to the student

The purpose of **Introduction to Teaching** is to acquaint those generally interested in the schools, particularly those considering teaching as a career, with the many facets of teaching. The most important subjects that should be of interest to the student are the process in the classroom and the nature of a teacher's responsibilities and incidental activities. This is the information on which one may determine the selection of a lifetime career. Academic subjects have many uses and means of expression but the study of a profession or vocation is specifically limited to the pursuit of a career.

No book may adequately describe the teaching process any more than a person may appreciate and understand the game of baseball, the processes of politics and management, or the practice of medicine, engineering, or law simply through reading. A book may supplement experience, or personal experience may supplement readings. The student should be seeking reflections of his reading in classroom visitations and observations, through conversations with teachers, and in the student-teaching experience. He should be searching for explanations of teacher reaction, pupil behavior, and classroom processes in his reading references.

This text does not attempt to present the student with everyone's viewpoint, interpretation, or bias. Instead, the author has taken positions in reference to a philosophy, specific theories, and interpretation of actual practices. Because teaching is an art, little about teaching is subject to scientific verification and a highly acceptable set of laws or recipes for action. However, the context is not merely idle speculation or chance opinion but the combination of experience and study of one who has chosen as his career the practice and study of teaching.

Students should challenge what they read in this book at least as much as in any other book. Any text should be a point of departure, not an end in itself. However, challenges should not be phrased in opinions; they ought to lead the student to further reading or an opportunity to test out ideas in a classroom. The student must question all dogmatism, *including his own,* and seek answers that are supported and supportable by a philosophical position, a theoretical concept, and the reality of the world in the classroom.

The "On Your Own" sections are intended to provide an opportunity to pursue a second "course" in the subject "the study of teaching." Many pertinent activities are proposed and questions are raised about the aspects of teaching discussed in the chapter. The student who follows the suggestions in "On Your Own" will have engaged in examining his own philosophical positions. He will know much about educational literature and be able to operate with dispatch and effectiveness in the library. He will be familiar with the content and scope of specialized books in education, psychology, philosophy, and pertinent areas of history, economics, sociology, and management.

Students of education are trying to resolve a series of contradictions that they have recognized from their own experiences in school. They may have seen youngsters humble male giants and obediently follow the directions of petite young ladies. They have been in classes alive with exciting learning experiences and in others smothered in boredom. Faculties have always seemed to be united against challenges from students, parents, and the public, yet there are signs that teachers disagree about philosophy and practices in teaching and about how they should organize and act in their own behalf. Teachers demand that pupils be reasonable in their behavior and moderate in their reactions, yet teachers come into conflict with school boards and engage in strikes and picketing. Many students are seeking to unravel such contradictions in a search for answers to their questions about whether or not teaching should be their career choice.

This book should aid the reader in finding answers to questions and in resolving some of those important problems that are in, of, and about teaching. Combining reading with investigation, participation, and speculation may aid in finding some answers. Combining information and experience is the means to answer any question or to resolve any problem; answers are available to those who truly wish to know.

acknowledgments

The author acknowledges with sincere appreciation the many colleagues and students who have shared with him their experiences and ideas about education, schools, teachers, learners, and learning. Two great teachers have had a particular influence: Dr. C. Gilbert Wrenn, University of Minnesota, and Dr. William H. Burton, Graduate School of Education, Harvard University. Edward W. Bechtel, high school principal in Fergus Falls, Minnesota was of great help to a beginning teacher.

The greatest aid and support in the actual writing of this text has been my wife, Shirley M. Ohles. She has been copy reader, critic, and typist. Her help and encouragement have been indispensable. Assistance is also acknowledged of Paul Nash, Boston University, Leonard Roberts and Mrs. Leonore Hauck of Random House, Inc.

contents

introduction to teaching

1

the nature of teaching

Education is a major enterprise in the United States. There are about forty-five million pupils in public elementary and secondary schools and an additional six million in private institutions. These fifty million youngsters are in schools administered by 125,000 principals and superintendents and in classrooms manned by two million teachers.

The influence of the home is crucial in molding the youngsters who attend school. The kind and degree of public support determines the adequacy of the school plant and instructional materials. School administrators select staffs, provide leadership, and facilitate instruction. But teachers are the keys to the effectiveness of the educational process. Of all the service occupations in this complex society, there is none that directly affects as many individuals or that has the potential for fashioning the future as teaching.

science or art?

The question has been raised as to the nature of teaching: Is it a science or is it an art? This question is not an idle or insignificant one, for the implications are of tremendous importance. If teaching is a science, then its scientific nature can and should be discovered, an organized pattern of operation should be established, and technicians should be trained to operate the program. On the other hand, if teaching is an art, then science may contribute a set of tools and offer suggestions for their use. Final success or failure in an artistic endeavor, however, rests in large part on the ability of individuals to utilize skill and insight in furthering an effective program.

Reason would tell us to search for an educational science. Much as science may threaten our very existence, it does offer abundant security in the belief that certain things about us—those specific things we do or see or experience—are fixed and scarcely subject to change. As things become "more scientific" we may become more secure in the results of our actions. The slaughter on our highways, for example, is a horrible tragedy and waste, yet the automobile is a symbol of security because it is generally available at our slightest whim. It cannot contract mysterious diseases. It is incapable of independent action and will never refuse to turn the corner or carry us off helplessly into unexpected adventures. The automobile is unaffected by anger, greed, frustration, or fear. There is security in knowing that when you turn a key the engine starts, as you push a button the horn blows, and when you step on the brake pedal the car stops.

A scientific education would become as mechanical and as dependable as an automobile. It would provide the data upon which the curricula to be executed by teacher-technicians would be structured. When the educational machine sputters and knocks, a standardized procedure would seek out and identify the problems; prescribed repairs would then be made. Thus the scientific emphasis provides the logical conclusion that youngsters can be *made* to learn. Problems of reading, understanding, believing, and reacting are soluble; they are dependent for solution only on the skill, interest, and willingness of the technician to tackle a problem.

In contrast to the masterful confidence of educational engineering, teaching as an art leaves questions unanswered and removes bulwarks of security. It casts doubts on finished products and provides few guides to the solution of problems. The skill of the artist does not depend on a single-minded ability to follow prescribed patterns but relies on a flexibility to adapt, change, and innovate. Teacher-artistry is a mysterious fusing of assorted processes. It uses the politician's skill in human dynamics. It calls into play the huckster's arousing of emotions and the criminologist's ability to suppress them. There is need for the psychologist's understanding of the internal individual and the sociologist's concern with external interaction.

The art of teaching is handicapped by the constant insecurity of not knowing answers in advance, of responding to a situation rather than creating it, and of not being able to make predictions about the nature of the product. In an age when we have become accustomed to the confidence with which technicians make diagnoses and predictions, we tend to become intolerant with those who cannot speak with equal certainty. The truth of the matter is that activities cannot be more scientific or more predictable than the factors within them. Thus, unless men can be expected to act in a predetermined manner, human affairs will never be as scientific as the meshing of gears, the orderly affairs of the universe, the regulated evolution of a plant, or the predictable response of an irrational beast. Teaching can never become a science; it must always remain in the realm of the arts.

If teaching is an art is there any reason to believe that teachers can be educated in the art? Perhaps we have to depend on teacher-artist as a self-made product. The first reaction against such a proposal is that there are too few "born teachers" to staff our schools. Many other arts, including medicine, are staffed through educational programs. Art and music conservatories and drama schools stand as evidence that the fine arts also find it appropriate to establish educational programs even though study alone cannot make artists of all those interested in the art. It would be a simple matter if every scholar automatically became a teacher; it is the nature of scholarship, however, to flourish more in isolation than in the interpersonal relationship that is teaching. One of the scarcest and most valuable combinations is that of scholar-teacher.

the benefits of science to art

Labeling teaching an art does not exclude the facilitating benefits to be derived from scientific endeavors. Perhaps B. F. Skinner phrased it appropriately when he spoke of a science of learning and an art of teaching.[1] Certainly this is consistent with the science of medicine and the art of healing, for example. Impressive scientific advances have extended the healing arts from the routine bleeding of a near-voodoo era to the complex surgical-pharmaceutical treatment of today. But even though it is aided by a highly technical medical science, healing success is still dependent on the diagnostic and practicing skills of the physician.

The fine arts reflect similar influences. Music, for example, is no longer dependent on the use of the voice alone or a simple reed flute; it has progressed to include the use of electronic instruments. Even the sculptor has added the welding torch to

[1] B. F. Skinner, "The Science of Learning and the Art of Teaching," *Harvard Educational Review,* 24 (Spring 1954), 86–97.

his array of tools, and the writer is equipped with the ball-point pen, electric typewriter, and dictating or recording equipment.

Like the other arts, teaching should be receptive to appropriate scientific advances and should be demanding more assistance from the sciences. The arts of teaching and healing are quite similar in one important respect: They both work indirectly. The physician does not personally heal but seeks to alter circumstances so that healing may take place; the major, if not the only, task of teaching is to aid the learning process. It is indeed possible for a teacher to go through all the actions of the instructional role with little learning taking place.

Science has been most intimately related to teaching through research directed toward analyzing and describing the teaching process. A major concern of educational researchers has been the attempt to identify the characteristics of effective teachers. The obvious advantages of establishing criteria for teacher effectiveness are to permit a more systematic method of teacher selection and to provide needed guidance to the content and method of teacher education programs. Unfortunately, half a century of effort has not solved the problem of what constitutes an effective teacher.

A more productive research topic has been the analysis of classroom interaction with special interest in the degree and kind of teacher behavior. Ned A. Flanders described an observational technique in which ten categories of interaction were recorded at three-second intervals for a period of about twenty minutes. The four hundred tallies that are recorded on a matrix can be analyzed to determine (1) the amount of teacher talk and pupil participation, (2) whether the teacher's influence was exerted directly or indirectly, (3) whether learning goals were clear or ambiguous to the pupils, and (4) whether pupil responses were dependent or independent of the actions of the teacher.[2] The OScAR (Observation Schedule and Record) is another instrument used to regularize classroom observation. The three factors it measures are the emotional climate of the classroom, the degree to which verbal activities are predominant, and the social organization of the class. Social organization is concerned with the amount of social grouping and pupil autonomy in the classroom.[3]

All these research efforts are particularly significant because they take into consideration an emphasis on pupil be-

[2] Ned A. Flanders, "Intent, Action and Feedback: A Preparation for Teaching," *The Journal of Teacher Education,* 14 (September 1963), 251–260.

[3] Donald M. Medley, "Experiences with the OScAR Technique," *The Journal of Teacher Education,* 14 (September 1963), 267–273.

havior and learning: they reinforce the concept that teaching is a subsidiary act in the classroom rather than a separate focus of the process.

the guiding of learning

The active process in the classroom is not teaching but learning; teaching is the activity that organizes, guides, stimulates, and assesses learning. Without learning, the teacher's efforts are futile and wasteful. Thus teaching is best defined as the organizing and guiding of learning activities.

When teaching is recognized as a subsidiary process that facilitates a more important individual and social process, then the true task of the teacher may be seen in a proper perspective and the tremendous responsibilities and opportunities that are the teacher's may be realized. Social, emotional, or psychological disintegration in a youngster or a group of pupils interferes with the learning process. Except for those limitations, however, the individual's ability to use basic skills, the attitudes he develops, and the manner in which he carries out the duties of the citizen in a democracy are to a significant degree a measure of the success or failure of his teachers. When there is an internal or external interference with learning, the disruption will minimize the role of the teacher and the influence of the educational process.

The teaching-learning question is far more than an exercise in semantics. The answer to it determines emphasis, methodology, and purpose. The teacher's attitudes in the classroom, for example, play a major role in the development of youngsters' attitudes. The way in which teaching-learning is defined also determines the evaluation techniques that are needed and the validity of the judgments on which the effectiveness of an educational program is measured. The teaching-learning definition is of crucial importance for it decides the process in the classroom; and what happens in the classroom is in substance what education is all about.

The emphasis on learning denies the possibility of "imparting" knowledge. There is no mechanical process by which an education may be foisted on an unwilling or unresponsive subject. The teacher may force a student to open a book but cannot make him read. An instructor can require the completion of an assignment but may not assume that solving problems confirms or even leads to knowledge of the process that is to be learned. A test may be administered but no one can correctly assess the motivating factors acting on the student or how he is interpreting the test items. We seldom know when a student is bluffing, guessing, or cheating or when he is smothered by an inability to learn or an unwillingness to achieve. We do not know to what extent a youngster has become a victim of outside forces that make achievement difficult or impossible. The teacher realizes success when students act and react in a carefully and often rigidly prescribed manner. Teaching is a process only to the degree that it activates the primary process of learning. Rather than simplifying matters, this indirectness of teaching complicates affairs. It requires a multiple approach and compounds attempts at evaluation. It increases the job of a teacher from a single interaction with one group in the classroom to a multiple relationship with many individuals.

teaching skills

The skills essential to the teaching art include inspiration, communication, learning, understanding, guidance, and methodology. Any attempt to derive a formula for priority of these skills would be artificial and presumptuous. All the skills are important; various successful teacher-artists may reflect diverse patterns of competence among the several proficiencies. Few teachers are complete masters of all the aspects of teaching; no successful teachers are deficient in many of them.

INSPIRATION As difficult as inspirational skills may be to define and characterize, they are basic to the art of teaching. Inspiration should not be equated with motivation, for it is a superbrand of motivation; it is directed and intense. The ability to inspire is subtle but crude. It is general and specific, purposeful and incidental—and extremely difficult to analyze. Teacher-artists may occasionally inspire an individual or sometimes a group. Periods of inspiration may be transitory or prolonged; they may be recognized or unnoticed. Inspired teaching channels individuals into areas of specialization; it is providential and becomes a milestone in the life of a mechanic, scientist, or president of the United States. Perhaps least aware of the tremendous powers of inspiration is the inspirer himself. To the dedicated teacher, evangelistic devotion and religious fervor are as natural as the sun and the rain. Inspiration is the transfer of an attitude; it is as learned as any fact, as taught as any value, and as mysterious in its workings as the forces of creativity. Yet in all its mystery, inspiration is a fact. It is a vital skill in the teaching arts.

COMMUNICATION The ability to communicate is of near-equal importance as inspirational skills. The ability to use the language in both written and oral forms is essential to the art of teaching, for whereas learning may be internalized, teaching is a form of external communication. Explanations, expositions, corrections, and instructions are all dependent on verbal communication. Words or phrases that are inappropriate to an age level, a social class, or a stage of mental maturity are barriers to teaching and obstacles to learning. No aspect of teaching has been as seriously challenged by mass education as communication. Educating all the children of all the people has brought into the classroom an almost unbelievable range from foreign-language-speaking migrant youngsters to highly literate, old-stock, native-born Americans. This range includes the near-genius and the near-moron, the culturally elite and the culturally deprived. If the teaching arts are to function, both group and individual communication must flow freely.

But aural and visual perceptions are not the only communicative media. Even the near-mystic "feeling tone" of a classroom is a process of communication. This concept is in reality a composite of a number of factors: tone, volume, quality, inflection, and accent of the voice; use of the eyes; slouch of the shoulders; pace and weight of the tread; curve of the lip; swagger of the hip; and even more subtle personal characteristics. Undoubtedly some communication has already taken place even before the teacher enters a room, including information about the teacher's reputation, the subject matter, the grade level, or the decor of a classroom. Even indirect communication plays its part. An individual mark, a report card, remarks made to a parent, the frequency and kinds of demands, requests, and suggestions made—all these play a role in communication between teacher and pupil. A particularly intriguing means of indirect communication is a youngster's judgment of the acceptance, by the teacher, of his remarks, questions, and actions. Thus there are various levels of communication, each one as significant as the next. One form of communication may conflict with another, but all combine to build unique configurations within each individual.

LEARNING SKILLS The communication skill is directly allied to learning skills, for the teacher must communicate something. Whatever the teacher communicates has been acquired through those same learning processes toward which his actions are directed now. An individual cannot teach without a broad knowledge of what is to be learned. The teaching art, then, requires continued learning on the part of the teacher.

The decision as to the level of learning skills necessary for a teacher has been historically in the hands of the colleges preparing teachers. Entrance and graduation requirements, as well as academic standards strengthened by the process of college accreditation, ought to be a fair measure of scholastic aptitude. Problems arise, however, when school systems attempt to force or encourage teachers to sharpen their learning skills. Graduate study may be a condition of employment and is sometimes rewarded by increases in salary. Unfortunately, enrolling a teacher in college courses does not necessarily make him into a better teacher. The key to encouraging teachers to continue to develop their competence in subject matter and methodology must be found in solutions other than threats or salary incentives.

UNDERSTANDING Only as the teacher has mastered the skills of the art of teaching already mentioned and acquired a commanding informational background in subject matter can he practice freely the skills of understanding. The concept of understanding has many facets: understanding a subject, child, community, method, or situation. A subject must be understood so that it can be explained. A child is another matter, however. One understands children through recognition of differences in age, sex, and level of ability. A child is a thinking, emoting, creative, bored, stimulating, absorbing, responding, reflecting, and refracting creature. Youngsters are in many ways simpler than their parents and in some ways more complex. They have not yet learned certain habits or inhibitions. While it is difficult to understand as complex a phenomenon as a human being, a degree of the skill is indispensable to the teaching arts. The child needs to be understood so that the other teaching skills may become effective instruments of learning. Inspiration cannot operate in a vacuum. Communication is completely bound by definition to understanding. Learning becomes inoperative without a purpose, while guidance and method are directed by and responsive to an awareness of what makes Johnny tick.

To understand a child one must be aware of his environment, his multiple-structured society, and his exposure to some groups or his lack of contact with others. Understanding in this context does not require the insight of a psychiatrist, the measures of a sociologist, the detachment of a historian, or the systematic arrangement of pattern of an anthropologist. It does, however, require awareness, for example, of the contrasts between a north side of Chicago and its southern sector or of the hills and the flats of Podunk. One should understand a society in order to gain understanding of the members of that society. Thus the middle-class teacher needs to appreciate his middle-classness with its strong ambitions, puritanical restrictions, and prudishness. He also has a particular challenge to understand the numerically limited upper class or the more numerous lower one. Psychologists, sociologists, and anthropologists have much information that is available to the teacher about individuals and groups in and out of his own immediate society. The supreme challenge to the teacher is to relate to the mixed society of the classroom and to the individuals within each subgroup in the class.

Appreciation of subject and child is not sufficient background for a teacher who must also be knowledgeable in the means, or methods, by which these two are to meet and coalesce. Teachers must be familiar with the techniques for presentation of learning experiences; they are the tools of teaching. A man with a hammer is a pounder or sculptor, depending on his knowledge of the use of the tool. Both creation and destruction are thus represented in a hammer; the outcome is dependent only on its use. Similarly the teacher is an artist only to the degree of skill with which he employs methodological tools. Like the man with the hammer, he may use his tools to build or destroy; he may hinder or facilitate learning; he may create or destroy interest; and he may aid or abuse youngsters by appropriate or inappropriate use of a method.

Important as they may be, the child, subject, and method are but aspects of a situation. The ability to accurately assess the situation, to weigh its components, to ignore and emphasize elements, and to constrict one factor while encouraging another requires a depth of understanding by the teacher. A teacher reacts to the situation that he has in large part created and is at any moment reconstructing. Construction of a situation and reaction to it are separate and distinctive skills even though both are directed toward the same condition. The situation aids or hampers learning. It determines the direction and degree of motivation. A moment in the classroom is structured by the teacher, pupils, administrators, and to some extent the community. The ability to assess a situation demands a profound knowledge of a subject, the community, a pupil, and a method; it requires a significant degree of introspection into each of them. Of all factors, introspection is perhaps the most difficult, for it asks an individual to figuratively stand aside and observe the situation while neutralizing both his ego and the emotions, values, and attitudes through which the world is perceived. Granting that the full exercise of this ability is at best rare and often impossible, teaching-learning is facilitated to the extent that introspection is accomplished by the teacher.

GUIDANCE The importance of guidance skills cannot be exaggerated. William H. Burton's famous volume on methods was aptly entitled *The Guidance of Learning Activities*.[4] The role guidance plays in the school is the basis for the differences in the traditional and modern labels that so glibly identify a philosophy, method, teacher, or school. Guidance is a philosophy and a method, but it is most of all an attitude. Central to the guidance attitude is the view of the role of the teacher: as a guide and leader rather than as a master and director. Guidance brings a subject to the youngster rather than a youngster to the subject. It recognizes that the differences among children are more significant than the differences between disciplines. A teacher's facility with guidance techniques determines teacher-class relations. It dictates whether fear or respect predominates and whether both the teacher and youngster are under a compulsion to establish conformity and to conform. Guidance suggests that there are group and individual objectives. It proposes direction and degree of action and reaction, the necessity for constant and periodic evaluation, and the need for flexibility. It suggests a willingness on the part of the teacher to lead rather than to direct and of the pupil to follow voluntarily with a desire to learn rather than to be coerced or pushed or challenged by the wish to please an adult. The burden for classroom success belongs to the teacher; he must find his satisfaction in the achievements of youngsters as learners rather than in his own accomplishments as a teacher.

By emphasizing the group or individual rather than a subject or teacher, guidance of learning thus has its impact on the curriculum—if not on the broad curricular pattern, at least within a classroom. It decides where a subject belongs in the

[4] William H. Burton, *The Guidance of Learning Activities*, 3rd ed. (New York: Appleton-Century-Crofts, 1962).

curriculum and where each learner should be with reference to that subject. It presumes the use of democratic procedures because the primary concern is for the individual, not because the sociopolitical structure is democratic. Effective leadership requires more consistent cultivation of individual responsibility, particularly when procedures are carefully adapted to differences in age, ability, and background. When directed by guidance principles, standards become measures of success rather than symbols of failure, methods become means rather than ends, and evaluation becomes a tool rather than a weapon.

METHODOLOGY The uniqueness of teaching involves the teacher's skill and understanding in methodology. Just as a brick layer is distinguished by his ability to lay bricks, a teacher is judged by his ability to teach. But though one may observe the laying of bricks and the growth of a building, he may find it is not as simple to observe the teaching process and a youngster's mental growth. Nevertheless, the job of the teacher is comparable with that of the brick layer. It is that special skill, the method, by which all other characteristics are put into play in the classroom, and as with other trades, the teacher's methods are learned. That some are born teachers would be akin to the idea that there are born brick layers and this is true only to the extent that a particular set of personality characteristics lends itself to self-instruction in a skill.

Proficiency in methodology does not only involve an understanding of methods but includes willingness to put them into practice, sensitivity to their effectiveness, and adeptness in changing procedures when needed. One of the greatest if unrecognized challenges for teacher-educators is to structure learning experiences in methodology for those preparing to teach. When the teaching art becomes subject to accurate measurement, it may be found that it succeeds or fails on the shoal of methods. That this is a truism in other occupational endeavors is seen in the case of the bright young man who, unfortunately, never sells insurance policies.

Evaluation of a process is critical to the use of methods. The salesman recognizes ineffectiveness; he analyzes procedures, markets, his product, his competition, and even his dress, voice, and personal habits; he then adjusts his methods to his findings. Similarly the teacher must evaluate learning, the learner, and the social structure; he must assess the classroom and its lighting, temperature, ventilation, and decor; and he must examine himself. Evaluation is as vital a part of methods as are preparation and presentation. Its end purpose is not to gather information and assign marks but to use this additional information to improve teaching and to facilitate learning. Evaluation points out the successes that need to be pursued and the failures that ought to be recouped and thereafter avoided.

In the future the profession may place a great reliance upon various technological assists to the field of methods. Television can offer some aid, although one wonders if it will be spared the ignominious fate of its relative, radio. Greater departures from practice may be expected in the future through the use of new devices such as the tool with the unfortunate misnomer "teaching machine."

The methods revolution carries with it enormous implications for the classroom and the profession. If there is any tragedy to the scientific encroachment upon education it is not the oft-repeated charge that new educational techniques are dehumanizing, but that educators are delinquent in adopting and using new techniques. The option a teacher faces is not the false choice of replacing traditional teaching procedures with new ones but that of incorporating newer methods into the older methods and of realizing an extensive flexibility in their use. The objective is to take advantage of divergent techniques that meet the learning needs of a highly differentiated society and not merely to be different or to innovate for its own sake. When schools learn to use educational television and programmed instruction effectively, it will be easier to develop and gain acceptance of new procedures to enrich the teaching tool chest.

OBSERVATION, INTERPRETATION, JUDGMENT Basic to the broader skills of teaching are the specifics of observation, interpretation, and judgment. Observation suggests more than perceiving; it is purposive, selective, and discriminative perception. A major purpose of observation is to identify signs of interest and the effectiveness of learning. Observation recognizes difficulties and seeks clues to the resolution of educational, social, emotional, and psychological problems. Perception includes seeing, hearing, and feeling, with the ability to detect the more subtle "feeling tone" the most important. Observation in itself is of no consequence unless it is used properly; proper use depends on interpretation and judgment. Interpretation has to do with the conclusions drawn from observations, while judgment is related to a subsequent use of the observation. Observed inattention of a youngster may be interpreted as lack of interest by one teacher or as a possible sign of health problems by another. Whichever interpretation is presumed, a number of judgments are possible, but among these are some that are as improper as others are suitable. Judgments are interrelated, for each one is dependent on previous judgments. Correct judgments are made only on the basis of adequate and reliable information; the more complex the problem, the more information is needed for a valid and useful judgment.

dynamic teaching

A successful art of teaching, like the fine arts or the art of healing, is dynamic. It is constantly doubting, experimenting, searching, adding, and subtracting. Dynamism does not suggest change for the sake of change but requires a systematic and progressive evolution. What some may identify as dynamism, however, can be a disorganized and aimless scrapping of established procedures for ill-contrived substitutes. No amount of knowledge is ever enough for a teacher. No method is ever perfect. No teacher ever becomes "good enough." To doubt, to seek, to find, and to doubt again make up the wanderlust to which the dedicated teacher commits himself. Teaching arts cannot tolerate wild excursions into experimentation as the fine arts may, for example. Education of future generations is too vital a function for society to permit reckless experimentation of classroom procedures. Teaching is not able to evaluate its efforts as effectively as medicine; medical failures are detailed in precise statistics. The burden that falls on pedagogical shoulders to build a dynamic education cannot be shirked or abused; it must be met and resolved.

To be engaged in dynamic introspection and experimentation, teachers must be secure in themselves, secure in acceptance of their efforts, and secure in the knowledge that their special abilities in their area of competency will be acknowledged. However, teachers act as though their positions are threatened. They may be unsure of their own competence in the academic realm or feel threatened when administrative judgments are based upon pupil performance on standardized tests. Their self-confidence is tested by parents who relate every success or failure of youngsters to their teachers and by employers and professors who tend to blame teachers for all weaknesses of employees or students. Teacher unrest is evidenced by the great mobility of the profession. Many teachers are engaged in a futile game of pedagogical musical chairs as they vainly search for security across a county line. Such concerns as tenure and fair dismissal procedures, the growing breach reported between administrators and faculties, public criticism of the schools, rejection of school bond issues, and the struggle for power and membership between teacher unions and professional organizations are evidences of the uncertain status of the teacher.

Experienced teachers report having taught in systems where teachers were told to resign, where public address systems were used as secret monitors in the classroom, where administrators bowed easily to public pressures, and where pupils' reports became sources of evaluation of teaching. In these situations it is difficult to envisage teachers engaging freely in self-evaluation or classroom experimentation. A profession may not be dynamic because it is not secure; at the same time, perhaps it is not secure because it is not dynamic. An activity must have a structure to be dynamic and to have a secure base.

There are some educators who suggest that the teaching arts cannot be regulated and are not subject to rules. It is true that an art cannot be tied to an infinite number of recipes or respond situation upon situation to a predetermined set of rules, an advantage enjoyed by the sciences. It is, however, inappropriate to suggest that teaching is nonregulated or nonregulative. Any discussion of teaching demonstrates that the process is highly structured, for the discussions are saturated with philosophical, theoretical, and practical rules. The teaching arts are regulated and systematic; there is nothing mystic or unworldly about them. Problems in and about teaching are frequently caused by misinterpretation of rules or ignoring them altogether. Inappropriate use of tools, attempts to extend rules beyond their rational limits, and efforts to regulate the more intangible and unpredictable human elements are evidence of misuse of a systematic structure, not of its absence. Whatever prestige might be gained by the artist from a proposal that his is a mystical command of the art is more than offset by the difficulties that would result from the assumption that the art is nonregulated and nonstructured. In such a situation truth cannot be isolated or identified. Within this framelessness, every artist becomes equal to the next and the layman unhesitatingly joins the experts.

The very nature of an art limits the extent to which it can be regulated, but the area of disorganization (or creativity) is not all-inclusive and occupies a limited if essential place. The key to effecting teaching artistry is methodology. The ease with or degree to which a teacher may go beyond the rules of methodology has to do with his skills of observation, interpretation, and judgment—all products of both the artist's learning and his experience. This flexibility is the ultimate expression of an art. The body of teaching is well defined by structure. It is only the refinements of the teaching process that are not regulated by a set of rules.

conclusion

Looking back over these pages one may ask, "But is this not an exaggeration of the complexity of teaching?" and the answer must be, "Far from it!" If anything, this short analysis has been an oversimplification. Each topic and subtopic might be a chapter in itself. Education has never suffered from an examination of its complexities but is seriously handicapped by frequent efforts to oversimplify its nature and problems. The simple answer may prove ineffective in solving complex human problems. Simple answers lead to the discrediting of one educational prophet, which is scarcely noticed in the rise of another, with the second usually as false as the first. It might seem that teachers, like Sisyphus, are condemned forever to roll one stone after another up the mountain; they have thus condemned themselves to a search for the easy way out of their difficulties. Obstacles seem to rise more menacingly with each defeat, but remedies can be found if educational problems are examined in a more reasonable manner, in a less emotional atmosphere, and without dependence on a simplistic analysis of the nature of the problems and a demand for equally simplistic solutions.

The science of learning and the art of teaching are more complex than medical counterparts. The physician treats the complaints of each suffering patient individually, but the teacher takes on en masse the educationally healthy as well as the ill. He does this without the variety and number of tools available to the physician. He is denied even contemplative privacy as administrators and the public look over his shoulder, shout advice, and quarrel with his techniques. All this confusion is found in a situation where it is impossible to document the patient's real ailment, the extent of his recovery, or the impact of a particular practitioner or treatment.

Teaching, then, is the most important career in the world. The future of the human race lies in conquering human problems as well as in meeting the challenges of science. Both scientific and human problems are most effectively and efficiently mastered through the knowledge and skills acquired in the classroom. Teaching bows only to learning itself as the major human activity and as the means to the future of civilization. Surely the magnitude of his task should humble the teacher, if he had the time for contemplation. But the demands are too great, the challenges too immediate for either humility or aggrandizement. The good teacher directs the conduct of youngsters better than many parents do and skillfully provides effective, diversified, and stimulating learning experiences at the same time. He is truly a superb artist who refuses to be overwhelmed by the enormity of the great art of teaching.

on your own

Teachers should be students of their craft. Skilled workers and artisans, as well as professionals, engage in formal or informal study, visit centers of the craft (field trips), exchange ideas with and observe masters of the craft (consultation), analyze their own work, its strengths and weaknesses (evaluation), and try this change or that new idea (innovation and experimentation).

The teacher, as a perpetual student, ought to be acquainted with means for informal study. A good public library will not specialize in professional education but should routinely add major works on education to its shelves. The card catalog under the category "Education" is the reference to such a collection. Periodical references that should be consulted are *Education Index, Readers' Guide to Periodical Literature,* and *Social Sciences and Humanities Index. Education Index* lists most of the major books and periodicals in education; one needs to become acquainted with the journals subscribed to by the local library. Less technical, popular literature will be covered by *Readers' Guide.* References to more scholarly journals will be found in *Social Sciences and Humanities Index.* The United States Office of Education publishes studies about teaching and schools. All federal government publications are listed in the monthly catalog of the *United States*

Government Publications and federal educational materials may also be found in *Education Index.* The monthly journal *American Education* is the major periodical of the Office of Education and also lists other government periodicals of interest to educators.

There is not an abundance of material about the nature of teaching, but students of education should consult "Education, General" in *Education Index.* The previously noted article by B. F. Skinner, "The Science of Learning and the Art of Teaching" (*Harvard Educational Review,* 24 [Spring 1954], 86–97) would be an excellent start. Among major references available in paperback are Gilbert Highet's *The Art of Teaching* (New York: Vintage Books, 1959), Jerome S. Bruner's *The Process of Education* (New York: Vintage Books, 1960), and John Holt's *How Children Learn* (New York: Pitman, 1967).

Notice has already been made of the articles on analysis of classroom interaction by Ned A. Flanders and Donald M. Medley in the September 1963 issue of *The Journal of Teacher Education.* The monograph by Flanders, *Teacher Influence, Pupil Attitudes, and Achievement* (Washington, D.C.: Government Printing Office, 1965), discusses research on teacher interaction in the classroom; other discussions of the topic will be included in Bruce J. Biddle and William J. Ellena (eds.), *Contemporary Research on Teacher Effectiveness* (New York: Holt, Rinehart and Winston, 1964).

On your own, you may raise the question as to the nature of teaching with college professors. The typical campus will find proponents for both sides of the issue. You may analyze your own learning, relating it to the role played by one of your instructors. Is your own learning process related to a scientific, psychological procedure? What differences may be found in the effectiveness of teachers? Are better teachers artists or scientific educators? How do superior instructors relate to a group and to individuals? By what means do they bring together learners and subjects? To what degree are they masters of subject matter as well as of the teaching craft?

additional references

Abraham, Willard. *Time for Teaching.* New York: Harper & Row, 1964.

Amidon, Edmund J., and Ned A. Flanders. *The Role of the Teacher in the Classroom: A Manual for Understanding and*

Improving Teachers' Classroom Behavior. Minneapolis: Paul J. Amidon Associates, 1963.

Ashton-Warner, Sylvia. *Teacher.* New York: Simon and Schuster, 1963.

Coleman, John E. *The Master Teachers and the Art of Teaching.* New York: Pitman, 1967.

Drake, William E. *Intellectual Foundations of Modern Education.* Columbus, Ohio: Merrill, 1967.

Full, Harold (ed.). *Controversy in American Education.* New York: Macmillan, 1967.

Hyman, Ronald T. *Teaching: Vantage Points for Study.* Phila.: Lippincott, 1968.

Joyce, Bruce R., and Berj Hartootunian. *The Structure of Teaching.* Chicago: Science Research Associates, 1967.

Maritain, Jacques. *Education at the Crossroads.* New Haven, Conn.: Yale University Press, 1960.

Skinner, B. F. *The Technology of Teaching.* New York: Appleton-Century-Crofts, 1968.

Whitehead, Alfred North. *The Aims of Education and Other Essays.* New York: Free Press, 1967.

2

What is a teacher? She is a tall, thin, sixtyish, thrifty old maid teaching in a small Midwest village school. He is a squat, bald, stockholding homeowner cutting a smart suburban swathe in his foreign sports car. She is a young graduate of a teachers college admiring an engagement ring and dreaming of caring for other children now, her own later. He is a bearded giant of forty commuting by subway and bus across city streets to an academic assembly line. Teachers are sons and daughters of factory owners, foremen, workers, and guards; of sellers of insurance, grass seed, and corsets; of graduates from schools of engineering, medicine, horology, and mortuary science; of farmers, miners, policemen, and of course, teachers. They are religious, irreligious, and antireligious; politically conservative, liberal, and radical; patrons of loan sharks, divorce courts, bowling alleys, and charity balls; frequenters of taverns, race tracks, art institutes, and libraries; educational traditionalists, progressives, and reconstructionists.

The only reaction appropriate to book, cartoon, movie, and television teacher-stereotypes is that they are all incorrect. Women teachers are not all bespectacled, frustrated spinsters who are unsophisticated and naive about children and men. Men teachers are not all absentminded, effeminate bachelors frantically escaping romance and the practical world. An average teacher is a typical parent or single man or woman, taxpayer, homeowner, voter, and user of Brand X; in essence, an average American.

But teachers *are* different. They are employees of public school systems hired by boards of education, generally upon recommendation of a principal or superintendent. Officially their working year begins early in September and finishes with the closing of school the last of May or sometime in June. Actually their working days during these same months include most evenings and many hours during the weekends. Elementary teachers find free hours during the school day only when a

those who teach

subject matter specialist in art, music, or physical education takes over the class; a secondary instructor may have one nonassigned hour in the daily schedule. Neither occasional nor scheduled free time, however, is sufficient to permit the teacher to plan tomorrow's lesson and correct that of today. He frequently carries home papers and books and spends many hours at home on schoolwork. The school day commences somewhere between eight and nine o'clock in the morning and ends about three or four in the afternoon. These six or seven hours are converted into, roughly, 190 pupil-hours each day.

Teachers *are* different. They were different the moment they made a commitment to teaching, just as his instant of decision differentiates a lawyer, physician, or plumber from people in other fields of work. The instant of commitment to teaching may occur at any time: at the age of eight after experiencing a first crush on Miss Jones, in high school as pressure mounts for vocational orientation, during a college career, or when a woman's family has grown and she seeks an outlet for interests and energies. Vocational choice for a teacher may be a mysterious phenomenon, with the term "calling" as correct a description as possible. Those who made this commitment have done so in the knowledge that teaching suffers in prestige and pay. There may be some who commit themselves in error, and many prospective teachers may not be aware of the personal and academic demands ahead.

education of teachers

There has been a revolution in teacher education as part of a general reformation in higher education. The criticisms that were leveled against the quality of prospective teachers in 1938[1] were hardly applicable a generation later. Colleges reported a great rush of applicants for the limited space of their classrooms, and the quality of students in teacher preparation improved significantly. Certification requirements for teaching increased from two to four years of college and some states established five years as the minimum requirement for permanent certification.

criticism of teacher preparation

James B. Conant channeled the various criticisms and frustrations of teacher qualification and preparation into a major

1 *How Good Are Our Colleges?*, Public Affairs Committee (New York: Public Affairs Pamphlet, No. 26, 1938).

indictment of teacher education.[2] His analysis of the problems was comprehensive and thorough, but his solutions were limited and questionable. Preparation of teachers is handicapped by the limitations that have been placed on the profession by assorted pressure groups and various entrenched interests. Teacher education is neither as deficient as its critics suggest nor as satisfactory as its champions propose. If critics like Conant, however, can move professional educators toward solving their own problems, they will have provided a major service to the schools. In the long run educators are the ones who must effect reform of the professional preparation of teachers, for constructive reform is usually initiated from within rather than imposed from without.

Scholastic background is not the only basis for admission to teacher education. Admissions officers credit the preliminary interview with helping to screen out of the professional program some who, for a number of reasons, are not serious teachers-college material despite impressive high school records. There are barriers to admission because of psychological, emotional, or physical deficiencies and the screening process—academic and nonacademic—continues through the college years. In regard to physical requirements, we become aware of the discrepancies, for there are reports of teachers or prospective teachers being eliminated from a job or a college class because they tipped the scales too heavily. However, one may recall a near-blind colleague whose classes were among the most stimulating, fruitful, and well-conducted in the senior high school. And there was the multiple amputee who amazed one in her ability to maneuver about education graduate courses; some years later she received a Handicapped-Person-of-the-Year award from the President of the United States. For various reasons and through a variety of procedures the teacher-in-preparation is continually screened; he is part of a highly select group. In scholarship, physical development, emotional and psychological stability, and personality characteristics teachers are above the national average. There is a high degree of motivation in public service for a major segment of the teaching profession.

2 James B. Conant, *The Education of American Teachers* (New York: McGraw-Hill, 1963).

professional education

A teacher's education is different, as is that of other professionals. One of the differences between the education of teachers and that of other specialists, however, is the variability in length and quality of teacher education programs throughout the country. In 1953–1954 roughly one-third of the nation's elementary teachers had less than four years of college preparation, while in one state, South Dakota, only one percent of the elementary teachers had a full four-year education. A decade later Wisconsin still had a score of two-year county teacher education programs. With such a wide variety of preparatory programs, some teachers had little education beyond high school, while others had earned graduate degrees. The trend is toward the elimination of all substandard programs, the adoption of universal minimums of four years of preparation, and the requirement by some states of five-year programs. But whether preparation for teaching extends over a few weeks or many years, the distinctive part of teacher education is and has been a concern for "pedagogy," the study of the art of teaching.

The unique and specialized substance of pedagogy is methodology. Less unique aspects are educational history, philosophy, psychology, sociology, anthropology, and measurement, all of which are studied as support and background for methodology. They provide a basis for the study of teaching method much as allied subjects support methodological studies in medicine, law, or engineering. The shorter the educational preparation for any profession, the heavier the emphasis on methods and the greater the isolation from other disciplines; the result is a limited and narrow-minded student. The inadequacy of programs for the education of teachers is not due to an emphasis on methods but often centers on the failure to instruct in supportive knowledge. The educational experience for a teacher should be long enough and broad enough to permit rich experiences in both classroom procedures and background to make the classroom a meaningful part of life and of society.

If the uniqueness of a teacher is methodology, emphasis on method centers about the use to which a teacher puts history, language, science, and so on. The same is true of every other user of the humanities, sciences, and arts. The lawyer and author, for example, each use the humanities, but differently; the engineer and physiologist each use the sciences, but differently. At the same time both the lawyer and the author have use for the sciences; the engineer and the physiologist have use for the humanities; and all of them have use for the arts. Methodology is what separates them from each other and the teacher from all of them.

In pursuing pedagogy, the teachers become facile in the use of "pedagese," the language of the art of teaching and the science of learning. It is a technical language and, like other technical languages, is abused. While essential to the degree that features peculiar to education need special terms (curriculum, ungraded classes, cumulative record, grade equivalent, etc.), pedagese is detrimental to the extent that the literature, particularly in some educational periodicals, is often crammed with meaningless verbiage. Many speakers at educational gatherings talk loud and long but say little. That this verbal misery is shared with virtually every other vocational group—the engineer, physician, barber, and filling station operator, for example, each has an overworked technical language—is of little comfort.

A teacher receives a liberal-professional education, but his liberal studies may be spotty in breadth and depth. He may be confused, moreover, about his professional education, both decrying the superficiality of professional courses and complaining that some essential topics had not been considered. Somehow he treasures hindsight about his professional preparation but is myopic toward the future. Still, teachers are not too disenchanted with the value of professional study, for they flock to teacher conferences at local colleges and to evening extension courses off campus or to summer courses on campus.

the employment of teachers

The graduating senior at a teachers college may have already secured a position (never a "job"), unless majoring in social studies or men's (not women's) physical education or holding out for a particular salary, area, city, or school within a certain city. The first teaching position is usually secured through a college placement office; the second, fourth, or tenth may be located through a private agency (usually at a cost of 5 percent of the first year's salary). Some applicants journey at their own expense to distant cities for inspection by administrators, the school board, and a committee of teachers; others are hired by mail. Occasionally, a position may be offered and accepted over the telephone.

Some educational professionals believe that utilization of a private teacher placement agency is a mysterious, even shameful, experience. While there is no doubt that securing a position through a college agency or placement services of a state education department or professional association is less expensive and no less satisfactory, many private placement agencies are equally reputable and may be more efficient. The teacher who seeks a special position, location in a particular area, or movement across the country may be served more satisfactorily by a good private agency. To many teachers the extra expense of employing a private placement agency is a worthwhile professional investment.

Like any job, a teaching position is a contractual agreement. Acceptance of a position may involve a written contract that is enforceable by law. The contract must be accompanied by a teaching certificate, for no one may teach without a document from that state's department of education showing complete satisfaction of requirements. If a person does not have the requisites, however, he may obtain a limited, a provisional, a temporary, or an emergency certificate. Although laws state that one may not teach unless qualified for that particular position, emergencies may necessitate adjustments in minimum requirements. Unfortunately there are always emergencies, and adjustments of a temporary nature sometimes become permanent. In times of teacher shortage, certification requirements have little meaning in many teaching situations. While education is not the only profession that has difficulty in setting aration requirements at the same time it seeks to establish a paths and chiropractors), it is in the most confused muddle. The profession is unable to completely enforce four-year preparation requirements at the same time it seeks to establish a five-year educational standard for certification.

Negotiation of a yearly contract suggests that teachers cannot be trusted to honor a nonwritten contract, that administrators are unreliable, that school boards are untrustworthy, or that all the parties involved may be irresponsible. A contract may be specific with reference to mechanics of its termination and renewal, to procedures about absences, and to teaching duties. The yearly contract, however, has been found deficient, for statutes to provide protection for the teacher against arbitrary dismissal, to set up in some states a "continuing" contract that binds the school employer further, or to establish firmer "tenure" provisions following "probationary" periods have been enacted. States have found it necessary to legislate minimum teacher salary laws as well. The most important development in the relationships between teachers and their school board employers has been representation of teachers by teacher unions (which engage in collective bargaining) and professional education organizations (which engage in professional negotiation).

The continuing teacher in a school system is a witness to the educational parade—every year new and eager faces, every year the dropping of a familiar figure. Where do they go, these subtractions from the roll? They may find their way into other school systems in an often fruitless pursuit for escape from something about teaching or from a particular teaching assignment. They may gravitate into college or private school teaching. They may escape from the classroom into industry or school administration.

There is concern over the movement of teachers, but there should be more concern about why they move. Those who leave because they find themselves unsuited to teaching depart both without regret and unregretted. Those who are escaping administrative weakness or excesses, public interference, or internal dissension may be among the profession's most perceptive, sensitive, and intelligent members. The profession is weakened if losing some good faculty prospects also means retention of others who are less desirable. The qualities of an excellent teacher place an impressive price on his services to business and industry, while an ineffective colleague is less eagerly sought by anyone. It is easier for the best to leave the profession if they choose to do so. However, it is comforting that many of the better teachers remain in the classroom, serving the future generations with distinction and exerting a positive influence to improve the profession.

financial considerations

There was a time when each teacher bargained individually with a school board for a salary and a contract. In this process the administrator was aloof from negotiations; he was in fact in the same position as his staff. Today enlightened labor techniques have spilled over into education. Teachers commonly share a salary schedule based on educational preparation and years of service, which is subject to revision each year. The administrator, while himself an agent for the board, advises both his employers and the faculty salary committee. On the one hand, he is faced with the realization that low salaries reduce the efficiency and morale of a faculty and tend to keep down the pay of administrators. On the other hand, he knows that weakness before a faculty is not appreciated by a tax-conscious board. Thus the administrator is in a position where he can gain little in the eyes of his faculty. He may be in a continually compromised situation between school board and teachers.

Public financial support of education is related to the attitude of the community toward the schools. The social or economic status of citizens affects their level of support. The knowledge of what the schools are doing may increase or decrease support by the public. As school public relations have flourished, administrators have bent more readily before the winds of public opinion. The public, sensing this, has blown harder. Educators may simplify the process of measuring public opinion and become more sensitive toward the vocal public than to the silent throng. One letter to the editor in a local newspaper can throw a school system into a panic even though there are no signs of a similar concern from the greater public. The sensitivity to bridge table gossip about local education has placed the administrator in the position of bringing grumblings from the home front to the attention of the teacher. There is confusion about the administrator's real role, whether it is to represent the public or a faculty. Frequently he cannot do both.

There are many who equate school finances with business financial matters. It is not unusual to have discussions about the support to be given to schools related to the efficiency of the school as a commercial venture. Education has thus taken on the façade of big business complete with paneled board rooms. The administrator has become more of a business manager and less of an educational leader. When the administrator is more business-oriented, administrator and faculty tend to grow farther apart. A principal who is bogged down with personnel problems in school buses, cafeteria, and boiler room, who is worried about scheduling, public relations, floor polishers, and pupil spectaculars in music or sports, may be isolated from everyday activity in the classroom. He has few opportunities to assist in the solution of individual instructional problems. Though the tendency is to place responsibility for difficulties in the school on individuals, it would probably be more correct to depersonalize issues and recognize that economic and social problems are at fault. The complex nature of the changing problems of the schools has not been met by necessary changes in the role and structure of school administration. Former United States Commissioner of Education Francis Keppel noted difficulties in school administration and proposed some directions toward which change could be initiated in the book *The Necessary Revolution in American Education.*[3]

Teachers are more successful in achieving their financial goals when they act as a united group. However, teaching staffs are often fragmented. The faculty-administration division is not the only one that splits a school system. There are subject matter, organizational, philosophical, and even sex conflicts. Special subject teachers, particularly those in music and physical education, frequently get involved in controversy with other teachers when a Christmas program or athletic event is in the offing. In many schools there is staff internecine warfare about the issue of teacher organization: Should there be a professional association or a union? There have been cases where a faculty has been split over that issue, with the two groups in the same building competing bitterly for members and power. Teaching tools and methods, joint teaching activities, and extracurricular programs are expressions of educational philosophies and become easy sparks to disagreement. Squabbles may be initiated by special salary provisions of an extra stipend for each man, or married man, on the faculty, but these arguments are sometimes confused by injecting irrelevant challenges as to whether men or women teachers have greater dedication to the profession.

While we have touched on the subject of money, it is appropriate that serious consideration be given to the matter of a teacher's salary. In many teachers' lounges or boiler rooms the next year's salary schedule is one of the most popular topics of conversation as the school year begins. The teaching profession is not richly rewarded by its employer-public, but then the public is a notoriously poor employer. Thus, when one undertakes to discuss the role of the schoolteacher, many other facets of teaching attributes, demands, responsibilities, and rewards should precede the question of the teachers' paycheck.

Teachers' pay is not a new issue in the United States, as is evidenced in this excerpt from a dialogue in an 1828 text in rhetoric:

[3] Francis Keppel, *The Necessary Revolution in American Education* (New York: Harper & Row, 1966).

It has always been surprising to me, that people in general are more willing to pay their money for anything else, than for "the one needful," that is, for the education of their children. Their taylor must be a workman, their carpenter, a workman, their hair-dresser, a workman, their hostler, a workman; but the instructor of their children must—work cheap![4]

There are few signs that the end of this problem is in sight despite the several devices in use by the profession to seek a solution.

The issue of increasing teacher pay includes some particularly sensitive matters about the profession. One cannot speak of improving a profession without casting reflections on the quality of the group as it is. To speak of better teachers suggests that a number of those presently teaching stand in need of improvement. The question is further raised as to whether inferior teachers will become better or adequate instructors with an increased salary; that is, whether they should even gain from a higher pay. There is a danger that increased pay for everyone may be construed as an award for simply being a teacher, good, bad, or indifferent. The issue of increased pay for the nation's teachers becomes mired in contradictions when the argument suggests that the immediate result will be improved instruction in the classroom.

The question of improving teaching skills has become so ensnarled in the matter of remuneration that many school systems provide extra pay for those who engage in advanced study. (Or is it those who seek more pay engage in advanced study?) With one eye on medicine, some members of the educational profession propose to equate years of study with pocketbook reward. It might be suggested, on the other hand, that if an engineer's starting and retiring salaries outstrip those of his teacher classmate, it may be due to demands of the labor market, willingness of an employer to pay higher salaries, or the fact that some college courses lead to better paying jobs rather than because he spent any certain number of years in college. One does not quarrel with the length of education deemed necessary for competence in a vocation. We confuse the issue by suggesting that graduate study alone should determine salary or that competence in the classroom is only a

[4] Caleb Bingham (ed.), *The Columbian Orator* (Boston: J. H. A. Frost, 1828), p. 165.

matter of adding a certain number of credit hours beyond a bachelor's degree to a teacher's personnel record.

One means of providing increased financial rewards for superior teaching is the "merit pay" plan. Under this proposal superior teachers are identified, frequently through administrative selection procedures, and are granted extra pay for this recognition. But while merit pay is applauded by the public and school administrators, it is less enthusiastically welcomed by teachers. Teacher opposition centers on the difficulty of identifying superior teaching. Teachers frequently charge that merit pay proposals will lead to competition among teachers for administrative favor. They allege that asking teachers to recognize superior instructors from among their midst would encourage interfaculty politics and in turn distribute the financial reward among the faculty power structure.

Another means of resolving the financial problems of teachers is in the organizing of teacher unions. A new challenge of teachers both in unions and in professional organizations is phrased in the question "Why not strike for higher pay?" Whether the discipline needed to engage in this type of organized effort can be achieved in this profession of independent thinkers has been answered in a resounding "Yes!" But if the issue digresses to the point where every action of the teacher becomes piece-work labor, teaching may become neither a profession nor an art.

Teaching enjoys the dubious distinction of being wooed by two different types of organizations, professional and union. The nature of the choice is evidenced by the bitterness between the two groups and the conflicting charges that the one is too docile and the other is too militant. In recent years the differences between teacher unions and professional organizations have become obscured as each group seems determined to demonstrate a greater forcefulness than its competitor in improving the teacher's financial position.

What should a teacher be paid? No salary is enough for a good teacher, for one whose contribution is not realized alone in skills learned but is evidenced in the ability of people to learn to live peacefully, govern justly, and work creatively. His influence is not measured in numbers of words correctly spelled. It is not limited by a classroom door or the ringing of a bell. A teacher's impact knows no intellectual, physical, or time boundaries. How much does society owe in pieces of eight to Michaelangelo, Pasteur, Jonas Salk, or Albert Schweitzer—or to their teachers? What should an inferior teacher be paid? Anything is perhaps too much!

We can, however, speak of the "average" teacher; what is the average teacher worth? He should be paid enough so that teaching attracts first the dedicated idealist and then enough superior pragmatists to raise the quality of the average in the profession. Teaching rewards should provide enough good to average teachers so that there is no room for the inferior, so that those who prove unsatisfactory may be eased out. The answer is not "what the traffic can bear" but what is appropriate to the profession in its place in society.

When will teacher pay be adequate? Short of gaining a promised millenium, adequate pay for teachers will not come about through persuasion, coercion, or legerdemain. It will come about when the public accepts the teacher as a skillful and efficient artist, and the public (collectively at any rate) is neither ignorant nor unrealistically romantic.

new teaching positions

Teachers engage in a massive game of vocational musical chairs each January through August. There is an estimated 15 percent of a faculty every year who leave the typical school. They replace each other, or their classrooms are occupied by college graduates from more than 240,000 students who have completed teacher education programs. Each veteran teacher who moves from one school to another and each college graduate finds adventure in the new position. Adjustments must be made to a new community, unique combinations of youngsters, another group of colleagues, and administrators who differ in backgrounds and the success they find in structuring the human relationships which are the essence of teaching.

Teaching positions are often casually selected, yet each new experience is a career gamble. A teacher's success in a new school may lead to long tenure in that building or in teaching. Lack of success may result in a move to another school or escape from the classroom.

Armed with a contract and fortified by statute, the new teacher reports to his school and is introduced to a room, textbooks, and the routine, commonly in the form of duplicated and bound "rules and regulations." A faculty handbook, like a students' handbook, is often phrased in negative terms. Its use is an advantage to those superiors for whom any problem may be quickly resolved by the question, "Didn't you read the black book?" to which there is no satisfactory answer. A teacher is seldom well versed with such documents, not only because of the pressure of time but because those matters that are of prime interest to an administrator may not be of equal interest to a teacher. The young teacher, whose first concern is the guidance of learning, finds he must become conversant with errorless roll-taking, with a fire drill trail, with a pink slip for referral to the nurse, a white one for excuse from study hall, a blue one for attendance at religious instruction, and so on.

The teacher becomes acquainted with the management outside the school. He may never have business relations with his school board employer, seldom confers with the board's agent, the superintendent, and will soon find that authority, if not responsibility, rests in the person of a school principal. While final responsibility cannot be delegated, authority for school management is delegated step by step from board to superintendent to principal. The tenor of a school system is set by the top status figure, the superintendent; the morale of a faculty and the feeling tone of a building are structured by the principal. There are many good principals who are dedicated educational leaders. They mold aspiring young teachers into professional artists and draw out the mastery of experienced instructors. Too many principals, however, drive promising recruits out of teaching and thus tend to retain inferior teaching prospects. The chain of responsibility breaks down when a school board accepts as adequate a superintendent under whose direction a school system seems to "run smoothly," or when the superintendent is happy with a principal whose school "gives no sign of problems," or when a principal puts a stamp of approval on the teachers whose classrooms are "quiet." An educational plant should be judged by the efficiency of the learning process, not by the neutralization of teachers or pupils. The structure of school administration, however, makes it difficult to determine whether a lack of disturbances in the school reflects repression by those in authority or open expression of teachers and youngsters.

The new teacher becomes concerned with meetings: grade or subject matter, schoolhouse, system-wide, curriculum, health insurance, Christmas program, salary, scholarship, social committee, or American Education Week meetings. They are called by superintendents, principals, or colleagues and at the request of business interests, patriotic societies, professional organization agents, or the PTA. There is believed to be a pattern to teachers' meetings: they seldom start on time, bog down in interminable argument unrestrained by parliamentary procedure, find resolution in administrative fiat, tend to create new problems as others are settled, frequently provide outlets for personal frictions, and end later than planned. Efficient and rewarding meetings are, of course, not unknown to teaching, but the traditional stereotype is one of confusion and bungling. As a means for evaluating a school system and a faculty the teachers' meeting is probably unsurpassed. If a school system is democratically oriented, a meeting of its teachers is an open affair, with frank discussion of common problems and a free exchange of ideas between individuals who respect one another.

The new teacher finds that instruction is not the full-time business of a school; sometimes it does not even seem to be the paramount task. Before instruction may proceed there is other business to resolve: absence and tardiness records; milk-money collection, yearbook fees, textbook rental, or school savings; distribution and collection of report cards or forms for polio shots; written permission requests to eat lunch at home or in school, to participate in field trips, religious instruction, or music lessons. Important decisions must be made before a textbook page is thumbed: Should Mary go to the dentist during school, Tommy to a funeral, Jane to the nurse, or Mark to the counselor? Must Susan make up work she will miss in advance of her two-week trip to Florida, on the way to Florida, or when she returns from Florida? And "Will you please announce that gym clothes must be . . . , music lessons are canceled for . . . , play tickets will be sold . . . , the bus will leave . . . , school will dismiss tomorrow . . ." Nor will the new teacher discover that routine is unimportant, for some teachers' careers have run afoul of clerical details. Let the experience of one New York high school teacher illustrate the point; refusal to hand in lesson plans two weeks in advance was ground for his dismissal according to no less authority than the state's highest court.

A teacher's personal behavior is subject to circumspection, an honor he shares with the clergy and others expected to exhibit model deportment. Such expectations of the teacher are justifiable if he is to be a guide and object of emulation of youngsters. Concern for teachers' conduct can be considered as complimentary recognition, provided restrictions on behavior are realistic and up-to-date. Modern ethical standards should no longer infringe on smoking or cocktail privileges, although frequenting the tavern may be out-of-bounds. Discretion suggests that the automobile has freed the teacher who wishes to make use of the anonymity of distance.

A certificate to teach is not permission to be other than a professional individual and the profession has concerned itself with "ethics." It is the ethics structured by the profession, by the teachers themselves, that should regulate a teacher's behavior, and these standards ought to be based on the needs of a classroom. Those who sit in judgment of a teacher's conduct should be fellow professionals and not a community's self-appointed censors. Teaching became an object of ridicule, for example, when the guardians over a great state's educational system reprimanded a teacher for indiscretion in writing a dramatic piece that, in modern style and contemporary language, was staged outside of school. Apparently a California teacher ought not, or may not, or in some circumstances cannot, be a member of the literary avant-garde!

personality factors

Much attention has been paid to personality characteristics of teachers. It is true that some personality types are not appropriate to the demands of the teaching task. Yet the often-repeated suggestion that there is a teacher personality type is not verified by the facts. While it is true that a teacher must have a genuine interest in people, a willingness to work, and tremendous reservoirs of patience, it seems to be equally true that he may be an introvert or extrovert, aloof or friendly, "strict" or "easy," or deep or shallow in emotions or humor. It is fortunate that various types of personalities can teach effectively, for the supply of potential teachers would be seriously limited if recruitment into teaching had to be restricted to a single personality configuration.

While it is correct that a sense of humor is a worthy attribute for a teacher, there is perhaps more truth in the suggestion that some funny people would not do well in a school. Many an outgoing personality operates much more effectively in the club than in the classroom. There are sympathetic souls who would be of greater worth in the church, social service, Red Cross, or probation office than before a chalkboard. It may be more correct to suggest that the criterion for the selection of a teacher is not the personality but the use that is made of it. There are personality factors, attitudes, and values that govern the adaptability of an individual and his ability to adjust to a situation. There are personality factors that restrict flexibility or that limit the effectiveness of one individual with another or with a group. Obviously there are extreme personality characteristics that are resistant to change and are undesirable in the classroom. It is not a healthy practice to subject students to unsatisfactory teacher personalities in the hope that there may be eventual improvement.

It is relatively simple to speak of good and poor teachers in the abstract, but in actual practice pointing the finger at an individual instructor with scorn or approbation is not a routine matter. A youngster in the classroom is not in a position to be objective about a teacher, even if he has the necessary maturity to make the judgment. A parent is even less qualified to evaluate a teacher on the basis of information relayed by Tommy. An administrator cannot detach himself from the situation for which he is primarily responsible. Personal observation by a supervisor is one haphazard sample of interaction in the classroom, for an observation is influenced positively or negatively by the very presence of the observer. A previously mentioned abominable practice that extracts information out of context without the advantage of observation is the use of a school's public address system to listen in on classes. Another reprehensible procedure, reported by the news media, is the use of tape recorders by pupils or parents to record instructional activities in the expectation that statements may be selected and offered as evidence against individual teachers.

Occasionally high school graduates become the judges. A sample of opinion from college students is the basis for the following discussion. Descriptions of students' "best" or "poorest" school teachers showed that the "best" teachers were equally divided between men and women, with the "poorest" teachers found more often among the men. This result might suggest that teaching may be a second vocational choice for men and a first choice for women. The sample showed no relation between the subjects taught and the quality of the instruction; every subject was reported to have "best" and "poorest" teachers.

According to the respondents, academic competency was not the shoal on which teachers floundered. Rather ability to make use of an education, methodology, and skill in handling discipline was what separated education's sheep from its goats. No superior teachers were credited with poor discipline, while the misfits were often in conflict with youngsters. Strict disciplinarians, however, were found in both camps. Pupil respect was a requisite for the successful teacher, lack of it was common to the failure. The superior teacher came to his task well-prepared and strengthened with enthusiasm, fair-mindedness, a willingness to admit errors, and a sense of humor. The inferior instructor was unprepared. He seemed to care little about youngsters, teaching, or the subject; he had "pets" and a short temper; and gave the impression that teaching was only a meal ticket or a sideline.

A good teacher's friendliness might become a poor teacher's overfriendliness. One teacher stimulated, another teacher bored. One was sympathetic, another sarcastic. One instructed in good habits and morals, another ignored or condoned cheating. One spoke proudly of his profession, another whispered of lost dreams. One tossed out challenges, another threw chalk, erasers, even ink bottles. For some teachers patience was a prime virtue, for others impatience was a major vice. Youngsters crowded into a good teacher's room after school; they entered a poor teacher's class with dread and learned to fear and hate subjects, teachers, and school. Students reported that several poor teachers had been teaching subjects outside of their major area of interest and specialization.

This opinion sample is a composite of the best and the worst, but a teacher may have been reported as superior even though he occasionally enforced attention by throwing an eraser and some failures were still remembered as "real nice guys." No single teacher personality came out of the analysis, but there was the unqualified suggestion that a teacher must have a dedication to the profession, a genuine interest in people and an ability to work with them, and the necessary techniques to activate learning. These are essential to effective teaching. The degree of commitment to teach determines the eventual success of the individual teacher.

Diverse personalities are found within the teaching ranks and the neophyte will soon learn that, while a faculty is an organized group, it is fractured and refractured by real or imagined divisions. Recent books about teaching, particularly in the urban ghettos, have served to spotlight the very real split between administration and faculty. While relations within the schools have deteriorated, education has become entranced with the practice of school public relations. Educational middlemen in the form of assistant superintendents, business managers, supervisors, coordinators, assistant principals, and department chairmen have isolated administrators from teachers, and as communication has broken down in this process, the educational leader and follower have less and less in common. An unfortunate circumstance is the imposition of additional duties and record-keeping that each new administrative service requires of teachers. When clerical processes pyramid, it is inevitable that time and effort for instruction must adapt to these demands upon the teacher.

What should a teacher be? Certainly, he cannot be all things to all people—happy as that prospect might seem to the pupil who wants a friend, confidante, and tutor; to the parent most happy with a master teacher, scholar, baby sitter, and miracle worker; to an administrator seeking an uncomplaining, hard-working, graduate student-policeman; or to a school board desiring a contented, permanent, innocuous, inexpensive employee. Teachers are expected to be imaginative yet staid, demanding yet considerate, friendly yet stern, communicative yet circumspect, consistent yet dynamic, personable yet dignified, and inventive yet conformist. They should be modishly dressed yet conservative, diligent yet untiring, and responsible yet unquestioning. In a sense a teacher should be inhuman yet superhuman. While a person cannot be all these things, it is not surprising that these are the expectations when teachers are considered to be servants of a community, public, school board, profession, administrator, pupil, and parent. Demands for excellence or impatience with imperfection is reflected by the public as employer to teachers as employees.

professional concerns

An effective teacher must be dedicated to the profession, at least to the extent that it is not secondary to a cabbage patch, maintaining a home, selling insurance, or tending bar, if not with the devotion of a missionary. Teachers must be willing workers, for teaching is hard work physically, mentally, and emotionally. The effective teacher is sapped at the end of a day, yet he carries home fragments from today's lesson and work to prepare for tomorrow. He must find pleasure in working with other human beings—student, parent, administrator, and fellow teacher. His hunger for knowledge in subject matter, psychology, philosophy, and methods drives him to a ceaseless reading, listening, talking, and observing. He evaluates his teaching self-critically, judges the effectiveness of methods, and is conscious of the atmosphere he creates. He uncomplainingly carries the burdens of the profession: the lack of perspective of its leadership and the rationing of support by its following. The teacher assumes professional responsibilities; he cajoles, pushes, and leads his colleagues. In the midst of this peripheral work he guides the learning of a most diverse mixture of youngsters.

Is this impossible? Not at all, for some teachers are doing just that. If our superior teachers can do it on their own energy and imagination and resources, there is hope that our less apt average teachers may meet the challenge with leadership from the profession and adequate support from the community. The quality of community support and professional leadership necessary to meet school problems is decidedly overdue. Part of the support that should be extended to every teacher is the acceptance by the public and use by the schools of technological assists in the area of teaching methods: movies, recorders, television, teaching machines, and the other multimedia techniques.

An effective teacher is intelligent and a user of his pupils' intellects as well. He is a master in his immediate subject matter concerns and also knowledgeable in others. Not only is the master teacher familiar with his own pupils and procedures, but he knows what the other teachers are doing so that his classwork fits in with previous instructional backgrounds and is preparation for the next experience. He exerts a subtle influence on colleagues through formal or informal discussions about the curriculum and whether the school experience is a properly cohesive program or a succession of more or less related exposures to ideas. He uses his intellect to gain personal understanding, to help pupils to understand, and to understand pupils.

A superior teacher is many things to many people, but he concentrates on structuring and preserving the learning situation. He controls the personal relationship with a youngster. He determines the extent to which an administrator, parent, or interested citizen shall infringe on classroom activities. He absorbs aid from all sympathetic individuals while repelling efforts of others to undermine him or his position. Recognizing human needs, he is inflexible in the face of undue pressure and adaptable to reasonable requests. He is a symbol of strength to weak youngsters and of sympathetic understanding to the fearful. He preserves his balance and does not become so embroiled in tangents that his classroom surrenders rich learning experiences. He resists the temptation to subordinate learning and convert the classroom into a psychological clinic or a means of social reconstruction.

The teacher is a citizen of a community, nation, and the world. He may relate to a church, a community service group, or a political party. An effective teacher is conversant with community problems and is acquainted with the local social structure and with the groups, cliques, and personages that comprise it. While not a party to them, he is a perceptive observer of the ethnic, religious, social, economic, and political schisms that divide and redivide a community. He is aware of national and international issues, their interaction with each other, and their impact on the local scene.

As a member of a profession, a teacher finds a concern for education beyond his own classroom, in the philosophy that directs it, the theories that explain it, and the practices that operate it. He checks theory by practice and philosophy by its theory. He is aware that whereas philosophy is constant and theory reflects philosophical premises, classroom practice is adaptable and flexible. For he knows that it is classroom practice that supports theories and gives life to a philosophy. Thus it is the teacher's professional role to pursue and substantiate a philosophy, to implement theory, and to perfect practice.

The teacher views his professional status as a means rather than an end and as a tool rather than a product. He perceives education as a means of bringing together many unique experiences instead of merging unrelated and insignificant segments. He believes that the worth of a profession rests on what it does rather than on what it says or proposes. Impatient with the busywork that takes much effort to accomplish little, the teacher adopts the greater challenges as his own, seeks to identify the true nature of educational problems, and aims to contribute his knowledge, skill, and experience to meaningful solutions of these problems.

The superior teacher is concerned with what should and may be done. He is not frustrated by failure and is not disheartened by the lethargy, ignorance, and obstructionism of colleagues, administrators, and laymen. He seeks to overcome apathy, to supply information, and to surmount barriers to progress to make teaching that which it can and must become. He cannot wait for a revolution in public attitudes toward values concerning education and educators. The teacher never pretends to evoke miracles in the classroom; he does not give lip service to simple solutions for complex problems. Recognizing the enormity of his task, he goes about his job with self-confidence. Knowing the practical limitations imposed by social and personal problems, he still aims for the ideal.

conclusion

The real mark of the ideal teacher is the skill with which he guides the development of youngsters. His first and major concern is with the development of his students' intellectual skills. Accordingly a teacher's efficiency ought to be measured by the degree to which every youngster reaches his own unique academic potential.

A superb job in guiding learning involves the physical, psychological, social, emotional, and attitudinal growth of youngsters. These are incidental benefits from the major school task: They facilitate learning but are not destined to take its place. The superior teacher thus creates the situation in which learning flourishes, provides opportunities for rewarding experiences, and makes use of tools and techniques most appropriate to each individual's skill and previous experience.

It is a challenging enough task to tutor one youngster; teaching thirty becomes the striving for an academic symphony with a teacher-conductor creating harmony out of diversity: criticizing this child, praising that one, frowning at this performance, and smiling at another. A successful teacher-conductor is a master salesman, organizer, counselor, technician, and artist.

While the perfect, ideal teacher is a fiction, that is what every good teacher is striving to become. The ideal need not be attained, but it is the challenge toward which every educator ought to devote his professional life.

on your own

Repeat the procedure mentioned in this chapter by writing descriptions of the poorest and best teachers you had before college. What do you find to be the characteristics that explain the extreme differences between them? Have some of your friends do the same, and compare the differences described by the group with those in the text. Looking at college teachers, why do some seem to be "best" or "poorest"?

Education Index may be consulted for further information

under "Teaching" and "Teachers." Additional sociological studies may be indexed in the *Social Sciences and Humanities Index,* where information on teachers in foreign countries also may be found. Popular periodical items on teachers, their characteristics, and their problems may be included in *Readers' Guide to Periodical Literature.* A useful source of information is the *Saturday Review,* especially the education supplement issues. *The New York Times* (with its *New York Times Index*) contains articles on education; it frequently covers stories on instances of teachers in trouble with school boards, administrators, parents, or the public over matters covering a wide range of potential conflict, from philosophies to practices to discipline and to religious, political, economic, and social issues. For concise accounts of educational news, including information about teachers, weekly news magazines (*Time, Newsweek,* etc.) are of value.

In professional literature the *Journal of Teacher Education* is the periodical most concerned with the evolving teacher and his selection and preparation. James D. Koerner's theme was reflected in the title *The Miseducation of American Teachers* (Boston: Houghton Mifflin, 1963). A significant (and controversial) report was that of James B. Conant, *The Education of American Teachers* (New York: McGraw-Hill, 1963). The publication of Conant's book unleashed a veritable flood of arguments, answers, proposals, and counterproposals about the preparation of the American teacher, which may be found in scholarly, professional, or popular literature.

A useful exercise for the teacher-to-be is to list factors considered essential for teaching success, to compile an honest analysis of one's own strengths, weaknesses, experiences, and potentials, and to plan the means whereby one may gain the characteristics, experiences, and knowledge necessary for success and happiness in the classroom.

additional references

Crow, Lester D., and Alice Crow. *Mental Hygiene for Teachers.* New York: Macmillan, 1963.

Elam, Stanley (ed.). *Improving Teacher Education in the United States.* Bloomington, Ind.: Phi Delta Kappa, 1967.

Jersild, Arthur T. *When Teachers Face Themselves.* 2nd ed. New York: Teachers College, Columbia University, 1957.

Kinney, Lucien B. *Certification in Education.* Englewood Cliffs, N.J.: Prentice-Hall, 1964.

Peterson, Dorothy G. *The Elementary School Teacher.* New York: Appleton-Century-Crofts, 1964.
Ryans, David G. *Characteristics of Teachers.* Washington, D.C.: American Council on Education, 1960.
Stinnett, T. M. *A Manual on Certification Requirements for School Personnel in the United States.* Washington, D.C.: National Commission on Teacher Education and Professional Standards, National Education Association, 1967.

3

those who learn

What are they, these expectant little tots with runny noses tugged uncertain into a kindergarten at the end of a mother's leashlike arm? How are they to be described as they stumble through a succession of grades to present themselves before the college gates at last? Surely they must be something more than the third boy from the rear in the last row, the girl caught cheating on the history exam, or this year's high school salutatorian.

All students, from kindergarten through graduate school, are fellow human beings. Each one is subject to common emotional, social, and physical forces. All are in need of the same satisfactions and are beset by similar worries and frustrations. Consequently, each student should meet the same opportunities, be subject to similar moral restrictions, and be treated with an equal dignity and respect. But as a person, he has progressed through a fantastic evolution from cells that differ only in genetic structure into the unique individual that he is. He will therefore be as different from his fellow students as he is similar to them.

The pupil is a human being in a human situation controlled by older fellow human creatures. His entrance into school is an experience without a parallel. With no free choice of his own or of his parents, he is required to leave the security of his home and enter a centrally located public building where there are many other youngsters. With some of them he might not otherwise find a common contact; some of them, in turn, might be excluded from his company. A child is the product of the genius who shapes our world or of the peon who sweeps it. His parents practice law or usury; they seek to preserve life or destroy it; they cut across the entire range of human strengths and frailties. A youngster lives in a shack or a mansion; he may take dancing lessons or learn the rudiments of petty thievery. He may accompany his parents to a concert hall or a tavern. He may be pampered or abused by these same parents, and admired or hated by his neighbors. At school he may be welcomed or rejected by his classmates and teachers.

No school finds the entire spectrum of citizens in its classrooms, but every school has part of the distribution, including at least a few examples of those society best accepts or most easily rejects. Some youngsters rise above the gang in the slum and probably a similar number fall from suburban heights. Many more might rise out of the slums, however, if opportunities were provided for them to alter attitudes and find means to realize potentials.

Somehow the school must, and to an amazing extent does, embrace this diversity within its classrooms. The ability of a school to meet this challenge depends on the awareness by school board members, administrators, and teachers of the similarities and differences of the children in the school. To the extent that individuals are similar, group processes are appropriate; to the degree that people differ, instruction must be selective and class work must be varied and flexible.

individual characteristics

As a human being, each pupil is a reacting, emoting, creating, behaving, and developing individual. Psychotics react, even though it may be by complete withdrawal from the group or failure to respond to what is going on. The nonpsychotic is continually reacting to a situation, motivational factors, other personalities, himself, and a world that challenges or frightens him. However irrational his reactions may be, they do meet his own standards as to what constitutes an appropriate response to the situation about him. It is therefore nonsense to discuss a lack of response on the part of a student; rather, it is realistic to identify the response and, by recognizing the conditions responsible for the behavior of the youngster, to proceed to make analyses of it.

reacting to the situation

A pupil reacts to a situation that is not of his own creation and over which he has little control. The classroom has its traditional fixtures: books, chalkboard, desks, students and teacher. An architect designed the room, an administrator furnished it, and a teacher makes use of both the room and its furnishings. To the extent that the room is poorly lighted or ventilated or is acoustically inadequate or inappropriately designed, the architect has constructed a disruptive part of the student's situation. To the extent that there is a neglect of janitorial supervision, that uncomfortable desks and poor texts have been ordered, that organizing faults—such as a divided class period sandwiched around a lunch program—have been scheduled, the administrator has structured a disruptive part of the learning situation. For while the administrator may be seen infrequently, his influence permeates the school. He selects the faculty. He sets up the guidelines, which result in interpersonal relationships that lead to happy or disgruntled teachers, rewarded or frustrated youngsters, and satisfied or complaining parents. He shares with the public, school boards, and teachers the responsibility for a stagnant or evolving curriculum and for a relaxed or repressive atmosphere. The way the administrator exercises his responsibility is a crucial factor in the effective operation of a school, for he is most directly involved in structuring the school environment.

The pupil structures the situation to the degree that he makes his presence known in the classroom. He is unaware that his reactions are reflections of the values he has learned primarily from his parents and peers and, to a lesser extent, from the newspaper he reads or the programs he views or hears. Thus, even as the youngster structures part of the classroom situation, he does so with little control over his contribution. Because he is personally involved in his own behavior and is without a frame of reference on which to evaluate himself in the classroom, he is generally more aware of what is happening to him than how his actions affect other people. Also, because of his immaturity, his perception of what he does and what is happening to him is far removed from adult interpretations of the same situation.

reacting to the teacher

Certainly it is the teacher who exerts the greatest degree of control over the classroom, and the youngster appreciates this more than anyone else. While youngsters have found some excellent learning situations in the jungles of the large city through the efforts of some teachers, there are other classrooms where students leave as untainted by knowledge as when they arrived. A building provides space, an administrator provides the means for teaching and learning, and a pupil provides the raw material, but it is the teacher who joins them together.

To a large degree the youngster is reacting to a teacher-dominated situation: he responds to the teacher as a personality, an adult, a source of stimulation and of punishment and reward, and a poser of questions and source of answers. The student also reacts to the teacher as a parent-substitute, a figure of authority, an experience-derived stereotype of "the teacher," and an instructor of a subject toward which the pupil's attitude may have been evolving. A child's attitude in school may form a complex pattern, for a particular youngster may be suspicious of teachers, negative toward his parents, rebellious toward authority; yet he may respond positively and strongly to a specific instructor. Various student-reacting patterns have been neatly and negatively stereotyped in our schools. Youngsters are typed as stupid, lazy, dishonest, sullen, troublesome, immature, uncooperative, ad infinitum. Like all stereotypes, these labels are oversimplifications; they are misleading or incorrect.

Labeling a youngster "stupid" leads to a negative emphasis that solves no problems but does create some. Stupidity suggests a negative characteristic that is a barrier to learning. Contrast this characterization with one concerned with a level of intelligence (low intelligence, if you wish) that presumes a positive ability to learn, even if limited or slow; it still suggests a means to some action rather than a barrier to all. What about the youngster who "can't learn," but may, without a second's hesitation, rattle off the batting averages of his favorite big league baseball players? "Stupid" is hopelessly ineffective as a label; it is a nondescriptive epithet that serves no useful purpose; it merely places an immovable obstacle between teacher and pupil and between the pupil and learning experiences.

Just as no youngster is stupid, none are "lazy." Laziness is a characteristic of an individual that interferes with action, is internalized, and is not subject to influence by others, except perhaps through force. Substitute motivation for laziness and a truer picture is drawn. Motivation is both an internal and external process and is a responsibility of the teacher. It is a tool of learning rather than a bar to it.

Meet the candidate for the laziest high school student. He would have won the title of laziest student without a doubt, and according to the record, he had practiced the art well through the grades. Refusing to do any significant class work, he had edged his way up grade by grade, pushed through by the automatic promotion countenanced by teachers unwilling to tolerate *this* one for another year—surely a dubious form of recognition. As you might guess, he tended to be surly and untrustworthy in school; he could not be recommended for any responsible situation. It puzzled some (those who took the time to wonder) that he could be so lazy in school when he traveled country roads before dawn collecting milk for delivery to a local dairy. And how could one explain this loafer as he packed groceries and filled shelves in a local supermarket after school? Lazy? No! Motivated? Yes, but not in the direction we might wish during school hours. "Lazy" like "stupid" is a hopeless term, a nonsolution to the misrepresentation of a human trait.

"Dishonest," "sullen," and "troublesome" are also terms lacking in meaning and completely negative in effect. They are insoluble barriers to desired responses. Each oversimplification ignores the true nature of individuals and reduces the likelihood that they will find acceptance in the classroom or gain acceptance of themselves.

"Immature" is another indefensible stamp to place on youngsters. A child is by definition immature; each conscious effort to hasten his maturity beyond its logical development is as cruel as it is unrealistic. Judgment of a pupil's maturity, as well as consideration of questions regarding a youngster's cooperativeness, ought to be seriously undertaken by the teacher. For cooperation is a two-way relationship; measuring cooperation also involves a particular kind of a value judgment—one that forces the teacher to judge himself. Such a judgment requires an assessment of the motivation and intellectual capacities of the youngster and of the emotional undertones of the situation.

In the misuse of language, teachers are tempted to label youngsters with terms that are mired in hopelessness, that serve to build barriers to learning and destroy bridges to classroom communication. Teaching requires a unique combination of realism to see things as they are and the idealism to push toward things as they ought to be. Nowhere is this combination of greater importance than in the personal relationship between a teacher and a youngster and the language that is used to make realistic appraisals about children.

Enticing as it may be for teachers to try to assess a student's motivational factors, the attempt to do so is not only as fruitless in the classroom as in other noninstructional endeavors, but it is potentially of greater harm. To assess motivation infers an ability to measure unseen, even unidentifiable, factors of which the individual under observation is hardly aware himself. It is a simple matter to observe a one-celled animal's reaction to light, a more complex process to analyze a bird's migratory habits, and a relatively difficult task to unerringly judge a chimpanzee's reactions to an experiment in space travel. Efforts to categorize the behavior of irrational creatures are not comparable in complexity to attempts to outline the causes and results of human behavior, as witness the frantic efforts of a mother ministering to the cries of a week-old infant. The ability of humans to react to and interpret stimuli, to select from among various stimulating factors and place values on them, to carefully screen possible alternatives before reacting, to alter reactions to a changing pattern of stimuli, and to evaluate previous reactions and prepare for future action makes the task of analyzing human behavior an extremely difficult enterprise.

A dramatic illustration of the pupil within a situation is the problem of cheating. The typical reaction of the teacher is to focus blame and responsibility on the cheater, who is assumed to be dishonest, untrustworthy, and somewhat immoral. If we can view the problem a little less emotionally, we may see cheating as a logical behavior fulfilling pupil needs and appropriate to a situation.

Let us first note the structuring of the situation. Generally teachers place a great deal of stress on satisfactory marks in school. Evaluation in the classroom is usually based on group competition without regard to individual abilities. Caliber of class work and performance on tests determine marks. Teachers use marks as one form of incentive to learn. Additional incentives for learning are provided in the form of penalties and punishment for deficiency in class work or failure to pass tests. Awards or privileges for satisfactory performance receive less notice or emphasis in the classroom than penalties for unsatisfactory behavior.

Frequently classroom assignments must be completed outside of class. Failure to complete class work successfully is reflected in disapproval by the teacher, with an assessment of penalties from staying after school to solemnly writing a few hundred times, "I will do my homework." When disapproval or punishment await, when opportunities to copy assignments abound, and when classroom crises about the necessity to pass tests administered to large groups arise, inducements to cheat are rife. Thus, when there are many pressures for cheating, the need to cheat becomes overwhelming for some youngsters. Every pupil seeks the approval of his teachers; the poorer students seek it perhaps a little more desperately. And if some children are less concerned with approval, they *are* anxious to avoid disapproval and punishment. Various needs of approval, affection, and security push many youngsters into cheating in the classroom.

While cheating is only one example of a negative process with a child in a classroom, it may be typical of others. The tendency to place the burden of proof for his behavior on the pupil may neither aid in a real understanding of a problem nor provide guides for logical and appropriate means of facing issues. It is important to understand youngsters. It is vital to recognize the effective elements of a situation and to structure the situation so that the appropriate needs of the youngsters may be met and the desired behavior will be forthcoming. Among the unrealistic limitations placed on youngsters is the expectation that they shall or must react positively to other personalities. A colleague once explained his reason for seating two troublemakers together in a study hall: "I'm going to make them learn to sit like this without causing trouble." And so the battle continued!

classroom interaction

A very human privilege is to react to other individuals. The student responds to the teacher and other students, perhaps to an administrator, and occasionally to a bus driver or a custodian. His reactions may be to personalities, social class, religion, color, ethnic background, or sex. Of all the possible patterns of reaction in the classroom, interaction with other people is among the least understood, yet it is one of the most important. A major objective of the school is thus to help pupils learn to accept fellow pupils as human beings. The greatest influence for classroom mutual acceptance is the example set by teachers in their relations with pupils as demonstrated by their ability to accept and respect every youngster.

To understand something is not to condone it. This might be noted particularly with reference to the interaction of youngsters based on prejudice. While part of an education must be an understanding of others, young people take many of their cues from adults who reflect their own frustrations in the damnation of identifiable groups. It is thus not a simple matter to ask that youngsters react more reasonably than their elders. Tolerance may be demanded toward those we reject, but full acceptance of everyone else cannot be forced upon a youngster when adults are seen to have the privilege of choosing friends or selecting associates. The real test of the success in learning tolerance is in whether individuals are able to recognize differences in associates, to like some and dislike others, and to react positively or negatively to personalities without depending on artificial, nonpersonal factors or group identifications as criteria for judgment. This is difficult for adults; it is a matter of equal concern for the evolving adult.

A pupil's personal and social development in the classroom may be measured in terms of his own personality and in his relations with other pupils. Some youngsters swim in the security of knowing that their approval is sought by many; others flounder in cold isolation from everyone except another youngster who is similarly rejected. Youngsters in the greatest difficulty in school are those who are also teacher-rejects.

A typical use of personal interaction in the classroom is stimulation of competition in the learning activities. A question could be raised as to whether a youngster is not really competing for the teacher's approval—either direct approval or in the form of a mark on a report card. While it may be easy to fool adults about competition in the classroom, children are not so gullible. In a short time a youngster knows better than anyone else what his competitive prospects are. He knows whether he can outspell Johnny or outrun him. Rapidly assessing the situation, a child will protect himself from failure, if not in the teacher's eyes at least in his own. The three or four youngsters in a class who have a chance to earn the highest marks may fight it out, while the rest of the group tends to look on in bored silence, seldom bothering to cheer for a champion. Only if a classroom is divided into groups, with each group containing participants able to compete among themselves, can the flavor of competition be shared; but everyone cannot participate when competition is a room-wide process. This is not an unusual situation even outside the classroom. Johnny's dad, for example, may fight for commissions and sales prizes on the used car lot, but he will never consider competing with the president of General Motors or even with his district sales manager.

A youngster is seldom free to create his own interpersonal

relationships in school. District boundaries dictate his school, chance his room assignment, and a teacher's purely arbitrary decision where he sits and with whom he is teamed in group work. Of all teacher-constructed situations the least objectively contrived is the alphabetical seating arrangement, which ignores every factor about youngsters except a chance initial; it even ignores the fact that Tiny Tom may be seated behind Enormous Elmer. One might more logically suggest shoe size or weight as criteria for assigning seats in the classroom.

An important factor in an individual's relationship with others is the way in which he assesses his human environment. Appraisal of others is dependent on the way in which an individual appraises himself. A person is able to know his own capacities and to measure his own performance better than other people, but such judgment is dependent on a realistic knowledge of oneself. The success of a self-appraisal depends on an ability to correctly measure the ease with which one grasps ideas and improves skills, particularly as contrasted with the speed and efficiency with which classmates learn. To the extent that he can do this relatively dispassionately, a youngster is able to measure with some accuracy his own capacity to learn.

It is possible for extraneous factors to creep into the picture. Excessive demands by parents may give a youngster an undeserved feeling of failure or an unrealistic idea of his own capabilities. Membership in a minority group may transfer group feelings of abuse so that a student may attribute his failures to skin color, religious affiliation, nationality, or economic status. One cannot leave the subject of the self-image without mentioning historical examples of the compensatory mechanisms that are alleged to have been aroused by feelings of inferiority, as in the cases of Hitler, Bonaparte, and Toulouse-Lautrec.

Along with acceptance of himself and others the individual reacts to the world about him. For some, rejection of the world leads to criminality, political rebellion, religious fanaticism, withdrawal from society, or escape into fantasy. Acceptance of worldly challenges activates the classroom politician, the junior scientist, the budding mechanic, and the apprentice businessman. The basic tendencies and attitudes that shape the adult are forming in the child and adolescent and are abetted or hampered by society in general and the school in particular.

The timid soul, generally suspicious of the world, is not aided in his adjustment by a school that penalizes nonconformity, demands superior performance from the less capable, and conducts its affairs with the stern determination of an office management apportioning routine assignments to its employees. Strongly motivated youngsters are frequently held in rein by a school's limitations in facilities and opportunities. The more numerous "average" children and the conformists happily survive in classroom anonymity. Of all youngsters, the individualists are the ones who eventually may contribute the most to society or impose the greatest penalties on the world.

emotional characteristics

Abilities, values, and prejudices are not isolated and unrelated factors. They are in large measure born and bred, controlled and expressed, maintained and altered, by means of emotions. The educative process is facilitated to the extent that the student accepts and understands his emotions and the teacher accepts and understands the emotions of the students and of himself. The impact of emotions in the classroom is eased by the general flexibility of a group of students and is further aided when a teacher is able to bend with the emotions of students.

Youngsters are highly sensitive to minor changes in the school environment, to the mood of the teacher, and to a change in the weather. Children's emotions are purer in expression than their parents': their emotions are less subject to artificial repression; they are more freely expressed and quicker to change. A routinized classroom tends to establish a more consistent emotional pattern, but rigid control over emotions is not necessarily indicative of a dynamic learning situation. Skillful instruction minimizes the debilitating emotions and encourages the positive ones. It avoids extreme emotional expression and a rapid vacillation between emotions.

fear and hate in the classroom

Unfortunately fear-anxiety emotions are often played upon heavily in the classroom. An extreme form of a child's fear of school may be expressed in school phobia, a psychological phenomenon involving physical illness and frequently stemming from hostile-dependent relations between parent and child. While it is based on problems outside the school, school phobia finds symptoms related to alleged causes within the classroom. In this extreme, if infrequent, situation school officials often reject the "silly" and "imaginary" actions of a youngster, but such reactions by adults intensify the problem. School phobia is an example of the confused nature of problems in the school that are related to the home or the street as well as to the classroom.

If school phobia is the most extreme form of fear-anxiety in the classroom, it is by no means its only expression. Fear is the most widely used emotion employed to "maintain discipline" and to "motivate" youngsters. While fear is acknowledged to be among the least satisfactory means of achieving school aims, it is still in common usage. Youngsters are encouraged to fear a failing mark because it will mean parental and teacher disapproval or occasional taunts by classmates. A low mark will certainly lead to warnings of difficulty in entering a college in the remote future, to a possibility of repeating a grade or a subject, and to more immediate penalties in required study during lunch periods or after school.

Fear and anxiety are important emotions to every student who looks on learning as a serious business. While less fortunate classmates are worrying about failure, gifted pupils are constantly fearful of falling from the top or of receiving other than the highest marks. The bulk of youngsters, who are between the two extremes of the class, are also operating under the influence of fear. Fear is a powerful incentive; it may induce pupils to unexpected defensive behavior and is in a large sense the root of cheating, lying, and truancy.

Youngsters fear; they also hate. Fear and hate are related; we often hate that which is feared. A youngster may hate school and become a truant, or he may dislike a subject or a teacher. He may tend to say he hates when he means he dislikes, but the learning results are affected in similar ways. Pupil dislike of a subject is learned; it may be related to unhappy experiences in the subject area. A teacher may foster dislike of a subject by a youngster through the teaching methods he selects or because of negative personality characteristics.

There are various personality types in the profession. A wide assortment of motivating factors draws a variety of people into teaching. It is probably because of the flexibility of youngsters' reactions to various conditions that so many pupils are able to ride through several personality storms during a school day without serious damage to their intellectual interests. Whether a youngster's dislike of a teacher or subject develops into a temporary or permanent disenchantment with teachers or subjects depends on the personality characteristics of the pupil and on his succeeding experiences with other teachers or classes of that subject content.

It is an oversimplification to blame dislike for a subject solely on teachers. The student who experiences difficulties in mastering a skill or in remembering facts may become frustrated and thus acquire a profound dislike for the subject, the cause of his problem. Much of the ultimate responsibility for a lack of interest in school may in fact be out of the hands of teachers. A curriculum that imposes inappropriate subject matters on youngsters (such as economic theories in the ninth grade) or that forces irrelevant repetition upon classes (such as the study of American history in grades five, eight, and eleven) may take much of the thrill out of learning. A textbook may be poorly written and a dull textbook may lay the foundations for frustrations and dislike. How many students have found texts that make the study of grammar, for instance, cold and laborious? It may be a mark of the intelligence of a youngster that he comes to dislike a subject that is ineffectively organized and poorly taught. It may similarly be a tribute to the wisdom of the slow learner who, perhaps subconsciously, identifies the school, teacher, or subject as the source of his frustrations. In his reaction the slow learner may be functioning as efficiently as his faster learning classmate; and they both may come to abhor the classroom.

Should we really be confused by the pupil who hates the school that seems to resent him, that regiments an important segment of his life, and that forces him to study things he finds unchallenging while it denies him opportunities to explore the challenges he would wish to pursue? A child's youthful simplicity and his naked honesty stand out in sharp contrast to the sophisticated blindness of adults. It is the adult who is naive when he demands that children uncritically accept what they prefer to reject and reject what they would choose to accept.

school as a happy experience

The youngster who experiences fear and hatred in the classroom should also come to know the pleasanter loves and likes of the school experience. It is an indication of negativism that we find "hatred" a more appropriate descriptive label than "love" in speaking of school. It is liking that oils the learning gears and leads to successful students, happy schools, and contented teachers. To a large measure a student likes a subject, or teacher, or school, that in turn "likes" him. This is not a plea for a teacher to lavish affection on youngsters, for a child cannot be given in a school the love and security that may be found only in a home. Homes bereft of love and affection deny a youngster a birthright that he can find nowhere else, and much as a teacher may attempt to be a substitute parent or a school to serve as a substitute home, teachers and schools cannot take the place of honest parents and real homes.

A youngster likes those things from which he gains satisfactions and through which his needs are met. As he is successful in school or in a subject a pupil is apt to enjoy his school experience and to like the subject in which he does well. A youngster's success in school comes when he wins approval from a teacher, satisfies report card-conscious parents, recognizes an improvement in his skills, or derives satisfaction by meeting challenges and finding answers to his questions. A youngster will recognize as sympathetic a situation that accepts him as he truly is, that poses challenges he can meet, and that recognizes the same measure of success that he does. There is a great similarity between the way an adult likes his job and his community and the way a youngster likes learning and his school.

It may be as difficult to structure a classroom that youngsters will like as it is easy to create one they will fear. Children find it easier to love than to hate. They come into the school situation with an inclination to like and be liked, but whether they do like and are liked by the time of their eventual exit from school will depend on their fortunes or misfortunes within a series of classrooms. They come as clay to be shaped and leave a well-hardened mass to be admired or rejected. They have been spun on a potter's wheel that is the classroom, shaped in good part by teachers, and hardened in a kiln that is the school.

the place of emotions in the school

Something of the eloquence with which a principal explained to a student teacher the phenomenon of a pupil's "crush" on a teacher will be lost in the retelling, but the point must be made. Through the grades an occasional student becomes emotionally attached to a teacher. This is the "golden opportunity" for the teacher to aid the youngster in gaining a healthy attitude toward school and in finding a strong and worthy motivation for the pursuit of his studies. The teacher must be careful not to take advantage of the youngster, but to give him the full advantage of the situation. The pupil can be helped most by being given neither undue encouragement nor rejection; his fascination for the adult will pass in time. Like any "true love" the strong attachment for a teacher is a pure and sudden and surprising experience for a child. Because such behavior is spontaneous and unplanned, it occurs when a teacher unconsciously demonstrates an honest interest in a youngster and concern for his welfare. The teacher who seeks to cultivate emotionalized responses from children must find disappointment, for their reactions will then be as forced and as artificial as was the teacher's encouragement.

Other emotions also have their place in a youngster's makeup. The child has the same emotions as the adult, but a youngster's emotions are more spontaneous. He has not yet had the experiences that lead to repression or exaggeration of emotional response. A youngster should be permitted the luxury of anger in school, at least occasionally and when appropriate; the same is true for a teacher. A pupil may have occasion to experience jealous feelings toward classmates; however, jealousy should not become a teacher's weapon to be used against a youngster under the false label of "competition." Joy and sadness are essential emotions throughout life and have their place in a student's reactive pattern. Classrooms have, or ought to have, their moments of joy. Sadness is perhaps less useful, although the facts of life cannot avoid unhappy moments. In some situations one youngster's joy is another's sorrow, but use of this joy-sorrow combination should not be necessary in carrying out learning activities. The youngster who is depressed in school may have brought his problem from home or from the street. The teacher should be sympathetic toward the dejected youngster, for, whatever the origin of his problem, it is as painful during classroom hours as in the setting from which it originates.

Every student has a right to live with and to express his emotions. Denial of this right only serves to create an emotional imbalance and to drive underground that which it is preferable to experience and accept. But not all emotional experiences are satisfying or satisfactory. The teacher who identifies a child with abnormal emotionality should refer him to experts who are qualified to make the necessary and expert evaluation of behavior.

the creative experience

Each youngster in the classroom is reacting; he is subject to emotions; he is creating. While we tend by definition to reserve creativity for a privileged few, this definition is correct only if we confine ourselves to a narrow meaning of creativity. If, however, the term is broadened to include an ability by anyone to produce something unique for himself, even the pupils with the lowest level of ability are creative. The most important creative experience for every individual is his own perception of the world about him. For the secure individual the world is broad and expansive; for the less secure it is narrow and confining. The youngster is in the center of his world. About him are framed his hopes and fears, his real and imagined friends and enemies, and his most treasured values and accomplishments. Somewhere in this structure are the school, the teacher, the family, and acquaintances. These worldly aspects are perceived not as they really are but as they seem to be.

The important and manipulable creations for a youngster are the things he has produced: crayon drawing, homemade valentine, or secret poem. The end product of this creativity may violate the rules of architecture, be hardly identifiable, appear messily pasted, or be ill-rhymed, but to the creator his work is a distinctive and true accomplishment. A child's creative efforts will never cease, even if discouraged and unrewarded. Unacknowledged creativity may be driven "underground" or even forced into the hidden recesses of the imagination. The basic interests and abilities of a youngster should be recognized and utilized in the classroom. The casual observer may be unaware that every individual is also a creator (even if mediocre), yet this is one of the differences that separates human beings from the rest of the beasts.

pupil behavior

Pupils are constantly behaving, and in this context we are concerned with personal conduct, acceptance of rules, and pursuit of moral precepts. While one might take comfort in the knowledge that Joan Dunn's *Retreat from Learning*[1] does not reflect the level of pupil deportment in many of our smaller schools, the failure of children to learn is a tragic judgment on the educational system in our largest city (and probably others as well). The author reports a frustrating teaching experience, with most of her time spent policing a classroom in New York City.

A student's behavior is a result of many factors. Behavioral development begins with the tender care of an infant and builds day by day, just as the evolving personality responds to the relative inflexibility of highly developed adult personalities. A behavior pattern is being shaped when a baby is never permitted to cry, is allowed to whimper indefinitely, or is continually alternated between excessive fondling and semiabandonment. These early experiences merge with genetic influences to unite into that indefinable characteristic called "personality." The first school experiences take place against the background of previous nonschool experiences. Behavior in school develops within the evolving situation in a classroom, in the meshing with other and diverse evolving personalities, and in relations with a relatively strong adult personality, the teacher.

The school cannot be construed as a second home environment. The behavior that a youngster acquires in a school is unique to the school; it mirrors conduct learned in the home only to the extent that behavior developed at home is exhibited and condoned in the classroom. Home-bred reactions are reinforced in school to the extent that a single teacher is able to be concerned with one of thirty youngsters at a given time. New school behavior of a youngster is molded under the influence of twenty-nine other youngsters and an adult.

Whispering, lying, cheating, shooting spitballs, passing notes, or open rebellion (the entire range of school behavior problems) are learned in school. No youngster enters school as a "bad school citizen" for the simple reason that he has not had the opportunity to become one. Many children leave school as problems after having had negative experiences in the classroom, but it is absurd to presume that a six-year-old enters a schoolhouse determined to become a failure.

Behavior patterns are constantly in flux in school and, up to the point where a teacher rejects an individual for his conduct, are subject to change in a positive direction. The influence of a teacher on behavior is obvious. Instances of "bad

1 Joan Dunn, *Retreat from Learning* (New York: McKay, 1955).

eggs" fitting into one classroom and "good citizens" running amok in another are numerous.

The conduct of an individual is reflected by his acceptance or rejection of rules. Acceptance of rules requires a willingness to accommodate oneself to them and is related to one's assessment of the values involved. If the penalties for ignoring rules are offset by the laughter of classmates or if a teacher's disapproving attention is better than none at all, the rules become significant only when they are broken. For the less rebellious youngster a rule becomes objectionable when it is seen to be unjust, improper, or unnecessary. Perhaps one of the most interesting examples of lack of general acceptance of classroom regulations among teen-agers is toward rules forbidding gum chewing. After teaching both in schools where chewing gum has been permitted and where it was forbidden, one gets the eerie feeling that more gum is chewed surreptitiously than legally. Gum chewing has become the issue of a schoolhouse Eighteenth Amendment.

The school cannot assume the responsibility that rightly belongs to the home, church, and community for construction of a moral code. Application and interpretation of the community code differ from subgroup to subgroup, but the individual youngster is able to adjust to the varying interpretations that he encounters in his community. The hand that steals from the local merchant and divides the loot equally with a gang may piously take up the church collection and honor personal property within the home. The knife that carves initials on a school desk and rips theater cushions may peel potatoes in the kitchen at home.

When behavioral codes vary, the school can neither assume the role of arbiter of morals nor simply defer establishment of rules to everyone else. A suitable subcode should be established for the school. Pupils learn the interpretation and application of moral codes and the school is obliged to provide instruction in an appropriate code of school conduct. "Appropriate," in this case, must apply to the school as a learning environment, to teachers as sympathetic adults, and to youngsters as citizens of the school society and as immature learners. The school cannot impose an adult code upon youngsters. It cannot enforce a code that is authoritarian while attempting to establish democratic attitudes in children. Nor can teachers expect to demand a middle-class puritanism of lower-class youngsters or, for that matter, of many middle-class pupils as well.

student development

A youngster's schoolhouse conduct is governed by his estimate of a situation, by the interpretation he makes of the effect of his own actions upon peers and teachers, and by his unconscious attempts to satisfy his basic psychological needs. A pupil looks to others for cues, for suggestions for his behavior and approval of his conduct. His development through school takes many directions and every direction is guided by external as well as internal forces.

PHYSICAL The physical development of a growing youngster is most obvious to an observer, for physical development has an influence on other aspects of growth. The small youngster may compensate by excelling in his academic efforts, or if he is of limited academic potential he may seek to gain attention by early use of cigarettes or engaging in petty thievery. The class giant may find his size a key to athletic success, or he may turn into an accomplished bully. Chronically ill or physically handicapped children may become intensive scholars, or they may develop emotional problems.

Both the largest and smallest youngsters in a class may be judged by their size. A teacher may equate size and maturity; he may expect the large pupil to be more mature in behavior, while the small youngster may be spared the same demands. Anger and its consequences may be denied to those of large physical stature. Physical development is placed in its proper perspective when it is accepted as incidental to other characteristics and unique among them. More than any other attribute it works its influence on youngsters, for responding to size is among the simplest of reactions. Unequal and erratic growth patterns of some pupils find them experiencing a development in which they are larger than the median of the group at one age level and average or smaller at other levels.

Physical evolution is related to emotional development throughout school, but it is of critical importance during puberty. In the adolescent years youngsters are in the volatile situation of being both or neither child and adult. While puberty is the most crucial period of emotional development, pre- and post-adolescent years are also of significant importance. Emotionality is a dynamic process: it is always operating and always subject to change. A teacher is in an unusually advantageous position to observe the emotional development and stability of children. His special service is to contribute to emotional stability through his own personality characteristics and by making reasonable demands on each student. A teacher cannot minister to severe emotional problems but must be able to make suitable referrals when necessary. The best cue to the teacher in identifying possible emotional difficulties is frequent irrational behavior by a youngster. The obvious case is the child whose behavior is disruptive in the classroom, but the teacher should also be aware of abnormally introvertive personalities who may have severe emotional problems too.

ACADEMIC Academic development is less obvious and more difficult to assess than physical or emotional growth, but it is still the most vital school task. There has been no greater challenge to education than schooling for the masses. Mass education is the social revolution that can free all men for all time. The perpetuation of the aims and methods of selective education in the schools prevents the realization of the promise and potential of universal education.

Educators cannot establish the goals that were appropriate to the education of an elite as the ideal academic development in mass education. The average individual cannot be subjected to the same demands that are placed on the educated man under a system of selective education. Every child may not be expected to understand Shakespeare's sonnets, read Virgil in the original, or master the Pythagorean Theorem, but ideally he should develop academic skills to his full potential. The major task of the school is to ensure this. Limits to academic development should be found only within individuals and not in teachers, the school, a subject, method, or curriculum.

The student who is endowed by nature with the capacity to make significant contributions to society should be required to do no less. Those who have limited ability should learn to the maximum of their potential. If a child's reading limit is at the sixth-grade level, he should be able to read that well. If his ultimate achievement is to add and subtract simple numbers but not to multiply or divide, he should learn his simple addition and subtraction as well as his ability allows. A child must not be denied that which is within his grasp. If the school does not have the means to fulfill this noble ambition, the changes necessary to meet this goal should be a major educational task.

It is not the responsibility of the youngster to decide what he should learn or when he has attained the limits of his potential, but he should have the opportunity to learn as an individual. The pupil does not want, expect, or demand to be his own master in the classroom. To foist such a responsibility on the child denies him that very security in adult leadership that children so desperately seek. Adults who accept youngsters' demands for license might consider the possibility that cries for independence might be pleas for the security of sympathetic and experienced guidance and control.

Students expect to realize academic progress. Grumblings from college students who look back on wasted opportunities in the classroom as well as complaints from the unskilled who feel that they were cheated out of academic knowledge in school leave little doubt that all had expected to learn in school. A youngster knows when he is not learning. Classroom problems are often traced to the frustrations of those who are willing to learn but are unable to do so. Behavioral difficulties are common among older youngsters who have come to accept their own limitations in the classroom and, experiencing only failure, have given up. The assumption that the child who tries and cannot or who has tried and quit has no interest in learning is too questionable to warrant its present acceptance in and out of school. Even if mottoes are trite, that of the State University of New York still has a ring of truth in it: "Let each become all he is capable of being." The individual does not bear the entire responsibility to learn all that society believes he should learn, nor is it the duty of the school to force learning upon him. A youngster's desire to learn is realized when the school provides the guidance, the means, and the opportunity to fulfill his educational goals and to meet his personal needs to know about himself and his world.

PERSONALITY While it should not preempt the academic responsibility of the school, personality development has become an important by-product of the school experience. In the wake of selective education we still operate as though there were a standard personality to be attained, as though everyone must become equally educated. It is obvious that all cannot attain equal academic heights. The expectation that every youngster is to develop a standard personality is both unrealistic and undesirable unless we presume to create the controlled puppet that is more appropriate to other political philosophies and cultures. We must tolerate the introvert, the extrovert, and those between. Some personality variations that may be looked on with suspicion in the classroom are necessary in order to maintain a diverse society. We do not expect the research chemist to share the same personality with a city taxi driver or the corporation president with the union agent. We can recognize differences in adults; it should not be difficult to accept variety in their children.

A youngster's right to his own personality may be violated when he is graded on "class participation" or in any class other than language arts on skills in oral presentation. A teacher is measuring personality attributes when he includes in a mark factors of cooperation, attitude, or ability to get along with classmates. Is a timid or reticent pupil uncooperative? an extrovert rowdy? a nervous child fidgety? a relaxed child indifferent? Is someone who is quick to laugh noisy and one who displays a subdued humor sullen? Is a profound thinker moody and a shallow thinker flippant? Is every youngster who deviates from the average a problem to society, to a school, to a classroom and a teacher, and to himself? The school seems to place a premium on the child who is a nonentity, until he also becomes a nonparticipant in the intellectual arena; then he is identified as a classroom problem. Rather than spending school time trying to mold every youngster into the "ideal personality," educators should be expending their efforts on the world of intellectual stimulation.

Every youngster is in a continual process of developing a moral code which is in part that of his family and gang but is essentially unique to himself. There is a tendency to magnify group control of codes and to ignore an individual's ability and willingness to be different as well as to be a conformist. Many people share an exaggerated belief in the ability of the teacher to personally direct general moral development far beyond the actual influence he has.

In structuring the schoolhouse moral code the teacher is in the pivotal position, but his influence is dependent on what he does rather than on what he says. Every unconscious pressure leading a student into classroom dishonesty carries far more weight than admonitions not to cheat. Of particular concern to youngsters is a teacher's "fairness." "Fair" is a nebulous term that is nevertheless a constant factor in a youngster's evaluation of a classroom. A fair teacher gives fair (reasonable) assignments and administers fair (appropriate and understandable) tests. He treats every pupil fairly (has no "pets"), is fair in applying discipline (is not unduly harsh in punishing and does not punish innocent bystanders), and evaluates fairly (a youngster gets the mark he has earned). Each of these assessments is a subjective judgment by youngsters, but a teacher who is aware of youngsters' criteria and has a reasonable set of criteria of his own will be "fair." Every youngster's complaint does not become a *cause célèbre* in the "fair" classroom; gripes are fairly heard and fairly judged. Other indices of a teacher's moral code should not be ignored, such as promises that are or are not kept, willingness to admit to errors, and recognition that one does not know everything. Youngsters are aware of the discrepancies in "do as I say, not as I do." They are, in fact, excellent judges of human nature and human values and can relate them to a stated moral code, to the code that is practiced, and to standards of their own.

SOCIAL School life is an academic existence for some youngsters and rebellion for others, but it is a social context for all. The school is a highly structured and highly regimented society. It has a greater caste system than the society about it, for it is here that every social group meets every other group in the school district, with no chance for escape. Parents may ride side by side on a bus and they may stand in queues at the supermarket with scarcely a common glance at each other. Their youngsters, however, find extended periods of contact with everyone's children and come to know even the intimacy of sharing a shower or sitting together at mealtime. In addition to forced togetherness, there are voluntary divisions in choosing partners or sides, in exchange of valentines, in the invitation to an after-school birthday party, and in recruitment into membership in the informal street gang or its more formal sorority counterpart.

While the school may assume responsibility for encouraging social democracy, there may be confusion as to whether it is more democratic to establish voluntary social groupings or to force membership in a common school society. The school permits and encourages both. The issue of social development raises the most difficult questions, which are generally left unanswered. Should one or a few youngsters be social outcasts in a classroom? If the answer is no, how successfully can the school encourage, scheme, or force acceptance of every pupil by the ingroup? Should the parallels in adult society be those that govern the school social system? If the role of complete social acceptance is a genuine school objective, the means of measuring a standard behavior present serious problems. Should there be any recognition of individual deviation from the standard, or would deviations lead again to a school caste system? While the adult ponders the questions, students live with the problem. Some find in the school ready resources for social adjustment, while others find in the same school rejection, frustration, and heartache.

ATTITUDINAL Development of attitudes is basic to all the other forms of individual growth mentioned above. The meanings a child finds in his physical, emotional, and personality development and the ways in which he uses these developmental forms are expressions of the youngster's attitudes toward himself. Social and moral development reflects the ways in which one perceives others as well as oneself. Academic development depends on a complex attitude toward oneself and others and toward learning an assortment of academic disciplines. Attitudes are basic to success in school; they are acquired and expressed in mysterious ways.

The greatest difficulty encountered in dealing with attitudes is that they are easily verbalized. Like other learned habits, attitudes are highly resistant to change, to the process of unlearning and relearning. Those attitudes considered to be most important should be learned first rather than relearned later. It is necessary that teachers know that attitudes, even those with reference to school, are to a large extent acquired outside of school.

Some youngsters come from families whose vocation, social status, and personal preferences are oriented away from academic interests. These pupils may live in homes where few books are found, where reading is confined to comic books and pulp magazines, and where the social environment is strongly anti-intellectual. If these antischool forces have not registered an impression before entrance into school, they beat their ceaseless tattoo through the school years. Yet even from this group come youngsters with a deep interest in learning, with a strong desire to squeeze the last precious drop of knowledge from school. In *Manchild in the Promised Land* Claude Brown recalled his struggle with and triumph over a tragic slum environment where negative influences were pushing him away from the greater society and its expectations.[2] A half continent from Brown's slum home, one may recall an attractive girl from a restless migrant farm family who voiced the hope on entering school in midyear that for once she might finish out a year in one school. Early the next spring she followed the family to another community. Little wonder that this fifteen-

[2] Claude Brown, *Manchild in the Promised Land* (New York: Macmillan, 1965).

year-old was sporting an engagement ring and seriously considering marriage before the summer's end!

In addition to negative outside forces, there are influences within a school that forge destructive attitudes toward learning. There are uninterested and uninteresting teachers whose personalities, demands, and methods wreak havoc with some youngsters. There are school administrators who find satisfaction in silent but sterile buildings, in schedules that take care of all problems other than learning, in regulations that repress the majority for the sins of a few, and in a curriculum that once established shall not be changed. We cannot write off casually the influence of nonstudents who disrupt classes, bully the interested, and sneer at teacher, school, and the world in general.

To keep an honest balance, we must give credit to the inspiring teacher, the enlightened administrator, encouraging homes, and most of all to the individual who may be determined to become immersed in the academic swim despite unfavorable circumstances. If this discussion seems to have emphasized the negative aspects, it is because it recognizes a general tendency to exaggerate the positive and is attempting to strike a balance.

Finally, it is an oversimplification to point out the complicated process of attitudinal formation without recognizing that one attitude may interfere with another. A youngster's attitude toward himself may conflict with his attitudes toward his peers or school. If he lacks confidence in his own abilities, he will reflect this in his attitude toward school. At the same time, if his negative appraisal of himself should change into a positive one, it is also possible that he may develop a more favorable attitude toward school. Considering the complex nature of the human creature, it is obvious that simple solutions are not adequate in resolving educational problems. The question of attitudes of youngsters and especially attitudes toward school and learning comprises one of the most difficult instructional problems.

conclusion

Many of the answers needed to explain teaching are not yet available, but this does not mean that there are no answers. The solutions awaiting discovery will be as complex as the problems they seek to resolve. The answers will be found only after painstaking research based on a realistic and faultless appraisal of people, events, and processes. Progress is impossible without the acquisition of additional knowledge about learners and learning (and we should not confuse knowledge with opinion). Increased knowledge does not suggest that the atom has become less complex but only that man's knowledge has increased. Although teachers will not solve all the complex problems of human behavior, they must believe that many answers will be found. There are no easy resolutions to problems of educating complicated human beings.

It is appropriate to emphasize the role of the teacher as a perpetual student, as one who is continually increasing and modernizing his knowledge of the physical, scientific, human, and artistic world. It is even more important to point out that the teacher must be a student of youngsters as groups, as products of homes and societies, as members of social classes, as learners, and as individuals. It is of the greatest significance that a teacher be mindful of the fact that schools were built, staffed, and organized for youngsters, not for administrators, teachers, parents, or the interested public. There is no reason for education, schools, or educators to exist other than to serve those who learn.

on your own

Those preparing to teach have the benefit of specialized information about school children through psychological study of children or adolescents. The serious student, however, never quits the pursuit of knowledge.

Because every individual is unique, study of a youngster's behavior at any particular time and in any particular situation may lead to new understandings and insights. A most informative experience is concentrated observation of a preschool child, for here one may find the nearly "pure" learning situation, uncomplicated by the teaching function. The youngster piling blocks, building in the sand, and coordinating eye and hand movements demonstrates the play of motivation, trial and error, success or failure, and the variability of the attention span.

Knowledge of those who inhabit our schools as learners must include information of youngsters beyond the learning environment. A most significant description of forgotten Americans is Michael Harrington's *The Other America: Poverty in the United States* (New York: Macmillan, 1962). Purposeful study by American educators cannot ignore the teacher's frustrations in slum schools as depicted in *Retreat from Learning* by Joan Dunn (New York: McKay, 1955) or the familiar *Blackboard Jungle* of Evan Hunter (New York: Simon and Schuster, 1954). Nor can one ignore the personal story of slum life in Claude Brown's *Manchild in the Promised Land* (New York: Macmillan, 1965) or impersonal studies such as that of Frank Riessman, *The Culturally Deprived Child* (New York: Harper & Row, 1962). Many well-written treatises on the impoverished and their problems have been published; the teacher should consider them an essential part of his educational background. Included among them are Kenneth B. Clark, *Dark Ghetto: Dilemmas of Social Power* (New York: Harper & Row, 1965); Charlotte Leon Mayerson (ed.), *Two Blocks Apart* (New York: Holt, Rinehart and Winston, 1965); and two books by Patricia Sexton, *Education and Income: Inequalities of Opportunity in Our Public Schools* (New York: Viking, 1961) and *Spanish Harlem: Anatomy of Poverty* (New York: Harper & Row, 1965).

Concern for the gifted youngster was a pioneer contribution in the recognition of differences among schoolchildren; the monumental work in this area is Louis Terman's (and successors) *Genetic Studies of Genius* (Stanford, Calif.: Stanford University Press, 1925–1959), Vols. I–V. Well recommended, also, is Willard Abraham's *Common Sense About Gifted Children* (New York: Harper & Row, 1958). The mentally retarded is by no means the forgotten child and an abundance of material is available on this sector of special education.

Current literature is rightfully concerned with the schoolchild in his many aspects and roles; reference should be made to *Education Index, Readers' Guide,* and *Social Sciences and Humanities Index.* Look under "Children," "Delinquency," and "Slums."

additional references

Baldwin, Alfred L. *The Theories of Child Development.* New York: Wiley, 1967.

Breckenridge, Marian E., and E. Lee Vincent. *Child Development; Physical and Psychological Growth Through Adolescence.* 5th ed. Phila.: Saunders, 1965.

Dunn, Lloyd M. (ed.). *Exceptional Children in the Schools.* New York: Holt, Rinehart and Winston, 1963.

Erdman, Robert L. *Educable Retarded Children in Elementary Schools.* Washington, D.C.: Council for Exceptional Children, National Education Association, 1965.

Gallagher, James J., Mary Jane Aschner, and William Jenne. *Productive Thinking of Gifted Children in Classroom Interaction.* Research Monograph B5. Washington, D.C.: Council for Exceptional Children, National Education Association, 1967.

Goodman, Paul. *Growing Up Absurd: Problems of Youth in the Organized System.* New York: Random House, 1960.

Grambs, Jean D. *Intergroup Education: Methods and Materials.* Englewood Cliffs, N.J.: Prentice-Hall, 1968.

Greene, Mary Frances, and Orletta Ryan. *The Schoolchildren: Growing up in the Slums.* New York: Pantheon, 1965.

Holt, John. *How Children Fail.* New York: Pitman, 1964.

Kohl, Herbert. *36 Children.* New York: New American Library, 1967.

Nordstrom, Carl, Edgar Z. Friedenberg, and Hilary A. Gold. *Society's Children: A Study of Ressentiment in Secondary School Education.* New York: Random House, 1967.

Rosenthal, Robert, and Lenore Jacobson. *Pygmalion in the Classroom.* New York: Holt, Rinehart and Winston, 1968.

Sigel, Irving E., and Frank H. Hooper. *Logical Thinking in Children: Research Based on Piaget's Theory.* New York: Holt, Rinehart and Winston, 1968.

Strom, Robert D. *Teaching in the Slum School.* Columbus, Ohio: Merrill, 1965.

Webster, Staten W. (ed.). *The Disadvantaged Learner: Knowing, Understanding, Educating.* San Francisco: Chandler, 1966.

4

The school is an instrument serving the special interests of its particular society. Public schools serve "the public interest," parochial schools a certain religious group, and private schools the special interest of a particular set of parents (usually concerned with preparation for college, although at times with preschool training or education of deaf, blind, slow-learning, or crippled children). The school is a social institution established by a society to provide education or training to further the objectives of the sponsoring group. When a society is a single-minded, cohesive entity the purpose of the school is direct and relatively obvious. As the society increases in complexity (includes a greater variety of viewpoints and special interests in the areas of social or economic class, religious beliefs, political philosophy, and national or racial differences), the purposes of the school are less clear-cut and are subject to the pressures of conflicting groups.

Americans are united into a national society, vague regional interests, and state and local entities. The political society has created the school system as a means of promoting the body politic, but other societies—religious, merchant, and industrial—have exerted significant influences upon the public educational system and have created schools of their own when dissatisfied with the public schools. As schools were established and particularly as they became universal in the larger social order, a growing educational "establishment" came to have a special interest in the schools, in the uses made of them, and in protecting them against outside influences. Educators have become the greatest champions of the schools and are the most active in maintaining traditions and in effecting change in the schools.

society's schools

A school is the result of a response by society in general or an economic or other specialized social grouping to provide an organized learning situation. The public school thus becomes a center for the meshing of social forces. The social group controls the schools, as the power clique sees it, for the interests of the greater society, and various social subgroups send youngsters into the school. Teachers represent a homogeneous social grouping that is at one time or another in conflict with every other social segment—including its own middle class. This conflict centers, occasionally, on matters of curriculum and, more frequently, on matters of special, egocentric concern to teachers, such as teaching salaries or related school responsibilities.

historical development

Schools were established when the burden of transmitting the culture or preparing the future generation to survive in the society became too complex or too burdensome for the family. A frequent occasion for the establishment of schools was the development of a need to teach religious doctrine, particularly as religion came to dominate every phase of life and as it became highly complex in character.

In the United States schools were first established to perpetuate a sectarian religious heritage. Early settlers in Massachusetts adopted the proposition that schools were to be established by parents in order to educate youngsters in religious doctrine. Many youngsters received elemental schooling under a voluntary school system, and in 1647 the Massachusetts Act made schooling compulsory, with the avowed purpose of promoting the theocracy. Over two centuries later religious influence was still obvious in the schools as shown by selections in *McGuffey's Fifth Reader*. These included "Respect for the Sabbath Rewarded," "The Goodness of God," and "My Mother's Bible."

early patterns of education

While the fanaticism that brought those first small groups to the New World centered life on religion and led to the establishment of religious schools, the growth of commerce and industry soon increased the emphasis on ciphering and brought about more extensive academic and vocational demands on education. In the early colonies children attended dame schools or common schools. The former were run by widows or housewives within their homes, while the latter were conducted in one-room schoolhouses, which were "kept" by colonial schoolmasters. An immediate need for further schooling for the few who would become clergymen and colonial leaders resulted in the establishment of a Latin grammar school in 1635 in Boston; a year later Harvard College was established. The Latin grammar school was modeled on similar schools in England, with a curriculum centered on classical studies, primarily Latin and Greek. Harvard College was almost exclusively an institution for theological training as were the other early colleges, William and Mary (1693) and Yale (1701).

While the New England school model exerted the major influence upon the development of American education, different patterns developed in other colonial areas. In Pennsylvania, which was typical of the middle colonies, religious tolerance and differentiation resulted in a parochial school pattern, with the various sects setting up schools for their memberships. The southern colonies, with their scattered population and plantation system, followed the English patterns of education. Tutors and private schools were organized for the wealthier citizens, and the rest of the population was schooled in apprenticeship programs or pauper schools. The Anglican Church played an important role in education in the South.

Increasing educational needs and the changing nature of the population led to the establishment of a unique American secondary school, the academy, with a broader instructional program than the Latin grammar school. Benjamin Franklin's academy at Philadelphia (1751) is considered to be the first of its kind. The academy rapidly replaced the Latin grammar school, reached a peak in development about 1820–1830, and declined dramatically after the Civil War.

Even less traditional than the academy was the public high school, which was first organized in Boston in 1821. The permanent extension of public education through the secondary level became a reality in 1872 when the Michigan state courts in the Kalamazoo Case ruled that monies raised through taxation could be used to finance public secondary education. The public high school developed as the universal extension of the common school and eventually enrolled the majority of youngsters.

The last major change in the public educational pattern

was the establishment of the junior high school, of which the first is recognized as that of Berkeley, California, in 1909. Innovations on the junior high school in the form of middle and intermediate schools are currently a matter of concern to American educators.

systemizers of instruction

Religious influences upon American education have been noted: theocratic in New England, divergent sectarian in the middle colonies, and Anglican in the South. As schools became secularized they came under new influences, at first European and later American in origin. A monitorial system of instruction, credited to Joseph Lancaster in England during the 1790s and called the Lancastrian system, was adopted in New York City in 1806. Under this plan, one teacher taught a large group with the help of older pupil monitors. The normal-school idea for the training of teachers had existed in Europe for a century before it was first introduced in the United States in 1823. Johann Heinrich Pestalozzi (1746–1827) in Switzerland became the model in 1859 for Edward Sheldon at the Oswego (New York) Normal School in establishing the "object method" of teaching. The kindergarten, initiated in 1855, developed from the German movement attributed to Friedrich Froebel (1782–1852). Psychology in education as taught by Johann Friedrich Herbart (1776–1841) was adopted in America in 1890. These Herbartian influences moved education and teaching away from the limited perspective of faculty psychology into scientifically acceptable theories of instruction. They also broadened educational objectives into a concern for the society and its citizenry.

Horace Mann (1796–1859) and Henry Barnard (1811–1900) provided important leadership in the organization and conduct of education in New England and influenced educational development in the United States. Mann believed that education ought to be free, universal, and nonsectarian. He moved toward greater organization of schools under state guidance and played a leading role in establishing normal schools for the preparation of teachers. Barnard was less of an innovator and a philosopher, but he provided leadership for better schools. From 1867–1870 he served as the first United States commissioner of education.

The most important figure to emerge on the American educational scene was John Dewey (1859–1952), who became a major influence in his own country and gained recognition throughout the world. While principal of the Laboratory School at the University of Chicago, Dewey became a spokesman for educational change, but it was at Columbia University that he dedicated himself to a long and distinguished career of teaching and writing. The words and works of Dewey led to a major reassessment of educational philosophy and practice in the United States. Borrowing largely from Dewey, progressive educators embarked upon a questioning of educational practice and belief that resulted in the most experimental era in the history of American education. An effort was made to have teaching become child-centered rather than subject-centered, and schools engaged in an expansion of educational activities. Advances in the study of psychology led to the emergence of testing as a means of measuring individual aptitude and achievement. Guidance programs could now use testing information to aid children in adjustment to school and the world. New instructional patterns were explored and an assortment of methods of teaching was suggested and sampled. Education became a matter of general concern. Some schoolmen even came to believe that public matters were subject to educational influence and educationally initiated reforms.

governmental influences

The most recent influence on America's schools has come from the federal government, whose new role was primarily determined by the Supreme Court decision of May 17, 1954, in which segregation of races in schools was declared unconstitutional. In historical retrospect, involvement of the federal government in enforcing the court's decision may be credited with the sudden resolution of problems hampering federal aid to schools: passage of a federal aid to education act in 1965 ended twenty years of conflict over the church-state issue in the use of federal monies for schools; a National Teacher Corps was established; and markedly increased financial support for higher education was voted by the Congress.

mass education

Most countries are engaged in a process of mass education, although few aim to educate their populations beyond early adolescence and the acquisition of the most elementary knowledge and academic skills. The United States has been unique in attempting the mass education of the later adolescent. At least two-thirds of American youth are now graduating from high school, and there is considerable concern and much agony over those who drop out. There are abundant signs that mass education shall be extended into the colleges and universities.

Mass education first developed from the belief that the individual must acquire at least an elementary knowledge and some skills for his religious and commercial welfare. Later the greater society deemed mass education essential for the benefit and protection of the social order. Schools have become a nationalistic tool for the preservation of capitalist, socialist, democratic, and totalitarian societies. They are the means by which highly developed societies maintain their technological leadership and through which underdeveloped nations hope to make the leap from primitive status to modern statehood.

As the industrial revolution engulfed society, it became essential to educate workers for the new technology. Even the farm became a complex, mechanized business, and a high level of education became a requisite for competing successfully in rural areas. It is appropriate to note that schools reinforced the laws prohibiting child labor in industry by requiring every youngster to be in school up to the age of sixteen or eighteen. Today it is important that the members of an industrial society have the educational background to man the technology. In the future it will be absolutely essential for every individual to reach his maximum educational level so that the total scientific potential for the entire population will be realized.

While mass education is a necessity to the industrialized society, it is also a human luxury. Never before has a nation presumed the right of each of its citizens to a full twelve years of publicly financed education. For a society to attempt such a task requires an affluence far beyond previous experience. Educational growth in the United States is financially feasible to the extent that (1) American national wealth is geared to an efficient and expanding technology and (2) this technology is promoted by the process of mass education. The eventual ability of a nation to continue the expensive process of mass education may depend on the efficiency of that educational process.

At the present it would seem that the limits to the technological evolution will be reached when every individual has been educated to the limit of his ability and is able to function at his peak. Yet the possibility that scientists can develop machines to substitute for human knowledge and skills (or even go beyond them?) suggests that the apparent limits may not be the real ones. Reports that human potential might be extended through biochemical processes open the way for an extension of human academic endeavors beyond original limits. It is enough to stagger the imagination to project the potential benefits for mankind through an effective mass educational process.

Even though mass education is an impressive near-reality and its potential may be awe-inspiring, it does have problems. Mass education has created new situations in the schools: all social classes are brought into the schools and retained for longer periods. Individuals who have little in common outside the school share classrooms and learning experiences. A greater variety of value standards, interests, and abilities come together in the schoolroom. Both the child with high ability and the one with low ability, the ready and the reluctant learner, are placed in a common situation. These new social structures have created new group situations and new demands on the teaching process. Few changes have come about to meet these problems. As a result, the teacher's greatest concern is frequently classroom discipline rather than classroom learning. Important problems in the management of mass education beg for solution before the schools may realize their fullest objectives.

control of public schools

The society that creates schools must provide some system for operating them. Historically the original colonial compulsory education laws required parents to educate their children, but those who made the laws were not able to provide the means to carry out the mandate. As a result, groups of parents provided for the education of their children by pooling resources to construct one-room schoolhouses or to seek out a woman in the community who would be willing to establish a dame school in her home. Where schools were built, residents contributed of their wealth, from money to whiskey to firewood, and boarded the schoolmaster successively in parents' homes.

The new schools were financed, operated, and controlled at the local level as an accidental result of a dispersed population, meager social needs, and little desire or power on the part of the colonies or states to engage directly in conducting enterprises that could be handled by the local citizenry. In this sense education was not unique, for few services were performed by the early central governments. Even such vital needs as health regulation, road building and maintenance, and law enforcement and legal processes were primarily local concerns. Rather than describe this delegation of function as "grass-roots democracy," it is probably more correct to note that it was impossible for the weak and distant colonial or state government to control its small and scattered population.

A variety of patterns of school management and control has developed throughout the United States. Every state has an education agency, which is responsible for its schools. State boards of education are elected by the public, appointed by governors, or nominated by the governor and confirmed by the legislature. Political patronage may influence appointments or nonpartisan selection may serve the public interest. State commissioners of education or superintendents of public instruction are named through the same variety of procedures that are used for state boards of education, hopefully with prime emphasis on potential for educational leadership. The quality of education in a state is in large part determined by the quality, purposes, means, and values of the agency governing the state's schools.

The direct management of schools varies in organization from the centralized state control of Hawaii to the local traditions of New England, where small local school districts are governed by school boards or school committees and where school budgets and other important matters may be decided by the citizenry in open town meetings. The Southern pattern for the development of local government resulted in an organization of schools by county geographical units. Some states have combined the New England and Southern patterns with a system of populated areas served by local school districts and rural areas organized through a county agency. There have been special provisions for the governance of some large city schools in which urban schools may be under the control of the municipal government or under the partial control of municipal authorities. In some cities, an otherwise independent school board is dependent upon the city for local financing of the schools and the school budget is a part of the general municipal budget.

The division of responsibility and authority between the state and the local school districts forms fifty different patterns, one for each state. States restrict the powers and activities of local boards and also mandate actions and programs for local schools. School districts are limited as to the means of raising money for the schools, the tax rates they may assess, and the ways they may utilize the money. They are held to a strict accounting of their financial affairs. States impose instructional programs on the schools and dictate curricular offerings. These must then be established by the local authorities and supported, at least in part, through local taxes.

local control

There is abundant evidence that local control of schools was not successful. A critical New York State legislative committee report appeared as early as 1811. This criticism was followed a year later by the establishment of the position of superintendent of public instruction to oversee the state's schools. Soon every state had a state educational agency that gradually and doggedly encroached on mediocre local programs of education. This process is very much in evidence today as localities continue to fail to meet educational challenges. It might be noted that relatively few complaints about state restrictions or mandates on local school systems originate from those schools that are acknowledged to be engaging in superior educational programs. The complaints of the better schools are usually directed against the rigidity and awkwardness of the workings of the bureaucracy rather than the standards imposed or programs mandated by the states.

Local control of education has nevertheless served useful purposes. During the extension of frontier life and before the dominance of urban industrialization, it was the localities that provided for the special needs of youngsters. Even isolated rural societies grouped efforts and resources to educate their children.

However, in the swift change that is the order of society today, local management of the schools does not meet current needs and cannot anticipate the demands of the future. The daily press too frequently reports local boards of education embroiled in controversy over curricular affairs, the raising of taxes, the issuing of bonds for new construction, or the hiring and firing of staff. The correct and final relationship between the states and localities as to the management of schools is yet to be determined but the process is under way.

A persistent problem for both public and private education has been financing their programs. The costs were originally equally divided among the parents. Teachers received some cash and the remainder of their salary in kind: shoes from a shoemaker, clothes from a tailor, or room and board from parents in general. Difficulties in collecting from parents, increased population of districts, compulsory schooling, and the extension of school services led to public support of education through real and personal property taxes. Local taxes soon proved insufficient to maintain adequate schools, and state subsidy programs contributed to school budgets. The demands on education grew even faster as society became urbanized and industrialized. Local concerns became state concerns, which have since become national concerns. The federal government has become an important means of subsidizing the schools, particularly in the equalizing of educational opportunities among the states.

the role of the state

The role of the state in education has gradually and persistently become a matter of major political importance. Whereas Hawaii, on the basis of its territorial development, already has a state system of education, other states are moving more or less rapidly in the same direction. The greatest resistance to centralized state control is to be found in the structure and tradition of local control of education. The states have only reluctantly moved into the school takeover as their financial obligations to education have dramatically increased. While the state role has grown and the proportion of state financial support has increased, localities have been pushed to continue and increase their financing of education. Education was not mentioned in the Constitution of the United States and the states have maintained that constitutional responsibility. By delegation or default the states placed the schools under local authorities, and the present trend toward state central control is a recall of state powers. If it can be assumed that the quality of educational leadership will be maintained at the present high level in some states and improved in the others, the movement of control from localities to the states will not be the tragedy that is envisioned by some.

An early state concern for education arose over the qualifications and training of teachers. The initial program in the United States for the preparation of teachers was a private enterprise, a teacher-training school established by Samuel R. Hall at Concord, Vermont, in 1823. *Lectures on Schoolkeeping,* a compilation of Hall's teaching lectures, was the first text in the United States for teacher education. In 1839 a state normal school was established in Lexington, Massachusetts, by Horace Mann, who had become the first secretary of the State Board of Education of Massachusetts two years earlier. Gradually, as old problems intensified and new problems arose, the states entered more and more into matters of curriculum, finance, physical plant, and the qualifications and working relationships of teachers.

Few problems have come to the attention of state agencies that have not been met by increased central control and direction. Recruitment of poorly qualified teachers has led to state certification laws. Arguments over what was to be taught have resulted in state-mandated curriculums. Dissension over content in textbooks has prompted state-approved lists of school books. Deficient physical plants have forced states to establish schoolhouse standards. Irresponsible firing of teachers has brought about state teacher-tenure legislation. In the present generation problems arising from the relations between teachers, administrators, and school boards are creating situations that must be resolved on the state level.

federal involvement

The federal government first appeared in force on the educational scene with the passage of the Morrill Act of 1862, which granted federal lands to the states. The proceeds from these lands were to be used to stimulate education in agriculture and the mechanic arts. Colleges that benefited from the Morrill Act came to be identified as "land grant colleges." In 1867 Congress created a National Department of Education (later the United States Office of Education) headed by a commissioner and authorized to collect and disseminate information on education. The first commissioner was Henry Barnard, a pioneer in teacher education in Connecticut and Rhode Island.

The next federal involvement was primarily with vocational education programs under the Smith-Lever (1914) and Smith-Hughes (1917) acts. Under Smith-Hughes federal influence was extended into the high schools, where federal funds aided programs of vocational and agricultural arts and home economics. But important national involvement in the schools did not occur until after World War II, when the G.I. Bill of Rights introduced mass education to returned veterans, primarily in colleges and universities but also in trade schools. Congress debated federal aid programs to relieve financial burdens on school systems that had postponed building programs until after the war and were now facing a postwar burgeoning population. School lunch programs were initiated on the national level, serving both an increased demand for school services and the problems of agricultural surpluses.

It was not the politicians who thrust the federal government into education on a grand scale, but the Supreme Court. In its role as the enforcer of federal laws and judicial decisions, the Eisenhower administration brought troops into Little Rock, Arkansas, to demand the integration of its schools. For the first time the federal government became a major factor in internal school affairs. It was under the same administration that the United States Department of Health, Education and Welfare was established in 1953; education thus shared cabinet status.

The first President to claim a significant role for the federal government in meeting educational problems was John F. Kennedy, who determinedly pushed for the integration of schools and who appointed and gave support to the first commissioner of education to play a major role in educational affairs, Francis Keppel. Under the guidance of President Lyndon B. Johnson, Congress finally resolved the issue of federal aid to parochial schools and massive federal funds were voted for educational purposes throughout the nation from preschool through postgraduate levels. The federal government was seriously involved in school matters and was there to stay.

The major long-range result of federal involvement is in the distribution of federal funds. This will in fact amount to a redistribution of resources so that wealthier states will be contributing to the educational systems of poorer states through the medium of the federal government. Once initiated, this process would seem to be endless. In addition, integration of races within the schools will probably continue to depend on the involvement of the federal government. Further, a question that has concerned several people and may eventually become the most important in federal-state-local school relations has to do with the quality of education throughout the country, the setting of national standards, and the possible establishment of national school programs.

differences in schools

The wide variety of school organizational forms in the United States is paralleled by the extremes that exist in the quality of schooling available to youngsters. Differences in the quality of physical plant, instruction, teaching resources, and administration are to be found regionally, by states, within a state, and even between one school and another in the same school system. There may be profound differences in the instruction that takes place in adjoining classrooms.

The most distressing educational problems are found in schools in "disadvantaged" areas, those rural or urban areas that contain concentrations of the unemployed and the underemployed. These schools serve those who share the misery of inadequate housing, insufficient diets or even malnutrition, and the lack of those basic material possessions generally accepted as essential to a minimum standard of living in the American society. Deprived of adequate medical care and sanitation facilities, sharing poor law enforcement and unequal justice in the courts, the rural and urban slums are forced to accept substandard schools and schooling for their youngsters. In many rural areas there are still one-room schoolhouses staffed by inadequately prepared teachers. Many of these schools have bare walls, pot-bellied stoves, and lack running water or toilet facilities. Inferior rural schools are found regionally in the South and in the Appalachian Mountain area or are scattered locally throughout the rest of the country.

Whereas rural areas often suffer from a scattered population, lack of wealth, and the inability of the citizen to make a living off marginal farm land, the large cities, centers of population and of industry and finance, suffer from the inability to meet the demands of their teeming multitudes. Here the not inconsiderable wealth of the center city drains off into affluent neighborhoods and suburbs. The city does not suffer from a lack of population but from its surfeit, not from a scarcity of wealth but from its displacement. There are too many youngsters in the slums so that the schools are overcrowded, the classes oversized, and the teachers overwhelmed by the magnitude of teaching too many youngsters with too many social, learning, psychological, and health problems. New schools in the city frequently relieve the increasing school enrollment without retiring old, inadequate buildings. One older school in New York City was described as follows:

> There is falling plaster throughout the 50-year-old building, and in nearly every classroom the blackboards are broken. The principal . . . said that dead rats had been found in closets and classrooms. . . .
>
> [The school] is heated by four old coal-burning furnaces. On

cold days the temperature in the stairwells of the five-story structure has been recorded at 38 degrees. In a few classrooms, however, it is so hot the children have a difficult time keeping awake. In these rooms there are no window frames. Many of the classrooms have broken window panes.[1]

Most cities are engaged in school building programs, but the task is nearly overwhelming. The suspension of nonmilitary construction during World War II led to a school physical plant deficiency that was never made up in the postwar population boom, growth of slums, and shift of the middle and upper classes into the suburbs. Efforts to meet urban educational needs have been projected into plans for educational parks where complete school plants from kindergarten through college are proposed to service thousands of students. In recognition of the cost of city land, other proposals suggest joint school and commercial or housing construction in which office buildings or apartment houses may be built above public schools. Portable school buildings may be utilized for temporary relief of the shortage of school buildings. The probability is that urban school deficiencies will eventually require massive use of federal as well as state funds.

The most affluent suburbs demonstrate a generous use of local funds for the construction and maintenance of schools. Suburbs enjoy the advantage of relatively cheap land, the absence of existing and outmoded buildings, and the dispersion of their population. Suburbs also benefit from the higher level of income of their residents. Suburban schools are relatively new and they generally provide rich school experiences with abundant materials, well-prepared teachers, and relatively small classes.

Teachers eagerly seek the higher paying positions in the affluent suburbs, where the expensive new schools are built. They read about these schools in the professional literature for the most exciting instructional innovations are reported from favored suburbs. Teaching materials are abundant and up-to-date. Well-educated and experienced administrators operate with enthusiastic and generous support of the public in the knowledge that they are insulated from serious school problems by a comfortable dollar gap.

[1] Martin Arnold, "P.S. 178: Study in Disrepair," *The New York Times*, February 28, 1968. Also recommended is Jonathan Kozol's *Death at an Early Age* (Boston: Houghton Mifflin, 1967).

Suburban youngsters have their own share of problems, but difficulties are more readily met in small classes and teachers have qualified specialists at hand for consultation and assistance. If parents are busy spending money away from home, they also have available funds to hire specialists if problems do arise with youngsters.

Suburban teaching is not without its demands, however. Higher pay means higher expectations in classroom efficiency and non-classroom responsibilities, as well as greater participation in professional studies and graduate degrees. In some suburbs, teachers must commute for they cannot afford to live in the community. Thus they are not able to become part of the community in which they teach.

Somewhere between the affluence of the privileged suburb and the impoverishment of the large city and marginal rural area lies the small city, the village, or the moderately priced suburban housing development. These population centers may be typified by the village, which generally keeps abreast of its educational needs and is satisfied with an educational program that is adequate but seldom engages in innovative or experimental programs. The average salaries of its teachers are above those of the poor districts and below those of the suburban schools. The teachers are adequate if not superior in the classroom. They have classes of reasonable size, a moderate amount of materials and resources, and access to some specialized services. These village schools are uncertain about the support of the community. They lack both the assurance of the favored suburbs that money and support are readily available and the absolute hopelessness of the impoverished areas that few are concerned about their problems and little help or support is to be expected.

The typical village-in-the-middle operates with mixed success. Some bond issues for school construction or maintenance of educational programs are approved, others are rejected. A few citizens can be counted on for school support, a few are expected to oppose the schools, and the large majority seem to be disinterested. School elections elicit moderate interest; parent-teacher meetings attract a dependable nucleus of parents. The youngsters in the community are a mixed batch. Some are highly school-oriented, some disinterested in schooling, and the large majority operate with interest in some classes or subjects, a neutral attitude in other situations, and disinterest at still other times.

school and the social order

The school is considered to be a reflector of society, but it seldom serves as an effective social mirror. Only in largely homogeneous areas, such as large city slums or remote rural communities, does the school approach being a microcosm of the larger society. A pluralistic society that tends to maintain its pluralism by separateness in housing, in social gathering, and in interests and value systems is not accurately reflected in the commonality of the school, where divergent social, economic, and religious groups are brought together as equals and placed into unique cooperative situations.

Perhaps the school best reflects the greater social order in school politics. Here the power structure that bends local municipal or county governments to its will controls the schools as easily and completely. Social class differences find the middle class enforcing its values upon the rest of the student population in dress, personal appearance, behavior, and school achievement. A particular source of friction among groups in school develops in the financial demands that are imposed on youngsters. Favored economic groups exert financial pressures upon poor families in matters of dress. Required materials for school use and such "optional" items as field trip costs, school photographs, club dues, and admission fees to sports or social events demand the same amount of money from the youngsters of families on welfare rolls as those from split-level neighborhoods. The school is particularly ruthless in the financial demands it may levy on youngsters and parents. Groups that are able to seek protection in the larger society by isolating themselves from the demanding power group are unable to find such isolation in the school. Even the slum school is dominated by middle-class teachers.

Education is frequently described as a means of passing on traditions and culture, and the school meets this role extremely well. By choice and under various pressures, the school lives more in the past than the present. The rigidity of the curriculum, control by the middle class, and conservatism of educators serve to emphasize the past. A serious instructional default in the areas of science and social studies is the outdating of textbooks even as they are printed. A second deficiency in instructional materials is the emphasis on content that is familiar and acceptable to the power structure. The schools tend to serve most effectively the special interests of the dominant social group.

Schools sometimes become the tools of special interest groups. Patriotic societies have been instrumental in obtaining a recurring emphasis upon American history in the school curriculum, in introducing instruction in state history, in requiring a daily pledge of allegiance and saluting the flag, in achieving removal of teachers suspected or accused of unpatriotic actions or teaching, and in defending against criticism teachers they consider to have been especially patriotic. Political interests, particularly the extreme left or right, have sought to exert a political influence through the schools.

Economic pressure groups are highly active in affecting school curriculums and textbook materials and in policing the education of teachers. They also inundate schools with instructional materials furthering their particular interests. Materials supplied by individual businesses and industrial councils are numerous and influential. Other types of organizations including cooperatives and trade unions are also active in propagandizing through the classroom. The problem that teachers face in using free or inexpensive instructional materials is to sort out valid learning from brash or subtle indoctrination.

Religious groups that were once primary in school management are still influential in educational affairs. Church groups play a particularly pertinent role in what is taught and what practices are carried out in the schools. Subjects such as the Reformation or evolution are responsive to religious pressures. Despite patriotic pressures that require pledges of allegiance and saluting the flag in schools, religious groups have obtained court support in exempting youngsters from these patriotic gestures. In some states compulsory prayers were recited in schools until the practice was ruled illegal in 1962 by the United States Supreme Court.

The courts have been asked to rule on religious issues in the public schools. Nuns have been allowed to teach in some public schools. Compulsory prayers have been outlawed. Youngsters have been excused from pledging allegiance to the flag on religious grounds. Complaints have been registered against Christmas observances in public schools and against the use of church buildings for classes from overcrowded public schools. Some religious groups have been critical about organized activities after school that infringe on time set aside for religious instruction. In practice, the doctrine of separation of church and state operates principally to keep the state out of religious affairs but not to exclude religious groups from exerting significant and often successful pressure on public agencies, including educational institutions.

religious schools

Private schools include the parochial schools which form an important part of the nation's educational structure. About one child in six attends a nonpublic school, in most cases a Roman Catholic school. To limit consideration of parochial school systems to the Catholic Church, however, is to ignore the numbers of schools operated by Protestant denominations and by Jewish bodies.

Public schools were largely Protestant-oriented in the 1840s when the growing Catholic population sought public funds first from New York City and then the state for the education of Catholic youngsters. After a violent public debate the New York legislature amended the state constitution to forbid use of public funds for religious schools. Other states followed suit. Catholics later set a goal of providing from their own resources religious schooling for every Catholic child, and they were eventually able to enroll about half of their youngsters in church schools. Other smaller religious groups including the Amish, Seventh Day Adventists, and some Mennonite sects have been more successful in providing schools for most or all of their youngsters, although they have been concerned with far smaller numbers of pupils who usually live in closely knit communities.

The large size and scattered nature of the Catholic school system has led the church to seek financial relief and concessions from the public. The smaller sects, on the other hand, have sought isolation from the general public and freedom from regulation and interference in the management of their schools. In 1965 financial aid to parochial schools was provided by the federal Elementary and Secondary Education Act, to be channeled through local public school officials. Earlier concessions won by religious groups have provided released time from school for religious instruction, public busing of parochial school pupils, and the establishment of shared-time programs in which the public schools provide instruction in some subjects for youngsters otherwise enrolled in parochial schools. An attempt to provide extensive public aid to religious schools in a revision of the New York State constitution in 1967 was considered to be a factor in the defeat of the new constitution in a public referendum.

The attempt by small sects to retain their independence has had mixed success. The Amish schools in particular have been under almost constant attack by public education authorities in various states. Primary targets of the state or local authorities have been the desire of the Amish to discontinue schooling after the eighth grade (despite compulsory school attendance laws) and the use of Amish teachers (who usually do not meet state certification requirements). Occasionally, as in the case of a Swedenborgian school in Bryn Athyn, Pennsylvania, in 1965, a church school is eliminated by state action (in this case, the church school was affiliated with the local public school system).

other private schools

About 2 percent of children of school age are enrolled in a wide variety of independent private schools. Most of these institutions are coeducational day schools and some of these, such as the Rhodes School in New York City, have earned reputations for their excellence. The most famous independent schools, however, are New England boys' prep schools. Among the more renowned boys' schools are Hotchkiss (Lakeville, Connecticut), Phillips Academy (Andover, Massachusetts), and Phillips Exeter (Exeter, New Hampshire). They have low student-faculty ratios, excellent resources (instructional, library, and recreational), and a very carefully selected student body from among the large numbers seeking admission. By tradition, their graduates are expected to gain success at Harvard, Yale, and the other prestige colleges and universities.

The rest of the independent schools include a wide variation in character and quality. They may represent an extremely limited group, such as the Capitol Page School for the United States Senate, House of Representatives, and Supreme Court pages. There are military schools, which are commonly associated with the armed services and may be the means for admission to commissioned rank in a branch of the armed forces. Some private schools are modeled on unusual educational innovations, such as the Montessori method of instruction or the Summerhill experiment.[2] Private schools are sometimes looked on as a means of avoiding contact with the mob, as a sure path to college, as a substitute for crowded or unsatisfactory public schools, or as an escape from racial integration.

[2] See Maria Montessori, *The Montessori Method* (New York: Stokes, 1912) and A. S. Neill, *Summerhill: A Radical Approach to Child Rearing* (New York: Hart, 1960).

basic role of the schools

Both public and private schools have traditionally been assigned the role of teaching "the three Rs": reading, writing, and arithmetic. Educators have found little competition in teaching these essential skills except for those occasional parents who pose the challenge that they are able to educate their children better than the schools. Whatever criticism there may be that the schools are not effective in teaching basic skills, there are no serious proposals to assign that responsibility to any other agency. The demand is that schools continue the process but improve the results.

It is generally acknowledged that success in school is dependent on the degree to which the basic educational skills have been acquired. Most particularly, if the youngster has serious reading problems in the first years at school he may be expected to have continued and intensified problems in the upper grades. The high school senior reading at the fourth-grade level is for all practical purposes a functional illiterate.

In many respects schools are led to emphasize the nonacademic aspects of their programs. Under federal programs, for example, most particularly the Smith-Lever and Smith-Hughes legislation, schools have extended their academic concerns into vocational training. While special vocational schools have been established in some communities, most public schools provide industrial arts, home economics, and business instruction in junior and senior high schools.

Vocational programs have tended to be used as "safety valves" for the nonacademically oriented students, for those youngsters who do not share a scholarly interest, attitude, or ability. A typical school program sets up various "tracks" through which students pursue college preparatory, industrially oriented, or business skill programs, each of which leads to a common diploma. For example, New York State youngsters who pass Regents examinations are recognized as having completed a college preparatory program at a high order of school achievement. There are efforts both to equate all high school diplomas and to distinguish among them.

The pressures applied on the school by special interests in the community have extended the curriculum. A particularly interesting instructional program is driver education. In this instance, the school has become a convenient centralized institution for providing instruction in a skill that reflects no academic interest, has only the slightest relationship to a vocational program, and is usually justified by statistics suggesting that driver training instruction reduces automobile accident rates. Automobile manufacturers who subsidize driver training programs, insurance companies, and organizations such as the American Automobile Association have been instrumental in promoting driver education in the schools. In some schools driver training is a requirement for graduation. Another example of schools being used to promote commercial interests is the school banking program, whereby arrangements are made to have the school act as an agent for a local bank in opening student accounts and periodically collecting deposits.

In its efforts to perform many diverse (even contradictory) services, the school experiences problems, successes, and failures. It would be unrealistic to presume that a school system may perform obvious educational functions and also accept the responsibility for any other social, personal, or developmental problem whenever another social agency experiences difficulties with it. The attempt to supplement religious or moral or value precepts of church, home, and neighborhood in a pluralistic society involves the very difficult task of selecting those particular precepts that shall be adopted by the schools.

conclusion

Who shall decide these very serious and complex educational issues? Shall the "public" decide? which public? how? Should the decision be a matter of national concern or may each state establish its own unique pattern? To impose one unique and common standard upon each state might lead to contradictory and conflicting practices from state to state. To suggest that the federal government assume the total responsibility for education conjures up the picture of a grandiose bureaucracy that would dwarf the Post Office Department. There is an apparent need for varying kinds and levels of decision making and for mechanisms to coordinate educational decisions across local, state, regional, and national lines.

At times, the task of selecting the duties and responsibilities that should be assumed by the schools is alleged to be the prerogative of parents and pupils. Parent-teacher organizations are one means by which parents may influence teachers or teachers parents. Frequently parent or citizen advisory councils are organized to assist in the resolution of school problems, including curricular matters. Often the truism that learning should relate to youngsters' interests is distorted from the study of child and adolescent psychology to a sampling of expressed feelings of youngsters or their parents. Thus a superficial verbalism may be accepted as worthy evidence on which important educational matters are resolved.

Professional educators too may seek to have a primary responsibility in determining the roles and objectives of the schools and the means and techniques for achieving them. On the grounds that the expert is sought out to play a major role in seeking solutions to social, industrial, and governmental problems, the educator may demand the same right to make use of his special competence in the evolution of the schools.

An interesting comparison may be made between education and other public endeavors. Seldom in matters of law enforcement or public services (water, sewage, etc.) does the public or an individual taxpayer become personally involved in operations beyond general policy matters that govern the daily routines of a public service. Perhaps universal education has made the individual citizen more conversant with the schools than with the police station or water purification plant. It has been alleged that as public services in general have become more centralized and distant, taxpayers have centered resentment toward bureaucracy and increased taxes upon the schools as the major public agency where an individual may still exert his influence.

It would be difficult to defend the proposition that public schools can be aloof from public needs, desires, or purposes. It is equally difficult to substantiate a defensible position in which school attendance provides particular knowledge about the complexities of education any more than use of other public services provides similar competencies or frequent visits to a dentist or physician give special insight into dentistry or medicine.

The logical relationship between the public and its schools is to assign to the public, through representative and responsible agents, the overall purposes and objectives of education. Essential to a responsible involvement of the "public" in public education is the establishment of safeguards preventing the imposition of selfish purposes by special interest groups and of personal feelings, individual bias, or conflict initiated for its own sake or as a means of establishing a local power position. Democratic schools for a democratic society cannot be realized when schools are dominated by political, economic, social, or religious pressures or when professional educators assert their authority to operate the schools outside the concerns or interests of the public, parents, or pupils. As a cooperative social entity, the schools must serve the general public and its elected representatives, while professional educators, parents, and youngsters assume reasonable roles to play in carrying out the grand design. Each group must accept responsibility, delegate appropriate authority to others, and cooperate with all other groups. Only when all join together in a common effort to ensure that mass education can succeed in a democracy may the schools fulfill their obligations and potentials to society with dispatch and efficiency.

on your own

Students interested in further study of educational history may consult Bernard Bailyn, *Education in the Forming of American Society* (Chapel Hill: University of North Carolina Press, 1960). A study of the progressive movement in education, *The Transformation of the School: Progressivism in American Education, 1876–1957* (New York: Knopf, 1961) by Lawrence A. Cremin, is recommended reading. In the history of ideas, Robert Ulich, *History of Educational Thought* (New York: American Book, 1950), and Paul Nash, *Models of Man: Explorations in the Western Educational Tradition* (New York: Wiley, 1968), are suggested. Philosophical references include as a matter of necessity John Dewey, *Democracy and Education* (New York: Macmillan, 1916), and the writings of Israel Scheffler. Other authors in the field are Theodore Brameld and Kenneth Benne.

The role of the school in American society is the topic of Grace Graham's *The Public School in the American Community* (New York: Harper & Row, 1963). Urban problems are the focus of James B. Conant's *Slums and Suburbs* (New York: McGraw-Hill, 1961), and Joan I. Roberts (ed.), *School Children in the Urban Slum: Readings in Social Science Research* (New York: Free Press, 1968). The public schools in a rural community are an important theme in *Small Town in Mass Society* (Princeton, N.J.: Princeton University Press, 1958) by Arthur J. Vidick and Joseph Bensman.

From your own point of view, background, values, and school experiences, what do *you* think should be the role of the school in society? Should it lead the society? If so, in what directions? Should the school be the tool of society? If so, who is to decide what functions or what services the school should perform? What role should be served by minority groups? Which ones should have what kind of influence? If the school is to play a role in religious-moral issues, whose religious beliefs should exert an influence? if political issues, which political group? if economic, whose economic theories?

List the ways in which you think the school should serve society. Does it perform these tasks well? sufficiently? poorly? In those areas where improvement is desired, how may progress come about and under whose leadership? For whatever successes you perceive or for the failures you find, who is to blame, who must accept the responsibility, and who has the authority to mend the school fences?

Finally, as a teacher and a citizen, what do you see as your role in perfecting the process of education? Where do you expect to find opportunities to serve the future of education? What do you believe to be the obstacles that will limit your action in seeking better schools? What do you consider to be the barriers to educational progress? What advantages may you have?

additional references

Bernstein, Abraham. *The Education of Urban Populations.* New York: Random House, 1967.

Best, John H., and Robert T. Sidwell (eds.). *The American Legacy of Learning: Readings in the History of Education.* Phila.: Lippincott, 1967.

Bolmeier, Edward C. *The School in the Legal Structure.* Cincinnati: W. H. Anderson, 1968.

Conant, James B. *The Comprehensive High School: A Second Report to Interested Persons.* New York: McGraw-Hill, 1967.

Dentler, Robert A., Bernard Mackler, and Mary E. Warschauer (eds.). *The Urban R's: Race Relations as the Problem in Urban Education.* New York: Praeger, 1967.

Fuchs, Estelle. *Pickets at the Gates: The Challenge of Civil Rights in Urban Schools.* New York: Free Press, 1966.

Gittell, Marilyn, and T. Edward Hollander. *Six Urban School Districts.* New York: Praeger, 1968.

Grooms, M. Ann. *Perspective on the Middle School.* Columbus, Ohio: Merrill, 1967.

Havighurst, Robert J. *Education in Metropolitan Areas.* Boston: Allyn and Bacon, 1966.

Hodgkinson, Harold L. *Education, Interaction, and Social Change.* Englewood Cliffs, N.J.: Prentice-Hall, 1967.

Krug, Edward A. *The Shaping of the American High School.* New York: Harper & Row, 1964.

Meyer, Adolphe E. *An Educational History of the American People.* 2nd ed. New York: McGraw-Hill, 1967.

Norton, John K. (ed.). *Dimensions in School Finance.* Washington, D.C.: Committee on Educational Finance, National Education Association, 1966.

Perkinson, Henry J. *The Imperfect Panacea: American Faith in Education, 1865–1965.* New York: Random House, 1968.

Read, Katherine H. *The Nursery School: A Human Relationship Laboratory.* Phila.: Saunders, 1966.

Rippa, S. Alexander. *Education in a Free Society: An American History.* New York: McKay, 1967.

Selakovich, Daniel. *The Schools and American Society.* Waltham, Mass.: Blaisdell, 1967.

Shuster, George N. *Catholic Education in a Changing World.* New York: Holt, Rinehart and Winston, 1967.

Smith, Bob. *They Closed Their Schools: Prince Edward County, Virginia, 1951–64.* Chapel Hill: University of North Carolina, 1965.

Tyack, David B. (ed.). *Turning Points in American Educational History.* Waltham, Mass.: Blaisdell, 1967.

5

The school is a unique social institution. Nothing similar to it exists in the greater society. It is artificial and conflict-initiating; yet it is the most hopeful device in transmitting democratic traditions to the future generations. As a means to freedom, independence, and democratic processes it may be found to be restrictive, domineering, and autocratic. As a social entity, the school is aloof from the real society; it is contradictory and indispensable.

Because the school includes most of the divergent, divisive, avoiding, and conflicting groups within the larger society, it establishes a distinctive social configuration. It is an experience in the use of political power that some individuals will later exercise in serious control of society. Others will dutifully cast schoolhouse ballots and may even occupy positions of responsibility, but they probably will not actively engage in the political arena in their adult life. For some youngsters school guarantees social, political, and academic success, but for many it is the center for frustration and failure.

Except for those whose financial privilege permits them to escape identification with the common herd or whose unique needs, especially religious, are not met in public institutions, the populace comes to the school society. There is little evidence that twelve years of schooling has a democratizing influence on the school population other than the fact that the greater society continues to live, struggle, and wage war against both internal and external enemies while continuing in a politically democratic mold. While the upper class tends to avoid the schoolhouse mixing of social groups and the lower economic groups seek to escape as soon as laws permit, the measure of contact seems to breed enough familiarity, sym-

the school society

pathy, and understanding to perpetuate the system. Some might argue that history documents continual conflict between the privileged and the deprived, between labor and management, and between those who have and those who have not, but the fact remains that the American experiment has been a phenomenal success.

school administration

The school society is a complex, multilevel system with responsibility delegated from higher authority to lower authority at the various levels. Every level of school administration tends to be structured within a totalitarian framework. Authority rests in those whose life tenures are commonly subject only to continued good behavior or to a voluntary withdrawal from positions of power. On the pupil level, use of democratic processes is dependent on the whim of a benevolent despot (the teacher), whose own freedom of action is subject to the paternalism of another higher school authority.

In the real sense a school is not governed but administered. By nature and structure the school is a nondemocratic institution with democratic responsibilities. Confusion about the nature of school administration arises from the suggestion that authoritarian procedures are democratic or when an attempt is made to superimpose self-governing mechanics upon an autocratic structure. Professional educators are appointed by the local school board to administer the school and to manage the educational enterprise. Most of them are former teachers who have selected school administration as a major for their masters degrees. Ambition, financial consideration, or discontent has encouraged them to move from the classroom to school management.

levels of administration

First and foremost, the school is regulated by state law. The state department of education supervises the things that must be done, may be done, or cannot be done. The board of education or school committee controls the local school system.

The school board varies in size and may be appointed or elected. It is a lay group that meets to supervise the conduct of the schools. This governing body is charged with the responsibility for making school policy, providing the local financial base for the schools, and appointing and dismissing staff. In practice, the pupils, school faculty, and lower-echelon administrators seldom come into contact with the school board. Many school teachers have never bothered, or had the opportunity, to sit in on a school board meeting, although most board meetings are open to the public. Other teachers may meet the board at an annual dinner meeting scheduled for the end of the year to provide an outing for the staff, to honor those who are retiring, and to recognize others who are leaving the system.

The school board appoints the superintendent, who is the chief school administrative officer and agent of the board. The superintendent serves at the pleasure of the board, carries out its policies, functions as the manager of the school system, and is the educational leader of the schools. The job of the superintendent has evolved into an impossibly complicated position, with the superintendent often caught between serving the board, representing the schools to the public, and acting as liaison between the school board and the faculty. Depending on the size of the school system, the school superintendent may be an immediate member of the school society or a remote manager represented by numerous intermediaries. Through his influence on the school board and its determination of policy, the means by which he seeks to implement policy, the nature of the staff he recruits, and the kind of leadership he provides, the school superintendent is the major figure in the conduct of the schools. He determines the atmosphere of the school system and the morale of its staff.

As interpreter of the schools to the community, the superintendent spends much of his time in public relations activities. He is a community leader, enjoys membership in the more influential community and service organizations, is included in active social circles, and is expected to serve church, community, and charitable institutions. Professionally, the school superintendent may belong to the state, national, and perhaps local educational associations, but his special affinity is to the state association of school administrators and the American Association of School Administrators. He may attend the AASA annual meetings as his major professional activity.

The school principal is at the level of direct administration of a school, although he may be subject to intermediate personalities in the larger school systems. While the superintendent is responsible to the entire community, the school principal identifies his constituency as that of the immediate area which is serviced by his school. In larger communities the principal identifies with neighborhood social organizations and area service groups. Bel Kaufman has written about a distant and seldom-seen principal.[1] In many schools, however, the principal is in close contact with his faculty, plays the major role in the establishment of the school morale, and directly regulates the conduct of daily affairs in the building.

A principal is an intermediary in a line-and-staff relationship. He is akin to a business branch manager or an army platoon sergeant. The principal heads a unit that has many businesslike characteristics but lacks the restraining influences of profit and loss figures, the commercial factors that defer or initiate action. At one and the same time, a principal enjoys the prerogatives of management and is freed from the tests of managerial efficiency. Much as a teacher is granted wide latitude in the conduct of a classroom behind a closed door, the principal is granted wide authority in administering his school. And just as there are no direct means for a student to seek redress from the actions of a teacher, there is seldom a direct means for the teacher to protest the actions of the school administration.

administrative efficiency

Criteria for judgment of the efficiency of any school administrator tend to be superficial and aloof from the educative process. For a superintendent of schools the test is frequently the skill with which he can relate to a school board and interact with it. The board may be more sensitive to the acceptance by the public of board action or inaction than toward a concern for the efficiency of classroom production. Administrators come under criticism of their boards when parental or taxpayer complaints rise in volume and in frequency or when protests come from certain powerful groups or individuals. Conversely, school systems are often considered to be successfully administered in the absence of much or powerful protest. School administration may thus act to ensure a community that can be soothed by a public relations program or a faculty that can be persuaded or coerced into cooperation. Administrative problems are eased by pupils who can be controlled by a variety of persuasions or parents who accept the school program, either through knowledge of school activities or because of ignorance of them.

Administrative efficiency is sometimes related to the ease

[1] Bel Kaufman, *Up the Down Staircase* (Englewood Cliffs, N.J.: Prentice-Hall, 1964).

with which colleges admit the graduates from a school system. Schools may be judged by comparison of achievement test records with other schools or evidence of activity by teachers above and beyond the call of duty. Schools are too frequently judged by what youngsters do rather than by what the school itself has done with or to or for young people.

Management is only part of the role played by school administration. Superintendents and principals are expected to provide educational leadership for the school community. The educational leader influences the public by interpreting the educational purposes and programs of the school system. He may be given the responsibility for explaining the schools' financial needs in solicitation of support for taxes and bond issues. He aids the board in development of a philosophy and determination of policies. He represents the policies of the board to the faculty and the thinking of the faculty to the board. He initiates curricular changes or implements those proposed by the staff. In recruitment of staff and in the weeding out of unsatisfactory teachers, he regulates the quality of instruction and seeks improvement in the classroom process through in-service programs for the faculty. By assuring that educational materials are available to teachers and that tools are kept in repair, the educational leader facilitates teaching and learning.

As a business leader the administrator is expected to conduct a well-run establishment free of problem teachers, problem youngsters, problem parents, and problem taxpayers. As a public employee he must of necessity exert some political leadership, responding to public desires and resolving problems posed by conflicting publics. As an educational leader he influences the quality of instruction and maintains a dynamic school program. An honest appraisal of the leadership functions of schoolhouse management suggests that school administration is a configuration of contradictions. Business considerations of a school system may not coincide with political needs, nor either of these with educational requisites. It is not unreasonable to suggest that there are not enough skilled administrators who can perform all of these duties.

One significant obstacle to administrative aims, desires, purposes, and objectives is the teacher social subgroup that exists within the total adult school society. Teachers as a group recognize clear distinctions between administration and teaching staff. They seldom accept administrators as "equals"; they are too painfully aware of the instruments for teacher control in the hands of administrators. Administrative judgment is reflected in occasions of tenure, merit raises, and letters of recommendation for placement purposes. Teachers are assigned classrooms, grade levels, hall duties, and committee assignments. They are dependent on administrative cooperation for new textbooks, school supplies, and audio-visual budgets. They must seek permission for occasional absences whether for personal reasons or to conduct class field trips. Occasions arise when administrative backing is needed to aid a teacher in handling youthful problems or parental complaints. Administrative practices may lead to a faculty united with a principal or in opposition to him. Or, if a principal is indecisive or vacillating in his relationships with the teachers, a splintered faculty situation may result. In such a case advantage may be sought by maneuvering the power structure of the moment, sometimes through the principal, sometimes in complete disregard of him.

Each individual school society is directed by the principal, and school policy is carried out by the teachers. In smaller schools the principal directly controls school affairs and supervises instruction. In larger schools assistant (or vice-) principals carry out certain responsibilities, while the principal is concerned with overall policy and major problems. A large school may find the principal insulated from school problems by a layer of intermediate administrators. He may be assisted by school counselors, attendance officers, nurses, sociologists, and psychologists.

Many schools are organized into academic departments, with departmental chairmen serving as intermediaries between the instructional staff and the administration. The departmental chairman may be appointed by the administration or elected by the teachers in the department. He may enjoy certain privileges, such as increased pay or reduced instructional responsibilities. Some larger schools seek the advantages claimed by smaller schools through the organization of the school into smaller units, with subgroups under the administration of "unit principals."

Professionally, school principals may belong to a local organization that represents their interests in large school systems, and they may affiliate with state or national associations of elementary or secondary school principals. Teachers may identify with an area of academic specialization and may belong to the local professional organization or teachers union. Educational organizations or unions are organized on the bases of individual school buildings, a school system (sometimes a county or region), and state and national levels. If the teacher belongs to various organizational levels, he may experience conflicts between local and broader interests and problems. Teachers may resent the cumulative financial demands of multiple memberships in the various educational organizations.

administrative democracy

There is much talk of democratic and authoritarian school administration, but administration is basically an authoritarian relationship with possibilities for various degrees of paternalistic relaxation of authority. Paternalistic, or pseudodemocratic, relationships do not depend on the form of administrative structure but are related to the personal attributes of individual administrators. In the American public school one seldom finds a periodic review of administrative-faculty-pupil relationships. Nor is it customary to find school problems resolved through the use of techniques such as the secret ballot or the town meeting. These observations are simply further reflections that schools are administered, not governed.

A distinction should be made between governing and administrative democracy. Governing democracy depends for fulfillment upon individual and group attitudes. It requires a formalizing of structure, the establishment of means for determining the common needs, and mechanics for selecting leadership. Governing becomes anarchic without structure; there is then no governance. Administrative relationships, however, are not anchored to structure. They may operate in a paternalistic or democratic fashion regardless of the formal organization. The school administrative structure establishes a hierarchy of status between teacher and administrator that may reflect the paternalism of unequals rather than the democracy of equals. Whether or not a school is administered democratically is related to the willingness of the school administration to share responsibility, to its desire to honor individual human dignity, to the beliefs it holds in collective wisdom, and to the attitudes of each administrator toward himself and others.

the teacher society

Faculties form social units. The structure of a faculty society is dependent to a significant degree upon the principles and practices of the school administration. Teachers form groups on the basis of shared backgrounds and interests and of vocational orientation. While there may be divisive elements within a faculty, there are also cohesive factors centered about common employment, common problems, and shared working quarters. The faculty boiler room "lounge" is a legendary and literal fact, although newer school buildings include "teachers' rooms," where faculty members can congregate in off moments. The boiler room or teachers' room is a meeting place where the faculty society is informally organized. This is where communication within the faculty is carried on and where protective strategies are devised or group plans initiated.

In smaller communities the teacher society tends to be perpetuated outside of school. Common interests pull teachers together and those teachers who are not products of the community may be the subject of a subtle form of rejection on the part of the townspeople. Teachers are sometimes looked on as interlopers and transients in a small community. Comfort in the social status quo encourages many villagers to maintain the unity of their closed society. They make it difficult for newcomers to gain social acceptance. Teachers as a group are often excluded from the select membership of a community. Undoubtedly this practice encourages the migration of teachers and reinforces their transient status. In larger communities, however, there is less cohesion of teachers outside of school as more and larger social subgroups provide for greater acceptance of teachers who may seek social congeniality through a church, social organization, or in neighborhood groupings.

Just as there are cohesive influences on faculties, there are also isolationist pressures. Not only may lack of interest by townspeople lead to group isolation of teachers but faculties tend toward the formation of splinter groups within themselves. Teachers divide into groups by grade level, subject, room assignment, sex, and marital status. There is also a tendency for teachers to isolate themselves within their classrooms, sometimes for protection against both administrative surveillance and colleague curiosity. In situations where an administration is particularly authoritarian the faculty may divide into power cliques, with each group centering its interests and activities on currying administrative favor. On the other hand, a democratic school society will emphasize issues, tend to reduce group rigidity, and strive to solve problems on the basis of a common philosophy and through a careful discussion of the facts.

While the adult school environment may present a united front to youngsters, it is crossed and recrossed by real and imagined divisions. Traditionally, the division among teachers has been between the common or elementary school and the Latin grammar, academy, or high school. The tendency to form separate groups of men and women teachers is in large part a continuation of that early division in which the teachers of young children were commonly women and the teachers of adolescents were primarily men. Emphasis on subject matter has also been a barrier between teachers with differing academic interests. The most recent basis for the division of teachers is through membership in professional organizations and teacher unions and between teacher-militants and teacher-conservatives in both organizational types. The common elements of teaching, however, are usually stronger than the divisive forces and faculties are more united than fragmented, although occasionally, and unfortunately, a group of teachers may be found who are dominated by internal conflict.

On an individual teacher basis, youngsters face an adult school society that varies widely from room to room. Length of tenure on a faculty may be reflected in the degree of satisfaction with which teachers accept the school society. Those who have persisted over the years to mold a school into their own image form a firm status quo and enjoy the support of those parents and administrators who tend to equate tenacity with success. Others, who are more recent recruits into a school system, may be in the process of fighting tradition and the seniority power structure.

organizing pupils

Since the abandonment of the one-room school the traditional organization of the school society has been on a grade basis, which is determined by age and achievement, with each grade separated into classes of manageable size. A school building is divided into areas according to age of youngsters or subject matter. The extremes in maturity and size between first and sixth graders in an elementary school provide a logical basis for separating classes or age groups. Physical differences are reflected in the size of classroom furniture and the height of water fountains.

In many schools selected youngsters are placed into formal structures, or student councils, which emulate adult legislative processes and supposedly engage pupils in their own governance. Most student councils are under strict adult supervision, and teachers frequently exert influence in the selection of classroom representatives. A classroom may be organized formally, with election of class officers by the pupils. Committees may be appointed and classes may engage in social or learning-related activities. The school society may be further organized on a formal basis into extraclass or extracurricular activities, with youngsters enrolled into Junior Red Cross chapters, language and science clubs, musical organizations, and athletic teams.

Youngsters are highly organized in school. A classroom may be rigidly structured about the way pupils come into class, where they sit, how they behave, the ways in which they respond to the classroom procedures, and the manner in which they leave the room. They may be required to move from one room to another in an orderly, quiet single file through halls that are monitored by students or teachers. Traffic may be directed by arrows painted on hallway walls or by student guides. Stairways may be designated for up or down passage.

The school society exerts strong controls on children in scholastic activities. Uniform and continuous direction by adults follows every action of the youngsters from their entrance into the school to their exit from it. Noon lunch periods, playground activity, and auditorium programs are particularly closely regulated. While much control of behavior and structuring of the immediate environment is necessary to protect the children against accidents or negative influences, the net result of all this extreme regulation and paternalism is an oppressive authoritarian school framework for many young people.

It may be difficult to ascertain whether the school is administered with primary emphasis upon the control of the youngsters or on the provision of learning experiences. Learning, of course, cannot take place in a situation dominated by anarchy or turmoil. The romantic ideal of teaching suggests that the suitable learning atmosphere is structured by enthusiastic teachers and exciting learning experiences. The unromantic reality, however, is a dependence on the use of authority to maintain behavioral patterns appropriate to the classroom.

Rigid structuring of the school begins even before the start of instruction, when a complex routing and scheduling of buses brings distant children to school. Traffic posts on streets near the school are manned by adults or by youngsters who are members of a school safety patrol. A variety of techniques are employed to control behavior as children arrive at school. Pupils may be required to wait outside the building or in a hallway or to congregate in an auditorium, cafeteria, or study hall until it is time for the teachers to be in their classrooms. Pupils may then "report to their homerooms" or stop at their lockers. A youngster is assumed to be under the control of a teacher once he is in the classroom.

Control over youngsters is exerted over their conduct in the school, where they may go in the school, and the promptness with which they carry out responsibilities. In most schools pupils must receive permission to go to a rest room, to the guidance or nurse's offices, or to make a phone call. A "tardy bell" may signal the time children are to be in a classroom, and lateness may provide automatic disciplinary action. A high school schedule rigidly specifies the room a pupil is to be in and the subject he is to be studying. Even the self-contained elementary classroom may be organized on a time instructional schedule.

Some schools profess to have authority over the actions of youngsters in the interval between home and school before and after school hours. There are efforts on the part of schools to suggest kinds of experiences to take place in the home to supplement the classroom, including the amount of time expected to be used for home study. The school is able to require that parents provide certain medical treatment for their youngsters. School influence may be extended to the disqualification of a youngster from participation in a school athletic program if he has engaged in other organized competitive athletics during a summer vacation. Girls who marry may be excluded from school.

Much controversy centers about dress and appearance codes imposed on youngsters by school authorities. Length of skirts, tightness of trousers, and length and style of hair are carefully regulated by many schools. It is probably an irrelevant argument to point out that a Franklin or an Einstein would not have acceptable haircuts in many schools or that George Washington's trousers would not meet with school approval. However, the argument that school behavior is dependent upon dress and appearance ignores the equally strong possibility that school attitudes and behavior are related to success in the learning-teaching process. Nonconformist dress and appearance may be symbols of a search for independence and expressions of rebellion against society in general rather than just a purposeful defiance of school authority.

Controls exerted on youngsters by the schools are often related to the school organization and pupil social class rather than to the needs imposed by the learning process. Changes in school building design and greater flexibility in determining class size may prove more useful in structuring healthy learning environments than elaborate systems of regulation. Repression in school, particularly of lower-class youngsters, is not effective in ensuring the success of mass education.

The school society into which children are enrolled includes a myriad of personalities. Each child comes into intimate contact with a wide variety of these—whether child or adult, classmate or teacher. A youngster's personal success in the school society is dependent on the chance nature of his personality structure and those of classmates and teachers. Children are a captive audience and their behavior is related to the way top administration structures the greater educational environment, a principal establishes the feeling tone in a single school, and a teacher dominates a group of youngsters. Youngsters are assigned by chance to the love of some adults and the mercy of others. The school society is a fairly stable and immovable environment to which a pupil adjusts and submits or against which he rebels. Frequent mention is made about the adjustment of a youngster to the school, but the question seldom is raised about the aptness with which the school accommodates youngsters. The youngster is expected to be flexible. The school, on the other hand, may be rigid or, as is often stated, a "consistent" and stabilizing influence.

organization of schools

The school environment is more than a grouping of adults—it is a structure in which youngsters are organized for instruction along a grade division. This compartmentalization has some relationship to age, but it is not a finite division. In addition, grades have some relationship to size of youngsters, but this relationship is highly irregular. There is also some relationship to school ability and achievement, but this condition is often violated. The higher grades within a school are accorded special privileges and in some cases are expected to assume certain responsibilities. There is a snobbishness about a sixth-grader, a ninth-grader, and a high school or college senior. The old story of seniority rights and protection of the status quo is repeated within every separate division of the school society. It is fortunate that seniority rights for an individual youngster at any level persist for only an academic year.

divisions of the school experience

The traditional grade division is rigidly set to the calendar. It admits individuals to the school on a carefully observed age criterion and then operates upon a nearly automatic, yearly progression. Movement through the grades is excepted only by the occasional falling back of a failure (the lowest of low achievers) or the forward leap of the far scarcer accelerate (the most successful among the gifted). A knotty problem, apparently settled for the time, has to do with grosser divisions of the introductory school experience. We begin first by a division into preschool: nursery school or nursery school and kindergarten. Kindergarten experiences are considered preformal schooling; the nursery school, prekindergarten. Americans have agreed upon six years as the appropriate entrance age into school, five into kindergarten, three or four into the nursery. Public kindergartens are common, but public nursery schools are less frequent and in many communities the nursery schools are private enterprises.

Concern for school readiness is a matter for the early elementary grades, an issue that may be of lesser concern in those European countries where school begins at the age of seven. The elementary school has been organized to include the first six grades; previously, the first eight grades comprised the lower school form in the United States. This arbitrary division of elementary schooling is supposed to end with early adolescence although adolescence begins at different times for different youngsters. The length of the elementary experience is an arbitrary delimitation that finds some upper elementary youngsters well launched into adolescence and some first-graders educationally or socially immature.

The early adolescent experience in the junior high school constitutes three years, followed by three senior high school years. The junior high school has been a relatively inconclusive experiment. Originally designed to provide an orderly transition from the elementary school to the terminal high school program, the junior high school has tended to continue elementary school processes through nine years or to extend secondary school departmentalization downward. In recent years the junior high school has been criticized for its failure to provide the transition between elementary and secondary schooling. One alternative plan is to set up a "middle school" encompassing grades five through eight, with the ninth grade placed in the high school. Change in school structure alone may not resolve any serious educational problems, but the move is an acknowledgment of the fact that the common academic division continues to provide for a unity among the last four years of school.

Although questions have been raised about the organization of the school, only slight consideration has been given to extending the basic twelve years of schooling. Both the school schedule and the basic curriculum have remained markedly unchanged despite the fact that the traditional pattern of nearly a century fails to acknowledge an amazing expansion of knowledge. A present tendency in education is to push content and learning experiences earlier into the school progression. This is a worthy proposal for young scholars but may not be relevant to later-maturing or slower-learning youngsters. Another proposal is to extend mass education into institutions of higher education. It is to be expected that the school year shall be lengthened through the summer, but there is less evidence that the school program will be extended by increasing the number of years of high school.

grouping

We group youngsters in school by developmental levels and more specifically by age levels; we further group them classroom by classroom. There is such a concern for grouping that even the haphazard age-success category is called heterogeneous grouping. When the criterion that educators use to group youngsters follows patterns of class or caste division in the greater society, the nonschool social distinctions tend to be imported into the school, with the consequence that the democratizing effects of the school are reduced. If the contacts between differing social groups that meet in the school are slight and incidental, the results are as inconsequential as the meeting of social classes in the supermarket. In an effort to reduce the isolation of slum youngsters, particularly blacks, some urban area schools bus students from one school to another and thus increase the mixing of classes and social or ethnic groups. Busing is said to reduce the effects of "de facto segregation" by equalizing educational opportunities between schools serving differing social groups.

We group because we are certain that placing youngsters in like groups improves the learning and teaching process. Ability grouping frequently follows patterns established by measures of intelligence, aptitude, or achievement or by combinations of these. Sometimes a teacher's subjective judgment plays a role in assigning youngsters to groups. Administrative considerations also enter into the problem of grouping. If groups were set up to conform to a normal distribution, there would be an oversized group in the middle and undersized groups on the slow-learning and fast-learning extremes. The common solution is to increase the size of the top and bottom groups by adding to them from the large population in the center. As a matter of convenience we seldom regroup for different learning experiences, even though it is agreed that individuals differ in their abilities, experiences, and achievement, particularly as we move away from the two extreme groups. There are some who suggest that the larger instructional problems are solved by grouping alone, although more enlightened individuals are willing to adjust methods, teaching materials, and the curriculum in order to solve the difficulties of teaching and learning.

Grouping in school tends to create castes and, of course, rank (caste) has its privileges. The school society's most conspicuous reactions to grouping procedures are found on the secondary level, where status relates to those groups that are labeled college preparatory "tracks." Here frustration meets the aspirant who fails for the assignment or his neighbor who enters the select group as a borderline case and then does not realize success. Any school grouping that is not heterogeneous implies that school objectives are related to a qualitative selective process in organizing for instruction. Levels of quality lead to status, status leads to caste, and caste leads to rank, privilege, and problems.

There are several grouping adaptations that seek to resolve problems of traditional procedures. "Ungraded" classes seek to replace the early grades with a three-year unit, which is divided into semesters. Each child proceeds at his own pace and may enter the fourth grade as early as four semesters beyond kindergarten or as late as eight semesters. He may thus complete the traditional first three grades in as little as two years or in as many as four years. Numbered semesters substitute for grade levels and a teacher may find several semesters represented in her class. The faster learners tend to catch up with their slower, but older, compatriots. Once the child is in the fourth grade, there is a reversion to traditional grade procedures. An alternative to "ungrading" is the "multigrade" plan, which uses three-grade divisions (1–3 and 4–6) and includes three grades in each classroom, thus keeping youngsters with the same teacher for three years. This is a return to some of the situations found in the one-room rural school.

A modification of the practice of organizing the school into grades provides for ability grouping without reference to grades in some subjects and the traditional pattern of grouping by age levels in other school activities. This is the "dual-progress" plan, in which grouping is related to "cultural imperatives" (language and social studies), which determine basic grade placement, and to "cultural electives" (mathematics, science, music, and art), in which students are instructed in ungraded groups that are organized on an aptitude-achievement basis. Special grouping arrangements offer a variety of ways in which youngsters are placed into instructional groups; each grouping technique changes the criteria for grouping. Grouping innovations result in differing combinations of pupil personalities and lead to a rearrangement of the school society. Each system is credited by its proponents with having particular and overlapping benefits for the educative process.

Are there advantages to grouping? Of course there are advantages, and every school finds some way of grouping: by age, ability, sex, or reducing the range of abilities in a group. By eliminating the most extreme differences in ability or achievement within a classroom, learning processes may become more uniform and teaching procedures more standardized.

To the degree that grouping in the classroom frees youngsters from an inability to function in learning, there may be outlets for motivation and success in attempts to solve learning problems. Freeing a child's potential to perform can release the fuller expression of a pupil's ability. Moreover, extremes of behavior and reaction may become less extreme when youngsters are divided into groups that are more alike than they might otherwise be.

Grouping is recognition of both teacher and pupil limitations in adapting to a situation. Grouping may permit learning to become more personal and more meaningful, with the quality of learning enhanced by reducing the range of differences among the pupils. Grouping does not eliminate differences, but it may make them more manageable.

Grouping has problems as well as benefits. No group is truly homogeneous. The complex of uneven ability patterns among youngsters and the variation of achievement levels within a subject area exist even when classes are grouped by the ability or achievement of the pupils. Differences between personalities, emotionality, maturity, and motivation of individuals serve to limit uniformity within any group.

Grouping can increase problems for some youngsters if selection procedures recognize only age or grade levels without including a concern for the possibility that a youngster should be able to find success. Grouping that reflects social distinctions opens the doors to school achievement to a chosen few and slams them shut on others. It creates frustrations and social friction. Youngsters who are labeled "best" may acquire aristocratic bearings. Those labeled "slowest" may believe the label and accept an inferior status.

The borderline cases are affected most seriously by grouping practices, for some pupils might become the persistent bottom of one group or the favored top of the next lower group. Sometimes parental preference dooms a youngster to continuous frustration in the halo of a "higher" group instead of placing him in the easier success of a "lower" group. The assumption that borderline cases can be moved back and forth across the arbitrary grouping division as circumstances change is seldom borne out. The "downward" movement from one group to another occurs more frequently because it is easier to pick up a slower pace of instruction than to catch up with a quicker one.

Is grouping democratic? No less than the division into unskilled, skilled, supervisory, and managerial labor. No more than the social stigma placed on individuals in a group or on an entire group. Grouping is democratic to the extent that through it youngsters will learn to know, live with, work with, and accept those dissimilar to themselves. It is a means of artificially structuring social units, and if wisely used, it may contribute to the solution of individual social problems while it seeks to resolve instructional difficulties. As far as efficiency of instruction is concerned, grouping moves the schools in the correct evolutionary direction. The full potential of grouping for instruction will be realized when we group in the ultimate, in terms of the individual. If learning can proceed on an individual basis, the way in which the larger class group is made up or the means by which pupils are placed in a group may be irrelevant. Differing groups and individuals may be purposefully placed in some larger instructional groups to further democratic ideals. Learning of some subjects may take place through individual instruction while other subjects may be more adaptable to large-group lecture, film, or televised instruction.

the pupil society

Within the framework of the school society, pupils form their own social relationships. The pupil society is a highly rewarding experience for some; a mixture of happiness and unhappiness for many; and an experience of dark, cruel, unrelenting despair for a few. The broad forces at work in the school community tend to stabilize relationships, reinforce the elite, continue the cohesiveness of the mass, and increase the isolation of the outcasts. Unhappily for our democratic professions, the school's adult society often lends its support to a pupil status quo that is socially selective and repressive.

The pupil society operates under two sets of objectives, those of the school and those of the pupils. The school's objectives favor the establishment of basic conditions of order, elimination of disorder, and unobstructed learning procedures. Those schools that concentrate on a struggle to effect order in the presence of unstable adult leadership or in the face of overwhelming rebellion on the part of youngsters accomplish little in effective learning. Pupil objectives are primarily concerned with satisfaction of youngsters' needs, with gaining acceptance and approval, and with a defensible personal relationship to peers, adults, and the school society. Some children find acceptance and approval with relative ease, particularly when they fit both socially and academically into the school environment. Others have mixed success and stray occasionally into less acceptable behavior patterns to satisfy their needs. The unhappy minority may vacillate between withdrawal to avoid reproof of their conduct and aggressive behavior in a vain effort to gain some kind of recognition for their actions.

ingroups and outgroups

The pupil society establishes definite but unstable ingroups and outgroups. The prevailing larger society provides the bulk of the ingroup, although it is possible for individuals from society's fringe areas to gain acceptance on the basis of unusual personality characteristics. As youngsters find acceptance in the framework of school objectives, their admission into the inner circle is facilitated. It is possible for the star athlete out of a lower-class family to be accepted by a middle-class school power clique. One of the most intriguing factors about class isolates is that misery does not love company. Isolates are separated from each other as well as from ingroups. The same factors that repel rejects from the socially accepted majority repel them from each other.

Much as they may wish, teachers cannot force the ingroup of a class to accept outsiders. In their control of the classroom environment, teachers can regulate the degree and nature of contact among youngsters. They also have opportunities to aid pupils in recognizing, identifying, and countering negative social or personality factors. They can only guide; they cannot push youngsters into change or force change upon them. In the area of social relations, the teacher's most important roles are to provide opportunities for contact and cooperation among individuals and groups and to serve as a model in accepting all youngsters as social equals.

As in any social structure, power positions evolve within the pupil society. Hopefully, the power niche is occupied by a "nice" boy or girl who is deadly serious in classroom affairs, unselfish, and neither domineering nor aggressive. Realistically, of course, the classroom ward heeler is molded by the school environment. He or she also may be rebellious, a secret plotter, or the protector of the rights of a small, determined, scheming minority. Whether a group is cooperative or insurgent will depend on the realities of the pupil society in a classroom, for the classroom is a part of the school society, which reflects the greater community.

competition versus cooperation in the classroom

Competitive situations structured within a classroom may act as an unconscious ally to classroom conflict. If, in the name of scholarship or free enterprise, a teacher's grading procedures, classroom privileges, or grouping arrangements emphasize competition among the youngsters, with only a few able to survive the competition, the pupil society may take on all the negative attributes of life in the jungle. The school society can demonstrate the values of a healthy combination of cooperation and competition. Classroom procedures may be guided by those human relationships identified with the democratic ideal —concern for the rights, feelings, desires, needs, hopes, and fears of every happy, miserable, intelligent, stupid, clean, unwashed human being. If cooperative striving centers on solutions for individual and group problems, and if competition is structured so that everyone may succeed (at least in competition with himself), the school society may reflect that high degree of social cooperation essential to a democracy.

The pupil society tends to emulate the formal groupings of adult social patterns that are related to socioeconomic backgrounds and accepted measures of success. Success on the adult level may be related to a job, membership in select groups, the size and location of a home, or the number of automobiles owned by a family. Measures of success in school may be related to a youngster's athletic or extracurricular achievement or to success in boy-girl relationships in the secondary school. There are informal social groupings that may consolidate a class in opposition to a teacher or that unite youngsters across grade lines to evade administrative fiat. In more legitimate activities a school society may exploit athletic abilities, strive for quality in dramatic or music presentations, or seek to enlist parental support for special projects. Irregular grouping on an informal basis in school continues only as long as need for the formation of the group exists. There is something strangely adult in the willingness of youngsters to make use of an individual for convenience's sake or for an individual to offer himself to the group for an expedient moment even though he may expect later rejection by the group.

regulating the school society

The school society is constantly being regulated by administrators, teachers, or pupils and sometimes by a combination of two or more of these. When an all-school policy is established and reinforced, the principal is in control. To the extent that he is able to influence classroom rules and procedures, he dominates the school society. If the atmosphere, practice, and pupil morale vary from room to room, teachers are in control of the environment. One occasionally witnesses positive regulation in a school by youngsters through a student council or classroom government. Within the bounds set by the administration or teachers, youngsters may find the freedom to settle many of their own affairs.

In addition to formal procedures, there are informal processes of control in a school. Fear of an adult exerts pressure on youngsters whenever it is possible that the particular adult may be within seeing or hearing distance. Pressures on a faculty by administrators or on an insecure principal by his teachers may be controlling factors in a school. Pressure by a few parents, many parents, the school board, taxpayers' groups, or news media may have a negative impact on the school environment. Youngsters have their own forms of pressure. They may fail to cooperate with school-management attempts at regulation. They may erupt into aggressive behavior by writing on desks or on washroom or hallway walls. They may engage in aggressive behavior among themselves. Active young minds may operate in innumerable ways to undermine the mechanisms of adult control.

The school provides constructive educational experiences for some youngsters and missed opportunities for others. Of prime significance on the positive side is the opportunity to break social, economic, racial, and religious barriers by a greater exposure of children to people unlike themselves than they would experience in the narrow confines of the home. In many smaller communities the breaking of these barriers is accomplished far better than in urban situations where the neighborhood school enrolls youngsters from the same ethnic or socioeconomic groups. The amount, type, and success of contact between groups varies with the skill of the adults who structure the school environment; but there are always opportunities in every school to breach nonschool barriers.

Each pupil has a certain number of positive educational experiences as he progresses through school. The better student thrives within this new environment and even the slowest pupil leaves school changed somewhat. There is abundant evidence of the success of the American school, even as there is of its failures. The promise for the future rests with the educational triumphs, for in each successful schoolhouse product is the story of a series of alternatives of success or failure. In an improving school system the number of youngsters who achieve success in school ought to increase every year. The most common failures of the schools are in those areas where the school society is molded by adult philosophy, principles, and practices that conflict with the real needs of youngsters. But for every autocratic alternative employed by an adult in the school there are paternalistic or democratic substitutes. For every negative action there are many positive alternatives. The school is in a position to mold the attitudes toward education of future parents by the way it educates each present generation of youngsters.

An unfortunate aspect in the school society concerns those extracurricular programs that reinforce the characteristics they are supposed to remove or reduce. When an athletic program exploits youngsters for adult entertainment or when music programs merely supplement athletics, youngsters are deprived of the real purposes of these school programs. When club activities reinforce positions of privilege they were intended to counteract and when democratic structures legitimatize adult authoritarianism, these functions perpetuate the exclusiveness and the hatefulness of the school society.

Schools are plagued with the related problems of truancy and high dropout rates. Yet there is seldom a purposeful and sincere effort to determine the reasons for this revulsion of formal education. Instead the answer is found in criticism of the youngster and through him of his parents and neighborhood. If the school is to be a significant social instrument, there must be a niche for each of its junior members regardless of who or what they are, where they live, or the status of their parents.

conclusion

There is a need to structure the ideal school society as a means of judging what we have and of achieving the ultimate objectives toward which we strive. The characteristics of an ideal structure are not hard to evolve. We must start with an adult society in the schools that is intelligent, competent, and democratic in philosophy and practice. From this adult core must come the framework upon which every younger citizen becomes an equivalent human being in the eyes of both adults and peers. Free from meaningless stigma related to race, color, or religion and devoid of the sheen of select parents or the tarnish of a neglecting home, each child is the worthy possessor of a body and a mind that are acceptable as they stand. Every youngster shares the same emotions and needs of all his classmates. Beyond a total acceptance of each imperfect individual we shall require the school to perfect the means, methods, materials, and techniques through which full expression of the capabilities of every young person shall be realized.

on your own

A useful exercise in considering the society within the school is to critically, unemotionally, and as accurately as possible reconstruct your own school social structure, the governing ingroups and the outgroups and the individual isolates. Even the most effective faculty runs into student resistance and conflict. Considerable reflection and some concentrated reminiscing ought to reconstruct fairly a past political-social student body.

The faculty power structure and interpersonal machinations are out of the experience of nonteachers. There has not been much in the way of earnest research in this area. However, you may refer to some aspects of the question through Myron Lieberman's *Teaching as a Profession* (Englewood Cliffs, N.J.: Prentice-Hall, 1956) and James M. Hughes' *Human Relations in Educational Organizations* (New York: Harper & Brothers, 1957). An occasional explosion within a school system is reported in educational or popular periodicals or infrequently in a book, such as *This Happened in Pasadena* by David Hurlburd (New York: Macmillan, 1951). The role of teachers in the educational process is of concern to Arthur T. Jersild in *When Teachers Face Themselves,* 2nd ed. (New York: Teachers College, Columbia University, 1957), and Nathaniel F. Cantor's *The Teaching-Learning Process* (New York: Dryden Press, 1953). An important aspect of the situation is the topic of *Mental Hygiene for Teachers* by Lester D. Crow and Alice Crow (New York: Macmillan, 1963). Previously recommended reading is applicable, such as Conant's *Slums and Suburbs,* Dunn's *Retreat from Learning,* Kozol's *Death at an Early Age,* and Kaufman's *Up the Down Staircase.*

Behavior of youngsters in the classroom is a particularly sensitive and difficult subject, which may be further studied through the child development approach, such as Marian E. Breckenridge and E. Lee Vincent's *Child Development; Physical and Psychological Growth Through Adolescence,* 5th ed.

(Phila.: Saunders, 1965), or by consulting bibliographical references, such as *Education Index* under "School children," and seeking out articles like G. Noar's "Nature of Human Relations in the Classroom" (*North Central Association Quarterly,* 39 [Fall 1964], 196–199). *Adolescents and the Schools* by James S. Coleman (New York: Basic Books, 1965) is an example of perceptive studies of youngsters and the classroom.

A highly significant aspect in future school development is the rapid trend toward urbanization and the growth of the megalopolis through such factors as developments in transportation, communication, automation, cybernation, and the ever-greater movement into industrial agriculture. What does this trend mean for the future teacher in terms of teaching as a vocation, changes in curricular needs, changes in individual and group values, and behavior of youngsters? Should there be changes made in the structure of schools? For example, do we need a new form of junior high? Should the school calendar be changed from its rural orientation to one geared to an industrial society? How may the teacher promote, plan for, and help execute the changes you deem necessary for the future? How is the changing character of the school youngster to be met and served?

The best way to analyze the school society is to visit a school and attempt to measure the vague "feeling tone" in a building. Beneath the traditional veneer, what are the true feelings of faculty members toward youngsters, parents, the community, school system, administrators, colleagues, and themselves? Does one find happy and productive youngsters and teachers? Is the building alive with eager learning or ever-present tension? A look at classrooms and student councils in operation may suggest whether power is administered for or against children. An hour in the teachers' lounge may reveal more of the human relationships within a school than many hours of interviewing administrators or teachers.

additional references

Anderson, Margaret. *Children of the South.* New York: Farrar, 1966.

Beggs, David W., III, and Edward G. Buffie (eds.). *Nongraded Schools in Action.* Bloomington: Indiana University Press, 1967.

Douvan, Elizabeth, and Joseph Adelson. *The Adolescent Experience.* New York: Wiley, 1966.

Dunn, Lloyd M. (ed.). *Exceptional Children in the Schools.* New York: Holt, Rinehart and Winston, 1963.

Hentoff, Nat. *Our Children Are Dying.* New York: Viking, 1966.

Kirk, Samuel A. *Educating Exceptional Children.* Boston: Houghton Mifflin, 1962.

Lifton, Walter M. *Working with Groups: Group Process and Individual Growth.* 2nd ed. New York: Wiley, 1966.

Long, Nicholas J., William C. Morse, and Ruth G. Newman (eds.). *Conflict in the Classroom: The Education of Emotionally Disturbed Children.* Belmont, Calif.: Wadsworth, 1965.

McGeoch, Dorothy M. *Learning to Teach in Urban Schools.* New York: Teacher's College Press, Columbia University, 1965.

Miller, Harry L. (ed.). *Education for the Disadvantaged.* New York: Free Press, 1967.

Nordstrom, Carl, Edgar Z. Friedenberg, and Hilary A. Gold. *Society's Children: A Study of Ressentiment in Secondary School Education.* New York: Random House, 1967.

Smith, Louis M., and William Geoffrey. *The Complexities of an Urban Classroom: An Analysis Toward a General Theory of Teaching.* New York: Holt, Rinehart and Winston, 1968.

Taba, Hilda, and Deborah Elkins. *Teaching Strategies for the Culturally Disadvantaged.* Chicago: Rand McNally, 1966.

6

In the business and process of teaching and learning housed by the school, the curriculum comprises the total of the structured learning experiences. It consists of content, methods of teaching, materials for learning, and techniques of evaluation.

the school curriculum

The curriculum is the basis for realization of the school objectives. Quite naturally, definitions of the curriculum differ according to the way objectives are defined. Those who propose that the school shall be involved solely or primarily with scholarly academic pursuits would limit the curriculum to traditional subjects: social sciences, natural sciences, the humanities, and, perhaps begrudgingly, physical education. Those who envision the broadest purposes for the schools would include, in addition to traditional subject matters, health education, driver training, vocationally oriented subjects, athletic programs, and even peripheral club activities. An extreme definition of the curriculum encompasses all the activities in the school, although much daily time and energy are taken up with routine procedures and the school may be a place where inappropriate or antisocial learnings occur.

Youngsters learn to dislike teachers, subjects, and school. Inner city schools report "zip guns" being made in industrial arts classrooms. It would thus seem suitable to exclude from the definition of the curriculum nonplanned, nonregulated, and nonstructured learnings as well as athletic and club activities. Some inconsistencies result when basketball is curricular in physical education classes and extracurricular in an interscholastic athletic program. To be meaningful, a definition of the curriculum must be relevant to educational objectives, incorporate a distinguishable content, involve purposeful teaching and learning, and be subject to continual evaluation in terms of basic objectives. The importance of stating the extent and

what to learn

limits of the curriculum lies in the accountability of the schools to the greater society for fulfilling the schools' assigned objectives. A poorly defined curriculum is difficult to assess. Schools may be handicapped in demonstrating their effectiveness when there is confusion about what does or should occur in the school and which of these activities are the responsibility of the school.

Because of the expressed dislike by youngsters of subjects and the antisocial behavior reported in the classroom, it sometimes is suggested that the school curriculum ought to reflect the wishes, desires, or interests of students. It is believed that when youngsters are involved in activities built about their interests, aggressive behavior will be reduced or eliminated. This rationale, however, ignores the fact that to dislike something necessitates some sort of experience. The youngster entering school may dislike the institution only vaguely and on the expressed dislike of others. Personal dislike must relate to experience.

A more suitable approach to content of the curriculum would be to select subject matter that has meaning to youngsters and will be of use to them. Assuming there is meaningful and functional subject matter, students dislike school or a subject because of the way they are treated by teachers and fellow pupils and by the frustrations they find in classroom activities. It is also necessary for the curriculum to represent a content that fulfills the objectives the society has delegated to the schools. Youngsters should be taught the traditions and culture of the society and the skills needed for productive and useful citizenship. Attention must then be focused on the interpersonal skills and teaching techniques of teachers.

If students find the classroom exciting and a source of success and satisfaction, interest in the subject and school will be fostered. It is then reasonable to expect that aggressive and antisocial behavior will be reduced. Because each youngster is an individual with his own personality, home situation, peer relationships, aptitude for school, aspirations, desires, and fears, it would be unrealistic to suppose that there should be no behavioral problems in a school.

subject matter content

The school curriculum is engrossed with a segment of subject matter content. It builds upon knowledge acquired before attendance in school and is extended by additional learnings after exit from the school experience. Some learnings are highly limited to the school (frequently true of a foreign language) while other learnings are unique to nonschool activities (sectarian religious beliefs and practices). The school curriculum presumes a relatively high level of efficiency in vocabulary and language usage as a basis upon which school learning experiences take place.

Language is essential to exploitation of the school curriculum. It is also the major subject content of the school, beginning with reading readiness exercises in early school experiences and continuing through learning to read and write and the study of native and foreign literature. Language instruction is the most intensive and extensive course of study in the schools. An early second topic of study is arithmetic, although the arithmetic-mathematics sequence may be terminated before completion of the high school program. Historically, the social studies program has ranked second to language as a persistent requirement in the curriculum. The sciences have been gaining emphasis in recent curricular developments, particularly in the lower grade levels.

Special subjects—art, music, physical education, health, safety, driver training, home economics, or industrial arts—may be required of all youngsters with the expectation that they will exert an influence on personal development or for purposes of exposure or appreciation. In the upper grades differences in courses and their content are reflected in the name given to a curriculum: college preparatory or vocational (business-oriented or industrial arts subjects). Some subject matters, particularly art and music, are taught to all youngsters in the elementary and early secondary schools and become by election or selection limited to those of particular talent in the later school years. High school subject content may invade areas commonly reserved for college level instruction (calculus) or is oriented toward extremely modest educational objectives (business arithmetic). Efforts are made on the one hand to involve students in complicated academic activities and on the other to provide routines that seem to be concerned primarily with a desire to keep youngsters occupied even if significant or functional growth in understanding or skills is not realized.

citizenship training and group guidance

In addition to teaching subject content, the schools are committed to citizenship training for all youngsters. The responsibility for citizenship training is assigned to social studies classes in the belief that knowledge of the country through study of its history, government, customs, and tradition is instrumental in acquiring citizenship attitudes and skills. A student council may provide experiences in democratic processes for a few youngsters, but this cannot be considered a curricular method of general training in citizenship for the mass of the school population. Occasionally a school will establish a program of student participation that extends into a democratic organization of each homeroom or elementary classroom. Some schools include in the curriculum a carefully structured group guidance program, which is aimed toward facilitating individual growth and the improvement of group processes.

moral training

While the school assumes a role in moral training, the curricular means through which this objective is to be achieved is not clearly defined. Not only is there disagreement as to whether moral training must be allied with religious instruction, but there is no single subject that is particularly adaptable to instruction in morals. Some people, particularly among the clergy, consider that the major means for a school to engage in moral training is through released time religious instruction, an arrangement between schools and churches in which pupils are excused from school for religious instruction at their church or synagogue. Others believe a school should provide periodic lectures concerning moral issues or should make use of appropriate posters or displays furthering certain moral positions. But the major instrument for moral instruction in the school is the individual teacher. His influence is reflected in the way he reacts to young people and to a situation. Too frequently a teacher depends on correction or punishment of youngsters rather than positive instruction and guidance in attempting to meet the school's responsibilities for moral education. Many teachers tend to be quite moralistic and include much preaching in the teaching as their method of incorporating appropriate moral values and behavior into the curriculum.

extracurricular or cocurricular programs

As noted previously, there is disagreement as to whether to include extracurricular programs or activities within the formal curriculum. Some prefer to identify such activities as "cocurricular," or sharing an equal status within the regular school program.

However such activities are categorized, the kind and extent of extracurricular programs vary greatly from school to school. An elementary school seldom has a very extensive program beyond a student council, a few clubs, and seasonal athletic competition for the upper grades. Some schools sponsor school safety patrols and scout or Camp Fire groups, and they may provide leadership and facilities for after-school recreational programs. Secondary schools commonly have student councils, well-organized athletic programs, cheerleaders, vocal and instrumental music groups (usually scheduled within the school program), Junior Red Cross or other service organizations, special interest clubs (some allied with subject areas), and school newspapers and yearbooks.

The quality of these activities and the degree to which they are carefully and purposefully planned as learning experiences vary from some superior programs to others that are highly disorganized and of limited value. Some programs include many or most of the pupils; others involve a relatively small proportion of the school population. Extracurricular or cocurricular activities present a spotty picture as effective aspects of the school program.

construction of the curriculum

However basic, the statement that the schools are society's schools and the curriculum is society's curriculum is yet an oversimplification, for those who control the schools select from among various pressures and interests to interpret the needs and demands of society into the realities of the curriculum. Out of the amorphous glob that is the society and from the cacophony of conflicting segments of society comes the framework within which the school curriculum is built.

pressures from outside the school

Political pressures have influenced state legislatures to decree much of the curriculum. While state guidelines may be suggestive rather than mandatory, they do serve as a guide for the publication of textbook materials, have an impact on teacher education programs, and exert an influence on the evaluation of school programs by state officials. The degree of conformity to state guidelines may be reflected in the level of state financial support awarded to a school district. Often the mere threat to withhold or reduce financial aid is a powerful weapon against a local school system. The curriculum is influenced by Congress through federal support programs, such as those in the areas of vocational or home economics education. No school system is required to subscribe to a federal program and yet few can ignore the bait of subsidies, even if this means surrender of some control over the content of the program and qualifications of the staff. The control of the local society over the school curriculum is limited by an externally directed framework. The curriculum represents a combination of social objectives as determined on national and state levels and by the local school district.

Special interest groups both expand on and contract the curriculum. Patriotic groups have been instrumental in the repetitious placement of American history in the school program and have insisted upon instruction in state history and government. Economic groups have influenced the editing of textbooks and secured the incorporation of appropriate courses of study in the schools. Banking interests have been effective in setting up school savings plans. Churches have successfully prevailed on public schools to provide released time programs. Religious groups have forced revision of textbooks espousing ideas, such as evolution, which are contrary to those of the group. Organizations have restricted teaching about communism, forced revision of reading lists, led to adoption of certain texts or the blacklisting of others, and influenced instruction in the most direct manner, through the firing of an instructor.

the influence of tradition

Probably the strongest influence on the curriculum is adherence to tradition. The stubbornness with which Latin persists as a regular school subject is perhaps the greatest demonstration of the strength of tradition. The lag between progress and the curriculum finds vocational agriculture instructing excessive numbers of future farmers during a period when the number of farms and farmers continues to decline. Business courses are slow to incorporate modern business practices.

Industrial arts programs engage in outmoded instructional techniques and seldom have appropriate equipment. There is a tendency to rely on the "tried and true" subjects in the school as standards for the core of the curriculum, thus depending on the familiar and comfortable for guidance to change. Basic changes in the curriculum are often late in meeting the needs of a dynamic society and, even when effected, may be half-hearted at best.

As social needs change, objectives of the school also must change. Social or industrial progress may be rapid, particularly under the impact of war, depression, or scientific break-through, but reflected change in the schools follows a deliberate pattern. Educator reaction to change is initiated by those schoolmen who are critically evaluating the society and the schools. These are the professionals who propose the means by which curriculum and teaching techniques may meet new challenges. Educator criticism and reform proposals are usually expressed in articles published in educational periodicals, seldom in book form, and occasionally in the popular literature.

In contrast to the educator's concern for the solution of internal problems within the school, nonprofessional critics are generally concerned with the solution of out-of-school problems through the schools. The noneducator reaches a mass rather than professional audience by publishing in popular literature and popularly written books. The noneducator may be unreasonably critical of the schools, naive about the true nature of school problems, and simplistic in his proposals for change. Some educators, on the other hand, are extremely defensive about the schools, apologetic in their analysis of problems, and overly cautious in their solutions.

Considerable discussion generally precedes action in making significant changes in the schools. Innovation is initiated on a trial basis in some school systems and frequently draws a number of quick and easy converts. To the extent that the new idea gains approval, it tends to reach a maximum acceptance and then to level off on a numerical plateau. At the plateau level the movement is supported by an enthusiastic but small hard core population; a larger number of schools adhere somewhat skeptically to the basic idea; and an indeterminate number of schools adopt and discard the innovation in a fairly rapid turnover. Legislative action or the lure of significant financial subsidies is commonly needed before an innovation gains general acceptance. The adoption of new objectives for the schools comes about rarely, slowly, and painfully.

At times, unmet demands of societal objectives for the school curriculum lead to structural changes aimed at achieving school reform or increasing efficiency in learning. The junior high school, for example, was designed to meet the special educational, social, psychological, and emotional needs of the early adolescent. Now, under charges that the junior high school has been a failure, the middle or intermediate school has been introduced as a new, superior structure to accomplish the same ends. Another structural change is the move to departmentalize the elementary school in order to improve learning and to upgrade the level of instruction. Subject matter content may be reorganized: history, geography, political science, and economics combined into the social studies; social studies and language arts combined into a core class.

The curriculum may be altered by the addition of new content. Economics education was added to the curriculum to satisfy the special interests of people concerned about the lack of instruction on our economic system. Driver education has become an accepted school subject. Advanced mathematical concepts have been introduced at an earlier age in school, and calculus has moved from the college level into some high schools. Failure to recognize the Negro's contribution to American society has led to courses in black history and literature. Changes in global realities have led to the introduction of Russian and Chinese language instruction and courses in Far Eastern and African area studies. Discussion and debate rage about the advisability or necessity of including sex education in the schools.

Efforts to realize the objectives of the school include the adoption of new teaching methods. Thus, the core curriculum frequently includes use of special teaching procedures, which recognize, in particular, the need to build instructional content and learning activities around the interests of students. Audio-visual techniques—the use of films, filmstrips, and tape recorders—are intended to improve instruction. Educational television and programmed instruction serve to fulfill curricular objectives.

An interesting innovation is the Trump Plan. J. Lloyd Trump, associate executive secretary of the National Association of Secondary School Principals, headed a research investigation into improved teaching suggestions for the NASSP and the resulting report (1960) was identified with his name. It proposed a reorganization of the secondary school so that instruction will be conducted in large-group instruction, small-group discussion, and individual study. Teachers are to be organized into teaching teams and the schedule would become flexible, so that instruction could utilize short or extended time periods. Teaching assistants are to aid in preparing and conducting instruction and a variety of teaching techniques and audiovisual tools are proposed.

the role of the teacher

The teacher is one key to effecting a curriculum and realizing its objectives. Although the teacher's role is commonly recognized and may be exaggerated, the teacher himself may not realize that his influence in the curriculum spreads across many subjects, various skills, and assorted activities. To be most effective, his teaching is related to a carefully structured sequence through twelve years. The superior teacher recognizes his place in the curriculum as a builder upon previous experience and an important contributor to a future progression. He identifies the horizontal relationships across the curriculum and makes use of opportunities to relate his special interest to other areas, including in his instruction the use of other subjects (art and music, for example) as aids and accessories to his own.

The direct responsibility of the teacher is to his own area of specialization, especially to his own classroom, subject, teaching, and youngsters. In accepting a position the teacher contracts to teach a particular grade or subject. His teaching responsibility may be spelled out in general terms, but the more precise detailing of subject content, organization of learning procedures, and the actual carrying out of the teaching process is delegated to the teacher himself. As yet, there is no definition of malpractice in teaching as a means of judging skill or integrity in carrying out the teaching assignment.

In the process of teaching, classroom teachers may be held responsible for maintaining certain records, handling housekeeping duties, caring for the physical well-being of pupils, and providing information (such as attendance reports and lesson plans) to the administration. Administrators may expect the teacher to utilize school-provided teaching materials and audiovisual equipment, to conduct field trips, or to supervise behavior in the halls, at lunch, or on the playground.

As a member of a profession the teacher assumes a responsibility beyond his own classroom. Ideally he seeks to carry out the grand social aims of education through participation in professional activities that advance the curriculum. He brings to bear political pressures so that the necessary financial means, structure, consultant services, materials, and procedures are provided to carry out the educational objectives. He endeavors to set standards of excellence for admission to the profession and for conduct in performing professional duties. His concern for the curriculum leads to vertical and horizontal coordination with teachers in other grades or in the same grade or subject. Service on departmental or school or system-wide committees involves him in an advisory capacity concerning policy and administrative matters, revision of the curriculum, and the proposing of or participation in research activities.

The elementary teacher should display concern for the curriculum at all levels of instruction as a broad professional interest. The secondary teacher, commonly enamored with higher education, should be involved with critical assessment of the elementary curriculum, which fashions the future secondary student.

In his concern with the whole curriculum as well as his own classroom, the teacher seeks to improve the efficiency of the learning process and to realize the school objectives at their highest level of performance. In the light of the fantastic increase in knowledge, the structure of the curriculum and the skill with which it is realized become of ever-increasing importance as more learning must be accommodated into the school experience. These objectives will be realized through an appropriate administrative structure, under enlightened leadership, and with skilled teachers who are highly educated in the learning process and flexible in the use of teaching procedures to effectuate the curriculum. In an era when large numbers of teachers are unqualified or at least not certificated (about 20 percent in the state of Ohio) and when the dropout from teaching is disturbingly large (about 12 percent of Ohio teachers leave the classroom annually), the role of the teacher in perfecting and activating the curriculum is of less consequence than it ought to be.

state and local supervision

State departments of education differ in their structure and in the extent to which they regulate the curriculum. A typical state department has curriculum specialists who propose revisions of state syllabi, commonly acting in consultation with lay and professional groups. Some state departments of education (for example, New York) publish frequent and comprehensive curriculum guides. In addition to maintaining responsibility for proposing or mandating the curriculum, the states engage in evaluation of instructional programs.

Local school districts are commonly required to forward information about their instructional programs to state authorities. Most states maintain supervisory personnel whose functions on the local level are both supervisory and consultative. Their duties include ensuring that state regulations are observed. State department of education personnel also seek to provide ideas and suggestions for the improvement of the local program. One practice that is gradually being discontinued is the administration of statewide achievement tests in secondary school subjects. In addition, many states exert a direct influence on the curriculum by requiring school districts to provide special services, such as remedial reading specialists, in the schools.

On the local level, larger city school systems employ curriculum specialists, who, like their state counterparts, assume responsibility for proposing curricular revisions and supervise or coordinate instruction in the classroom. A large city may (and smaller city systems are likely to) establish committees of teachers, administrators, and perhaps laymen to study the curriculum and propose changes. Frequently, course of study outlines detailing changes in the curriculum come from these deliberations. Local curricular processes may claim to enjoy the benefit of meeting special local needs, whereas the national studies are said to be particularly useful in setting national standards and in seeking to eliminate narrow parochialism.

the textbook

Despite the continued and energetic criticism of the textbook, instruction still centers about the use of a book as a general resource. Stilted as it may be, the textbook read-recite-test instructional pattern is still used in the schools. However, the text should not come under unwarranted criticism, for the facts remain that teaching requires youngsters to use the same sources of material; group instruction demands shared resources; and demands on the time and energy of the individual teacher frequently make it difficult or impossible to break free of the text. To the degree that the textbook is the major instructional resource, it represents curricular content in the classroom. It is therefore not unexpected that special interest groups take particular notice of the content of school textbooks.

Some teachers are permitted to select textbooks for their own classes. Other schools provide for the adoption of texts by district. In some states textbook selection committees provide for statewide adoption of several books, and there is still one instance of a state practicing statewide adoption of a single text. A populous state that limits the selection of books for its schools may influence the content of all books competing for that market. Many publishers of textbooks are particularly influenced by the opportunity to market their products in those states where adoption procedures limit the competition. If the addition or deletion of content in a book will enhance chances that a text will be placed on the adoption list of a populous state, the publisher may yield to temptation.

The importance of the textbook in setting the curriculum is demonstrated by recent efforts to influence secondary school instruction on a national level. The American Institute of Biological Science sponsored a curriculum reform of high school biology which resulted in the Biological Science Curriculum Study comprising three textbooks for biology classes published in 1963. Other national groups have provided curricular guidelines through production of textbooks in chemistry, physics, and mathematics. The American Council of Learned Societies has demonstrated an interest in the development of the humanities and social studies curricula, and similar concern has been shown in the teaching of English by scholars in that discipline.

In whatever form the curriculum is constituted as it enters a classroom and from whatever authority it is structured, the success of the operant curriculum (the actual learning experience) is dependent on the personality, knowledge, and ability of the teacher in the classroom. An excellent teacher may put life into a drab instructional pattern; he may bring order out of chaos. An inferior instructor, however, may negate the most carefully designed program. The eventual realization of educational objectives is subject to the qualifications, integrity, and whim of an individual teacher, a fact which suggests that an enormous responsibility is placed upon administrators. They must provide leadership to teachers, fulfill supervisory responsibilities, and conduct in-service training of staff.

sequence of the curriculum

The teacher needs to understand the grand design of the curriculum, to know the educational progression in some detail, and to understand his own role in the process. As suggested previously, it is essential that the teacher recognize the school experience as a logical, sequential structure through the twelve years and accept a responsibility for the entire program as well as for his specific area of interest and concern.

the preschool and elementary curriculum

Every level and every grade in school is of equal importance: an older child may become a school dropout; a younger child may become a functional dropout and stop exerting effort to learn. A vertical building of learning experiences requires that each level will build from previous experiences and provide a base for the subsequent learning. The crucial school level for any youngster is that in which he is currently enrolled.

In a progressive and sequential experience, organized preschool and the elementary school are basic to the total learning experience. The urban crisis has focused attention on the inner city school and the problems of youngsters in adjusting to school, particularly those from slum and ghetto areas. The limited background of experiences that some children bring to school makes the transition to the classroom that much more difficult and learning that much less efficient and effective.

The first matter of importance in the sequence of the curriculum is the development and exploitation of prereading and introductory reading exercises. We may expect that the nursery and kindergarten experiences will receive greater stress now that the Head Start Program has pointed to the importance of preschool experiences for the underprivileged in society and by implication for all youngsters. One of the primary objectives at the introductory stage of curricular development is effectiveness in communication. It is essential for the culturally deprived youngster to have experiences equivalent to those of other children in order to form a basis for understanding and communication among all who attend school and to allow teachers to function effectively regardless of the social class or home environment of youngsters. The more formalized kindergarten seeks to facilitate learning and talking skills, increase vocabulary, provide experiences in handling books, and start instruction in letters.

In the first grade teachers initiate the development of reading skills. Oral reading, introduced in the first grade, is continued at least into the third year. By the fourth grade, variations in reading skills are evident and, of greater importance, efforts are made to aid youngsters in gaining the necessary background and skills to read in most of the subject areas. Many schools adopt commercial reading programs to facilitate the learning process.

Handwriting commences in either the first or second grade, first in manuscript style and then in cursive form. Elementary grades involve youngsters in creative writing exercises with both prose and poetry. Spelling commences with writing and may involve learning over 4,000 words by the sixth grade. Emphasis on individual skills should not obscure the fact that elementary school experiences also involve youngsters in drama, interpretive reading, and group discussion techniques. The sixth-grader may add to his learning tools oral reports, artistic expression in the designing of posters, participation in formal group-speaking exercises, and practice in committee processes. In addition to instruction in the vernacular, schools may provide foreign language instruction as early as the third grade.

Acquaintance with numbers may begin in the formalized kindergarten experience and be extended to counting to two hundred and writing numbers to one hundred in the first grade. By the third grade multiplication and division may be included in the curriculum and decimals, particularly money values, are introduced. Most arithmetic processes will have been taught by the end of the sixth grade. The trend in mathematics has been to move concepts downward in the graded progression and to engage in learning the principles of mathematics rather than to limit instruction in arithmetic to learning facts and drill exercises in procedures and skills.

The child has experiences in social situations before entrance into school, but it is here that he develops social skills and learns to adapt to social interaction. In a broad sense, social education of school-age youngsters involves the entire intergroup situation of the school. In terms of formal instruction in the social studies, however, the classroom learning activities first center on the family and local services. Initial instruction is directed toward the immediate environment, and field trips are often used to provide realistic learning experiences. Interestingly enough, there is seldom a serious effort to explain that most immediate of social services, the school itself. By the sixth grade the youngster will have advanced through what is, in effect, sociology and government to formal studies in American and state history and geography. At this stage the introductory study of the society has been concluded, but the training of the future citizen continues through the secondary school. Because the social studies are generally organized on a spiral curricular pattern in which instruction is conducted on several levels, each of which is more complex and more significant than the previous ones, there is limited breadth and depth of social studies instruction in the elementary school.

Science education as an organized subject in the elementary school suffers from confusion about the grade placement of subject matter and from inadequate preparation of many elementary teachers in science subject background and instructional methods. Because it is less systematically structured than the language arts or arithmetic, science instruction is not strictly organized and responsibility for areas of study is not well delineated. In the early grades science instruction is still dominated by practices related to the traditional nature study. In the upper elementary grades, however, science instruction has become a matter of better planning and teaching. Some schools make use of educational television to compensate for the limited backgrounds of many teachers, while other systems have resorted to departmentalized instruction in science matched with departmentalization of social studies or arithmetic in grades five and six. Occasionally such an effort is labeled a team-teaching enterprise, although the term "departmentalization" more aptly describes the practice.

Of the special subjects, art is the first in the curriculum, not as a formal study but as a form of communication, a means of expression, and a way of stimulating activity. Music is also a common but less formal activity in the introduction to the classroom. Many school systems employ art and music teachers in the elementary schools and classes are scheduled for periodic instruction, either in special rooms or within regular classrooms. In addition to the art forms as means of expression and opportunity to develop talent, experiences in art and music are considered important in providing opportunities for emotional release and for the development of social skills in group activities. Some schools begin instrumental music instruction in the fourth grade, with teaching centered about performance on wind rather than string instruments. Elementary schools that do not have the services of art and music specialists may provide inadequate instruction in those subject areas.

Physical education is introduced early in the elementary grades. Schools employ full-time or part-time specialists who may divide their efforts among several school buildings. Both individual and group activities are promoted in the programs, and organized athletic activities may be initiated by the fifth grade. School systems that are particularly committed to a strong athletic program assign coaches to elementary schools and arrange regular schedules of competition. An elementary athletic program may include cheerleaders, cheering sections, and the awarding of trophies. Schools that do not employ elementary school physical education specialists depend on the regular classroom teacher for instruction, but in this situation the quality and breadth of the program may be open to question. The same problem concerning quality of instruction raised in the absence of art or music specialists in the elementary schools also applies to physical education.

Increased interest has been shown in health and safety instruction in the elementary grades. A frequent practice is to pair health and science instruction, alternating lessons on a daily or semester basis. Considerable emphasis in health instruction is placed on personal hygiene as well as general information about diseases and their prevention and cure. As youngsters, particularly the girls, enter puberty, health classes become vehicles for describing and explaining physical change.

Traditionally considered to be an important role of the family, providing instruction in personal health and hygiene finds uncertain reactions among teachers and parents alike. Questions that are slow in resolution include whether sex education should be taught in the schools, at what grade level it should be placed, what the appropriate subject content should be, and what qualifications would be necessary for those responsible for the instruction. While the discussion continues, more schools are experimenting every year with teaching sex education.

articulation between grade levels

At one time a matter of considerable professional discussion was articulation between grade levels, the elementary grades and the junior high, and the junior high school program and that of the senior high. If less is heard today of this topic, it may be due to frustration in attempts to resolve the problem or accommodation to reality rather than to a solution of the problem. While the curriculum ought to be a twelve-year educational program with a smooth and orderly transition between segments, the elementary grades may be recognized as building educational experiences up from the introductory to the more complex, and the senior high school as taking its cues from the colleges and building toward the college instructional program. The junior high school is caught in the middle and is somewhat ambivalent about its position and purposes, although it tends to aim its program more at the senior high school. One result of the vertical confusion between administrative segments is a fragmented, disorganized curriculum. The confusion is compounded by tendencies in the elementary school for one grade to be isolated from another and on the secondary level for each subject to be separated from the others.

the secondary curriculum

A discussion of the secondary curriculum must take into account contradictions in the secondary structure that are evidenced by criticism of the junior high school. While the administrative structure of secondary education is generally a three-three division of grades seven through twelve, the academic program is divided into a two-four structure. Grades seven and eight are closely allied to the general content and objectives of elementary education. The upper academic progression is organized from grades nine through twelve and is directed toward specialized programs of study. Little progress has been made in establishing a smooth progression of twelve years of education, despite efforts to diminish or erase children's difficulties in adjusting to changes in structure, purpose, content, and methods from one school level to another.

The secondary curriculum provides two basic programs, a college preparatory program and terminal formal education that is sometimes vocationally oriented and at other times geared toward a general, nonvocational preparation for living. In the reflected glow of status accorded a college education a hierarchy of prestige has developed, in which college preparatory instruction selects out the superior student and the favored teacher. Unfortunately these pressures push into academic programs some who would find greater satisfactions in terminal programs. For others, failure of assignment to the precollege curriculum or lack of success in the college preparatory program becomes a personal or family tragedy. The exaggerated emphasis upon preparation for college by the high school has been more a reflection of middle-class standards of college-educated teachers than of the values of many youngsters in school or of their parents. This is particularly true in the small village or rural schools and the larger inner-city school systems.

English instruction on the secondary level is geared toward improving basic skills: reading, writing, listening, understanding and speaking. Except for the likelihood of emphasizing the literature of the United States (frequently in the eighth grade) or England (often in the eleventh or twelfth years), the subject content and teaching techniques may be scarcely indistinguishable through the last six years. Persistent and intensive repetition of instruction in grammar, spelling, and the mechanics of written expression through the school experience suggest either the difficulties in learning to understand and use the vernacular or the weaknesses of curricular organization and teaching techniques. The extensive absorption with communication fundamentals reduces the opportunity for significant study of non-English literature, a worthy venture in the modern world.

Electives in English may be offered in the senior high: public speaking, journalism (the journalism class usually publishes the school newspaper), dramatics, creative writing, and world literature. Proposals for the reform of English instruction include the core curriculum in which literature and social sciences are integrated into a common course of study. History and literature comprise the content, while writing and speaking become the vehicle of instruction. A modern twist to the core curriculum idea is the organization of humanities courses in which language instruction is combined with the teaching of history, art, and music. Recent proposals favor inductive learning of literary analysis or composition skills and concentration on the interrelationships of language, literature, and communication. Attempts to increase the amount of writing include the use of lay readers to relieve the classroom teacher of burdensome correction of compositions.

While secondary English instruction is taken up with the building of skills, instruction in the social studies emphasizes content. A common pattern includes seventh-grade instruction in state history, geography, economics, and social institutions; American history in the eighth and eleventh grades; world history in the tenth. The ninth- and twelfth-grade curricular offerings show wide variation: The lower grade may include economics, vocations and group guidance, or geography. The last grade may have a second year of American history or government, economics, or current problems.

Pressures are exerted to move away from the social studies approach with its emphasis on commonality of content and objectives to instruction in the separate disciplines. Curricular change in the social studies is slow and belabored. Difficulty in updating the social studies may be due in part to the watchdog activities of self-appointed patriots who aggressively resist any change in the curriculum as a devious attack on the national heritage and a direct threat to the nation. In contrast to other subject area specialists who have joined together to revise curricula, social studies teachers have been engaging in a wide search for improved methods and organization of content.

The junior high school follows the ordinary pattern of arithmetic instruction established in the elementary school with repetition of basic arithmetic processes extended into the seventh grade. An introduction to geometric forms and introductory experiences in geometry and algebra occur in the eighth grade. The minimum expectation in mathematical achievement for the average noncollege-bound student is knowledge of the facts and skills of basic arithmetic that are included in the general mathematics course of the ninth grade. College-bound students study elementary algebra. The continuing mathematical sequence includes plane geometry in the tenth grade, intermediate algebra and trigonometry in the eleventh grade, and advanced algebra and solid geometry in the twelfth grade. High school students who are interested in a science-mathematics-engineering preparation commonly complete the mathematics sequence. In some schools they may advance into calculus. Other college hopefuls may drop the mathematics progression beyond the ninth or tenth grade. An elective arithmetic extension is provided in some high schools with instruction in consumer or business mathematics.

In contrast to most subjects, the major influences on the mathematics curriculum have been effected in the elementary grades. It may be that a reformed secondary mathematics program will result from the cumulative changes in learning that accrue from the "modern math" instruction in the elementary school. The weakness of arithmetic-mathematics instruction has been evidenced by the extended necessity to teach and reteach basic arithmetic through the ninth grade and by the large numbers of capable students who drop out of the sequence early in high school.

The common junior high science program has been organized as general science courses. Each year pupils study selected topics in biology, chemistry, and physics. Advanced students in the ninth grade may take a course in earth science, while the typical college-bound student may study, without following any particular sequence, biology, chemistry, earth science, or physics in grades ten through twelve.

Science curricular reforms are the result of proposals advanced by study groups appointed out of the disciplines, such as the Biological Science Curriculum Study, Chemical Education Material Study, and Physical Science Study Committee. Significant changes were not sought in the basic structure of the curriculum, but emphasis was placed on the organization of content within each subject and the refining of teaching methods and materials. The unified efforts to improve learning in the science areas may be contrasted with the fragmented efforts in the social studies.

Modern foreign language instruction may commence in the elementary grades, in grade seven or eight, or, more traditionally, in the ninth grade. Latin instruction is usually restricted to the last four years of high school. The language available to students may reflect the locality—Norwegian in a Minneapolis high school—or the area—Spanish in the Southwest, French in New England—or the evolving world—Russian or Chinese in select school systems. A particularly encouraging aspect of foreign language instruction is the use by some schools of language laboratories utilizing taped instruction. Students may use tape recorders to practice the use of oral language and to improve pronunciation.

Art and music are offered as required courses in grades seven and eight (and sometimes nine) and as electives in the other high school grades. In the senior high school, art is elected by students who have a special interest and aptitude in applied art. Music, on the other hand, has become allied with the extracurricular program, and the school band frequently dominates the instrumental music program. An order of first priority for the band may be memorization of musical selections for parade and exhibition purposes. In many schools youngsters spend hours perfecting marching formations for a football game. Vocal music tends to emphasize group performance, although individual potentials may be developed and given experience in school programs. In some schools vocal music programs produce commendable operettas or musical comedies. Occasionally, elective courses may be offered in music theory and in music or art appreciation or history.

Health instruction is provided in the junior high school either as a separate subject or as a unit of instruction in biology, home economics, or physical education. Physical education is often a required subject through the secondary school. Youngsters are taught recreational games, sport skills, and dancing in physical education classes and swimming when facilities are available. An intramural athletic or recreational program may be conducted by the physical education staff, which may also be responsible for the interscholastic athletic program. Occasionally a school system may provide camping experiences as part of the school program. Any projection into the future would suggest that the school recreational program, especially in individual and small-group activities, will experience expanded objectives and activities and that particular attention in physical education and athletic programs will be directed in the area of spectator skills and appreciation of efforts by the experts.

The vocational education curriculum is first introduced in the school as general education and personal development activities. Classes in industrial arts and home economics begin in the seventh and eighth grades. At this level instruction is provided in general programs, with limited experiences in the various skills for all youngsters. Beginning with the ninth grade, instruction is offered in specialized subjects. Industrial arts and business curricula may be pursued in larger cities in separate vocational schools or as part of a regular high school program. A broad variety of vocational skills may be learned through the industrial arts program, which may include courses from automobile mechanics to electronics, machine shop, and printing. Schools report the construction of boats and even complete houses by industrial arts classes. Agricultural education is often scheduled in small schools in rural areas and may involve introductory classes in the seventh grade. The specialized vocational agriculture program is offered in the ninth through twelfth grades and may be extended beyond the high school in federally subsidized programs. A distributive education program finds the school actively involved in an apprenticeship-style program with the business world. In this program students spend part of the day in school, the rest at work in the community. While the school does not provide instruction in each new skill that evolves in the world of work, it may establish some new programs to meet business needs, as was the case with computer programming.

Home economics instruction is initiated by some elementary schools on a limited basis. Other schools provide introductory instruction in the seventh and eighth grades. Sometimes boys are assigned to homemaking classes or are permitted to elect them. Beginning in the ninth grade, the homemaking progression may continue through the twelfth grade. At various times emphasis may be on food preparation, clothing, home furnishing, family relations, or personal development.

Business education is usually provided on an elective basis beginning in the ninth grade. The advanced program is offered in most high schools as well as in vocational schools. Basically, business curricula are designed to teach skills in stenographic, clerical, typing, and business-management procedures. Students may gain practical experience in part-time clerical jobs under the supervision of the schools in the distributive education programs.

In a category of its own is driver education, frequently offered to all students and sometimes required of all. Most schools hire full-time instructors, who have completed a special program at a college or university. Instruction is provided first in the classroom, then in an automobile. There is probably no school program as highly recommended by noneducators (particularly law enforcement agencies and the American Automobile Association), as enthusiastically supported by parents, and as distant from the traditional objectives of organized education.

special services

Among other special services provided by many schools are classes for slow learners and the mentally retarded. Some states mandate establishment of instruction for the slow learner, supporting the program with subsidies and prescribing means and criteria for assignment to such classes. Larger communities provide special instruction for the physically handicapped and the deaf and blind. New York City has established special "600" schools for particularly difficult behavior problems and offers a program for the superior academic student at the Bronx High School of Science. Adult education classes are a common service rendered by school systems. In some states junior colleges have been under the aegis of school districts.

evaluation

The curriculum stands subject to evaluation, improvement, and change. The curriculum in the classroom is evaluated by the teacher using testing and observation techniques. Standardized achievement tests are administered in many schools. Comparisons may be made on an individual or class basis with the norms provided with the tests. The real test of the curriculum is in how well it fulfills the grand social objectives of the school. The terminal program, for example, should prepare the young generation to live in the changing world, to staff the business and industrial community, and to meet citizenship responsibilities. The college preparatory program should equip youth to meet the requirements of higher educational programs and provide the knowledge and skills to cope with the dynamic world and the requirements of citizenship.

It is a well-established and relatively simple procedure to evaluate achievement in learning of facts and the ability to use them. Teachers measure growth in absolute terms, as in physical development, or in relative terms, as in social relationships. Some skills, such as study habits, typing, or performance in athletic activities, lend themselves to ready evaluation, while the more abstract skills, such as making generalizations or applying academic knowledge, and the processes through which one solves new problems are less subject to measurement and analysis. It is particularly difficult to effectively evaluate the development and growth of attitudes toward oneself or others and attitudes toward knowledge or institutions. The opportunity to evaluate the outcomes of the educational experience on an individual or group basis is centered in learning of facts and the development of selected skills.

The evaluation of the larger outcomes of the curriculum is another matter. Rather subjective appraisals of high school graduates are made by manufacturers, office managers, or college professors who tend to mix their own perception of expectations with the degree to which a young adult has mastered shop procedures or typing or composition. There is a temptation to equate the general nature of society and its progress and deficiencies with the educational system while ignoring the role of other institutions and forces in molding and directing the society. The curriculum cannot be judged by the success or failure of broad social objectives and processes. It is particularly awkward to sort out partial responsibility, assign a portion of it to the curriculum, and effectively measure that part.

The evaluation of the curriculum must be based to a large degree on an inferential process in which the weight of an educational experience is balanced against the influence of other social institutions. The evaluator must often operate on little more than unsupported opinion (which, however, may be subject to investigation through social research methods) in determining what influence may be expected from the school. A more useful means of evaluating the curriculum is to engage in several procedures: assessing the pertinence of courses of study; experimenting with structural changes in the schools to determine the influence innovation may have on the learning process; accelerating the adoption of new teaching methods through teacher education programs as well as through improved educational leadership in the schools; and marshaling forces to upgrade the evaluation process so that more accurate assessments may be made of ability and achievement. The curriculum is also evaluated by seeking and applying radical departures in tradition and practice to meet the crisis situation of urban education and by actively promoting the movement from group teaching and evaluation processes to individual procedures in pursuing the belief that social objectives must be realized in terms of the individual.

conclusion

If the school is to be relevant and responsive to the changing society, the curriculum must be dynamic. A dynamic curriculum changes with the needs of society and adapts to advances in methods of teaching. It places new demands on school buildings, administrative leadership, and teaching personnel. The evolving curriculum and the changing needs of youngsters ought to dictate the structure of the school, the sequence of the educational experiences, the placement of subject matter, and the appropriate instructional techniques. Every teacher should be a curriculum specialist. The primary measures of the effectiveness of schools and individual teachers should center on the nature of the curriculum and the success with which curricular objectives are achieved.

The school curriculum is an essential study for every teacher in his own area of specialization and it is a superior challenge for those who seek to shepherd the schools into the future. There is abundant literature on the curriculum by specific subject areas as well as in general.

In professional periodical literature, reference should be made to *Educational Leadership,* the journal of the Association for Supervision and Curriculum Development, *Childhood Education, Elementary School Journal, Grade Teacher, The Instructor, Journal of Secondary Education,* and *High School Journal,* among others. The many publications that serve special interest areas include *Arithmetic Teacher, Mathematics Teacher, The Reading Teacher, Modern Language Journal, Elementary English, English Journal, Journal of Geography, Social Education, The Social Studies, Art Education, Music Educators Journal, Business Education, Journal of Health-Physical Education-Recreation, Journal of Home Economics, Industrial Arts Teacher, American Biology Teacher, The Science Teacher, Journal of Chemical Education, American Journal of Physics, Speech Teacher,* and *American Vocational Journal. Education Index* will provide additional references. Many general or special interest educational associations also publish research journals and subject-centered yearbooks.

The teacher-to-be should have experience in relating to the school as a totality, including the observation of grades above and below the special interest area. It is necessary for the elementary specialist to become acquainted with the needs and procedures of secondary education and for the secondary teacher to become acquainted with the evolving elementary school. There is a need for one first-grade teacher to communicate with another and for a corresponding horizontal familiarity across the secondary spectrum with a special emphasis on a dialogue across individual subjects.

The serious student of the curriculum may begin with B. Othanel Smith, William O. Stanley, and J. Harlan Shores, *Fundamentals of Curriculum Development,* rev. ed. (New York: Harcourt, Brace & World, 1957), the National Education Association report, *Deciding What to Teach* (Washington, D.C.: National Education Association, 1963), G. W. Ford and Lawrence Pugno (eds.), *The Structure of Knowledge and the Curriculum* (Chicago: Rand McNally, 1964), Arthur R. King, and John A. Brownell, *The Curriculum and the Disciplines of*

Knowledge, A Theory of Curriculum Practice (New York: Wiley, 1966), and Dwayne Huebner (ed.), *A Reassessment of the Curriculum* (New York: Teachers College, Columbia University, 1964). An introduction to the elementary school may be found in Robert S. Fleming (ed.), *Curriculum for Today's Boys and Girls* (Columbus, Ohio: Merrill, 1963), and to the secondary school in Harold B. Alberty and Elsie J. Alberty, *Reorganizing the High-School Curriculum,* 3rd ed. (New York: Macmillan, 1962). In addition, books discussing the curriculum and methods of instruction are published in every teaching field.

additional references

Alpren, Morton. *The Subject Curriculum: Grades K–12.* Columbus, Ohio: Merrill, 1967.

Bouwsma, Ward D., Clyde G. Corle, and Davis F. Clemson. *Basic Mathematics for Elementary Teachers.* New York: Ronald, 1967.

Chall, Jeanne S. *Learning to Read: The Great Debate.* New York: McGraw-Hill, 1967

Crosby, Muriel. *Curriculum Development for Elementary Schools in a Changing Society.* Boston: Heath, 1964.

Hocking, Elton. *Language Laboratory and Language Learning.* 2nd ed. Monograph #2. Washington, D.C.: Department of Audiovisual Instruction, National Education Association, 1967.

Inlow, Gail. *The Emergent in Curriculum.* New York: Wiley, 1966.

Jarvis, Oscar T., and Lutian R. Wootton. *The Transitional Elementary School and Its Curriculum.* Dubuque, Iowa: Brown, 1966.

Kieth, Lowell, Paul Blake, and Sidney Tiedt. *Contemporary Curriculum in the Elementary School.* New York: Harper & Row, 1968.

Michaelis, John U., Ruth H. Grossman, and Lloyd F. Scott. *New Designs for the Elementary School Curriculum.* New York: McGraw-Hill, 1967.

Nixon, John E., and Ann E. Jewett. *Physical Education Curriculum.* New York: Ronald, 1964.

Taba, Hilda. *Curriculum Development: Theory and Practice.* New York: Harcourt, Brace & World, 1962.

7

When the question is raised at the dinner table, "What did you learn in school today?" and the answers are "We had a test in American history;" "Our class saw a movie of Japan;" "Today we started another reading book;" "A new boy came into our class," it is evident that there is, indeed, confusion on the part of the masses as to what learning really is.

Learning is basically a psychological process through which an individual accommodates to and exerts controls upon his environment. At the infant stage, learning is highly egocentric and primarily concerned with physical development and adaptation. At the adult stage, learning is extended in breadth to social concerns and is largely intellectual. Only after a baby has succeeded in gaining a high degree of control over his physical world does the emerging individual concentrate on efforts to communicate, to develop mental skills, and to seek to meet others on an interpersonal basis.

The exact nature of the psychology of learning is often described in unverified hypotheses, but it is probably a physical-chemical-electrical process centered in the nervous system, regulated by emotional-glandular stimuli, and highly dependent on the senses for selection and gathering of data. Human thought processes have become more meaningful as the cybernetic revolution has developed sophisticated electronic computers that suggest how human mental activities may be programmed and executed.

In the classroom learning is an individual process that relates to individual experiences. Each experience is dependent for meaning upon an individual's pattern of previous learning, with each experience building a new pattern of reaction. The way an individual learns is limited by the speed and efficiency

the process of learning

of his reactions. Any group-teaching procedure is directed to as many learning situations as there are youngsters. Evaluation of class learning should recognize that the group is only the sum of its individual parts, that a class measure is a central index with most of the class above or below it. On the one hand, group learning may inhibit the progress of an individual by setting a pace that is too slow or too fast, or by constricting types of experiences. Exhibiting an object to thirty youngsters may limit opportunities to handle, smell, rap, lift, or drop. On the other hand, group processes may stimulate the individual by providing additional clues appropriate to a youngster's performance level and by generating peer approval.

Learning is commonly and correctly referred to as goal-directed activity. Learning goals of students are those of the individual and may be different from those of the teacher. The teacher's goals for the youngsters include the learning of facts; the development of reading, study, generalizing, application, and problem-solving skills; and the growth of attitudes toward oneself, school, peers, society, and the world. While the teacher's goals may be admirable, idealistic, and farsighted, a youngster's goals are practical and directed to the here and now: answering gnawing questions, permitting or facilitating some planned accomplishment, fostering parental and teacher approval or, at the least, warding off disapproval, gaining peer acceptance, winning the special attention of a particular classmate, fulfilling a requirement for membership in some status group, or gaining permission for an unrelated activity. Learning is a serious proposition for the teacher. To many youngsters it is a game to be taken as seriously as any other game and to be dropped as lightly for the next interesting activity that may come along.

Teachers sometimes remind youngsters that learning is "hard work" and emphasize the virtues of ambition and persistence, both accepted middle-class values. Whatever parallels a teacher might perceive between school and the adult world of work should be balanced by the inconsistencies. Adult employment is voluntary and individually and personally selected and solicited. The adult derives financial rewards from his employment and uses this money to maintain himself and his family and, hopefully, to purchase some nonessential materials or services. If "hard work" is equated with "unpleasant" tasks, it has little relevance to youngsters' goals. Teachers should emphasize the goals and rewards of learning rather than the demands of the process. One would seldom find an employer who places a greater emphasis on the unpleasant aspects of a job than on the rewards that may be realized in his employment.

The particular goal toward which a youngster strives affects the strength of the learning effort. Learning that is directed toward the learner's goals, either as a means to solve a further problem or as an end in itself, is learning most seriously pursued, most easily mastered, and most lasting. Teacher goals that coincide with student aims create opportunities for learning, encourage students along their own lines of least resistance, and provide a self-promoting momentum. Teacher aims may tend to accentuate less desirable and durable student objectives, such as the avoidance of unpleasant consequences. Most skillful teaching and most successful learning concentrate on goals that are appropriate to the individual's capacity to meet them and are suitable to the evolving subject matter.

ability to learn

The confusion generated in the past few years about the nature of intelligence, the stability of the IQ score, and the influence of cultural bias on school performance has not only undermined the intelligence quotient, which is appropriate, but has created undue consternation about the concept of ability in general. Just as there are differences in physical structure, in manual dexterity, in bodily control, and in rhythmic sophistication, there are differences in the ability to do mental tasks, in the capacity to learn. While the poorly coordinated person may increase his agility, he will not develop abnormally high manipulative skills. Similarly the mentally ill-coordinated individual may increase his mental efficiency, but he cannot become an intellectual giant. The limitations of ability measures, particularly in precisely assessing the same basic abilities within differing cultural situations, do not deny the fact that some have lesser ability or the likelihood that there is a built-in limit to any ability. An unknown factor in discussion of ability is the degree to which maximum ability is measured or even measurable. This involves individuals making judgments about concepts that may be outside their own experience and beyond their limits of comprehension. There are some suggestions that ability (or its expression) may be elevated by external influences, for example, drugs. However, even if outside factors may extend ability or increase learning efficiency, a basic potential that is measured in perfection of cellular development, speed of chemical-electrical action, and extended practice has its limits.

Regardless of how ability is perceived, how well it is measured, or the degree of efficiency in classroom processes that is attained, experience in any group-learning situation demonstrates differences among individuals in speed and effectiveness of learning and in types of ability to learn. Some individuals can best understand a concept deductively, that is, by moving from the broad learning experience to its component parts. Others learn best inductively, or by building upon specific experiences toward a general understanding. Listening skills are particularly important to some youngsters, whereas others rely on reading, and still others on seeing and handling. The thrill of discovering something new activates some learners, while others have difficulty in sorting out relevant aspects. The latter profit from the guidance of a sympathetic and skillful teacher.

To further complicate the situation, everyone does not learn every subject or even every topic with equal facility. A class of youngsters must be offered an assortment of experiences to provide for varying kinds of skills and levels of ability. An individual benefits from a variety of experiences in one type of learning situation and from numerous kinds of experiences in his several learning situations. Ability potential differs in kind and strength with the individual; the exercise or utilization of ability strengthens and realizes some potential and, in the process, fails to exploit other potentials.

Ability, like any other basic endowment, is unevenly distributed within each individual and among individuals. Some youngsters have broad ability patterns: physical, social, and intellectual. Others excel in some areas and are limited in the rest. Still others operate at a general minimal level, with limited capabilities in most areas. One only needs to recall an Albert Schweitzer to recognize the rare genius who is able to master divergent abilities as expressed in musical artistry, philosophy, and humanitarian medical missionary work.

The question posed to the schools by cultural bias is whether the availability of opportunities to engage in appropriate educational experiences outside the school is a crucial factor in learning in school. Bias reflects differences in attitudes in the home toward youngsters, in the attitudes that youngsters develop, and in the ability or willingness of a family to provide broad and varied life experiences for children. Slum youngsters may have failed to develop verbal skills because of limited speaking experiences in the home. Some youngsters grow up without substantial conversational experiences and are not accustomed to handling reading materials or having someone read to them. If youngsters are limited to the immediate environment, they may lack opportunities to see new things and to broaden a perception that the world does in reality extend beyond a known four walls. The federally sponsored Head Start program attempted to provide experiences for slum youngsters that would equalize their experiential backgrounds with other children and thus enable them to adapt more readily to the school experience.

The school is a place for the housing of many opportunities for learning, with each lesson a separate educational experience. The opportunity to learn within a single lesson is applied unevenly within a class. Youngsters with high ability may learn quickly. Those with limited ability may not accomplish the learning before the lesson is over and the opportunity is ended. But ability to learn is not the only factor that determines whether an individual may take advantage of a classroom opportunity, for there also are psychological or emotional problems that may interfere with learning. Interpersonal problems between youngsters or a personality conflict between a pupil and a teacher may reduce the opportunity for learning. Physical limitations and sight or hearing problems may limit an individual's operating effectiveness. The school as an environment may facilitate or inhibit realization of learning opportunities with adequate or insufficient light, heat, or ventilation within a stimulating or drab and uninspiring physical surrounding.

One learns through experience, direct or vicarious. Memorization is as true a form of experience as dissecting a frog. Reading, watching a movie, and observing a scientific experiment all provide vicarious experiences. To assign reading in the text, to set a group at work on written assignments, or to show a film or conduct an experiment does not guarantee that every pupil is actually experiencing the activity, let alone that those who share an experience are sharing it in a similar fashion. It is easy to hold an open book without reading it, to daydream during a movie, or to fail to recognize the pertinent aspects of a demonstration. Experience is a personal, not a group, phenomenon.

attitudes and learning

One learns through experience, and learning is itself an experience. Learning is satisfying or frustrating, depending upon the success of the learning. The youngster brings into the classroom an attitude toward school and learning derived from previous experience. The eagerness with which the average youngster first enters school reflects upon his earlier experiences with learning that were mainly unstructured, informal, and highly satisfying. Contrast this eagerness with his attitude ten years later, when he may have found learning to be difficult, frustrating, and unpleasant.

Effective learning is an egocentric, highly personal experience. Selfish, self-serving learning is not only appropriate to some disciplines but may be essential to excellence. The true scholar finds in his studies extraordinary satisfaction and a fascination that leads him to his desk or laboratory when others choose to relax. From his exertions come the little rewards of new knowledge, new insights, and new associations that propel him on.

For many others the egocentric drive becomes involved with the approval of others and is not centered in self-satisfaction. Interpersonal skills, democratic attitudes, and group processes such as committee work require the socialization of youngsters. There are pupils who need to be directed into increased individual activities and there are others who need to be guided into group processes. Both types of activities are necessary for required learning to take place.

By the time a youngster begins school he has already passed through his most intensive learning period. He has developed from a helpless infant to a highly animated child who has acquired a high level of language facility and a complex array of customs, traditions, behaviors, and beliefs. Crucial to success in school is whether a child has learned skills of interacting with other children and has developed positive or negative attitudes toward adults. Preschool children have been exposed to attitudes toward adults. They have been exposed to adult and peer attitudes toward social institutions including the schools, and they have developed attitudes toward themselves. The youngster enters the school with a strong or weak experiential background and with positive or negative attitudes. The school cannot go backward in time with a youngster to rebuild experiences and attitudes, but it must accept each individual as he is and move with him, hoping to build on (and thus retain and encourage) strengths while seeking to eliminate or compensate for areas of weakness.

The youngster brings techniques of learning to the school. As an infant he learned to handle, feel, bite, drop, throw, pile this on that, or place one object inside another. Through manipulation he found relationships, characteristics, potentials, and limitations. He learned that one may try and lay aside, try from another angle and once more quit, and then return again to eventually solve a problem. Experience has provided him with opportunities to learn that one may solve a problem on one's own or take a problem to someone else who will solve the problem or show how it may be done. He has found that adults may direct learning and be quite insistent and forceful in what, when, and how a youngster shall learn. He has probably experienced situations in which something to be learned has been stubbornly elusive and then has suddenly become obvious. This is related to what educators call the discovery method of learning.

The typical age for entrance into the first grade is six years, although there is not universal agreement that this is the appropriate age. Some tend to agree with many European educators that the appropriate age is seven, while others propose that five is more suitable. The important question, however, is whether a youngster is "ready" for school. Readiness is generally related to the expectation that a youngster has learned basic personal habits, has adequate command of the language, and can associate with other youngsters. The general assumption for learning readiness is that the individual has the physical and mental capabilities to do the task, has had the appropriate experiences and necessary prior learnings, possesses the proper attitudes toward himself and others, and is not emotionally or psychologically crippled; in other words, that he can handle the job. Reading readiness refers to a threshold position from which reading skills can be acquired, and it is in these terms that readiness is generally described. Unhappily for many youngsters, parents, and teachers, age alone is a poor criterion for developmental or learning readiness.

Parents who have compared the development of their own and other youngsters can provide worthwhile suggestions about differences in the readiness of children to sit, crawl, walk, talk, feed oneself, or become toilet trained. Unhurried and observable physical development is a factor in readiness for change and so is the unseen, psychological-physiological-emotional growth, which is as essential to learning. Ages, and therefore grade levels, are at best only averages. They are approximations for readiness for school as a grand experience or for specialized school tasks as pertinent experiences. Providing readiness experiences for children cannot accelerate preparation for a task but may facilitate it; these experiences can bring a youngster to the threshold. It would probably be a useful suggestion for one to "think physical" when considering the readiness of children for school learning experieces. Just as every youngster is not equally ready to bat a ball or high jump or swim under water, every pupil is not ready with the same ease to multiply by five or understand the dry cell battery on the day and at the hour called for by a lesson plan.

A child must want to learn; he must be motivated for learning to take place. Unfortunately, motivation has acquired some strange meanings. Some seem to believe that motivation is an electric switch that can be turned on when a teacher displays a picture or model or shows a movie or filmstrip. Motivation is not something imposed from without, but an internal force leading to action by the individual. This internal force may be aroused by the incentives of a teacher, such as an opportunity for recognition, or it may be activated by a personal interest in the subject. Internally aroused motivation may be generated by basic drives (such as fear or hunger) or needs (for recognition or success) or goals (the honor roll or admission to college). Among the most common external incentives are rewards and punishments. Rewards are positive and lead toward an objective. Punishments are negative and result in an avoidance reaction that may have little to offer in the way of constructive elements.

As the architect of a learning situation, a teacher plays an important role in the motivation of his students. He may engage them in exciting learning experiences that draw upon their personal needs and arouse their interest. He may attract them to a classroom with the feeling that learnings are functional, that they are pertinent to this day or the future. He may motivate through fear, the use of sarcasm, or the threat of failure. A teacher motivates through the atmosphere he creates in a classroom or by utilizing and emphasizing the dynamism of a living subject matter. He may motivate in an opposite direction by confronting the youngsters with the stultifying blanket of uninteresting and aimless teaching. The most important motivational factor in the classroom is the teacher, but he is never in full control, for motivation is involved with the entire situation into which young people are placed in school.

Each youngster in the classroom is in a unique motivational situation, which is in part physical, for each child is seated in a different immediate physical context. A youngster's motivational environment consists of his immediate neighbors, other members of the class, the teacher, the room decor, the weather outside, and the ventilation and light within. He is affected by a particular audio-visual device or the attitudes he brings into the class about the subject, school, peers, teachers, and himself. At any instance the individual may be the object of several motivational pressures and his action may reflect the influence of a dominant force or the compromise of several divergent factors.

Attitudes are predispositions for action and are crucial to learning. A youngster's attitude toward school affects his behavior in school; his attitude toward a subject influences his action in that classroom; his attitude toward a teacher arouses friendly or unfriendly action or neutral inaction. Perhaps the most important attitude is the student's attitude toward himself, toward his personal worth, toward his past, present, and future. A second most important attitude is interest, an attitude directed toward schoolwork in general and school subjects in particular. Interest in schoolwork is learned like any other attitude. It is shaped by experience, strengthened by success, and weakened by frustration or failure.

Attitude toward school is first shaped in the home and neighborhood before entrance into school. The child whose parents were eighth-grade dropouts, who knows of the fears, failures, and frustrations of brothers or sisters, and who views agents of society as natural enemies is not favorably oriented toward school. Unfortunately the school will probably not prove him wrong, for the concept of readiness suggests that a youngster who is not psychologically prepared for school will not find success in the classroom and will not profit from instruction. If the youngster who is most reluctant to attend school finds classroom success elusive and difficult, his reluctance will grow and rejection of school will increase. An unhappy youngster will communicate the rejection he experiences in school in his interaction with younger siblings and acquaintances. It is not that the school experience must be a failure for any particular youngster, but it will be that for some unless special concern is shown for each child and extraordinary procedures are devised to meet the particular needs and counteract the greater fears and insecurities of some pupils.

A significant aspect of interest development is that there is an undefined point where interest becomes self-generating. The student who has developed a strong interest in a subject and has become highly skilled and knowledgeable in it finds success and satisfaction, which further strengthen interest, increase motivation, and lead to pursuit of further success and satisfaction. The skilled athlete spends much time and energy perfecting skills that are already highly efficient tools; the budding artist is continually doodling and drawing; the future concert pianist spends hours in self-disciplined practice.

The fun that was preschool learning becomes work in school. Whether work is a satisfying or frustrating experience for a youngster depends on several factors: rewards attained through the activity itself, favorable or unfavorable reaction of others, tangible benefits from the work, and opportunities to progress through one's efforts. There are those who seem to feel that learning as work cannot be enjoyable, but a glance at youngsters hard at play suggests otherwise. The junior football player drags home exhausted and bruised. The treasure hunter digs energetically. The tree-house builder scrounges for lumber and lifts it into a tree. Success does not have to be divorced from work, and satisfaction may be related to substantial rewards stemming from substantial efforts.

Even as they are learned, attitudes may be changed. Positive attitudes may become negative and negative attitudes may become positive. However, it is not easy to alter an attitude, for change involves extinguishing one learning and establishing a new learning, or attitude, in its place. A favorable attitude should be learned at the beginning rather than changed from an unfavorable one later. The school-accepting, school-eager youngster has gained his acceptance of school and eagerness to learn at an early age. The much discussed "late bloomer" is a rare individual. He is scarcer than the school dropout or the functional dropout, who may cease to learn effectively as early as the fourth grade. Concern of the school and energy of teachers are directed more logically toward building and sustaining favorable attitudes and school success than toward attempting to reverse negative attitudes and to recoup lost learning experiences so that each youngster may experience success in school. Teachers should emphasize the equal and crucial importance of every grade and every classroom in the life of individual pupils and the necessity for every learning environment to provide wholesome and satisfying experiences for every young person.

speed of learning

An individual learns at differing rates according to the nature of the task to be learned. In a class of youngsters there is a wide variety of speeds of learning. These are as varied as the number of youngsters, although those in the middle of the group tend to cluster at similar speeds. Instruction is commonly paced to the "average" of the class, so that those who learn at a faster pace are artificially slowed in their learning and those who learn at a slow rate are exposed to a pace that is beyond their capacity to learn. Two major reasons for the tendency to repeat elementary learning experiences in the curriculum grade after grade are the failure of slow learners to achieve and the weak and unreliable learning of average students. It is difficult to ascertain whether the speed of instruction selected by a teacher is appropriate for that group.

One factor responsible for speed of learning is intelligence, or the basic capacity to learn; yet the supposition that mental capacity is the sole reason for learning effectiveness is an oversimplification. Another factor to be considered in the speed of learning is the physical condition, particularly those physical disabilities that may retard the learning rate. Some physical problems that affect learning speed are visual and hearing deficiencies. Ill-health, poor diet, emotional and psychological difficulties, fatigue, weaknesses in basic learning skills, and lack of interest may all be reflected in slow learning rates.

Significant differences between an individual's rate of learning and the pace of teaching lead to various kinds of behavior on the part of the learner. The student who could learn at a faster pace may become lazy and careless in his work, or he may develop an inflated and unrealistic opinion of his ability. If he loses enthusiasm in a subject and toward school, he may become a disciplinary problem. The student who operates at a slower pace than that set for the class will not be able to learn effectively. He will become frustrated with his lack of accomplishment and the awareness that his progress is prematurely terminated as the class moves on to a new phase of instruction. As he falls behind the learning pace, he may become discouraged and lose interest in the subject and school. He may withdraw from reality and find success in fantasy or he may seek recognition through aggressive action against peers, teachers, and the school. Youngsters who are functioning at or near the instructional pace react more favorably toward school, find substantial success in the classroom, provide a stable element in the group, and are considered by teachers to be hard-working, dependable, and well-adjusted to school. The school has, in fact, become well-adjusted to them.

The reality of the classroom, with its challenge of thirty youngsters and limited materials, limited assistance, and limited energy, time, and resources, suggests that for most teachers in most schools there are few pertinent alternatives to class instruction at a rate appropriate to the group, that is, to the typical youngster in the class. Most teachers, in any case, have difficulty in adjusting to the rapid rate of learning of some youngsters. They may seek to control the bright youngster by requiring him to do more of the same assignments, repeat certain experiences, or participate in "enrichment" activities, which may include studies in depth of the subject. Sometimes a bright youngster is used as a teaching assistant to help slower classmates or to take care of routine clerical tasks, and he may be expected to wait quietly and patiently for the others to catch up. The slow learner is least understood by those teachers who insist that lack of success is largely a matter of laziness and disinterest and that hard work and effort are the means for meeting all learning problems. This is a reflection of a safe middle-class value for middle-class teachers; it may not apply to upper- or lower-class youngsters or to many middle-class children.

reinforcement in learning

Skill or lack of skill in learning results in rewards or punishments for youngsters. High marks on report cards are considered to be rewards for quality work; low marks are punishments for slovenliness and inefficiency. High marks may be the source of additional reward by publication of an honor roll. Successful scholars may be excused from certain tasks and gain recognition from adults (if not from peers). Slow learning may result in a teacher requiring a youngster to report for help after school. A youngster may perceive this as punishment, as being retained after school for serious and persistent failure in the day's lesson. There are various types and degrees of reinforcement of learning behaviors, some internal and some external, some pleasant and some unpleasant, some fruitful and some hopelessly ineffective.

The first major form of learning reinforcement that is acquired by an individual is internal, the satisfaction of basic needs and drives. Through the school years internalized reinforcement is most useful for learning; it is constructive and motivating. Highly motivated learning builds upon a background of previous success with accompanying satisfactions and rewards; thus a strongly motivated youngster finds rewards for his efforts within the task. His satisfactions may be centered in small increments of learning at a high level of sophistication. He thrives on the excitement of discovering significant facts, new relationships, subtle meanings, and exciting new ideas.

The effectiveness of reinforcement on learning depends on the nature of the learning activity and the speed with which reinforcement is applied to learning. Vague rewards and distant goals, such as placement on an honor roll or admission to college, may be appropriate to broad learning experiences; for instance, a year's study of a subject. The more specific the learning experience is, the more closely related the reinforcement should be and the greater the necessity that reinforcement should be speedily applied. Learning the solution to a specific problem requires an immediate and closely related reinforcement. The product of two numbers, for example, needs to be immediately identified as correct for adequate reinforcement of that learning.

Reinforcement of learning is nowhere more highly regarded than in theories of programmed instruction. In addition to the need for immediate reinforcement, programmed instruction proposes the necessity for a carefully structured sequence of learning experiences: Efficient learning is said to require both early rewards for learning and an easily followed and understood program of instruction. Those who advocate the use of programmed instruction argue that the ordinary teacher cannot provide highly structured learning experiences for every individual, nor can the teacher supply the immediate reinforcements that are necessary to each of a class of thirty youngsters. Instructional programs are therefore presented in holders called teaching machines or in textbooks. Learning through use of a teaching machine or a programmed text, then, is an individual experience conducted through a series of short, logical steps, with the correct answer immediately available to the student as soon as he makes his response.

Some early proponents of programmed instruction reacted like many other educational innovators when they engaged in extravagant claims for programming. They failed to place sufficient emphasis on the necessity for highly skilled programming and to recognize the limited areas of learning appropriate to this type of instruction. Adverse reaction to the oversell and publication of hastily produced and unsatisfactory programs has retarded the acceptance of programmed instruction, but the basic theory is well conceived and supported by careful research. Programmed instruction may be expected to find a proper niche in the schools as it has already found a limited but important place in military and industrial training programs.

Applying some of the theories of programming to the entire curriculum, one may picture the school years involved with instruction in systematically structured subject matters presented to youngsters through individual techniques that provide for immediate learning success. Some parts of the curriculum do not fit into the programmed category, particularly group activities such as physical education, musical ensembles, drama, and journalism. In addition, subject matters that are essentially nonstructured or less structured, including literature, philosophy, and history, are poor programming risks. However, highly sequential school activities, such as mathematics, language construction and usage, and typewriting or shorthand, are ideally suited to program techniques. To gain full benefit from the use of programming in the learning process, schools must alter teaching and learning techniques so that some instruction is individualized and programmed, some is arranged to meet the needs of pupils in groups, and the rest involves incidental or enrichment learning experiences that may be organized either for individual or group instruction.

learning goals

Learning is a goal-directed activity. The content of learning objectives determines what the curriculum shall entail. The way in which objectives are expressed specifies the particular individual needs that will be met. The goals that are stated suggest the appropriate teaching techniques.

Learning takes place in differing situations and with a variety of teaching and learning techniques. Basically, learning is directed toward the mastery of facts, skills, and attitudes.

FACTS Facts may be loosely defined to mean specific knowledge, ideas, and opinions as well as tested, accepted, and verifiable facts. An opinion exists independently as a fact whether it is a true or false opinion. In some instances opinions have had a greater impact than verifiable fact, as evidenced by the tragic events evolving from the beliefs espoused by the Nazis or the significant events in American history that have been rooted in racial myths.

The most significant area of factual learning is in the vocabulary. It is easy for a teacher to overlook the importance and the extent of a vocabulary in learning, but without a common basis of language—the learner's major intellectual tool—functioning in school tasks is impossible. As an example, the basic vocabulary that is needed to understand the game of basketball, to be able to watch as well as play the game, includes: this is a basketball, that is the basket, the object is to toss the ball through the basket for one or two points; this line is an outer boundary, this one a three-second limit, this one to cross in ten seconds, and so on. The same command of vocabulary facts is essential to any learning situation.

While vocabulary forms the basic facts, there are many more facts that must be learned. Names may be both vocabulary and facts—for instance, Washington—and so are many special word arrangements—New York Yankees or *The Old Man and the Sea.* Ideas, opinions, generalizations, concepts, formulas, and poetry (that which is considered subject content) may be classified as facts and may be learned, retained, memorized, and forgotten. Memorization is frequently decried as an anachronistic exercise but many facts must be memorized, as, for example, shapes of letters and numbers, the meaning of symbols like plus or minus signs, shape and position of notes in music, combinations that are chemical symbols, and many others.

SKILLS An individual also needs to learn many skills, including the basic academic processes, such as reading, mathematical manipulation, induction, deduction, generalization, and synthesis. Among the essential practical skills to be learned are library usage, communication, social interaction, physical tasks, manipulative activities, and personal hygiene. Instruction in the development of skills depends upon the efficient learning of a basic and necessary factual foundation.

It is difficult to separate the learning of facts from the learning of skills, for the learning of skills depends on knowledge of facts and the learning of facts depends on sensory, academic, and other operating skills. Measurement of the degree to which facts are learned is a relatively practical matter, but the assessment of the learning of skills varies from ready evaluation of some study skills to the impossibility of measuring many subtle mental skills. The learning of facts as an end in itself is not a functional process, but those facts that give relevance to, find application in, and result in an increased level of performance skills are highly functional. An encyclopedic memory is scarcely of value as contrasted to a well-stocked library or a computer, but no substitute has been found for the use of human skills in the application of knowledge.

Problem-solving skills are particularly emphasized in the schoolroom. The problem-solving process is commonly outlined as setting goals, appraising the situation, setting hypotheses, testing hypotheses, discarding inappropriate answers, and pursuing fruitful answers to the solution of the problem. The procedures are similar to those ascribed to the scientific method. Problem-solving skills are acquired through instruction in systematic procedures and through practice in the solution of progressively more complex problems. The role of the teacher is to demonstrate problem-solving methods, to structure experiences in the process, and to supervise and guide youngsters in the learning procedures.

Critical thinking is a less-definable concept that is at times separated from problem-solving and at other times identified with it. There is uncertainty about the true nature of critical thinking, and the question whether it is basically a skill or an attitude remains. Fundamental to the concept of critical thinking is an expectation that the individual will seek his own answers to questions and his own solutions to problems. Even though the process of critical thinking involves use of the skills of problem-solving, the emphasis is placed on attitudes. Thus, the exponent of critical thinking rejects indoctrination and acceptance learning, but he does so in the face of a practical situation where it is essential to learn a large body of facts in order to understand relationships, skills, and attitudes. The nature of the learning process necessitates the acceptance of basic learnings and an ability to apply systematic techniques for more complex learnings. In the social context of education, freedom from indoctrination is worthy as a goal, but it is aloof from the world of reality.

ATTITUDES If facts are essential as tools and skills are indispensable for functional learning, attitudes effect the one and facilitate the other. Attitudes toward self, school, and subjects are instrumental in the learning of facts and skills and in learning other attitudes; the most crucial outcome of learning is attitudinal.

One of the classroom's most important attitudes is interest in a subject, and the teacher is largely responsible for building it. He exerts considerable control in interest development through his own attitudes, the teaching procedures he uses, the types of experiences that he provides for the youngsters, and the extent to which the pupils realize success in his classroom. The best opportunity to affect attitude formation in school is through those activities for which the school provides the first or major influence. Classroom influence in other attitudes may be limited but should not be ignored.

A youngster brings attitudes toward himself to school, yet the classroom provides particularly rich opportunities for individuals to find experiences in constructive self-evaluation. An important role of the teacher is to demonstrate his own regard for every individual and, by example, to encourage mutual respect among the youngsters.

CREATIVITY A particularly interesting concern for learning has been centered on creativity, that is, the development of ability to produce something unique, different, or original. There is confusion as to whether creative activities should be conducted on an individual or a group basis. If creativity is defined as whatever unique or unusual or spontaneous production any individual may engage in, creativity may be group-oriented. But if it is seen as a special talent reserved for unusual individuals who respond to a particular set of circumstances, it is inconceivable that a teacher would seriously assign a creative task to an entire class. The relevancy of artistic or creative classroom activities depends on whether creative learning is to encourage free expression for all or is aimed at identification and cultivation of individuals with unusual talent.

There is probably no aspect of learning more important than creativity, regardless of the particular definition used. It is a matter of social concern that truly creative individuals be identified early and given abundant opportunities to exploit their talent. At the same time, the rest of the school population should be given free expressive opportunities so that the process of identifying special talent may continue, the lesser talented are encouraged to develop appreciation of art forms, and everyone is permitted to engage in pleasurable recreational activities. Appreciative and recreational learnings may be provided through scheduled group activities, while provisions for the individual are directed toward informal situations that provide individualized stimulation, recognition, instruction, and opportunities for free expression.

Identification of creative individuals has been left largely to parents or individual teachers. Instruction for talented youngsters is provided through special classes in many communities or in specialized schools in larger cities. In recent years, however, increased concern for creativity has led to expanded efforts to provide creative experiences for youngsters. Creative evaluating techniques, such as the Minnesota Tests of Creative Thinking, have also been developed.

TRANSFER OF LEARNING A question that continues to bother learning theorists concerns the transfer of knowledge, skills, or attitudes from the limited framework in which learning takes place to other life situations. Early psychologists assumed that the mind was divided into faculties, which were strengthened through academic activities. Included among these faculties were continuity, destructiveness, benevolence, mirthfulness, calculation, and agreeableness. Schoolwork was believed to exercise the faculties and increase their strength and effectiveness. Although this psychology has long been discarded, many still believe that the study of mathematics trains the mind in orderly processes and that the study of history leads to acceptance of the duties of responsible citizenship. There is implied in the educational process a transfer of learning from the restricted context of the classroom to the world beyond.

School activities that are duplicated in other situations have large transfer realities. A person should be able to use the mathematical formula for determining area as he places an order for carpeting for his living room, but in order to make this transfer of information it is necessary to understand the principle involved and not just the mechanics of calculation. If a person is to make use of schoolwork beyond the classroom, he must act on highly efficient learning and must recognize similar elements between the learning and practical situations. One may be aware of instances where there is a lack of transfer, as when democratic attitudes that are taught in the classroom are displaced and youngsters engage in vandalism outside of school or even within the classroom.

Transfer of learning differs among individuals although the limits of transfer are not set just by the characteristics of an individual. The nature of the curriculum and methods of instruction may facilitate or hinder transfer potential. If appropriate changes were made in the social studies content, instructional methods, and sequence, for instance, the school might then realize stated objectives of teaching citizenship skills and attitudes that could transfer into adult life. More effective learning in the social studies would be achieved if youngsters were actually first taught about their own environment with the neighborhood as a learning laboratory. Basic established social and developmental principles should be extended to a gradually expanding world: the rural area or village or section of a city, the county or metropolis, a region of a state, the state, the section of the nation, the nation, a subcontinent or continent, and the world. A thorough building of concepts and understandings would lead to the elimination of the hopeless repetition of superficial experiences that smothers interest and never fully answers a youngster's questions.

Similarly it should be possible to instruct effectively in correct language usage and appreciation of literature in English classes that would then be evidenced in speech patterns and reading habits outside the school. Instruction in the language arts must move from the artificial and repelling drill of grammar and spelling to the acquisition through use of language facts and skills. Of particular importance is the acceptance of the youngster's own subcultural language as a prior condition to the building of a second language, that of the dominant culture. Use outside of school of the language acquired in the classroom will depend on how well the new language has been learned and whether there are opportunities to apply it in nonschool situations. Unrealistic or inappropriate learning objectives—such as improving the use of the vernacular through the study of foreign languages or solving nonscientific problems through laboratory science instruction or study in mathematics —ought to be discarded for reasonable and attainable goals.

success and learning

When a youngster's performance in the learning process is judged by marks on report cards, learning effectiveness is related to individual success or failure. Success has been noted previously as an important factor in motivating the individual and in establishing interest patterns. Failure, on the other hand, is frequently defended as a part of life, as an essential to survival in a competitive society, and as a necessary learning experience for every individual. Some suggest that failure in school is necessary so that an individual may adjust to the uncertainties of reality and as a challenge to be overcome (in the tradition of Horatio Alger). Sometimes the suggestion is made that it is the school that fails rather than the individual, but whether this is a defensible criticism or merely a sentimental cliché depends on the nature of failure in learning. Those who accept the role of reinforcement in learning may point out that failure is not reinforcing and is therefore not useful in promoting the learning process.

Learning in its most analytical form is demonstrated by the small youngster who is busily looking, listening, feeling, applying, and reapplying. The young learner does not experience a series of easy successes. The pile of blocks seldom stands long; the larger peg just does not go into the smaller hole. Yet these failures are not regarded seriously. Attention is easily turned to something else. The playpen and the classroom have differences that are more important than the similarities. A major difference is the role of an adult in continually structuring the situation in the classroom but exerting little influence on momentary events in the playpen. The classroom does not permit the individual to select when and how to try things, when to lay something aside, and when to return to the task. Serious failure and frustration may be avoided in the playpen by turning aside to something else. In the classroom, on the other hand, the teacher may insist on continued effort beyond the point at which a youngster would naturally seek to relieve the pressure. Frustration may thus be intensified into failure.

A major difference between the classroom and other learning situations is the traditional evaluation of an individual in school against the group. Failure in the classroom is not related to the success an individual experiences in various tasks but to his achievement in terms of the rest of the class. A bright student may be operating at a low level of performance, thus realizing little real personal success because the challenge is below his performance level. His effort may be limited and his feeling of satisfaction slight. Easy success in the classroom, then, may lead to shoddy work, carelessness, and lack of interest in school or in a subject. On the other hand, the slow learner is doomed to failure in the group regardless of his performance, for his slower rate of learning results in lesser achievement and the impossibility of competing successfully with the class. In contrast to the fast learner who may be the classroom champion with slight effort, the slow learner may be the class failure even when performing at a high level. Failure that is unrelated to effort but geared to an impossible standard is debilitating. It results in insoluble frustration and in eventual lack of interest and patent dislike of school. Failure leads the slow learner to become a functional nonlearner and frequently a behavioral problem, too.

When teaching is directed toward the class average, the resulting lack of learning for some youngsters may deny them the facts and skills necessary to function at a more advanced level. The problem most fatal to learning is the failure to progress in reading achievement so that reading materials gradually move beyond an individual's competence. Even subject matters that do not become progressively more complex cause failure as attitudes turn negative, the subject matter loses its meaningful challenge, and the classroom imprisons the spirit as well as the mind.

The test of success or failure to learn should be the same for a youngster after he has entered school as it was when he engaged in preschool informal learning. The standard that determined his success in initial learning experiences was how well and when he walked, talked, or became toilet trained, not how his activities compared with those of other youngsters as a group. Moreover, when such comparisons are made, the contrasts are drawn against the typical pattern of development of youngsters of the same age, not in a comparison with youngsters who vary in age among themselves by at least twelve months, as is the case in the classroom. Whether a youngster succeeds in school ought to depend on his achievement in relation to his own potential and not in comparison with the achievement of other youngsters.

The argument that life in the world requires competition, success, and failure is neither useful nor valid in the classroom. Adults do not compete with all other adults even in the same neighborhood, which is the nearest parallel to the classroom. The schoolteacher is seldom in competition with the village banker in either the occupational arena or the social swim. They may compete at the bowling alley or for the leadership of a local veterans' association, but these competitive situations are highly voluntary. Individuals seldom seek out competition unless the odds seem favorable or the penalty of failure is not great. Tradition has even structured some failure as a form of success: To run for mayor of a community is a measure of prestige whether or not one is elected.

Competition and chances for success or failure are suitable in the classroom when an individual senses an opportunity to engage in meaningful activity. A pupil may compete with others of equal ability and achievement, but he may more logically compete with himself—with his own record of accomplishment. Competition must not pose an impossible challenge. Failure in the classroom is acceptable, therefore, only if it is to result in effective learning. Failure that is challenging and a spur to action is a positive contribution to the educational process.

An important consequence of an individual's success or failure is the impact that it has on his self-perception. If success is undeserved or if failure comes despite heroic efforts, the individual sees himself as having failed to achieve a satisfactory level of performance. The most important evaluation taking place in the classroom is the self-evaluation made by a youngster. Despite the teacher's evaluation of the pupil, expressed by the encouragement, "You can do it if you try," the child is making his own evaluation that says, "I have tried and find I cannot," or, "Your judgment of what I do is incorrect and unfair." The pupil needs to engage in honest self-evaluation, through which he may correctly assess his standing and his possibility of achieving the expectations thrust upon him. Placing a youngster in competition with the class does not tell him in absolute terms what he is, what he could be, or what he should be doing. An interesting study about the way children react is *Pygmalion in the Classroom*,[1] a report on research that investigated pupil achievement in the classroom as it relates to a teacher's expectations of youngsters' abilities to learn.

In some respects the individual knows more about certain aspects of his achievement in school than anyone else does. He knows how much effort he has put into a learning task and whether it has been a meaningful endeavor for him. He knows how well he understood a problem, how easily or progressively he proceeded toward its solution, and whether his classwork was the result of his own efforts. He knows better than others his relations with peers, his sense of belonging, and his feelings of adequacy or inadequacy in the group. The pupil depends upon others, however, for the additional data necessary to make realistic judgments about himself and his schoolwork. He receives information from parents, teachers, and peers about their conception of him and his activities. The teacher provides

[1] Robert Rosenthal and Lenore Jacobson, *Pygmalion in the Classroom* (New York: Holt, Rinehart and Winston, 1968).

information about the correctness of solutions to problems, the quality of work, and the acceptability of his classroom behavior. Teachers propose learning techniques that may be used and suggest a variety of ways of attacking a problem. When the youngster is to be evaluated against the group, he must depend primarily on others for most of his information. The pupil's own perception of his status within the group may be highly unreliable if he improperly selects out of the group those persons to be used as a standard of comparison.

A pupil's self-evaluation of his progress in school is the single most important factor in learning success. On the basis of his feelings of success, the youngster will cultivate an interest in school or a subject matter. On this basis he establishes goals, particularly important long-range ones, such as being listed on the honor roll, graduating from high school or being admitted to college. On the other hand, he may decide that he cannot function in the school situation and will stop trying to learn and find success through approved classroom procedures. Unable to drop out of school because of compulsory school attendance laws, some youngsters become functional dropouts early in school. They simply pass the years in school doing little and learning less until they become old enough to drop out or are "graduated" from high school. These youngsters may become behavioral problems and, when there are many of them in a single classroom or school, they may be overwhelming and disruptive enough to make it difficult or impossible for others to learn.

As youngsters get older they become more selective in the use of their energies and they distribute their efforts unequally. The evolving student favors certain subjects in school or selected out-of-school activities. There are a few exceptional individuals with wide ability who become both honor students and star athletes, but they are selecting from an even wider range of possibilities some activities and passing over others.

Initial learning in school is dependent on preschool learning; later success is related to the effectiveness of previous instruction. Formal education requires verbal skills for success in school. There is an emphasis on developing speaking, listening, writing, and particularly reading skills.

Poor reading skills interfere with studying a textbook; that is obvious. The youngster who cannot comprehend reading material or read at the required pace may not understand written directions and will be limited in his attempts to answer test items. If limited in vocabulary, a student may not have the basic information to continue his studies. As instruction becomes more complex and requires a larger and more technical vocabulary, the student who has serious reading problems falls further behind the pace of instruction.

Learning is systematically structured and progressively acquired. Acceptance of the challenge of learning and success in the classroom permit advancement into more complex scholarly areas. Failure to achieve satisfactorily at any level obstructs further learning in general, for learning cannot be realized when success depends on experiences that were missed or inadequately handled. Thus limitations in learning arithmetic fundamentals interfere with achievement in advanced areas of mathematics. Weakness in reading skills inhibits much further learning, especially in the study of science, social studies, and literature. Every scholarly field has its areas of specialization that require prior competence in facts, skills, and attitudes. Loss of interest in learning sets limits to achievement, with failure to achieve at one level barring achievement at more advanced stages.

theories of learning

Because an explanation of the learning function is crucial to the structuring of appropriate educational institutions and the development of reliable methods of teaching, efforts to explain the phenomena of learning have produced various theories by psychologists and educators. Yet limitations imposed by the nature of human action and reaction make the proving of any theory difficult. While no theory is as yet scientifically substantiated, progress in the fields of psychology, sociology, physiology, and pedagogy has added substance to some theories and weakened the case of others.

Early theories of learning centered about departmentalization of the mind into faculties: It was proposed that the mental faculties should be exercised like muscles and thus strengthened and made more adaptable. Later, theories were advanced in which reflex arc and stimulus-response explanations established a connection between the brain and sensory organs. Experiments by the Russian physiologist I. P. Pavlov led to the description of the conditioned reflex, which associated a response with a new stimulus paired with an original stimulus. Edward L. Thorndike was among the first of the psychologists who developed behavioralist theories of learning, in which research became centered upon the study of the behavior of organisms. As a reaction to concentration on the single stimulus-response mechanism, field theories were proposed, of which Gestalt psychology was the foremost representative.

More recent concerns have been the reinforcement and programming work of B. F. Skinner and the cognitive theory emphasis, of which Jerome Bruner's influence is most significant. Whereas programmed instruction has found a more enthusiastic reception in industry than in education, the Bruner impact will exert an important influence on educational thinking and curriculum planning in the foreseeable future, particularly following the changes in the arithmetic-mathematics curriculum. Central to the Bruner thesis is the belief that any subject may be taught to any child at any stage of development. Emphasis is placed on the learner engaging in the methodology of the scholar and in discovering learnings for himself. Jean Piaget, a Swiss psychologist, is one of Bruner's most severe critics; he suggests that there is probably an optimal time in a child's development to experience a particular learning. Other emphases in learning theory have to do with special cases: creativity; gifted and retarded youngsters; programmed instruction and educational television; individualized, small-group, and large-group learning; ungraded or multigraded classes; departmentalized elementary schools and team teaching in high school.

Much of the concern for learning theory has been directed toward models of the structure of the classroom process and methods of teaching. Although theory and practice should be interrelated and highly interdependent, in the world of reality they are often treated as separate entities. The famous Trump Plan of team teaching, which emphasizes large- and small-group and individual instruction, seems to have little conscious relationship to Bruner, Skinner, or even Pavlov.

Learning theory has a long way to go before it gains wide acceptance among educational professionals or becomes the foundation upon which the school curriculum is structured. Because of the painful conservatism of the members of the teaching profession, much scientific evidence will be needed to overcome the obstacles that insecurity of teachers and pressures upon administrators create within the schools. It will not be an easy task to allay the suspicions of the public toward what is happening to schoolchildren as basic changes are made in educational procedures.

The effectiveness of the application of learning theory in the schools depends upon the process of teaching, which is limited by structure and tied to administrative decisions. The most restrictive aspect of the classroom is the inability to move out of the group instructional processes, which form an educational straitjacket. Only programmed instruction and phases of certain innovations in the structure of teaching provide for individualized learning, and there is still no profound discussion among schoolmen that the group processes ought to come under serious question and examination. One problem that arises from the use of instructional programs and from innovations in teaching for creativity or instruction of the gifted is that some youngsters are able to achieve at a rapid pace, while teachers and the curriculum are not able to accommodate to this accelerated educational progress. If a pupil is able to complete the requirements for algebra instruction in half the allotted time, he should progress to the next level, which may be geometry. If he should complete geometry before the end of that year, further instruction at a more advanced level should be available to him. The problem is not that such flexibility cannot be effected, but that few teachers are prepared for such an eventuality. Few schools are able to meet the challenge posed by the full impact of releasing the power of learning.

The momentum to propel the schools into individualized instruction may depend on the development of a needed concern for the efficiency of learning. It will not be possible to effectively man the increasingly complex technological and social world as long as there is a serious lack of concern for the efficiency with which learning is accomplished in the classroom. The expectation will eventually be posed that society and the individual are to be served fully only when each person learns to the practical limits of his potential, that in order to operate worldly concerns it is essential for every individual to perform at or near one hundred percent efficiency in acquiring learnings as well as in applying them. Whereas group potential is dependent on the high performance of the slow learner, genius, and man-in-the-middle alike, learning efficiency should be measured by the ratio of achievement to potential. Both measures need further refinement in order to provide sufficient and accurate data. In order to maintain high levels of efficiency, then, instruction in many subjects will have to be conducted on an individual basis. One might project a revolution in learning procedures in the next decade that will accomplish greater changes in the classroom than those that have taken place since the University of Chicago engaged the services of John Dewey. It can come none too soon, for the geometric extension of knowledge waits for no man.

on your own

The learning process is not a particularly simple subject for introspection, yet it would be a useful exercise for the student to analyze the means of his own learning. What conditions seem to be optimum for learning? Which subject matters seem to be more easily or less easily learned? Under what conditions is learning facilitated through group instruction? with the help of a tutor? by oneself?

Individuals differ in the interest they find in some subjects and the lack of interest in others. While these attitudes are long in building and are likely to be subtly acquired, a student should spend some time in reflection upon the development of his interest patterns; he should note whether they were cultivated in the home, in school, in a church or club, or through the influence of a relative, neighbor, or friend. Perhaps he could also date the period at which a particular interest or disinterest became significant or overwhelming and whether this attitude change was related to a course, teacher, field trip, book, or some unusual educational experience.

Introspection is not the only way to study learning. Observation of others in the learning process may provide essential clues to the means by which learning takes place. Study of a young child, for instance, ought to demonstrate that play is a serious progression of learning experiences, and this study may provide an opportunity to examine the nature of those experiences. The child at play experiences failures and frustration, success and the rewards that ensue from success. A particularly rewarding experience for those analyzing the learning process may be to move from play to school. Here are lower-grade youngsters in a contrived learning situation where frustration is greater and rewards are arranged (and thus shared with others) and are, therefore, less apt to be realized spontaneously. The contrast between the two situations centers on the introduction of adult direction and influence in the school. Observation of learning in lower and higher elementary grades, at junior and senior high levels, and in various subjects and activities may provide insight into children's reactions to learning, the effects of success and failure, and the development of attitudes and behavioral patterns that inhibit or facilitate learning.

There is enough literature in the field of learning for intensive study of the theory of learning. Previous reference has been made to the writings of B. F. Skinner and Jerome Bruner. Among journals with a special concern for learning are *Educational Theory, Journal of Educational Psychology, Journal of Experimental Psychology, Journal of Teacher Education,* and *Journal of Programmed Instruction,* as well as many journals that serve special grade or subject areas.

There are many excellent texts in educational psychology that include discussions of learning theory, while particular attention may be directed to Ernest R. Hilgard (ed.), *Theories of Learning and Instruction* (Chicago: University of Chicago Press, 1964), a yearbook of the National Society for the Study of Education; Arthur W. Melton (ed.), *Categories of Human Learning* (New York: Academic Press, 1964); B. R. Bugelski, *The Psychology of Learning Applied to Teaching* (Indianapolis: Bobbs-Merrill, 1964); and David P. Ausubel, *The Psychology of Meaningful Verbal Learning* (New York: Grune & Stratton, 1963). A charming reference is *The Teaching-Learning Process* by Nathaniel F. Cantor (New York: Dryden Press, 1953).

Special learning situations, such as creativity, have been given attention. Examples of educational literature on creativity include *Guiding Creative Talent* by E. Paul Torrance (Englewood Cliffs, N.J.: Prentice-Hall, 1962) and the research report of Kaoru Yamamoto, *Creative Thinking and Peer Conformity in Fifth-Grade Children* (Kent, Ohio: Kent State University, 1965). Well-recommended as a reference on the highly talented is Willard Abraham, *Common Sense About Gifted Children* (New York: Harper & Row, 1958).

A glance at bibliographies in special interest problem areas suggests that literature of learning follows cycles responding to the periodic concern with a particular problem. Every teacher is challenged by the realities in the classroom to become familiar with literature about the gifted, slow learners, or handicapped. Some teachers have a particular interest in the learning problems of retarded or gifted children, the emotionally or psychologically disturbed, or the physically handicapped. Such teachers may enroll in special educational programs for certification as teachers of exceptional children.

Barbe, Walter B. (ed.). *Psychology and Education of the Gifted: Selected Readings.* New York: Appleton-Century-Crofts, 1965.

Burton, William H., Roland B. Kimball, and Richard L. Wing. *Education for Effective Thinking.* New York: Appleton-Century-Crofts, 1960.

Combs, Arthur W. *Perceiving, Behaving, Becoming.* Washington, D.C.: Association for Supervision and Curriculum Development, National Education Association, 1962.

Cruickshank, William M., and G. Orville Johnson (eds.). *Education of Exceptional Children and Youth.* Englewood Cliffs, N.J.: Prentice-Hall, 1967.

De Cecco, John P. *The Psychology of Learning and Instruction: Educational Psychology.* Englewood Cliffs, N.J.: Prentice-Hall, 1968.

Landreth, Catherine. *Early Childhood Behavior and Learning.* New York: Knopf, 1967.

Lindgren, Henry C. *Educational Psychology in the Classroom.* 3rd ed. New York: Wiley, 1967.

Shulman, Lee S., and Evan R. Keislar (eds.). *Learning by Discovery.* Chicago: Rand McNally, 1966.

Stevenson, Harold W. (ed.). *Child Psychology.* Sixty-Second Yearbook of the National Society for the Study of Education, Part I. Chicago: University of Chicago Press, 1963.

Travers, Robert M. W. *Essentials of Learning.* New York: Macmillan, 1967.

8

Organizing and guiding learning are the two major aspects of teaching, with emphasis placed equally on both. Just as there is a romantic concern for the surgeon performing modern miracles at the operating table, there is an exaggerated enchantment with the picture of a teacher performing academic sleight of hand in the classroom. Whether in the operating room or classroom, office, store, or laboratory, however, the productive process depends upon careful and thorough planning. The disintegrating classroom may represent an elaborate set of plans without the skills to carry them out or a sloppy planning job that provides little worth executing regardless of the guiding skills available. The productive classroom requires effective execution of well-laid plans.

objectives of learning

The identification of objectives is essential to planning for instruction. All planning begins with establishing objectives, whether the action is to take place in the kitchen, on the highway, or in the classroom. Once the objectives are determined, the means for reaching them are established. The teaching procedure follows, and the learning is then evaluated to assess the degree to which the objectives have been attained.

Basically, educational objectives are concerned with the learning of facts, skills, and attitudes. The most serious effort to organize and classify educational objectives was that of Benjamin S. Bloom and associates.[1] Bloom classifies objectives

[1] Benjamin S. Bloom (ed.), *Taxonomy of Educational Objectives, Handbook I: Cognitive Domain* (New York: McKay, 1956). David Krathwohl, Benjamin S. Bloom, and Bertram B. Masia, *Taxonomy of Educational Objectives, Handbook II: Affective Domain* (New York: McKay, 1964).

the organization of instruction

in the cognitive domain—emphasizing recall and recognition of knowledge and acquisition of intellectual abilities and skills; in the affective domain—concerning interests, attitudes, and values of the learner; and in the psychomotor domain—concerning physical skills. *Handbook I* is useful for aid in establishing objectives in the cognitive classifications of knowledge, comprehension, application, analysis, synthesis, and evaluation. *Handbook II* is a guide for identifying objectives in the affective aspects of learning. Handbook III has not yet been published. Attempts by teachers to objectify teaching and learning will probably confirm the experience of Bloom and his associates that the most readily structured objectives are those about knowledge; the interest-attitude area is less easily formulated into objectives. Perhaps the emphasis in school upon factual knowledge reflects the reality that it is easiest to identify facts that are to be learned and to thus plan the curriculum. Even if they are more difficult to phrase into objectives and to evaluate, nonacademic skills and interests, attitudes, and values need to be included among the objectives established for the classroom.

There often is confusion between teaching and learning objectives. Not infrequently it will be argued that to distinguish between them is futile and useless. However, the major classroom process is learning, with teaching a subordinate, intermediate (and not always essential), adjunctive procedure.

Emphasis on teaching objectives places responsibility on the student to react to and benefit from a teacher-directed process. When the classroom activities focus on teaching rather than learning, the teacher is the center of attention. Concern may be shown for how well a lesson is organized and what the quality is of the teacher's actions. The assumption is frequently made that if the teacher performed well, the pupil should have responded. If the student did not respond, such failure may be attributed to personal characteristics, such as his ignorance, laziness, or refusal to cooperate. Emphasis on learning objectives, however, centers responsibility for learning on the teacher, who must teach, motivate, push, and cajole each learner in an effort to fulfill the objectives.

The logical schoolhouse progression is to structure the curriculum about those things that have been selected as priority learning, to seek to meet them through learning activities that are organized and guided by teachers, to evaluate the learning in order to determine how effectively the objectives have been achieved, and to make the adjustments that are needed to improve the process. Teaching and learning objectives may be similarly phrased but they differ greatly in meanings and consequences. For instance, to aid in the appreciation of Shakespeare's *Hamlet* or to appreciate *Hamlet* are objectives that are similar in phrasing. The first is concerned with aiding the student and the techniques of such aid, whereas the second is concerned with the student and his learning to appreciate a literary work.

To be effective in selecting and defining learning objectives, a teacher must be competent in subject matter and knowledgeable about the kinds of individual and group behaviors he seeks to encourage and teach. Thus the elementary teacher needs breadth across many subject areas and the secondary instructor needs depth in a specialty. The teacher of the elementary grades should also have a thorough knowledge of the teaching process at all other grade levels, and the secondary teacher must also have a strong acquaintance with the other subject matters that are taught at the same grade levels. All teachers must have extensive information about behavior and growth patterns. In order to make appropriate referrals to health, learning, or psychological specialists for problems relating to individual pupil behavior, all teachers must be able to identify nonconformist behavior that is acceptable and normative as well as behavior that is irrational and possibly neurotic, psychotic, or otherwise potentially disruptive or unhealthy.

Before a teacher can establish learning objectives, he must consult the syllabus that is the basis for a year's study and extract reasonable and meaningful objectives to fit the needs of his particular youngsters. A useful procedure is to divide the year's content into units, or intermediate segments, organizing a topic to be taught for a few weeks, and from that content to decide which learning outcomes are most important. Stating the kinds of learnings as objectives establishes the goals of instruction and suggests the content and teaching techniques that are appropriate to the teacher, class, and subject. Once the unit objectives have been determined, it is necessary to establish the specific learning objectives that should be planned for each day's instruction. Daily instructional objectives are specific, and for this reason the teacher plans each day's activities in detail. Teaching will thus emphasize the things to be learned and provide a variety of experiences so that all pupils may achieve the learning objectives.

The yearly-to-intermediate-to-daily organizing of learning activities is still geared to group instruction, although some school instructional schemes permit a more flexible organization of instruction and make it possible to meet the learning needs of individuals more adequately. Teaching youngsters in ungraded classes provides greater opportunities to tailor learning objectives and instruction to the individual child. It permits instructional planning to meet the youngster at his level of achievement so that a teacher may proceed at the pupil's pace of learning.

Teaching is basically a communicative process. Thus a major concern of organizing instruction is the need for communication skills and techniques. A constant reminder needs to be built into every teacher's consciousness that vocabulary and use of words must be appropriate to the group under instruction. It is a challenge to communicate at a given grade and age level so that both the slowest learners and the most advanced youngsters understand the language and all pupils are led to extend their vocabularies. Textbook materials appropriate to a youngster's reading achievement are a first essential in the classroom.

Communication, however, extends beyond the spoken and written word. A schoolroom communicates excitement or a bland atmosphere by the use a teacher makes of chalkboards, bulletin boards, arrangement of desks, and availability of teaching materials. The dress and demeanor of the teacher are also important in establishing a dynamic classroom. In addition, audio-visual services provide many instructional communicative devices for the classroom teacher. Much is communicated in teaching: facts, attitudes, enthusiasm, and the excitement of learning.

planning relations with students

Questions of mutual respect and a teacher's rapport with youngsters are too crucial to the fulfilling of learning objectives to leave to chance. The relations between a teacher and his class can scarcely be cast aside as incidental or accidental. Perhaps no aspect of the classroom process should be more carefully considered or planned than the type of interaction desired by a teacher to facilitate learning.

Instructions frequently given to teaching neophytes suggest the role of planning teacher-pupil relations: "The best thing to do is to start off tough and then loosen up." The great concern shown for problems of discipline in teaching leads to much consideration (perhaps even exaggeration) of what is to be done in order to effectuate satisfactory classroom relations, the kind of image the fledgling teacher seeks to establish, how misbehavior will be countered, and what means of punishment or correction are needed. While an obsession with discipline may result in neglecting other aspects of teaching, there can be little room for argument that effective learning does not take place amid chaos and confusion. This is not to suggest that an atmosphere dominated by fear is a satisfactory alternative or that the old-fashioned demand for a hushed silence is either natural or constructive. Good discipline is that conduct which facilitates learning. Poor discipline is conduct that interferes with learning.

In approaching the question of rapport in the classroom, a teacher must understand his own personality and its potentials and limitations. Whatever relationships a teacher seeks to establish must be in accord with his attributes: The introvert cannot hope to be a "personality kid" nor may the extrovert realistically seek to pose as a sober taskmaster. It is crucial that a teacher use his personality constructively in establishing classroom relationships and that he seek to create a positive learning atmosphere.

There are also other factors to consider in building personal relationships. The traditions and practices established in a school, for one, should provide a reasonable structure to which the individual classroom teacher can conform. A classroom that deviates significantly from the established pattern in a school requires too great an adjustment of the youngsters who move between that classroom and others. A second factor that must be included in the teacher's planning for an appropriate classroom atmosphere is the mode of conduct that is natural to the particular group of youngsters: The same expectations may not be made of undernourished mountain youngsters or children of the slums as of the privileged offspring in exclusive suburbs or the highly conformist child of the middle class.

A teacher has access to a number of aids that may extend and refine his relations with his students. An important reference for information about the school is the local teachers' handbook, which usually outlines a teacher's prerogatives, procedures, responsibilities, and duties in that school or school system. It may be important to distinguish between rules as written and as practiced. It would be advisable to consult teachers as well as administrators for information about actual administrative practices.

Of more significance than the handbook, however, are student personnel records, which are occasionally maintained by a classroom teacher but are more commonly found in the guidance office or with the main administrative files. A well-organized personal history of every schoolchild is collected in a cumulative record, which is simply a file folder upon which information may be written and within which reports may be kept. When it is correctly utilized, a cumulative folder will include an individual pupil's record of regular academic and health inventories, a running compilation of grades and attendance, results of periodic aptitude, achievement, and other standardized testing, and anecdotal records reporting unusual behavior or achievement. A teacher should be able to obtain from a cumulative record information about a youngster's home and family, learning ability and achievement, significant successes or problems in school, relationship with teachers and peers, and health and growth patterns. In addition to information about individuals, schools maintain records which provide information about classes and grades, including the ranges of scores and average measures of ability and school achievement tests and a comparison of these measures with other schools or groups of schools.

planning for instruction

Of particular concern to a teacher are his personal records, lesson plans and notes about his previous teaching, information he has compiled about youngsters, and the data he uses for evaluation in the classroom. The teacher must be acquainted with the school's procedures for reporting to parents. The periodic report card, check list, or letter to the parents requires particular information that the teacher needs to collect and record. Unit plans and daily lesson plans should be filed for future reference, most importantly so that they may be analyzed for strong points and weak spots in planning and execution and changes made to improve future teaching and learning. A teacher needs to plan carefully the means by which tests, assignments, and homework will be evaluated and recorded and to decide how important each measure of learning shall be in the evaluation of youngsters and the teaching process. It is a common practice of school principals to require teachers to file advance copies of lesson plans weekly with the central office to provide an instructional guide in case a substitute teacher takes over the classroom.

guidance and special learning services

The guidance and special learning services may have information or suggestions for the teacher which are important in planning for instruction. The obvious example is health information that limits the activities in physical education classes for the youngsters with heart defects or the epileptics or diabetics. There is other information that is less obvious but as necessary to other teachers. Some youngsters may have emotional or psychological problems which limit the experiences they should have. There may be some who are excused on religious grounds from saluting the flag, repeating the pledge of allegiance, or participating in class activities like a mock election. This information should be centered in the guidance office.

Remedial instructional services are most effective when they are related to activities in the classroom. The youngsters who are receiving remedial reading instruction may require special textbooks or supplementary materials and those in speech correction classes may benefit from special activities in regular classroom instruction. In addition to specialized information, the teacher may need assistance in selecting educational experiences and teaching techniques and in obtaining unusual or special equipment or materials.

A number of special services may be available to aid a teacher in planning for classroom instruction. A widely accepted special service is provided by the counseling and guidance personnel. However, this service is more common to secondary than elementary schools. Guidance personnel may be most useful to a teacher in providing special information about a youngster and by serving as a point of referral of pupils for aid in personal or learning problems. A counselor is trained in the interpretation of tests and in testing techniques and should be consulted in the selection, administration, and use of standardized tests. Serious psychological or emotional problems may be referred to a school psychologist, either directly by a teacher or through a guidance counselor. Some schools have school social workers who offer particular aid with youngsters' problems that are centered in the home. A helpful special service is performed by learning specialists, such as remedial reading teachers. A classroom teacher may aid a youngster who has been out of school for a prolonged period because of illness by working with teachers for the homebound, who provide instruction at the pupil's home.

Audio-visual services are highly useful in planning and carrying through instruction. They can provide information about films, tapes, transparencies, radio or television schedules, or pictorial representations. They may supply audio-visual techniques for a teacher's use or they may provide a complete program including delivering and servicing of teaching techniques. Some larger communities or regional organizations of schools maintain film, slide, or tape libraries. In other schools teachers are usually dependent on a more distant rental library for many audio-visual teaching tools. Whether the classroom has ready access to audio-visual materials or must depend on distant sources for teaching aids affects both planning for instruction and the actual teaching.

In planning to use audio-visual techniques, the teacher needs to know what tools are available and whether the classroom is suitable for the use of some devices or the class must be moved to another room or an auditorium. Some classrooms do not have shades to darken rooms. There are some classrooms that are without electric outlets, so that certain techniques may not be used in the room. The teacher should know whether there are opaque, overhead, film, filmstrip, or film cassette projectors, as well as tape recorders, record players, television and radio receivers, duplicating machines, and techniques for producing transparencies. There is frequently a need to schedule use of a physical facility as well as the audio-visual tool when auditoriums or special rooms are used for projection purposes.

Some classroom activities require special or extra materials. Colored paper, tagboard, spirit masters, or mimeograph stencils may be needed. Chalk, paint, or crayons may be necessary and a project may require costumes or even food. Plant and animal specimens are often used in classes. A biology lesson might call for an aquarium, a cage for animals, or facilities for growing plants. Other lessons may call for microscopes, experimental equipment, or models. Extraclass activities may use crepe paper, spotlights, dance music, or game materials.

library tools

Reference and picture books and periodicals are common tools in the classroom, and fiction may also contribute to the study of science, health, history, or most other subjects. Some schools have full-time librarians while others have individuals who work as part-time or volunteer librarians. Some schools use public libraries or bookmobiles and there are some that do not have access to a reasonable amount of reading materials. Every teacher has to know the library facilities that are available and whether there are funds for building classroom libraries. If the school has a library, the teacher should know the range of reading materials available, the system of cataloging used, and the willingness or ability of the librarian to participate in instructional activities.

Well-organized schools distribute lists of audio-visual and library materials available for instruction to teachers. The well-organized teacher will get acquainted with the available materials and equipment. Some schools include audio-visual specialists as well as librarians on the staff to assist teachers in learning which instructional materials are available and in planning for instruction. Multimedia rooms are associated with libraries or operate independently to plan and make transparencies, models, and displays or to prepare and duplicate teaching materials.

after-school studies

There was a renewed interest in homework for youngsters when the easing of emphasis on study at home by progressive educators was reversed in the post-Sputnik era and with the increased emphasis on mass higher education and the preparation of more youngsters for college. Teachers who believe in heavy homework schedules or who teach in schools where homework assignments are required by school policy must plan such assignments to avoid meaningless busy work, to utilize home study for its most logical purposes of drill on fundamentals and increase in skills, and to reduce conflict with other necessary nonschool learning experiences. Teachers should be aware that much of an individual's personal, emotional, psychological, spiritual, social, physical, and recreational development takes place out of school and in the home, neighborhood, club, and church. Homework has a legitimate place in the school program, but a youngster needs and is entitled to experiences that are not related to the school. His after-school hours should not be restricted to an extension of the school.

In contemplating homework and nonclass assignments, the secondary school teacher should not ignore the time a student spends in a study hall and the possibilities for making constructive use of time that frequently is wasted. Aside from an opportunity to do homework in school, most planned instructional use of study hall time should take place out of the study hall and in the classroom, library, or laboratory. Study hall boredom may give way to special projects or remedial instruction if there is adequate planning and staff. Similarly, there are opportunities to ally some extracurricular activities with classwork. The relations between athletic programs and instruction in physical education are as pertinent as those between the school newspaper and English composition and grammar. It should be as appropriate to relate a stamp club and world geography, a camera club and the art class, and the student council and instruction in principles of government.

utilizing the physical classroom

A teacher should aim for maximum benefit from the physical classroom in planning for instruction. If a room is adequate in size and contains a reasonable number of pupils, the desk arrangement should be planned to promote learning experiences. The traditional orderly row-on-row of desks serves to formalize the classroom, tends to center the teacher in front of the group, fosters a dependence on use of the lecture method, and places the emphasis on teaching as the major activity in the classroom. Informal desk arrangement may facilitate small-group or individual activities and place the emphasis upon learning rather than teaching. The walls of a classroom provide a challenge to convert four sterile surfaces into a stimulating educational environment. A chalkboard may be the place to record assignment of duties to youngsters, list textbook assignments, and write the names of those required to stay after school; or it may better serve as an area for graphic explanation of exciting learning by the teacher or as a means for self-expression by students. Any classroom should be large enough to house a plentiful supply of supplementary learning materials—books, programmed materials, crayons, water or tempera paints, drawing and construction paper, files of mounted pictures, pamphlets, and clippings—and there should be easy access to radio and television receivers, tape recorders, film, filmstrip, slide, opaque, and overhead projectors and maps, graphs, and charts.

The question of teacher judgment should be examined in analyzing teaching as a process. Planning for instruction is an exercise in the selection of options among learning objectives, subject content, teaching methods, and evaluation techniques. The quality of this judging process depends upon the individual teacher's knowledge of a subject area, the extent to which he understands and accepts the purposes of instruction, the awareness of the available teaching methods, competence in their use, and the ability to evaluate their effectiveness. The teaching process involves a succession of snap judgments rewarding or penalizing student behaviors, deciding how to evaluate the ongoing instructional technique, and choosing the time to alter classroom procedure. Unlike the more reliable purposeful judgment in planning, classroom split-second decisions are more subject to error and are related to a teacher's personality, his present emotional and fatigue state, and his depth of experience. It is important that a teacher find time to analyze and evaluate the snap judgments that he makes in the classroom to reduce obvious errors, to learn to anticipate the range of pupil responses, and to react more satisfactorily for the improvement of youngsters' learning.

The organization of instruction is the least exciting part of the teaching-learning process, but it is of crucial importance. It involves more facets than the teaching novice may recognize. As the blueprint for learning, planning permits or facilitates instruction. Good planning provides directions for purposeful activity and increases the likelihood of meeting objectives and of maintaining regulated, spirited, and successful classes.

classroom discipline

It has been pointed out that satisfactory discipline is essential for learning to take place. The frequent exposés of education in city slums picture the typical teacher as subject to the whims of violent youngsters: He seeks to quell group rebellion, to stop scuffling in pairs, and to inhibit individual exhibitionism. It is asserted that a few students learn despite the chaos, but for the majority of youngsters school is a three-ring circus, a prison, a center for social unrest, and a forum for organized anarchy. While the total picture may be less disintegrative than journal-istic essays suggest, it is not unusual to find an individual teacher in nonslum schools presiding over a disintegrating classroom. The discipline that is maintained in a classroom is an informal, noncommunicated arrangement between the teacher and his pupils, individually and as a group, as to whether the business to be conducted shall be at the behest of the teacher or in organized opposition to him or whether no organized learning procedures shall be permitted at all.

The crucial factor in satisfactory classroom discipline is the relationship between a teacher and a class. The heart of this relationship is the measure of respect youngsters hold toward the adult. Outdated naiveté suggested that respect by youngsters was automatically due to an adult—and especially to a teacher—but the experience of American teachers throughout history has demonstrated that automatic veneration of teachers has never been an established fact in the United States.

The first quality requisite to the earning of respect is the giving of respect. It is necessary for every teacher to accept every youngster, even if the child appears to the teacher to be obnoxious, negative, or disagreeable. Challenges to the middle-class-oriented teacher are the nonconformist, frequently lower-class, students from the core of the city and the outer fringes of the village or children from isolated rural or mountain families. It may be difficult, but the teacher must respectfully interact with every individual in his class.

In addition to showing regard for youngsters, however, a teacher must be knowledgeable and competent in methods of instruction. Youngsters are expected to behave courteously to the adult who is concerned about them, but they must also be able to recognize grounds for respecting a competent teacher.

Discounting the discipline that is maintained by a teacher through fear and the use or implied use of force, the code of conduct in a classroom is arrived at through a formal or informal agreement between the teacher and the pupils. While some persons regard the formalizing of teacher-pupil relations as unnecessary and negative, it may be argued that failure to establish commonly accepted limits of behavior requires that the acceptable limits of conduct be established by the experimentation of the pupils and through the teacher's reaction to their behavior. It is a negative process to establish acceptable patterns of conduct solely by trial and error and by repression at unpredictable and unexpected stages of developing behavior. A teacher and class can and should establish reasonable limits of conduct jointly as the class first meets.

The primary criterion for acceptable behavior is that the conduct of both the teacher and the pupil should facilitate learning. Both teachers and pupils will accept classroom limits that are reasonable and may be applied without prejudice. Disruptive behavior, from unregulated whispering to the passing of notes, interferes with learning; there is seldom disagreement about that. It is less clear, though, how a frequent source of conflict, gum chewing, applies under this criterion. In establishing limits of conduct, then, it should be recognized that some traditionally accepted standards, such as gum chewing and noise level, are of little aid in regulating the classroom. The noise level of a class, for instance, must be related to the learning activity before it can be applied as an index of acceptable behavior. In this way, the teachers and students may decide that there should be no talking or whispering during a test, other than explanations or clarifications by the teacher. Only one person should be speaking during a lecture or recitation. Class enthusiasm may raise the noise level during a discussion, and the noise level may be high when a learning game is in progress.

Once limits have been established, it must be assumed that they will be tested, not necessarily maliciously, but nevertheless tested. As soon as a limit is tested, it should be reinforced; if it is not enforced, the limit will be displaced. When a limit is displaced, it is necessary to establish a new limit. Failure to reinforce a limit may find youngsters moving from hidden whispering to open conversation to more disruptive behavior. If no checks are applied to a disintegrative situation, the classroom may explode. If a teacher delays making a response to the testing of a limit, a crisis situation may develop that necessitates use of strong repressive measures. On the other hand, if the teacher reacts swiftly to an initial testing of limits, a mild reaction may be applied by the teacher before a crisis has arisen. The superior teacher is well in control of the situation and reacts to deviant and potentially troublesome behavior unobtrusively with a glance or flick of a finger. To the casual observer there is a remarkable absence of random behavior by the youngsters in such a classroom.

For most teachers in most schools, there will be situations that result in punishment of youngsters. While a well-worn cliché would prescribe punishment "when a youngster needs it," the truth is probably served more aptly in the admission that discipline is applied "when the teacher needs it." The time for strong measures arrives when the teacher runs out of alternatives and succumbs to frustration. Regardless of the prompting to deal with an offender, the teacher must recognize that use of force or fear to control pupils is generally negative. There are few positive benefits in chastising youngsters in school. Assigning extra schoolwork as a penalty, for example, undermines a subject. Expulsion from a room or standing in a corner symbolizes the room as punitive and negative. Staying after school erodes the idea of school as a pleasurable place.

If punishment is negative and yet must be used, what should a teacher do? The reasonable and realistic teacher serves the pill with grace and wisdom. Perhaps the least specific negative symbol, staying after school, is preferable; the minimum time to effect the symbol (that is, about ten minutes) is sufficient. The teacher should remember that classroom problems are primarily his responsibility and that punishment is a final outcome of his frustration.

A teacher admits complete failure when he resorts to mass-punishment procedures. If a class is in unanimous opposition to the teacher, the situation has collapsed. The teacher who is at war with a class may win a few battles but has already lost the war. It is an abuse of his position of power when a teacher punishes the class in the expectation that conformist youngsters will apply pressures upon the nonconformists. The teacher is thereby assigning to pupils his own responsibility to keep order. The resentment, anger, and loss of respect for a teacher and a class that may be expressed by a student at any age level who has felt unjustly penalized is evidence of the disastrous consequences of mass punishment for individual misbehavior. Unreasonable attempts to force appropriate behavior incite pressures for aggressive retaliation. An effort to coerce youngsters into showing respect for a teacher may increase disrespect and reduce the possibility that attitudes will change.

Good discipline—that group and individual conduct which facilitates learning—results in a relaxed, happy, and satisfying atmosphere. It promotes the objectives for which schools are established; it fulfills the grand design of the society. A frequent suggestion for the resolution of the discipline problem is the proposal that "the best discipline is self-discipline." The difficulty with that solution is not just that this is a simple answer to a complex problem, but that it is an unrealistic oversimplification. It places the entire responsibility for discipline upon the shoulders of immature youngsters. It proposes adult values and behavior for nonadults. It assumes that educational objectives are accepted by all and supposes that only obstinacy by youngsters stands in the way of solving disciplinary problems.

selection of content for instruction

The process of planning for daily instruction begins with examination of the yearly program of instruction as outlined in a syllabus, although some teachers derive their plans directly from a textbook. After he is assigned the subject matter for the year, the teacher should establish approximate teaching objectives for specific periods of the year. Breaks in the school calendar—Thanksgiving, Christmas, and spring vacation—are used as guides for pacing instruction. The pace of teaching and learning should be related to the nature of the class and to the ability level and previous achievement of the pupils. A teacher is concerned with two dimensions of instruction: breadth—that is, the extent of subject content—and depth—or the thoroughness with which a subject is studied. Instruction may be adjusted to the needs of individual pupils by regulating the depth and breadth of the subject matter to be studied.

One may find that planning for instruction is an area peculiarly confounded by an overlapping and confusing vocabulary. The term "teaching units" has come into disrepute in recent years, although an equally satisfactory term has not been adopted to identify intermediate levels of planning. In this discussion "teaching units" will refer to the intermediate planning segments and is not intended to be limited in meaning to any rigid definition of the term. A further confusion persists with outlines for instruction, which may be called syllabi, curriculum guides, or courses of instruction. The term "syllabus" will refer to a proposed outline of content for a subject. "Resource unit" will be used to describe a compilation of suggested course content, possible methods of instruction, and abundant teaching and learning aids.

Broad instructional programs are divided into manageable segments called teaching units. A valuable reference for planning a teaching unit is a resource unit, which is a rich accumulation of suggested objectives, methods, and activities. A unit must be subdivided into daily lesson plans. It is advisable not to plan daily lessons more than a week in advance, as it is usually difficult and unrealistic to determine ahead of time the daily activities for a unit lasting several weeks. Pacing of teaching is facilitated by holding to a unit schedule; flexibility of scheduling, however, is provided by adjusting evolving daily lesson plans. Depth can be added to a subject or learning activities when teaching progresses faster than anticipated and the number or extent of instructional experiences can be reduced when the learning pace slackens.

Formalized definitions of unit planning suggest that it involves four aspects: introduction of the unit as a meaningful and challenging experience, conclusion of the unit through culminating and unifying activities, evaluation that measures learning and provides information to improve teaching and learning, and a variety of teaching techniques to meet the diverse ways by which learning takes place.

A copy of the daily lesson plan may be filed in the school office as a guide for a substitute teacher. The daily lesson plan is also of great value to the classroom teacher as a detailed outline of subject content, as a scheme to be followed, and as a close check that objectives are realized. As the best record of what has actually transpired in the classroom, the lesson plan is an indispensable reference for evaluating learning. Looking back on a lesson as it was planned and executed provides an opportunity for the teacher to ascertain strengths and weaknesses of the classroom process and to design and execute future teaching methods. This is a teacher's best basis for improving future instruction. The immediate purpose of planning is to ensure an effective instructional program, but long-range planning is essential for corrective purposes. Teachers must always be concerned with improving teaching procedures, identifying learning problems of groups or individuals, and making arrangements for remedial instruction.

the textbook

Despite frequent criticism of the reliance on a single textbook in the classroom, much of the teaching in American schools still centers about the textbook. Tradition is not the only reason for continued use of the text. There is a need in most courses for a common reference and for an access to organized knowledge whether or not it is in textbook form. The textbook often most simply and most satisfactorily fits these needs. Reform in the classroom through change of subject content and teaching methods may be furthered through the textbook, as has been the case in recent efforts to improve instruction in the sciences and mathematics.

The textbook has limitations that must be recognized by teachers. It includes just a limited selection of the available subject matter. For example, a world geography text represents only a small sampling of its subject. No textbook is sufficient as a sole reference either in the extent of subject matter or in the types of learning experiences that ought to be provided. Texts are also not satisfactory for motivational purposes because they are limited in depth of subject and the variety of learning situations they present. The greatest limitation of a textbook, however, is its inflexibility in meeting the range of reading abilities in a class. Typically written at a reading level somewhat below the grade for which it is intended, a text seldom challenges the reading interests or vocabulary of the superior reader, while it may prove to be beyond the reading skills and comprehension of the poorest reader.

A simple answer to reading problems is to adopt a multiple-text procedure. Publishers have begun to produce slow-reader editions of some textbooks, which permits "dual textbook" use, but there are still relatively few classroom situations for which textbooks may be found that are parallel in organization and written at both elementary and advanced reading levels to permit the use of several books.

Many textbooks are supplemented by teachers' manuals and pupil workbooks and may be considered self-contained teaching packages. There are even more elaborate combinations offered to teachers, with books, teachers' manuals, and workbooks supported by readings, paperback supplements, filmstrips, models, and transparencies. While it is possible for a teacher to rely upon the author's plans and to use the texts supplied, no means may be provided by a publisher to utilize the particular strengths of a teacher or to meet the particular needs of a community, school, or group of youngsters. The concern is not for a teacher's competence or lack of it, but for an adequate level of efficient learning in the classroom. Canned teaching from a text, manual, and workbook is sterile; it is unrelated to the reality of the classroom and can seldom be effective. There is talk of "teacher-proof" instructional proposals that are assumed to guarantee learning regardless of the deficiencies of a teacher. Packaged and teacher-proof instruction may compensate for mediocrity and incompetence, but it is a horribly pessimistic means to an optimistic end. The textbook is an important facet of learning, but it can never be sufficient to itself in mass instruction and is seldom satisfactory on an individual basis. At best it is a useful tool for an imaginative, competent, and enthusiastic teacher.

Significant improvement has been made in the writing of textbooks and greater progress may be expected in the future. Today's text is better written, more attractively styled, and better illustrated than the textbook of the past. Intervention by concerned academic specialists led to the formation of national committees that produced new science and mathematics textbooks. Pressures from civil rights groups and others concerned with the education of slum youngsters of all racial backgrounds resulted in the publication of new materials for reading instruction. Publishers now reject content based on the protected experience of the dominant middle class and produce elementary reading books that cut across social and economic class boundaries. Reading programs have thus moved out of the sterile Dick and Jane stories into the real world. Textbooks, however, are still very expensive and many schools use them after they should have been replaced by newer books. Certainly a text will become outdated if it is used beyond a reasonable period of time; this is particularly true in the areas of science and social studies, where change in content is particularly accelerated.

A teacher may occasionally select the textbook to be used in instructional planning and execution, although the choice is often limited to a state list of approved texts. Many teachers use textbooks that are selected by local school systems or by individual schools. Occasionally and unfortunately, a school board may intervene in the selection of a textbook.

The basic criterion of textbook selection is the subject content. The content in a textbook should follow the general dictates of the course of study or curriculum guide, which prescribe the factual or ideational content and the scope and breadth of the subject to be studied. The accuracy of the facts that are presented is essential to the content of a textbook. Where there is disagreement about facts or their interpretation by recognized experts in the field, a text may be sought that includes various interpretations, or the responsibility for introducing alternatives may be assumed by the teacher through lectures or in the inclusion of other teaching materials. The advantage of including varying interpretations in the text is the guarantee that the full truth will be taught. However, a book that attempts to present all positions in a controversial subject tends to be primarily a listing of content and is often bland and uninteresting. The alternative of relying on the teacher for the inclusion of additional instructional materials may permit a more positive and therefore more interesting textual presentation.

Multiple authorship and the number of textbooks available to the schools make it increasingly difficult to form satisfactory judgments about the competence of authorship. Textbooks continue to be revised and published in the name of the authors after the original writers have died. Books of retired authors sometimes are revised by younger writers who are listed as joint authors. In some textbooks multiple authorship obscures responsibility, making it difficult or impossible to determine how much or what an individual writer may have contributed to a joint endeavor. This is not to be construed as a blanket condemnation of all multiple authorship, for specialists frequently collaborate on textbooks with each contributing his particular expertise. With such a variety of procedures in use by authors and publishers, however, it is a complicated task to judge a multiple-authored text on the basis of the authorship.

Readability of a text is concerned with an author's writing skills as well as the appropriateness of the reading level. To garner full benefit from a textbook, a youngster should find the reading interesting and rewarding rather than merely tolerable. Grade level, reading achievement, or the personal preference of a teacher might favor one textbook format over another. The size and style of print or the choice of two columns of type on a page rather than one are considered important by some who select textbooks. Further criteria for selection may be the inclusion of assignments at the end of a chapter and the accompaniment of a special text for teachers with instructional suggestions or directions in contrasting type or color of ink. The durability of the binding is crucial to those schools that expect 900 days or five years of hard use by students (an exceptionally large order). The price of textbooks may be an important index to some schools, although the financial outlay actually may represent less than one cent per day.

teacher-pupil planning

Teacher-pupil planning is a much discussed and much misunderstood procedure. There is little opportunity to place responsibility for determining the content of the curriculum upon youngsters. There are, however, plentiful opportunities for joint teacher-pupil planning in deciding the methods of instruction to be used in the classroom. Teachers and pupils may work out arrangements for rules of conduct and social activities. They may make arrangements for field trips and select specific techniques of instruction. There is seldom a learning situation where only one teaching technique may be utilized. Generally a broad variety of techniques are suitable. A self-confident teacher who is flexible in teaching methods may leave the exact instructional procedure to be followed up to the group. Frequently the joint teacher-pupil decision process becomes a form of misnamed authoritarianism, with the teacher making the decisions and the pupils dutifully going along. Rather than engage in a sham that fools no one, the teacher should accept pupil suggestions. He even may prefer to have a student chairman preside over a planning session. Real teacher-pupil planning takes pupil interests into consideration in determining classroom procedures and is a useful experience in group processes and in practicing the democratic way of life.

evaluation

Evaluation techniques are important to planning for instruction as a means of determining the effectiveness with which learning experiences have been organized and the efficiency of the guidance of learning. To evaluate is to make a value judgment. Evaluation also involves measurement, which is the gathering of data, and this process is conducted both informally and through formal testing. In focusing evaluation on learning objectives, the teacher attempts to determine whether the learning objectives have been realized and, if so, how well they have been achieved.

Each school or school system adopts a system of evaluation that is uniform for all teachers in some areas of evaluation but which allows each teacher to exercise some judgment about the behavior and achievement of youngsters. The evaluation procedure is seldom controlled entirely from outside the classroom. The individual teacher is usually expected to conduct some testing procedures and may occasionally be responsible for most of the evaluation process. In addition, many schools provide periodic and system-wide standardized testing of all pupils. Whether evaluation is a formal or informal process is unimportant to the pupil, but it is essential that teachers understand the differences between the forms of evaluation.

Much of the evaluation process is informal. Teachers do much of their measuring and gather much of their data by observation. Such observation requires skills in the techniques of observation and in selecting the appropriate model against which the behavior is to be compared. A pupil's behavior, for example, may be considered humorous by one teacher, ignored by another teacher, and resented by a third. Although all these attitudes are informal evaluations of the same behavior, the differences among them evolve from the teachers' individual frames of reference and may be due to each teacher's previous experiences with the youngster. A teacher informally measures the quality of a youngster's answer in recitation or contribution in a discussion. The teacher may also judge the acceptability of a pupil's behavior, clothing, or personal appearance. Informal evaluation is inconsistent. It varies with the mood of the teacher, the mood of a class, or the moods of individual pupils. It responds to the happenings of the moment and the context within which these happenings take place. The model against which a teacher measures a response or a behavior is a vague concept, but the model is real enough to a teacher at the moment of judgment although he might have difficulty describing it.

testing

Formal evaluation uses special techniques or instruments to measure an experience. It requires the creation of data-gathering devices and makes deliberate comparisons with the behavior of a student against an accepted standard. An observation may be formalized as an evaluative device by using a check list to standardize the measures. Whereas informal evaluation relies on impressions or interpretations, formal techniques derive quantitative measures. Sometimes, too, a qualitative measure is expressed quantitatively: An "average" oral presentation is recorded as a C or 80; a better speech receives a B or 88; a superior effort is awarded an A or 95. Formal evaluation usually depends on the use of written tests, although oral tests may be used, and requires special and unique procedures.

Testing, then, is classified into subjective and objective procedures. A subjective test is one in which the data collected by the test—that is, the performances or answers—must be interpreted by the teacher as he makes an evaluation of performance. The teacher exercises judgment as he measures the behavior. An essay test is a subjective measure because the person who scores the test must judge the quality of an answer. An objective test, however, does not require the making of a judgment as it is scored. There is either a correct or an incorrect answer: This may be a word—"true" or "false"—a number or letter, or even a line drawn from a cue to a response. A common type of subjective evaluation is the essay test in which the pupil freely responds to the posing of a problem. Under the broad umbrella of free-response test items are completion or fill-in, problem, and essay items.

The line between subjective and objective tests can become blurred. If an arithmetic problem in a test is to be evaluated by the process a youngster used rather than by the answer that was derived, a subjective judgment is required. When only the correct answer is to be scored, the subjective judgment is relatively objective. Similarly a completion test item is highly subjective if it calls for a free response, but it is quite objective if only one answer is correct. Testing in the early elementary grades may involve oral tests, which are administered individually and which call for a free response. As youngsters learn to read, tests are duplicated and distributed to the class. Pupils are then given little individual attention during the administration of a test.

The first objective testing a youngster experiences is a matching exercise. He may be asked to draw a line from a picture in one column to a picture in another column. The mechanics of the matching test are complex at this early grade level and may be complicated procedures for many senior high school youngsters. True-false test items are relatively easy to construct and score, although a significant problem on every grade level is the use of confusing or ambiguous language. The true-false test is less discriminating than some other types because of the opportunities for the testee to guess the correct answer. The multiple-choice test is more discriminating; some authorities consider it a superior means of measuring achievement. Any printed test requires a considerable amount of reading ability, and reading skills are especially important in selecting answers to multiple-choice items. Pictorial items of the multiple-choice or matching types are often used in lower grades and may be used more frequently in the upper grades.

CLASSROOM TESTS The construction of classroom tests for competent measurement of achievement requires knowledge of the curriculum and thorough acquaintance with learning objectives. A teacher needs to consider subject content, previous experience of the pupils in testing, and the time available for taking and scoring the test in planning the kind and length of a test. The way a test is to be scored may dictate whether a special answer sheet is to be provided. Skill and care must be exercised in construction of test items. Administration of teacher-made classroom tests is as important as the administration of standardized tests and the same care should be taken that all pupils understand directions and can function in the testing situation. Scoring of tests demands accuracy. Highly developed judgmental skills are essential to scoring subjective test items.

When constructing classroom tests, the teacher refers to learning objectives to decide what to evaluate. Pencil-and-paper tests evaluate learning of facts and may be used to assess some selected skills. Most skills and attitudes, however, are evaluated by observation of behavior. A teacher selects the facts to be included in a test on a basis of priority and importance. Kinds of subject matter determine the test items that are most appropriate for evaluating learning. Some subjects, such as history and literature, are more adaptable to essay or completion tests, while others are more suitable to true-false or multiple-choice items. Pictorial test items are of particular use in some subject matters where illustrations, maps, or charts are utilized.

A teacher needs to plan the language as well as the techniques of testing. Reading level and vocabulary should be appropriate. Depth of the subject should be sampled so that the differences in the effectiveness of learning will be reflected in performance on the test. Breadth of the subject is tested so that an evaluation may be made of the scope of learning. In constructing a test a teacher should avoid ambiguity, confusion, or trickery, as every extraneous factor introduced into the testing situation dilutes the meaning of the evaluation. Complicated testing procedures evaluate a pupil's ability to react to the complexity rather than to measure his knowledge of a subject.

The teacher should decide how a test will be presented. Oral tests were once in general use but are now used infrequently since they are time-consuming and extremely difficult to evaluate. Oral tests are usually reserved for those with serious sight or reading problems. Some teachers write tests on a chalkboard or project them through an overhead projector, but this method is seldom as satisfactory as providing each pupil with a copy of the test. Most tests are duplicated and a teacher should be familiar with duplicating techniques. As many as 250 copies, for instance, may be reproduced using a spirit duplicator and thousands of copies may be printed on a mimeograph machine. Diagrams or graphs are reproduced with ease using the spirit duplicator but are difficult to place on a mimeograph stencil. There are recent developments, however, that use heat transfer processes to copy from a sheet of paper to a spirit duplicator master. A special machine makes a mimeograph stencil from printed copy. Eventually, sophisticated copying equipment will be in general use. Numbers of pupils, availability of materials, and the amount of clerical assistance available determine the way a teacher prepares a test to be administered to a class.

Teachers need to determine how test answers should be recorded. Writing answers on the test is less confusing for the pupil. Using separate answer sheets facilitates the teacher's task of scoring tests but introduces more complex processes to the students and increases the likelihood of error. Electrically scored answer sheets transfer the scoring task to a machine but reduce the opportunity to notice or identify errors. The teacher must determine the way that marks are to be derived from the scores that are made on a test.

The teacher should be familiar with rudimentary statistical tools for analysis of tests and the means to improve testing techniques. Simple measures such as the mean, median, quartiles, and percentiles should be ready tools of the teacher. Teachers who are more skilled in statistical procedures may find it useful to derive standard deviations, correlation coefficients, and standard scores. In order to evaluate individual test items and to improve the quality of classroom tests, a teacher should know the techniques of item analysis.

STANDARDIZED TESTS In addition to classroom tests, which are admittedly rough measures, many teachers and schools make use of standardized tests. A standardized test is distinguished by the derivation of norms; that is, the test had already been administered to a sample group, which is representative of the larger group that will later take the test. Standards are set for future testing from this administration of the test. The score achieved by the median seventh-grader in the third month of school during the normative testing procedure on an achievement test becomes the 7–3 grade norm. Seventh-graders who achieve the same score in later testing will be credited with achievement at the 7–3 level. In addition to being characterized by the derivation of norms, standardized tests are constructed by test experts and are subjected to statistical analysis. A manual is usually published for standardized tests. It includes norms for test scores, a description of the test, and reports on the statistical analyses that have been made to determine how well a test measures what it is designed to measure (that is, its validity) and the consistency with which repeated testing would render the same score (reliability).

Although the classroom test is a measure of achievement, standardized tests are designed to measure either achievement or aptitudes, interests, and social, emotional, or psychological stability. A familiar aptitude measure is the scholastic aptitude (IQ) test, which seeks to ascertain an individual's ability to function in school-like tasks. Another important aptitude test measures readiness for reading. There are also tests that measure musical aptitude, manual dexterity, and creativity. Personality tests purport to identify and measure personality traits. Attitude tests attempt to describe attitudes toward others. Tests using projective techniques seek to discover emotional or psychological problems. Interest inventories are used to determine patterns of interest for educational or vocational purposes.

The teacher ought to recognize the problems that arise in the use of standardized tests. Group tests are generally dependent on reading ability. Individual testing requires special training of the test administrator and is time-consuming. Scholastic aptitude tests are limited in application because of cultural differences among youngsters and variation of children's experiences in early development, particularly in large city areas. Some tests measure more accurately than others. Achievement may be measured more easily than aptitude, and aptitude is tested more readily than interests or emotions. Tests must have been standardized on groups that are comparable to the class to be tested. The greater differences there are between the normative group and the class, the less pertinent are the norms.

evaluating learning and assigning marks

Classroom evaluation involves two major aspects: evaluation of learning and the assignment of marks. The teacher may make value judgments about the depth, breadth, and efficiency of learning by analyzing the content of a test, measuring student achievement on the test in general and with particular items, determining the degree to which learning objectives have been realized, and comparing test results with measures of the abilities of individuals and groups. On the basis of this evaluation some teaching techniques will be retained, some changed, and others eliminated; the pacing of instruction may be accelerated or slowed; the content may be changed; and testing techniques may be altered and improved. On the basis of test results an individual youngster may be singled out for particular study and may be referred to specialists for examination or treatment.

An almost universal practice in school is to assign marks as a measure of pupil achievement. Mastery of subject matter or placement in the group determines what the mark shall be. Pupil achievement is periodically reported to parents through a report card, parent conference, or letter sent to the home. The letter-marking system assigns a label to the youngster relating to his position in the group. Those at the bottom of a group test are assigned a D or an F; the youngsters at or near the top receive an A or B; and those in the middle form the C group. To the extent that a pupil's position in the group is dependent on his intelligence and his ability to do schoolwork, his letter mark is predetermined. Numerical marks do not represent the degree of mastery of a body of subject matter but show how well a pupil has responded to a sampling of the subject. Percent marks measure pupil achievement by the proportion of correct answers rendered to the total number of items on a test. A final percent mark is derived by averaging several test scores. Percent marks are closely related to native ability, for those who are highly endowed intellectually will answer more items correctly than the slow learners. Marks seldom indicate how well a youngster has done in line with his ability, interest, and effort. A mark, however, does tell how well he has done in answering items on a test and how his performance compared to the group. Comparisons are made whether or not a student is able to compete with the group.

The teacher must recognize the importance of marks to parents and children. A youngster's achievement record may exclude him from an academic program or admit him to a college. It may serve as motivation to stronger efforts and superior school achievement or it may discourage further effort and turn a slow learner into a functional dropout.

evaluating the teaching process

In addition to making judgments about learning, the teacher must evaluate the teaching process. There is no direct means of doing this; teaching must be evaluated indirectly through the learning of youngsters. Classroom instruction, however, cannot be evaluated simply by obtaining measures of the class against a group standard, such as the norms of standardized achievement tests. Nor is teaching evaluated by the scores youngsters make on nonstandardized statewide achievement tests such as are still used in states like New York. Some schools misuse testing programs in the attempt to evaluate teaching when neither the tests nor the results warrant such judgments.

The teacher is in the most advantageous position to gather the data through which teaching may be evaluated. By comparing a youngster's learning with his ability to learn and by considering the teaching methods utilized, a teacher may decide which techniques worked with the particular child and how effective they were. The teacher should know why some methods were successful and why others were not. A teacher's evaluation is the best basis for improving teaching and increasing the efficiency of learning. Evaluation is an incomplete process until teaching success has been measured; it is not sufficient to stop with an evaluation of the learning of pupils. The process of evaluation should lead to the improvement of instruction.

The teacher engages in a highly subjective evaluation of teaching. By asking and answering questions, reading faces, correcting assignments, scoring tests, and supervising classwork, the teacher appraises the progress of instruction. Class behavior may be an index of teaching effectiveness. Youngsters' boredom leads to restlessness and efforts to ease the boredom. A child may be bored because he has already mastered the learning or because he cannot relate to teaching that is too advanced for him. A major criterion of teaching effectiveness is pacing instruction to the learning rates of children. Clarity of instruction is important, too, and may be determined by analyzing the reactions of youngsters and by asking individual pupils to tell what they have learned. The teacher must provide individualized assistance for those who do not fit the instructional pattern. The extent to which a variety of teaching methods has been used is ascertained by comparing teaching units and daily lesson plans with resource units. In order to appraise instruction the teacher must focus on the role of teaching as facilitating learning, for responsibility for success in the classroom rests on imaginative teaching and not on dutiful learning. The emphasis is correctly placed when the success of the teacher is reflected in the learning efficiency of the youngsters. The classroom process is learning, not teaching.

conclusion

For some teachers the past, present, and evolving teaching procedures are challenges to what might be. These teachers are interested in furthering the art of teaching; they want to engage in classroom innovation and research. Innovation is informal experimentation with classroom procedures, educational structure, and subject matter content or organization. Any teacher may innovate and many do. Little more is required than to have an idea, to possess the means to try out the idea, and to gain some knowledge or impressions of the worth of the trial. Research, however, is a carefully structured process utilizing the scientific method to establish a truth. Research requires trained personnel, strict application of precise procedures, exact collection of data, and application of appropriate interpretive processes. Research procedures bring together scientific methodology and the art of teaching.

Research is divided into three basic types: experimental, historical, and survey. Experimental research may test the effectiveness of new educational structures, determine the results of curricular change, or derive new teaching tools and methods. Historical research produces a record of the past and aids in understanding the present. Survey research provides a picture of present practices, attitudes, and beliefs and contributes the essential information about where we actually are. Sometimes it is said that historical research tells what was, surveys tell what is, and experimental research suggests what may be. A special concern in education is "action research," a relatively informal type of investigation that is more akin to innovation than to research. Hopefully, research in education may contribute significantly to the science of learning and the development of new learning tools. It will not contribute as fruitfully to the less scientific and predictable aspects of human interaction in education, to the administrative-teacher structure, or to the art of teaching.

on your own

The heart of the educational process is learning, and the student of education will center his efforts on teaching techniques in special-methods classes and student-teaching experiences. The emphasis is usually directed toward the guidance of learning rather than the more mundane planning.

Textbooks on elementary methods and special secondary methods invariably include a section having to do with planning for instruction. Occasionally a special form is suggested for unit or daily lesson planning. The most logical planning form would seem to be that which is most natural to the individual teacher. A reasonable requirement is that any form of a plan should include an outline of content, specific learning objectives, particular teaching methods, plans for evaluation, and a time plan for instruction. The logic and techniques of planning to teach could be compared with any other form of purposeful activity and should be found to be basically similar. In addition to methods texts, students may refer to special texts for student-teaching experiences, such as Alex F. Perrodin, *The Student Teacher's Reader* (Chicago: Rand McNally, 1966); Lester D. Crow and Alice Crow, *The Student Teacher in the Secondary School* (New York: McKay, 1964); and Everett T. Keach, *Elementary School Student Teaching: A Casebook* (New York: Wiley, 1966). Standard references for structuring objectives are the two taxonomies noted in chapter 8: *Taxonomy of Educational Objectives, Handbook I: Cognitive Domain* and *Taxonomy of Educational Objectives, Handbook II: Affective Domain.*

Many universities have instructional resource centers where syllabi, courses of study, curriculum guides, and resource and teaching units are available for use and where textbook collections are maintained. State departments of education, professional organizations, and local school systems sponsor curriculum studies and publish syllabi, resource units, and teaching units. Some states are active in the structuring and restructuring of the curriculum; their state departments publish frequent and excellent curriculum guides. Many periodicals, some in special subject fields, such as *Social Education,* and others of general educational interest, such as *American Education,* include references to curriculum materials. Educational problems, including discipline and teaching techniques, are favorite topics for the educational writer and publisher. Whether the published product is sense or nonsense is for the individual reader to judge—there are plenty of both. *Education Index* is a useful reference to periodical articles.

There is no substitute for actually drawing up teaching plans to gain skill in structuring daily lessons. Observation of classroom teachers in action provides an opportunity to note execution of plans, to analyze lapses of attention for deficiencies of planning, and to observe incidents of incorrect pacing when a subject is left hanging at the end of a class period or concludes early so that youngsters are instructed to "take out your books and study."

The role of the teacher should be studied in terms of an individual's personality, strengths and weaknesses, and command of subject matter and teaching methods. The future teacher ought to plan the appropriate relationships that he will seek to establish with youngsters. He should determine how effectively he might work with other adults, such as teacher aides, and whether it would be advisable to seek positions in team-teaching roles. Periodical literature includes frequent discussions on innovations in teaching; books also are concerned with new structure and processes. A few examples of available references include Judson T. Shaplin and Henry F. Olds, Jr. (eds.), *Team Teaching* (New York: Harper & Row, 1964), and Medill Blair and Richard G. Woodward, *Team Teaching in Action* (Boston: Houghton Mifflin, 1964), both in the area of team teaching; and in the area of ungraded classes, B. Frank Brown's discussion of the program of the Melbourne (Fla.) High School, *The Ungraded High School* (Englewood Cliffs, N.J.: Prentice-Hall, 1963), and Frank R. Dufay's *Ungrading the Elementary School* (West Nyack, N.Y.: Parker, 1966). An important reference to the core curriculum is Roland C. Faunce and Nelson L. Bossing, *Developing the Core Curriculum,* 2nd ed. (Englewood Cliffs, N.J.: Prentice-Hall, 1958). A review of interpersonal relations in the classroom is *Classroom Group Behavior: Group Dynamics in Education* by Mary A. Bang and Lois V. Johnson (New York: Macmillan, 1964).

An excellent reference for evaluation in the classroom is J. Stanley Ahmann and Marvin D. Glock, *Evaluating Pupil Growth,* 3rd ed. (Boston: Allyn and Bacon, 1967). A highly useful, if less comprehensive, book is C. M. Lindvall, *Measuring Pupil Achievement and Aptitude* (New York: Harcourt, Brace & World, 1967), and a book even more centered in classroom test procedures is *Teacher-Made Tests* by John A. Green (New York: Harper & Row, 1963). Personally helpful to a teacher is Ray H. Simpson, *Teacher Self-Evaluation* (New York: Macmillan, 1966).

Those seeking to carve out a new frontier in teaching through research should become acquainted with the research activities of the National Education Association through the *NEA Research Bulletin* and with individual or institutional efforts through the *Review of Educational Research.* Less technical than some but satisfactory as a reference to research techniques is Carter V. Good's *Introduction to Educational Research: Methodology of Design in the Behavioral and Social Sciences,* 2nd ed. (New York: Appleton-Century-Crofts, 1963).

additional references

Alexander, William M., Vynce A. Hines, *et al. Independent Study in Secondary Schools.* New York: Holt, Rinehart and Winston,1968.

Allison, Mary L. (ed.). *New Educational Materials: Pre-Kindergarten Through Grade Twelve.* New York: Citation, 1967.

Anastasi, Anne (ed.). *Testing Problems in Perspective.* Washington, D.C.: American Council on Education, 1966.

Black, Hillel. *The American Schoolbook.* New York: Morrow, 1967.

Brown, James W., Richard B. Lewis, and Fred F. Harcleroad. *A-V Instruction: Materials and Methods.* 2nd ed. New York: McGraw-Hill, 1964.

Dale, Edgar. *Audio-Visual Methods in Teaching.* 2nd ed. New York: Holt, Rinehart and Winston, 1965.

Diamond, Robert M. *A Guide to Instructional Television.* New York: McGraw-Hill, 1964.

Erickson, Carlton W. H. *Fundamentals of Teaching with Audiovisual Technology.* New York: Macmillan, 1965.

Lange, Phil C. (ed.). *Programed Instruction.* Sixty-sixth Yearbook of the National Society for the Study of Education, Part II. Chicago: University of Chicago Press, 1967.

Rossi, Peter H., and Bruce J. Biddle (eds.). *The New Media and Education.* Garden City, N.Y.: Doubleday, 1967.

Saettler, Paul. *A History of Instructional Technology.* New York: McGraw-Hill, 1968.

Sax, Gilbert. *Empirical Foundations of Educational Research.* Englewood Cliffs, N.J.: Prentice-Hall, 1968.

Spache, George D. *Good Reading for Poor Readers.* Rev. ed. New York: Garrard, 1964.

Yates, Alfred (ed.). *Grouping in Education.* New York: Wiley, 1966.

9

the guidance of learning

Organizing instruction is the prelude to the heart of the educational process, teaching and learning. Effectiveness in the guidance of learning rests on the skills of organization; the quality of instruction depends on adequate organization and, in addition, successful execution. Thus, the teaching process constitutes the two distinctive processes of organization and guidance of learning. At the same time, it is also concerned with their fusion, for to view them as separate and distinct entities would lead to an artificial and arbitrary fragmentation of the learning process.

To guide learning effectively the teacher must be skillful in human interaction, knowledgeable in teaching methods and theories of learning, and abundantly informed about the ability, level of achievement, attitudes, values, and motivation of youngsters. Guidance suggests skills of human dynamics that evoke cooperation rather than impose coercion; it is aimed toward leading instead of dragging or pushing.

motivational techniques

Studies in the psychology of learning have centered attention on motivation as an important aspect in the teaching process. The teacher's concern for motivation is to have pupils engage in learning activities willingly and, if possible, enthusiastically. Youngsters are motivated to perform certain actions or to learn specific attitudes. The teacher aims for the formation of positive attitudes, particularly those toward oneself, school, classmates, a subject, and a teacher.

The nature of motivation has already been discussed in chapter seven: It is a psychological phenomenon, an internal force that leads to action. Since motivation is complex and reflects a compromise of many forces, the teacher and his ingenuity provide limited influences among a wide variety of others. When the incentives provided by the teacher are supported by those supplied by a youngster's family and peer group and by his own attitudes, needs, and values, the child finds it easy and comfortable to engage in classroom activities. When the teacher's expectations and assignments seem to impose values that are not shared by the pupil or may conflict with motivating forces that are more important than those of school, subject, or teacher, the youngster will not respond satisfactorily to teaching procedures. When motivating forces are mixed between those that support and others that conflict with classroom objectives, the youngster's reaction is unstable and unpredictable. He may respond to a strong pressure, such as fatigue, or vacillate between combinations that are temporarily supportive and temporarily neutral or in opposition.

If the teacher believes that motivation is environmental as well as personal, he will consider the classroom an important motivating factor. A room may be neat, clean, and sterile; it may be disarranged and confusing; or it may be a well-planned dynamic atmosphere where meaningful bulletin boards, displays, models, or projects add to the learning materials and activities. An exciting atmosphere is maintained when the classroom environment changes with instruction. A teacher should not keep one bulletin board on display for an extended period of time just because it is exceptionally attractive. The classroom environment should be planned for pupils and learning rather than for administrative visits or the next PTA meeting. In addition, the teacher is a most important aspect of the environment. A teacher's dress is important, but more significant factors are his personality and the interest and enthusiasm he shows for youngsters, teaching, and a subject.

providing incentives for motivation

The teacher does not motivate youngsters directly, for motivation is an indirect process. The teacher provides incentives for motivation as he structures a situation that meets the basic psychological needs of the students. Most incentives focus on rewards or punishments. Marks are rewards for some and punishment for others. A star on a paper, placement on an honor roll, displaying a pupil's assignment on the bulletin board, and excusing a pupil from some tasks, assignments, or a test are rewards and comprise positive incentives. Negative incentives usually carry a threat of redoing an assignment, working extra problems, standing in a corner, staying after school, or writing "I will do my homework" one hundred times. Youngsters' responses to both positive and negative incentives are directed toward the incentives rather than to the learning experience. It may be argued that youngsters' reasons for engaging in learning activities are of lesser concern than their actual participation, but the argument does not stand up well when examined in the context of theories of learning. For example, motivation is essential for learning and the way in which motivation is directed determines what is learned. The youngster who completed an assignment to avoid punishment has directed his energies toward conformist behavior rather than toward learning the lesson. He will develop substitutes for effective studying, such as copying someone else's homework or skimming through a chapter to select out phrases or bits of information to answer questions. He may learn something of the subject, but his major learning has been to perfect subterfuges, to unobtrusively avoid that which is least agreeable to him.

structuring the learning situation

The most effective motivation is centered about the way a teacher structures the learning situation. When a teacher relates learning to the youngsters' previous levels of achievement, orients instruction to meet pupil needs, and communicates a feeling of significance and relevance to school and a classroom, students will be able to relate to the instruction with understanding and a belief in the worth of the enterprise. While this may seem to be a simple process, it is extremely complex and is rarely realized in all of its facets.

The deceptively simple matter of relating instruction to previous school achievement is seldom accomplished in structured subjects like mathematics, reading, and languages. In these areas learning is dependent on the acquisition of elemental knowledge and skills, and all youngsters will not have realized the same level of achievement. Science, social studies, and literature depend on the use of reading skills and do not require equal mastery of previous subject matter. One may study American literature without first learning about British prose and poetry. Psychological needs of children are easier to meet than intellectual needs, whereas intellectual interests vary more than the general needs of acceptance, recognition, or approval. It may be difficult to demonstrate to every youngster the significance of instruction in grammar or the relevance of squaring binomials, but every teacher ought to be able to explain logically the significance and relevance of his instruction.

Suggestions that teaching problems are readily resolved by motivating students to learn and by engaging in interesting teaching tend to underestimate the complexity of motivation and the range in youngsters' interest patterns. A major problem for the teacher is to help the students establish constructive attitudes about themselves. Research has demonstrated the importance of the expectations that teachers place on the learning and behavior of pupils. In order to tailor instruction to youngsters and to provide adequate and realistic expectations of them, a teacher must have extensive information about the interests, abilities, achievement, attitudes, and other personal characteristics of each child. He should know the previous learning experiences of his pupils.

the textbook as a guide

The teacher understands youngsters and knows the curriculum in the school. He must also be an expert in the subjects he teaches, the methods available for instruction, and the materials that should or might be used. The most common teaching and learning tool is the textbook. While the textbook is not the oldest teaching technique and learning tool, it has been a major instrument in the formalized schooling of classroom instruction. The textbook is abused when it becomes the focal point of instruction and the major means for children to learn in school. The solution to instructional problems, however, is not to toss the textbook aside as no longer relevant to a teacher or inappropriate to a student. Realistically considered, a textbook is an important common resource and reference, but it should not become the sole or major tool in the school. Our terminology frequently includes references to "supplementing the textbook" when discussing extension of teaching methodology. The inference is that the basic teaching instrument is a book that every pupil uses and that the classroom process may extend beyond it.

A common practice is to assign a set number of pages in the textbook to an entire class. Additional tasks may be required, such as answering questions at the end of the chapter in the book or in a workbook. A previous day's assignment may be the subject of a recitation, which is followed by more assignments and recitations, until the entire process ends with a test. Teaching from a textbook is a group process that aims instruction at the middle youngster in the group. It fails to stimulate superior students and rapidly outruns the slow learner. The textbook technique is a means of "covering the material," which is a process of exposure to knowledge rather than an assurance that learning is taking place. The read-recite-test textbook method of teaching is unimaginative and sterile and hopelessly limited as a learning process.

Highly structured, program-type subjects may emphasize use of a text, especially since these courses call for individual instruction and eliminate much classroom group instruction. More ideational subjects, on the other hand, are adaptable to flexible instructional techniques, including group instruction. An accurate appraisal of the classroom suggests that most subjects include both structured and ideational content; they differ primarily in degree. English-language instruction, for example, includes highly structured subject matter (grammar) and less-structured content (literature).

There should be a reversal of the traditional emphasis on supplementing the textbook: it should be one tool in a flexible and imaginative learning experience. When the classroom is freed from dependence on the textbook as the center of instruction, the text may be supplemental and elastic. It is possible to use a common reference, a book, apart from a rigid group process. It is also possible for individuals to seek answers to their own questions from a text while operating at different speeds of instruction. Of course, as suggested previously, a youngster must have the appropriate reading skills in order to benefit from textbook instruction.

The way a teacher uses a textbook may depend on whether he participated in its selection and had an opportunity to project its utilization in relation to his own perception of teaching and learning. Thus, the teacher's competence and experience in teaching will influence the use made of a text. In addition, administrators make decisions that are reflected in the way a teacher conducts instruction and the extent to which he concentrates on a text. In this way, teachers who are assigned several daily preparations or many large classes and who have little or no assistance may center instruction on a textbook. Instructors who have limited preparation in their subject area or those who teach outside their areas of competence will also tend to rely heavily on the text.

The teacher should never assign so many pages a day in a textbook or a chapter a week. Reading assignments ought to be regulated by the content that may and should be learned within a reasonable period of time. Grouping procedures reduce the range of abilities in a class and a teacher may be able to ensure that every pupil meets a standard minimal level of achievement. Teachers of ungrouped classes, however, are faced with the unhappy realization that the class instructional pace will outrun the learning of some individuals. The teacher is often forced to accept the frustrating reality that he is not able to meet the various learning needs and problems of all pupils. He is confronted by the pressure of a burgeoning curriculum in a static schedule. He must answer the question, for example, of whether to "cover the material" assigned for the year's instruction, knowing that the teaching pace will reduce the effectiveness of instruction and the efficiency of learning, or to engage in a reasonable and productive rate of instruction, which may fail to meet all of the learning objectives.

teacher-centered techniques

Learning procedures may be centered in the person of the teacher or the pupil. When it is teacher-centered, learning activity is performed or controlled by the teacher. When domination of the classroom by the teacher means that appropriate goals are selected and exciting learning experiences are conducted, the teaching-learning process is facilitated. But when teacher-centeredness limits the scope and variety of learning procedures and results in an active teacher and passive pupils, learning is hindered.

THE LECTURE A traditional companion to the textbook and antedating it as a teaching technique is the lecture. A lecture may be defined as a sustained presentation by one person; it involves individual activity and group passivity. The lecturer, whether speaking from a church pulpit or classroom lectern, makes a presumptuous assumption if he believes that every member of a group is hanging on to his every word. Every teacher who has been concerned with the seeming inability of some youngsters to understand verbal instructions can attest to the difficulty of a one-sided communication.

In the "pure" lecture situation the speaker is the sole source of the information. The most common example is an individual describing a personal experience. The lecture method is also appropriate when the lecturer has expert and superior knowledge about a subject. A lecturer should not repeat material that is found readily in other sources. The lecturer should ensure that the field of knowledge is being enlarged by what he is saying. He must also be concerned with his speaking techniques; thus he must speak clearly, distinctly, and loud enough to be heard by all, and he should not use technical language that is beyond the capacity of his audience.

The lecture is not a particularly effective teaching tool, whether it is used in the second grade to describe a bird's nest or in the twelfth grade in a lesson on the merits of the Federal Reserve System. Lectures progress at the pace of the speaker rather than the pupil. There is no opportunity for a teacher or a pupil to go back for clarification. The attention of older students may be divided between listening to the speaker and making notes for further reference. The lecturer gains no automatic feedback from the class and has little opportunity to measure the effectiveness of the procedure. A lecture is improved as a learning tool with the use of films, slides, exhibits, or other pictorial devices by which visual as well as auditory senses come into play.

In preparing a lecture the teacher should clearly define his objectives. A lecture is not appropriate unless it can contribute something unique to the classroom. This is true of any teaching technique. A teacher's purpose in lecturing is to give instructions, clarify an issue, share a pertinent personal experience, or utilize his expertise to expand knowledge beyond other readily available resources. A lecture as a sustained presentation by one individual is dependent for its effectiveness on the voice and speaking techniques of the lecturer, his vocabulary and clarity of expression, and the interest of his listeners in the subject.

The stereotype of classroom lecturing is the college professor reading from ancient and yellowed sheets of paper. Reading a prepared lecture to the unselected mass of elementary or secondary youngsters requires exceptional speaking talents. Although a prepared lecture may ensure the appropriateness of the content, the average classroom teacher can function as effectively from a well-organized outline. It is advisable to break a lecture with class discussion in order to initiate the necessary feedback so that understanding may be evaluated and the teacher may reiterate or emphasize aspects that are unclear.

RECITATION Only slightly less teacher-centered than the lecture, recitation is a successive question-answer procedure reviewing previous learnings. Recitation that depends on volunteering of answers by pupils may be dominated by a relatively limited group of youngsters. Another procedure is for the teacher to call on youngsters at random as the whole class tensely awaits the unknown question and victim. A ripple of tension may also follow a teacher as he proceeds through the class in alphabetical order or across the room by rows.

Recitation is very time-consuming and adds little to the learning process. It may encourage youngsters to study, yet there is little opportunity to evaluate how well the class has mastered an assignment. A teacher does not know, for example, whether one youngster answered the only question he knew or another pupil missed the only question he did not know. There is also little evidence to suggest that other youngsters benefit significantly from the answers of classmates. A "perfect" recitation would find every youngster answering every question: Presumably, every pupil would know every answer and the recitation would then be superfluous as a learning experience.

In preparing for a recitation, a teacher selects those facts, interpretations, or understandings that he considers of major importance in the lesson. A list may then be made of the questions. It has been pointed out that there are several ways in which the questions may be posed to a class. Each procedure, of course, has its own problems and advantages.

DISCUSSION While the lecture may be satisfactory as a learning experience and the recitation questionably so, a well-conducted discussion can be rich in learning outcomes. Classroom discussion is a structured process leading from a common base of information through a carefully guided succession of responses to a new learning experience. In contrast to the lecture and the recitation, discussion is an activity centered in the learner, guided by the teacher, and dependent on the group for spontaneous response to an evolving process. It is essential for an effective discussion that every member of the class will have experienced a common activity, such as a field trip, film, lecture, or reading assignment.

Discussion may be described as a mechanical process. It

involves a structured procedure and three previously determined aspects—a common base of information, the final learning goal, and the first question that leads from the common base toward the objective. Discussion is not a random, disorganized bull session; it is a learning process carefully shepherded by a teacher and is purposeful and regulated. The first question relates to the common base; the next and subsequent questions relate to the previous answer given and cannot be preplanned. In regulating the course of a discussion, the teacher initiates interaction, permits interplay within the class, steps in to redirect the procedure or to pick up a break in the progression, and concludes the discussion when the goal is reached. Occasionally a group or individual will pursue a tangent that leads away from the teacher's goal. A tangent may be followed if it is judged to be as valuable a learning experience as that originally planned, or it may be terminated by repeating or rephrasing the question that led to it in the first place.

Discussion is a particularly useful technique for deriving generalizations, developing attitudes, and drawing conclusions. It may facilitate certain kinds of appreciation better than any other method. For example, a discussion in a class in American history may lead to an understanding of the questions that faced a young person about to leave home and family in Europe to emigrate to a strange, unknown United States. Discussion is not a suitable technique for introducing new factual material, but it is ideal for the extended use of previously learned facts. A group discussion can be an exciting experience: It may find every youngster actively engaging in the process, mentally if not verbally. The interest and enthusiasm that are characteristic of a particularly satisfactory discussion may lower inhibitions and more introvertive pupils may become active participants. A good discussion can edge up the noise level, but it most importantly raises the interest and participation level and results in significant and satisfying learning. Primary limits to the use of discussion are the skill with which a teacher can lead the mechanical process, the inadvisability of operating without a common base, and the selected kinds of learning appropriate to discussion.

pupil-centered techniques

When learning activity becomes centered in the learner, the role of the teacher becomes very complex as he must supervise several activities at once. The task of the learner is also more complicated, for the pupil must have some skills and an independence of action that are not needed when the teacher dominates and directs the learning. The benefit, however, is in more effective learning and greater satisfaction for students.

THE PROJECT METHOD Unlike teacher-centered lecturing and teacher-conducted discussion, the project method centers activity in the learners. A project is a structured learning experience carried out by an individual or group, with the activity culminating in some form of measurable product. The range of activities is nearly inexhaustible, from murals, models, and skits to laboratory experiments, historical research, and the compiling of booklets. Project activities are excellent opportunities to engage in teacher-pupil planning. Projects require more (not less) organization and more (not less) supervision by the teacher. The teacher should ascertain that each individual understands what is expected, that youngsters have or will have the necessary tools and skills, and that materials or references are available. The teacher must often provide many of the materials, including paint, paper, tape recorders, and so on. The teacher is the consultant; he is the expert who knows where to get things, how to do things, or what further references are available to answer questions.

The richest learning experiences often result from individual students pursuing unique tasks, each performing at his own pace. Dependent on the teacher for guidance and support, the student is secure in the knowledge that whatever the outcome it is his own. Individual projects are useful, for each youngster may be evaluated as an individual and not on his placement in a group. The teacher who is shepherding thirty individuals and their projects has the greatest individual project of anyone—that is, the most comprehensive planning, and the most difficult problem of evaluation.

A recent emphasis upon individual projects, especially under the influence of team teaching and other innovations in instructional organization, is a concern for individual study. The rather informal, incidental, or occasional individual project has become a formal and systematic procedure. Independent study programs that permit acceleration of superior students may also be regarded as a means of engendering interest and success by average or slow pupils. Some programs are reserved for an "honors program," while others are an exercise assigned to all students. Individual study demands special competencies of teachers. Like other innovations, however, individual study programs sometimes tend to become ends in themselves rather than means to the facilitation of learning.

Individual projects challenge and service the individual, while group projects serve social objectives. Small groups may be organized into committees. The instructor, however, cannot retire, correct a mountain of papers, and expect the committees to operate automatically as a form of human learning machine. His first responsibility is to ensure that the pupils understand committee techniques, the duties and responsibilities of cooperative planning, and the responsibilities of leadership and followership. A frequent shoal upon which classroom committees flounder is the unwarranted assumption that pupils understand a process when they do not, with the result that when the classroom explodes, the blame is placed on the technique. There can be no uncertainty about whether members of a group understand the committee process; the teacher must know that they do. It should be a general axiom that youngsters need to be instructed in learning techniques before they can be expected to use the methods as learning procedures.

Essential to successful committee operation is the means that is used to select the members of a committee. Committee membership may be selected from class volunteers, from the seating arrangement or an alphabetical list, or by chance. The teacher should recognize the type of group process that evolves from each method of selection. A committee made up of friends does not improve the broader group process. On the other hand, arbitrary selection by seating or alphabetical grouping from the class book may create unnecessary problems by forcing together youngsters with personality conflicts. A teacher may aid the classroom social process by matching strong and weak personalities and extroverts and introverts. A teacher ought to use a variety of means for selecting committees in the expectation that the various groupings will serve different learning and social purposes. In the long run it is possible to serve both individual and group needs, those youngsters secure in the center of the social process and those isolated from it, the introvert and the extrovert, and the skillful scholar and the slow learner. Adequate planning is required to serve a wide variety of youngsters and the broad purposes of the school.

THE FIELD TRIP Of all teaching techniques, the field trip is probably the most effective. There are few subjects that cannot profit from a visit to the city hall, nearest museum, local newspaper, factory, or bank. It is more pertinent to visit the fire station, interview the labor union leader, or witness the printing of a newspaper than to read about it. Few schools make effective use of the field trip even though it is more reasonable to have classes visit the police chief, for example, than to expect him to visit innumerable classrooms. There is no substitute for field trips. Many of them ought to be a part of every youngster's experience.

The two major reasons given for the limited use of the field trip are the time involved in making a trip and the difficulties in arranging transportation. Neither argument weighs very heavily against that of the increased efficiency of learning which results from personal experience. Another problem cited is the legal responsibility of the schools for accidents. Yet this argument does not inhibit an active physical education program with its attendant bruises, an industrial arts program with the occasional hammered thumb, or the daily busing of students to and from school. Insurance that covers school accidents may be extended to field trips. Still another problem is said to be the difficulty in controlling groups of youngsters, but this problem may be related to excitement and lack of experience when learning trips are infrequent and unusual. There is no satisfactory reason for failure to provide adequate supervision for any group in or out of school. Perhaps the chief reason why teachers do not use the field trip adequately is the failure of school administrators to reduce unnecessary red tape, facilitate scheduling problems in the secondary school, and provide ready transportation. A slight switch in thinking from obstacles to means is often all that is required to make use of complicated but effective teaching techniques.

instructional devices and media

The superior teacher knows the many instructional devices that are available to the classroom and uses them with confidence. Dynamic and stimulating teaching emphasizes a variety of methods and techniques, not for the purpose of entertaining pupils but because any youngster may learn more efficiently when he experiences different learning methods and because different youngsters achieve the same learnings in different ways. When it is appropriate and possible, pupils should personally experience learnings as well as read or hear about them or see them in movies or on television. There is seldom just one way to learn. One technique is rarely sufficient for an individual or a group. Many teaching tools are included under the general category audio-visual or multimedia techniques.

THE CHALKBOARD The chalkboard is the veteran among audio-visual tools. The major advantage of the chalkboard is its convenience to the entire group, the ease with which it may be used for spontaneous writing or drawing, and its quick erasure. A major disadvantage is the tendency to center teaching in front of the chalkboard and to perpetuate a rigid, formalized, lecture-type atmosphere. Arithmetic and mathematics teachers make use of the chalkboard for student learning activities; other teachers ought to do more of the same. More recent extensions of the same general technique are the flannel board and magnetic board, each of which requires special, previously prepared materials. Although many schools have been slow to utilize these special boards, they have been eagerly adopted by industry for training or sales purposes. A suitable substitute for the chalkboard is the use of sheets of paper or tag board on which lessons are drawn with a felt-tipped marker. Often set up as flip sheets, the papers may be moved about a room and used to instruct small groups. Flip sheets may avoid the formal arrangement that is typical when the chalkboard is used.

OVERHEAD AND OPAQUE PROJECTORS The most recent adaptation of the chalkboard is the overhead projector, which projects images from sheet transparencies onto a screen. Using a grease pencil, a teacher may utilize an overhead projector in the same way he would utilize a chalkboard: he may draw, write, or erase as needed. The teacher faces the class when using the overhead projector. In addition to its use as a substitute chalkboard, a wide variety of transparencies may be projected through the overhead. Various photocopy techniques make it possible to reproduce materials from books or other sources for overhead projection. Colored transparencies may also be used. A succession of transparencies, called overlays, are effective in illustrating complex concepts or developing representations.

Extraordinary effects can be achieved by using polarized lenses with the overhead projector. The average teacher should be able to make extensive use of overhead projection in imaginative and stimulating teaching. Some schools provide professional help in making transparencies. There are, in addition, many commercial materials available to the schools for overhead projection.

An old veteran among projective tools is the opaque projector. Any opaque materials—papers, pictures, or pages in a book—may be projected onto a screen. The opaque requires a darker room than the overhead projector. An opaque projector can be used to make enlarged copies of maps or charts. In one instance, it proved to be a quick and painless way to make an eight-foot Santa. Some older opaque projectors generate excessive heat and a teacher should take care to protect materials against damage. Nevertheless, the opaque projector is still a valuable tool in the classroom.

STILL PICTURES The still picture is an important teaching device. It is useful in establishing a stimulating classroom atmosphere. If a teacher were to realize nothing more from the use of still pictures than a dynamic learning environment, the effort required to build a still-picture file would be well rewarded. Whether or not a picture is "worth a thousand words," visual presentation has long been accepted as an effective learning tool. A rich file of mounted pictures should ensure frequently changed displays in a dynamic classroom. Indeed every room ought to have a bulletin board which is changed regularly every week. A bulletin board is an opportunity for teacher-pupil planning or a challenge to youngsters to find means of expression and an outlet for their energies.

Other pictorial tools include charts, graphs, time lines, and maps, which are aimed at the serious business of learning rather than the luxury of promoting an atmosphere. However, the teacher must be sure that pupils can read and use these tools with understanding. The visual shortcut that may be available through the use of still graphics may prove a confused detour without the development of special reading and interpretive skills. Charts, graphs, time lines, and maps are each complicated representations of complex concepts. The difficulty, for example, of projecting graphic representations of land forms from a round surface to a flat one is an involved procedure, as evidenced by the various forms of map projection that attempt to resolve the contradiction. Still, even though it is an imperfect representation and may be difficult to read and interpret, the map is an indispensable learning tool.

SPECIMENS AND MODELS There are many opportunities in the classroom to use specimens and still other instances in which models ought to be used. Most subjects lend themselves to the use of models, and there are many commercially produced, high quality products available to teachers. Globes, models of the human ear, representations of atomic structure, geometric forms, and so forth, are on the market. Imaginative use of materials and the talent of youngsters should result in the addition of many homemade models and mock-ups for instructional purposes. In certain instances models for the classroom may not be available and have to be made locally. A class, for example, may build a model of the local community as it was in pioneer days or create representations of immediate geographical or geological features. Some projects may be combined with field trips and involve several subject areas. Social studies, sciences, art, and industrial arts may be combined easily for instructional purposes.

FILMSTRIP AND FILM PROJECTORS Another early projective technique was the lantern slide, which is now replaced by slide and filmstrip projectors. Slide projectors provide flexibility for the teacher who is an amateur photographer and who may add local and familiar or personal slides to the classroom collection. Commercially produced filmstrips are also available for use in the classroom. Filmstrips are easily stored, are simple in operation, and retain their sequence. Commercial filmstrips may use drawings as well as photographs. Some filmstrips are coordinated with a record or a taped explanation, usually punctuated by a "ping" when the next frame is to be shown. Some firms permit previewing of filmstrips prior to purchase, a method that increases the likelihood that those which are purchased will be suitable to the teacher and his subject. Purchase of instructional materials without an opportunity to examine them is a questionable practice, although many commercial firms are able to sell educational materials to schools even though they withhold the right of preview or examination. It might be speculated that unexamined purchases of educational materials serve to encourage the production of unnecessary and irrelevant materials and reduce the effectiveness of all teaching materials in the classroom.

Movies are by now well-established tools in the classroom,

although there is confusion among both teachers and pupils whether they are classed as education or entertainment. Part of the confusion results from the difficulty of incorporating films naturally into the classroom procedure. Frequently the convulsion required to move a class to an auditorium or a basement "theater" is not worth the effort it takes to view a fifteen-minute movie. A hopeful innovation is the cartridge-loading eight-millimeter film projection unit. The first cartridges were small and the film segments short, but with the development of larger cartridges and the addition of sound to the units, film cartridges will be useful to the teacher and classroom.

Film cartridges reduce one problem of the usual film program, the cost of sixteen-millimeter movies. Because of money shortages few school systems are able to maintain their own film library. Most films are rented and must be ordered early in the spring for showing the following school year, a fact that creates an impossible demand on scheduling. Many teachers are thus caught between the choice of basing the pace of instruction upon a film schedule or taking films as they come, regardless of the immediate content of instruction. Eventually some movies will be shown through television sets, and with the use of cartridges for frequently used films many of the problems in the use of movies will be resolved.

Audio-visual specialists have developed theories about the use of audio-visual tools. They have established as a clue to the effectiveness of a technique as a learning device the degree to which it approximates personal experience. However, criteria for selection of techniques may depend on practical matters in addition to the theoretical. There is the question of which resources are available to a teacher. Most schools have film and filmstrip projectors and a usable opaque projector. Projection screens are also available, although every room may not be equipped with a screen and movies may be scheduled in a "movie room." The difficulty of obtaining films to match classroom instruction was mentioned previously. Teachers may be forced to plan the use of instructional tools around what is available and convenient rather than what is preferred.

The first demand on the teacher who wishes to provide flexible and exciting learning is to inventory the resources available to him. This requires a thorough review of ordinary procedures and resources in the school and may suggest wandering through storage spaces where materials that were discarded once may find a new use. The community should be scoured to locate field trip possibilities and to make incidental use of commercial products or advertising materials: A drugstore's cast-off displays may provide materials for health or science units. Insurance agents may be helpful, for some of them represent companies that have published excellent educational materials. Commercial trash may provide instructional materials for art, science, or industrial arts. Every teacher should be acquainted with educational film and tape catalogs and published sources of free and inexpensive classroom materials; he should be supplementing the teaching tool chest through the mails.

Not only is the audio-visual area one to which the teacher may turn in selecting satisfying and challenging creative activities, but many audio-visual techniques provide opportunities to engage youngsters in productive efforts—making instructional materials or operating audio-visual equipment. Many teachers maintain files of still pictures that have been collected from magazine articles and advertisements. Newspaper front pages that record major historical and scientific developments are useful visual materials. Magazine articles provide the substance for a homemade reference library in many subject areas. A teacher who collects and uses his own materials will find that youngsters may become alerted to the possibility of classroom use of graphic or written materials. It is the perfectionist and shortsighted teacher who must personally set up or closely supervise every bulletin board display or other class-produced learning device. A little less "professional" work by a group of interested and eager youngsters may not be as pleasing to the critical eye, but more important benefits will be derived from the satisfactions and feelings of achievement of the pupils.

An opaque projector and a felt-tip pen can make available more charts, time lines, maps, and other graphic representations from anything that will fit into the projector. For more sophisticated or older youngsters, class-made slides and even filmstrips are possible and some schools have experienced success with projects in which pupils have written, directed, and filmed presentations. On an individual or group basis, youngsters can produce imaginative and creative models, murals, and representations.

EDUCATIONAL TELEVISION IN THE CLASSROOM The promise of educational television in the classroom is exciting to most youngsters and many teachers. Adaptation of television to the educational process has been slow and painful and the eventual outcome is still in doubt. Television instruction has been brought into the classroom through commercial stations, by exclusively educational stations, through cables in closed-circuit systems, and by airborne transmission in several Midwest states. To further increase the use of television in the classroom, efforts are being expended toward the transmission of educational television through a national space satellite system. There are some things that television may do uniquely: It may place the mass public at Presidential inaugurations or a space flight. It can be used to show a film to many classrooms at the same time or to increase the number of pupils who may benefit from live instruction of a particularly skillful teacher. On the other hand, there are some things television cannot do: It cannot provide personal experience and has little or no role to play in individualized instruction.

Some teachers react negatively and defensively to educational television, but one may imagine a similar reaction to the revolutionary challenges that were posed by the printing press or the first lantern slides. A teacher's attitude toward television in the classroom should be the same as that toward other teaching techniques, a determination to exploit the method to the fullest to further the learning process.

Some teachers resent the demands that television instruction places upon them. Televised science lessons sometimes suggest the need for class experiments and demonstrations or field trips, and the teacher may react negatively to these extensions of his instruction imposed by a vague figure on a cathode tube. A teacher's attitude is a reflection of his perspective. It is as logical to react positively toward the outside help of a science instructor as it is to react negatively to the relatively small demands that instruction might make on the classroom teacher. The teacher has an essential role to play in the use of television in the classroom. Without the active involvement of the classroom teacher, the potential of educational television in the school can never be realized.

Instruction through local educational television systems is a joint effort between classroom teachers and the television studio. Communication is sought between the classroom and the studio in an effort to adapt transmission to the classroom and classroom processes to studio technique. Emphasis is placed on the preparations that teachers make in the classroom to introduce youngsters to the televised lesson. The remote televised program does assume direction of a course of study, but this is also true of the remote textbook writer. The competent teacher is able to adjust televised instruction or a text to the needs of his class and individual pupils.

Televised instruction that serves supplemental or enrichment purposes in the classroom does not present unusual problems to the teacher. The teacher's role is to prepare youngsters for the experience and to summarize and incorporate the lesson into the total learning process. Total television teaching, however, such as instruction in a foreign language, is a new situation for many teachers. The elementary teacher may look on a televised French lesson in the same manner that he considers instruction of his pupils by specialists in music, art, or physical education. The substitution of a television set for the presence of a teacher, however, does pose two special problems in the instruction: the inability of the television instructor to assess the process and the matter of physical supervision of the lesson. The classroom teacher must therefore serve as the local eyes and ears of the television instructor. A teacher's comments on pupil reaction and suggestions about the effectiveness of teaching methods will permit the television teacher to make clarifications or alter procedures. The classroom teacher must oversee the learning procedure. If fourth-graders in a French lesson on pronunciation do not repeat the sounds at the direction of the television instructor, correct pronunciation will not be learned. The concerned teacher joins the class in learning French while he also supervises, encourages, and motivates his pupils.

RADIO AND RECORDING DEVICES Some use is made of radio as a school device, but it could be used more extensively. Those television lessons that fail to make effective use of the visual medium could be transmitted by radio. Some states or regions provide educational radio for the classroom, and teachers within range of stations serving these programs may elect to make use of broadcast lessons. Occasionally, local happenings of importance to a community are broadcast but not televised. A record player is also suitable for the classroom, although many of its uses have been taken over by the more versatile tape recorder. A teacher can record important broadcasts and build his own file of tapes for the classroom. A class can record its own version of the Constitutional Convention or the correct procedures for a job interview. Just as there are film libraries there are tape libraries that provide copies of tapes for classroom purposes for a reasonable fee. This service is rendered by commercial concerns and selected universities.

PROGRAMMED INSTRUCTION Most teaching tools may be classified as traditional or contemporary, but those who would seek a window on the future should acquaint themselves with programmed instruction and the computerized classroom. Programs are organized so that they require special holders, called teaching machines, and are printed in book form. The youngster who uses a teaching machine must be taught to move the program one frame at a time, record an answer, check against the answer given by the program, and continue to the next frame. Pupils who use a programmed text must follow instructions closely. A linear program in book form is organized to be read horizontally one frame at a time from page to page. A branching program poses a problem and offers multiple-choice answers. The pupil selects an answer and is referred to a page where the program is continued by an explanation or another problem. It is the responsibility of the teacher to select an appropriate program for each youngster, to assure that every individual is able to use the program, to supervise the program in use, and periodically to evaluate the learning.

In selecting instructional programs teachers should know that every subject does not lend itself to programming, even though programs are being published for most subjects. Highly structured subjects such as mathematics are the most logically programmed. Some topics in other subjects lend themselves to a careful structuring, but much of social studies and perhaps all of literature are inappropriate to a program. Even in subjects that are appropriately programmed, some programs are poorly written, fail to follow the need for short and logical sequences, or use inappropriate vocabulary. The teacher must select programs that are suitable to a subject matter, are well constructed, and are appropriate to a pupil's reading level. Programs are dependent on reading ability and the teacher must select programs that meet the reading abilities of individual students.

A teacher must know enough about a class so that supervisory time may be allotted properly, with the self-reliant pupils more on their own and the more dependent youngsters guided and supported. The use of programs and the individualization of instruction require that a teacher plan ahead so that when a fast learner completes one program he may move into the next level of instruction. One difficulty in using programmed instruction is the unwillingness on the part of teachers and administrators to accept the consequences of individualized instruction. It is an exercise in futility to permit a youngster to accelerate his learning and then make him wait for the class to catch up before moving into more advanced levels of instruction.

THE COMPUTERIZED CLASSROOM The computerized classroom is the extension of programming beyond the teaching machine and programmed text, with a learning sequence programmed into a computer. The pupil uses a typewriter or electronic panel to receive the program and to react to it. A computerized classroom will change the role of the teacher, for the computer will take over much of the process of guiding instruction. The teacher should be relieved of many clerical routines that now haunt the classroom. He may become a roving consultant and tutor during computerized learning situations. However, some aspects of nonprogrammed instruction will still be left to the skill of teachers. There never will be a machine or device that may satisfactorily substitute for the essential personal and human interaction that is the unique contribution a teacher makes to a classroom.

THE LIBRARY Hopefully every teacher will find a comprehensive library available in the school. In addition, a teacher may build a relatively inexpensive classroom library through purchase of paperback books. The library is an essential resource for a satisfactory reading-instruction program, but teachers should use the library for other supplementary instructional materials. The best place to learn about library skills and usage is in the library. Librarians will accumulate references on special topics for use in the classroom. Pupils may go to the library, and library references may be brought to the classroom. When both techniques are used, a teacher will have delegated responsibility to youngsters and given them an opportunity to develop individual reference skills, and he will have ensured that proper and abundant resources were available for use under supervision in the classroom.

Youngsters need help and guidance in the selection and organization of library materials and in learning to use several references rather than to rely on a single source. Within the framework of a cooperative relationship between teacher and librarian, the basic responsibility for teaching library and reference skills remains with the teacher, while the librarian is a ready and invaluable supplemental-resource person. This is not to deny the teaching services performed by librarians, but when library activities are initiated in the classroom and fulfilled there the teacher is in control of objectives, methods, and evaluation. The teacher has an obligation to supervise and guide his pupils in the use of the library. The library should not become a convenient place to "get rid" of youngsters. It is an essential learning tool.

innovations in instructional organization

The traditional role of the teacher to close a door and shut out the world from the classroom has been altered by certain organizational changes in the school. A familiar classroom procedure is the core curriculum, which requires that the teacher organize instruction so that two or more subject areas —commonly social studies and English—are joined in instruction. Some proponents of the core insist that the curriculum must be geared to the expressed interests of pupils. While the core idea tends to blur departmental lines in the secondary school, the opposite trend has come to the elementary school, where plans such as dual progress departmentalize the elementary grades. In some elementary schools classes are departmentalized in some of the instruction when two teachers are paired so that one will teach science and the other social studies to the two classes. The idea of the self-contained classroom and complete control of the elementary teacher over instruction has been altered to a situation in which the teacher is relieved of part of the traditional instructional pattern and assumes more responsibility in another area. Among the important ideas set aside by departmentalizing the elementary grades is the belief that the young child needs the security of identifying with a single adult in a secure and familiar classroom.

One way of organizing schools is through the ungraded classroom. Ungraded classes tend toward departmentalized instruction. Youngsters of differing ages are placed into instructional groups according to their ability and achievement. While there are no strict limits to the extent of ungraded instruction, the usual pattern is to group youngsters across two or three age levels. When instruction is departmentalized the teacher must adjust to larger numbers of youngsters in the total instructional day. In some ungraded classes a teacher may expect to have some youngsters for two or three years. As the older youngsters leave every year and younger ones take their place, group characteristics change. Multi-age groups exaggerate the variability of youngsters in a class in physical, social, and emotional development.

Perhaps the most drastic change of functions in the traditional classroom is the placing of the teacher in a cooperative relationship with another adult. One such innovation is use of a teacher aide, a relatively untrained adult whose major responsibilities are to relieve the teacher of clerical tasks and to assist in classroom routine. The teacher should acquaint the teacher aide with the noninstructional routines that are to be performed. Particular emphasis should be placed on those minor details that a teacher may logically delegate to someone else. The teacher aide becomes an additional factor in planning for instruction, for a determination must be made with reference to the classroom activities that may be assigned to the aide. A teacher must take care neither to exploit the teacher aide nor to reduce the quality of instruction by delegating unsuitable responsibilities to the assistant. An innovation that is similar to use of the teacher aide is the special instance where individuals outside the school are hired to correct compositions for instructors of English. The English teacher must standardize correcting procedures so that they will be equivalent to those in effect in the classroom.

A complex classroom relationship is found in some team teaching programs where there is a team leader, several teachers, and several aides. Team teaching calls for the greatest flexibility of a teacher who may work with large and small groups and instruct youngsters individually. Team teaching permits a teacher to become a specialist in method as well as in a subject. The multiple relationships between the teacher and pupil, parent, and administrator, and between a team leader and team teachers and teaching aides require that special attention be given to the call for special levels and types of interaction. Complex relationships in the school impose additional responsibilities on school administration and leadership.

conclusion

The teacher has an impressive array of teaching methods and tools to facilitate the guidance of instruction. He must become well acquainted with the differing possibilities in which any learning experience may be conducted. Success in teaching and learning is not solely or even primarily dependent on teaching methods or tools that are or may be available to a teacher. A teacher who must prepare for an excessive number of lessons, who faces unreasonable numbers of youngsters, or whose pupils share inordinate learning or social or emotional-psychological problems cannot effectively utilize teaching methods or tools. A curriculum that constantly increases its expectations of the classroom without making the necessary adjustments for the realization of those expectations renders the teaching toolchest relatively ineffective. Administrative decisions may involve the teacher in noninstructional tasks that conflict with the organizing and guiding of instruction. Budgetary restrictions limit the number and extent of materials or staff necessary to facilitate instruction. Unnecessarily restrictive policies and rules limit the kind and scope of classroom experiences, especially when administered by an unresponsive and unimaginative educational bureaucracy.

The school does not need a "teacher-proof curriculum" as much as it requires the guarantee of a reasonable opportunity for every teacher to be successful in the classroom. Until such assurances are forthcoming, the teacher must exploit his situation to offer his classes the broadest range of methods and variety of teaching tools he may muster. Guiding of instruction, which is the core of the teaching-learning process, is a difficult and demanding job. There is no method or technique that may ease the demands for exhaustive efforts by the competent teacher. The great benefit from the use of a wealth of methods and techniques is increased efficiency of learning and the assurance that a permanent and significant contribution has been made to society and to the future.

The teacher should exert his influence toward accelerating the educational evolution or revolution that will extend the effectiveness of his teaching. He should accept the role of educating administrators, parents, and the public in the needs of the classroom and he should participate in those educational organizations that seek to mold the schools of the future.

on your own

In pursuing information about teaching methods, the major references ought to be special methods textbooks. Periodicals are important sources of shared experiences: There are *The Grade Teacher* and *The Instructor* for elementary grades; and *Journal of Secondary Education, High School Journal, Clear-*

ing House, and various journals of special subject organizations for secondary teachers. Social studies teachers may refer to the *How To Do It* series of the National Council for the Social Studies. Many other subject areas are similarly active in providing information for the classroom.

From a variety of references available, one might suggest Robert E. DeKieffer's *Audiovisual Instruction* (New York: The Center for Applied Research in Education, 1965) and Jerrold E. Kemp's *Planning and Producing Audiovisual Materials* (San Francisco: Chandler, 1963), and from among pertinent periodicals, *Audiovisual Instruction.* In addition, Robert M. Diamond's *A Guide to Instructional Television* (New York: McGraw-Hill, 1964) may be of special interest or, in the area of programmed instruction, Karl U. Smith and Margaret Foltz Smith's *Cybernetic Principles of Learning and Educational Design* (New York: Holt, Rinehart and Winston, 1966) and J. L. Hughes' *Programed Instruction for Schools and Industry* (Chicago: Science Research Associates, 1962). Among periodicals available is *Programmed Instruction.* Particularly useful are specially prepared references, such as *A Bibliography: Selected Reading on Programed Learning* (Albany, N.Y.: The State Department of Education, 1963). The computerized classroom is of very recent concern: A useful introduction is John I. Goodlad, John F. O'Toole, Jr., and Louise L. Tyler's *Computers and Information Systems in Education* (New York: Harcourt, Brace & World, 1966).

The heart of the teaching process, educational methodology, is a lifetime challenge to the career teacher. An introduction may be made to a study of classroom teaching by reminiscing about one's own classroom experiences through the grades. The exciting classrooms and teachers may provide suggestions for successful teaching. Students may analyze the classes they attend. They should observe elementary or high school classes in action and must become students of the process of education.

additional references

American Council on Industrial Arts Teacher Education. *Approaches and Procedures in Industrial Arts.* Fourteenth Yearbook. New York: McKnight, 1965.

Association for Supervision and Curriculum Development. *Individualizing Instruction.* Washington, D.C.: the Association, National Education Association, 1964.

Biological Sciences Curriculum Study. *Biology Teachers' Handbook.* New York: Wiley, 1963.
Bond, Guy L., and Eva Bond Wagner. *Teaching the Child to Read.* 4th ed. New York: Macmillan, 1966.
Chemical Education Material Study. *Chemistry: An Experimental Science.* San Francisco: Freeman, 1963.
Cornfield, Ruth R. *Foreign Language Instruction, Dimensions and Horizons.* New York: Appleton-Century-Crofts, 1966.
Crank, Doris H., and Floyd L. Crank (eds.). *New Perspectives in Education for Business.* Yearbook of the National Business Education Association. Washington, D.C.: the Association, National Education Association, 1963.
Ecroyd, Donald H. *Speech in the Classroom.* Englewood Cliffs, N.J.: Prentice-Hall, 1960.
Fenton, Edwin. *Teaching the New Social Studies in Secondary Schools: An Inductive Approach.* New York: Holt, Rinehart and Winston, 1966.
Francis, W. Nelson. *The English Language: An Introduction.* New York: Norton, 1965.
Gans, Roma. *Common Sense in Teaching Reading.* Indianapolis: Bobbs-Merrill, 1963.
Glaser, Robert (ed.). *Teaching Machines and Programed Learning, II; Data and Directions.* Washington, D.C.: Department of Audiovisual Instruction, National Education Association, 1965.
Hatcher, Hazel M., and Mildred E. Andrews. *The Teaching of Home Economics.* Boston: Houghton Mifflin, 1963.
Heller, R. L. (ed.). *Geology and Earth Science Sourcebook.* American Geological Institute. New York: Holt, Rinehart and Winston, 1962.
Jarolimek, John. *Social Studies in Elementary Education.* New York: Macmillan, 1967.
Kaufman, Irving. *Art and Education in Contemporary Culture.* New York: Macmillan, 1966.
Kowall, Bonnie C. *Perspectives in Music Education.* Source Book III. Washington, D.C.: Music Educators National Conference, National Education Association, 1966.
Peterson, John A., and Joseph Hashisaki. *Theory of Arithmetic.* 2nd ed. New York: Wiley, 1967.
Physical Science Study Committee. *Physics.* 2nd ed. Boston: Heath, 1965.
Thomas, George, and Joseph Crescimbeni. *Individualizing Instruction in the Elementary School.* New York: Random House, 1967.
Van Til, William, Gordon F. Vars, and John H. Lounsbury. *Modern Education for the Junior High School Years.* 2nd ed. Indianapolis: Bobbs-Merrill, 1967.

10

The duty of a teacher is to teach. With that trite phrase few will argue. Yet it is the noninstructional "tail" that "wags the dog." George W. Denemark phrased it bluntly and realistically:

> The job of today's teacher has become virtually unmanageable. Unless something is done to remedy the situation, creative, competent teachers will find themselves hopelessly bogged down in technical and clerical duties which could be performed by others. Or they will be overwhelmed by so many complex and important things to do that few if any of the tasks will be done well enough to leave them with any sense of accomplishment. Potentially outstanding teachers are growing discouraged over their inability to find the time and energy to be educators rather than technicians. . . .[1]

teacher as a model citizen

The teaching role is in an accelerating evolution and the noninstructional role of the teacher has undergone a profound and continual change since World War II. The traditional stereotype of the teacher in rural and small-town America was that of a model citizen and a sterling character akin to the local clergyman. Because teachers worked to influence youngsters, it was expected that they would be first among the observers of legal and moral laws and should show avid interest in affairs of government in a politically inactive and nonpartisan manner. Immune from immoral temptations, they neither

[1] George W. Denemark, "The Teacher and His Staff," *NEA Journal,* 55 (December 1966), 17.

non-instructional roles

smoked in public nor drank in private. Never seen in questionable company or places, teachers faithfully attended church and contributed a substantial proportion of their time to civic affairs.

A short time ago some small communities maintained teacherages where single female teachers were permitted or required to live. While it might have been expected that teachers would break the routine by leaving town at the end of the week, weekend absences were sometimes viewed with suspicion and absence from the community interfered with other expectations, such as singing in a church choir, teaching Sunday school, chaperoning a school dance, attending a school play or concert, or working at an athletic event (taking tickets, supervising students, or simply showing a healthy interest in school affairs). While the clergyman was the arbiter of community morals and was expected to be above criticism, the teacher was to be a model to youngsters and a molder of their values and was expected to be as circumspect as the clergyman. The requirement that teachers be more correct than parents was strictly enforced and the implication that the influence of teachers on youngsters was of more significance than that of others in society was scarcely challenged.

Probably the major influences easing these pressures on the teacher have been urbanization, with its displacement of the establishing of value systems and behavior from the rural small town to the city-suburban areas, and the shortage of teachers. Growth of urban centers has permitted the teacher to enjoy anonymity through selection of housing away from the school locality and by the absorption of individuality in the press of the mass. The teacher shortage has served as a brake upon the determination of some school boards to enforce puritanical rules upon the conduct of teachers. Teachers as a group have become more militant. They are willing to challenge enforcement of traditional codes of behavior. They have gained some support in this challenge from selected state departments of education, which have the legal right and responsibility to review disciplinary action taken against a teacher.

In the broad sense the teacher is a representative of his profession within the community. While relieved from Victorian standards of conduct and the necessity to adopt a posture more correct than that of others in society, teachers are still judged by public stereotypes of teachers and teaching. There is an interesting ambivalence among many people who resent "moonlighting" by public employees but commend as evidence of industriousness the pursuit of a second job by those in private employment. There is also differentiation by some persons of the types of extra employment appropriate to a teacher. Bartending or selling insurance often is frowned on, while camp counseling and selling encyclopedias gain ready approval.

As a citizen in his community, the teacher should be visible in more important matters than the means he uses to supplement his income. A service the teacher should perform within a neighborhood or community is to interpret education and the schools to the public. This does not mean an unusual or inordinate responsibility to "talk shop" among acquaintances, but to be as willing to expound on education and to speak favorably about it as the insurance broker, bank employee, or machinist is to speak of his vocational life, its challenges and problems, the superiority of his product or services, the caliber of his employer, the integrity of his union, and the quality of his own efforts in his job. The subject of education and the schools comes up more often in ordinary conversation than insurance rates, computerized banking services, or the latest wrinkles in gluing cabinets or machining gears. Opportunities may come to the teacher to educate fellow adults in the facts of the educational structure, plant, technique, and product. By actions, affiliations, and civic performance, the teacher supports or refutes stereotypes of "the teacher," builds and strengthens new images, and informs others about education.

The teacher-as-citizen should not feel any special obligation or limitations on acceptance of citizenship responsibilities or prerogatives. Traditional restrictions against teacher participation in partisan politics or the right to run for political office are gradually giving ground, and more educators are becoming politically active. There is a matter of conflict of interest for the teacher who would consider running for the local board of education in the district where he is employed. In some urban areas there are teachers who are employed by one school district and live in another, where they serve on the board of education. As educated individuals, teachers should accept the role of the citizen in a community. They ought to reject improper restrictions on the fulfillment of citizenship responsibilities and should serve as liaison between the schools and the community.

As a taxpayer the teacher ought to represent the community in his concern for the proper expenditure of public monies. This is not to suggest that public funds are extravagantly appropriated to the schools, but even skimpy funds may be spent unwisely. It is the responsibility of the individual teacher to exert an influence so that money is used wisely to educate youngsters. When enriched education demands additional expenditures, the teacher's task is to support efforts to ensure that such funds are forthcoming. The teacher's responsibility goes beyond an individual classroom to a concern for the use of funds within a school system. He should be concerned that peripheral activities in the school are not rewarded to the detriment of learning procedures. As a representative of the schools, the teacher is able to interpret bond proposals for school purposes to the public. He seeks to ensure that proposed bond issues are appropriate to educational needs and then actively supports those issues at the polls. The most pertinent use of political power by teachers is to become involved in educational politics to support the approval of bond issues and to be active in the election of school board members.

teacher as a faculty member

The teacher has several roles to play as a member of a school faculty. He recognizes the legal responsibility of the state governments for the education of the citizenry. Constitutionally the control over education rests in each state and it is to the governor, legislature, and state department of education that teachers must look for the real and eventual power over education. Most states have delegated much power over the schools to local boards of education. States have prescribed responsibilities to school boards and have granted them certain powers to set policy and to levy taxes to finance the school program. School boards have been granted the authority to appoint a staff and to delegate specific duties, responsibilities, and authority to administrators and teachers.

In many circumstances particular delegation of responsibilities by boards to the school staff are ill-defined, and uncertainty about duties and authority leads to conflict and confusion. It is important for a teacher to know the authority that is exercised by the board, what power has been delegated to administrators, and what duties are expected of teachers. Hopefully such information is provided to the teaching staff, but if it is not, the teacher has the responsibility to ascertain areas of authority and responsibility before initiating action. Such information may be obtained from experienced colleagues, although the first source of information should be the principal of a school. The ultimate resource and the most authoritative source is the office of the superintendent. Only in unusual circumstances should a teacher consult with board members about school problems and even then it should be with the knowledge of administrators, having first sought answers from them.

The role of the teacher in the chain of command is spelled out in general terms by school board policy and in a broad administrative framework that is structured by the board's agent, the superintendent. Teacher duties and responsibilities conform to the role description shared by all teachers in all schools and are primarily a matter of tradition and practice. Specifically the teacher operates in line with assignments made by the principal and rules enforced by and sometimes made by the principal.

The teacher looks to the principal as the primary transmitter of new policy or changes in the old as determined by the board. The principal serves as the interpreter of the means by which policy is to be carried out in a particular school. Principals are responsible for the resolution of instructional, extracurricular, maintenance, scheduling, and disciplinary problems and in the delineation of duties among the staff. Whether the principal exercises this leadership through democratic or autocratic means is dependent on his philosophy, his experience, and his skills in the conduct of human relationships.

The actions of a school board, superintendent, or principal facilitate the teaching job or obstruct it. Conflict situations within a school system seem to be brought to public notice more frequently than the affairs of efficient and happily operated schools simply because conflict is newsworthy. News media may keep the public informed on those school systems where internecine warfare fragments a school system or a community. Schools that are governed in harmony may be more prevalent but they seldom catch the eye of newsmen. Key to the degree of harmony in any school is the principal. Teachers usually learn through the principal of the restrictions or assistance granted to instruction by the school board and administration. The principal has the responsibility to advise teachers of board decisions dealing with noninstructional aspects of the school. It is as important that information be transmitted from teachers to administrators as it is that information about policy be passed from principals to teachers. The teacher should forward to the principal requests for new instructional materials to meet special needs of pupils and advise him about other problems that go beyond the classroom, such as the need for psychological assistance, remedial instruction, or special health services.

As a faculty member a teacher ought to assume certain general responsibilities toward the school physical plant and the broad educational program. Principals make assignments designating which teacher is to supervise the hallway adjacent to the classroom, a nearby lavatory, or a section of lockers. An individual teacher may be designated to represent a group of teachers who teach a particular grade or subject or are located in the same area of the school building as a means of centralizing requests for supplies, audio-visual materials, or other special services. Individual teachers must assume a responsibility for the entire school environment by reporting emergency situations and supervising youngsters when necessary to protect property, prevent injury, and maintain order. Teachers should identify with their school and the entire educational program rather than limit their interest and influence to a single subject area, classroom, or wing of a building.

As one among several and an equal among equals, the teacher has an important role to play in his relations with his teaching colleagues. A superior faculty finds the teaching novice seeking assistance from veteran colleagues and the experienced teacher volunteering aid to another instructor who is in difficulty. Learning is fostered and enriched when staff members pool ideas and resources and join together for activities beyond the scope, time, or energy of an individual teacher or classroom. A sharing of information and experiences in working with individual youngsters may ease the path of both teacher and learner, just as the sharing of knowledge and experiences or teaching procedures promises more vital learning and better coordination of the educational program.

The concerned faculty finds teachers voluntarily assisting in emergencies, with teachers making arrangements among themselves to take over a class when a sudden illness strikes. The way in which individual teachers perceive the role and status of their colleagues and the means by which they strive to relate to the whole environment determine the "feeling tone" of a school, the esprit de corps of a faculty. This spirit is a vital factor in structuring the degree of cohesiveness and purpose among the pupils as well as among the adults. It may be trite to suggest that happy teachers forge a well-run school and promote happy youngsters, but it is true.

In some schools the colleague relationship among teachers is not left solely to chance but is structured in essential aspects by the administration. In many secondary schools departmental chairmen are appointed to preside over subject matter areas. Elementary schools may organize teachers by grade, with one teacher designated as chairman. Committee procedures are used in most schools where committees are appointed to administer flower funds, provide for staff coffee and snacks, organize instruction or a subject, plan a curriculum, or carry out a research project. On a broader scale, committees may be appointed to represent the teachers in matters relating to school administrative matters or policy determination and many faculties are represented by a committee in salary negotiations with the board of education.

Most faculty members perceive what they call professional obligations. These relationships may range from perfunctory membership in a local, state, or national teachers' association or teachers' union to active participation and holding office in professional groups and seeking to exercise professional leadership. In addition to general teacher organizations, there are special interest groups representing subject areas, grade levels, or narrow specialties, such as the study of comparative education or the core curriculum. The professional relationships of teachers vary from a refusal on the part of some to affiliate with any organizations, to others whose membership is designed to "support the profession," and to still others who share an expectation that organized efforts are essential to the solution of the narrow interests of teachers and the broad issues concerning the education of youngsters. It may still be true that teachers in some schools are coerced by administrators into joining professional organizations, but the impression is that more teachers are demanding action by professional groups to solve educational problems and are supporting such action by voluntary membership in professional organizations. Many teachers are accepting a role as active members of an organized profession seeking not only to defend themselves against what they consider to be outmoded restrictions on personal behavior but as a means of attacking the system itself. Without operating through legal channels or through the state legislative processes, they strive to force upon resistant school boards a surrender of part of the board's power and authority to the organized teachers.

For some teachers a challenging and satisfying activity is to participate in programs sponsored by colleges and universities.

Many superior instructors find supervision of student teachers especially rewarding. They claim as one benefit that the teacher-in-the-making provides stimulus and ideas for improving an experienced teacher's classroom. Other teachers cooperate in the execution of research projects sponsored or directed by colleges and universities and report exciting, if demanding and exacting, experiences.

control of youngsters' behavior

As a faculty member, the teacher has a broad role to play in the behavior of all pupils. Teachers have policing (more accurately, supervising) responsibilities. They react to problems that arise throughout the school and on the playground. However, there may be confusion about the authority and responsibility that a teacher should have over youngsters in transit to and from school.

The teacher's most obvious responsibility for pupil behavior is within the classroom. The basic rule for the behavior of youngsters is that they engage in conduct which facilitates learning. There are intervals before school begins, however, when formal instruction has not yet started and the teacher is occupied with routine tasks in the preparation of the day's instruction. Some children come to school early and have little to do but wait until instruction begins. A satisfactory resolution to the problem of the early arriver may be to assemble the children in a gymnasium where they may play under supervision. A less satisfactory arrangement permits youngsters to gather in a school entry or hallway to wait for "the bell to ring." The least satisfactory practice is to lock youngsters out of the school until just before classes begin. The justification sometimes given for refusing to let youngsters in the building even in foul weather is that parents should not send children to school too early. This fails to take into account the many and varied home situations that may provide valid reasons why some youngsters arrive at school before some teachers might wish. Regardless of how, why, or when youngsters come to school there is no justification for locking them out of a building on cold or rainy days, but there should be no objection to expect children to wait outside school for a reasonable time in fair weather.

A teacher should organize youngsters as they arrive in the classroom so that inappropriate behavior is avoided. "Inappropriate" in this case is directed primarily toward physical activities that may lead to injuries, tearing of clothing, or damage to school facilities. Many activities may be arranged to occupy youngsters. Pupils may listen or dance to a record player. Chess, checkers, cards, or other games may be permitted. Some youngsters could be active in assisting the teacher in preparing for instruction. Formal club activities can be scheduled before school and individualized projects may be pursued by some pupils with a minimum of supervision. Particular sensitivity to noise level in this type of an informal situation does not seem relevant. Reasonable noise is more adequately resolved by proper acoustical facilities than by persistent monitoring by teachers.

During playground or recess periods, legal requirements and common sense dictate that a responsible adult be assigned to supervise youngsters. In these periods of relaxation, preference is shown for informal activities and the emphasis on supervision is to prevent injuries or damage. Access to the playground during recess periods provides a respite for youngsters from the absolute domination by the teacher in the classroom as well as an opportunity to engage in physical activities in contrast to the physical inactivity of the classroom.

On the junior and senior high school levels, scheduling of classes and assigning of staff result in unassigned periods for youngsters and resort to the use of study halls in which more than 100 pupils may be confined for a long, formal, and restricted period. All youngsters are expected to be actively and energetically completing homework assignments in the study hall. The concern for individualized differences in youngsters and the recognition of a range from nonreader to avid reader with meager to highly developed study skills are lost in the mass problem of keeping youngsters in a study hall under control. For many teachers study hall duty represents their most hated schoolhouse chore. They complain that the relations with youngsters necessitated in the study hall are contrary to those desired in the classroom and that negative experiences between teachers and pupils outside of class may undermine interaction in the classroom.

Most schools have a school lunchroom, frequently a cafeteria. Teachers are assigned responsibility for the conduct of youngsters at lunch. They supervise their own class or are responsible for the group in general. Of all the artificial situations in school, the cafeteria and study hall present the most difficult behavioral control problems. In both instances children are engaging in activities seldom experienced outside of school and they are placed in groups whose size makes effective organization difficult.

The lunchroom is another example of an informal situation where noise level is irrelevant, although the level of noise may be exaggerated by an unsatisfactory acoustical environment. Many cafeterias are large rooms with hard walls, hard floors, and hard ceiling surfaces, which amplify all sound. A more reasonable design provides eating facilities that are broken into smaller areas with acoustical ceiling tile and walls covered with drapes. Sometimes music is piped into the lunchroom through the public address system, serving to neutralize conversation and the rattling of dishes and utensils.

Most school buildings include an auditorium or a room that serves as a combined auditorium and gymnasium or cafeteria. Schools produce their own entertainment which is presented in the auditorium and in addition may use the room to schedule programs that are booked through commercial lecture services. A casual observer might be reminded of a penal rather than an educational institution by the manner in which some youngsters are marched to and from an auditorium, assigned individual seats, checked to see if they are present, and kept under close and severe supervision during a presentation in the auditorium. A teacher may find supervision of school entertainment as trying a task as study hall or lunchroom duty. The reaction of youngsters in a large auditorium reflects in part their attitude toward society and school. Their response depends on their maturity, personalities, home background, experiences, values, and interests. Pupil behavior can also be affected by the quality of the program they are required to attend.

Teachers may volunteer to be chaperones for youngsters' parties or dances and are often directed to do so by the principal. The chaperone role is sometimes interpreted by the teacher as one of preventing mayhem, enforcing codes of propriety, and seeing that everyone is started on the way home. The major role of the chaperone is to provide a presence and to fulfill the legal requirement that a reliable person be in attendance at school functions and responsible for the safety of those participating. Teachers may forget that youngsters conduct their own informal social activities outside of school at a generally acceptable level of behavior without supervision. Unlike other activities that are unique to the school, social activities are an extension of the real world. An artificial aspect of school social activity, however, is the enforced association of those who might not seek each other out because they live in different neighborhoods or identify with differing social groupings.

The greatest faculty responsibility in directing and maintaining satisfactory behavioral patterns by youngsters is through establishing and enforcing appropriate general rules or patterns of conduct. An apparent lack of interest in the behavior of pupils by a faculty is an open invitation to students not to set any standards, while rigid, harsh, and unrealistic expectations create tension, lead to silent or secretive rebellion, and foster a repressed and unhappy student body. A difficult behavioral situation for youngsters is an erratic pattern of rule enforcement, with pupils encountering some teachers who demand strict enforcement of repressive rules on behavior and others who completely disregard youngsters' conduct. One of the most important roles of a faculty and of its individual teachers is to establish a uniform pattern of reasonable expectations of youngsters.

classroom management

The school is in large part a human environment, but it is also a physical environment. A teacher has no control over the greater physical environment—the neighborhood or the school building. He can do little about dirty hallway interiors or unwashed windows, but he controls the immediate environment of his classroom.

maintaining the classroom environment

An important subsidiary task of the teacher is to maintain a pleasant and challenging classroom. The schoolroom comprises a learning atmosphere that is either stimulating or repressive. The basic physical room—the color of its walls, the size and style of the windows, the placement of chalkboards or bulletin boards, cabinets, teacher's desk, and work tables—is largely beyond the control of the teacher. An imaginative instructor, however, can create a dynamic atmosphere in spite of a poor physical environment. In addition to exciting and frequently changed instructional displays, the teacher must recognize the importance of the arrangement of the teacher's and pupils' desks and work tables. Neat, straight rows of desks may suggest rigidity and formality or they may suggest order. Haphazard arrangements can suggest flexibility or disorder. But it is not room arrangement alone that suggests whether school furniture is placed correctly. The combination of room arrangement and the type of learning activities that are being engaged in determine which physical order is best. The teacher should be free to arrange the classroom in the most suitable manner for the learning activities that are planned.

It is the responsibility of the administration to provide the materials necessary for instruction and learning and the duty of the teacher to make these needs and desires known. Through professional reading, attendance at meetings, conferences and workshops, or in additional formal study the teacher keeps abreast of recent instructional procedures and is acquainted with developing teaching aids. The teacher ought to know which new instructional innovations and devices or materials might be helpful to his class and he should have information about prices and names and addresses of suppliers where orders should be placed. The teacher must know the procedures of the school system for ordering teaching materials. In practice, some teachers have no trouble ordering materials and are encouraged to keep their classrooms up-to-date. Other schools operate with inadequate budgets. Their teachers struggle with insufficient materials and inferior resources and experience difficulty in equipping the classroom. Whether a teacher has adequate teaching devices and materials is not dependent solely on the size of a school budget. There are many teachers who make extensive and skillful use of teacher-made and student-made learning aids and there are others who misuse and waste expensive resources.

Teachers are responsible for the use of teaching materials and for the working condition of school equipment. Misuse of available materials interferes with learning as much as failure to use materials. Equipment that does not or cannot function is of no value in a school or classroom. The teacher should ensure that youngsters learn to take care of school equipment and that they do not scratch their names on desks, carelessly waste instructional materials, or use equipment improperly. Teachers must supervise pupils as they use equipment and report breakdowns and losses to the administration for repair or replacement. But while school equipment should not be misused, it must be considered expendable because energetic youngsters from a wide range of backgrounds and with a spread of personality types place a strain on school materials and equipment.

The teacher should be a major influence in effecting

changes in the school physical plant and in the equipment and materials used in instruction. Improvements in lighting, heat, or ventilation are requested by the teacher who finds problems in the classroom environment. While major physical changes in school buildings are infrequent and even new coats of paint are applied at unhappily long intervals in some schools, the teacher ought to be a force behind basic changes and maintenance. As an expert in teaching techniques and subject matter and as the sole expert in the needs of his pupils and his own interests, abilities, and experience, the teacher is the logical person to propose requisition of new teaching materials and equipment.

A teacher is able to make recommendations about the placement of youngsters. It might be necessary for the teacher to recommend moving a youngster from one class to another, from one group to another, or from one grade to another. A competent teacher asks that a youngster be transferred from his class to that of another teacher when a serious personality clash becomes evident between the teacher and the pupil.

The teacher is a housekeeper and a teacher of housekeeping to youngsters. A vital, exciting, and variable learning situation may cause a room to become cluttered and disarrayed. The disarrangement of one activity must be cleared away before another activity may begin. A variable learning situation may find a formal arrangement for a lecture or the showing of a movie followed by the organization of small groups into committees. In carrying out committee plans a classroom may become a drama workshop, a science laboratory, or a construction site, with the consequent disarray.

Schools do have custodial services, but it is not unusual for a teacher to be expected to wash his own chalkboard, arrange pupil desks, and adjust windows and shades. The days when teachers cut wood, fired a stove, and swept and cleaned a one-room schoolhouse are over, but there are still too many teachers who are expected to perform menial housekeeping tasks.

Teachers shepherd the belongings of youngsters. They retrieve stray textbooks and collect forgotten mittens and caps from odd corners. They maintain caches for lost and found articles in the classroom and send to the office stray articles found outside the room. Showing concern for children's care of their belongings, teachers may note inadequate clothing on some children and seek suitable replacements. They teach youngsters how to care for personal as well as school property.

keeping records

The teacher is a keeper of personal, pupil, and administrative records. These records are necessary for the teacher to analyze his teaching procedures. They aid the teacher in interpreting pupil progress or problems to parents, administrators, specialized school personnel and responsible nonschool specialists. They provide the basic data on which a youngster, teacher, or school system is judged.

The teacher's personal file ought to include a comprehensive account of his own teaching experiences, the tools and techniques that were used, resource and teaching units that are available, previous and current lesson plans, and the failures and successes of the lessons. An effective teacher maintains notes on promising teaching techniques he has read about or observed. He lists films, filmstrips, recordings, books, booklets, and other visual materials that may be useful. Professional documents, teaching certificates, correspondence, administrative directives, and notes from parents ought to be on file and available for ready reference, although some personal papers are stored more suitably at home than in school.

There may be questions with reference to which records or materials that have been accumulated by a teacher are his property and which are the property of the school system. In general, those things provided by the school and paid for out of school funds are the property of the school; those collected and paid for by the teacher belong to the individual. It is a commendable contribution of a teacher to supplement classroom materials from his own collection, but the teacher who is compelled to supply essential or useful teaching materials because the school refuses to provide for the minimal instructional needs is subsidizing the teaching process.

Probably the most important records kept by a teacher are those containing information about youngsters. The teacher is the major source and consumer of information about pupils. A teacher's evaluation criteria and techniques determine how the achievement of a youngster is expressed. The teacher has sole knowledge of classroom deportment and class social relationships. He is in the best position to estimate youngsters' interests and motivation. The alert teacher maintains files for the collection of information about youngsters including anecdotal records, which are reports of special, unusual, and important events concerning pupils. The teacher's classbook is the record of classroom assignments and test scores and often includes tardiness and absence tabulations. Some schools maintain separate absence and tardiness "registers," which may be complex and time-consuming accounts. Attendance reports are sometimes viewed as impressively important records and may even have standing as legal documents. They are carefully checked for accuracy in the school office and when wrong are returned to the teacher for correction.

Some teachers are responsible for keeping cumulative folders and are expected to record information on them. The care and skill with which cumulative records are kept, the ability of teachers to record accurately data concerning pupil behavior and achievement and to identify information of pertinence, and the speed and accuracy with which information is forwarded to administrators and guidance and health personnel facilitate or limit the degree to which special services may be utilized to aid youngsters. One of the first things with which a teacher should become acquainted after the initial introduction to a new school and a new classroom is the cumulative folder system and the amount of information that is available about the youngsters in the school. Many mistakes may be avoided in dealing with children in the classroom if the teacher makes intelligent use of the information that is available in a cumulative file. Unfortunately, center-city schools, which may be burdened with serious educational and behavioral problems, may not have satisfactory pupil records because of the high turnover of youngsters in the schools. In some areas there are classrooms with a pupil turnover rate of more than 100 percent each year.

guidance responsibilities

Teachers engage in group guidance procedures. Directed toward resolution of general problems of youngsters at an age group and within a particular school context, group guidance serves to meet individual and group problems on a group basis. Group guidance procedures engage youngsters in a depersonalized analysis of common problems and permit open discussion that may lead to suggestions for general solutions to problems. Adjustment to school, relationships with peers, problems of growing up, matters of relating to adults, and the necessity for preparing for later educational experiences or for life beyond school are group guidance concerns. Among techniques proposed for group guidance experiences—in addition to discussion—are lectures, films, books, booklets, and sociodrama.

Teachers engage in individual guidance, in aiding individuals to meet their personal, social, or educational problems. Teachers may identify problems and seek to aid youngsters, or troubled young people may seek assistance from teachers. A teacher must know his own limitations, provide direct aid to youngsters only when it is within his capacity to act, and refer serious problems to those specialists who have the training, experience, and competence to meet the problems. It is as essential that a teacher know where to go for professional assistance for youngsters as it is that he be able to identify problems. The one becomes futile without the other.

Administrators may require teachers to collect information for office use: the name and address of the family physician; who, other than parents, should be contacted in an emergency; record of vaccinations and inoculations; which special religious requirements or prohibitions apply to which youngsters. A principal who seeks information on space allocation, budget planning, projected staff assignment, or curricular needs may call on the teacher for information about youngsters, physical plant, curricular plans or trends, or instructional needs. Teachers also receive requests for information to serve community surveys, school board investigations, administrative curiosity, or anyone's research project.

serving as financial agent

Among the least justifiable noninstructional tasks of a teacher are those many and minor services that may be quite worthy endeavors. Each service evokes just a small effort and "only a few minutes" of a teacher's time, but the aggregate of many small tasks may be a large and tedious job. Teachers are charged with collecting and recording contributions to charitable organizations. There may be few who would quarrel with the merits and record of the American Red Cross or the many other noteworthy volunteer organizations that fight disease, hunger, and human misery throughout the world. Yet one may question the propriety of "volunteer" contributions in a situation where strong efforts are exerted to achieve complete pupil participation. Classes may be placed in competition with each other over the totals collected, and names of contributors may be published as much in the expectation that pressures to conform may be applied to delinquents as to honor those who contribute. Charitable contributions in school should be collected through centrally located collection boxes where donations may be offered anonymously and voluntarily. In such a way not only would "charity" be removed from coercion of children, but teachers would be relieved of the task of collecting and recording contributions.

Teachers are assigned the responsibility of serving as agents for patently commercial enterprises. In some school savings plans teachers become bank tellers and collect and record deposits made by youngsters. Teachers collect insurance payments and sell photographs taken by commercial photographers in the schools. Band instructors sell instruments and music to youngsters. Physical education teachers collect money for purchase of gym uniforms from a local store. Some companies that sell school insurance to youngsters collect premium payments through the mails. It would seem appropriate that any commercial venture that is approved to operate in the school should staff its own enterprise. A teacher should not have to serve as an agent for a business firm in the classroom.

There are other school activities that place the teacher in the role of a financial agent. Youngsters are assessed class dues, book rental fees, or laboratory fees. Athletic tickets, yearbooks, and school newspapers are sold in classrooms and classes of youngsters are sent into the community selling candy or magazines to finance a music or athletic program or the purchase of a school organ or movie projector. Whether the school program should be subsidized through this form of an indirect tax is a philosophical question worthy of consideration. The need to reduce the collecting and accounting responsibilities of teachers, however, should not be subject to much argument. If there are school expenses that should be financed by the pupils, collecting and accounting for this money may be delegated to youngsters or conducted by the school office staff, but should not be foisted on the teacher.

Sometimes a school is rocked with the scandal of the theft of money from a teacher's desk, and news media occasionally report the burglarizing of a school office. School funds should never be left in a classroom and there is no justification for accumulation of money in a school office. When money is collected in school, arrangements should be made for immediate deposit in a bank. In the case of pilfering from a teacher's desk, one might question whether the careless teacher or the tempted youngsters should bear the blame.

extracurricular activities

The assumption by the school of social as well as educational responsibility for developing youngsters is reflected in many extracurricular activities in the school. There are some activities that are related to the close association found in school and to the general amenities common to accepted social practice. An elementary classroom or a secondary homeroom may celebrate birthdays, organize occasional class parties, or celebrate Christmas or, in some schools, Hanukkah.

Teachers frequently oversee or even assume all the responsibility for class social activities. Highly organized classes may elect officers, appoint functioning committees, and even collect dues, which are used to finance activities. Gifts may be exchanged among youngsters and traditions have been established in some schools of classes presenting gifts to teachers. Middle-class teachers may be oblivious to the financial stress that frequent and persistent small expenditures place on some youngsters.

The question of sectarian religious observances imposed on atheists, agnostics, and those with divergent religious beliefs is usually ignored. Some teacher time and effort ought to be directed toward improving social relations among youngsters, but the tendency toward exaggerated attention to class parties, particularly the excessive celebration of Christmas in many schools, should be regulated closely or curtailed.

Performing and club activities are often organized and sanctioned by school policy. In many schools "major" activities, such as school newspapers and yearbooks and drama, music, and athletic programs, provide additional income for teachers. There are some school systems where any teacher involved in nonacademic programs receives extra pay for the activities. Comprehensive activity programs may incur extensive managerial and accounting responsibilities and involve the collection and expenditure of large sums of money.

Extracurricular programs may be scheduled within the school day and all youngsters may be required to participate in some activity. The burden is then distributed among all the teachers and may be incorporated into regular instructional planning and the execution of plans. When the activity program is conducted outside of the school schedule, some teachers spend a considerable amount of time in supervising activities. It is common to find a large part of the faculty involved when youngsters perform in musical or dramatic presentations, when competitive athletic programs are organized between schools, or in the event of a parent visitation evening or the conduct of a science fair or a school fund-raising activity.

Schools often publish school newspapers. Ordinarily one teacher is assigned as the adviser, some teachers may aid in the collection of news, and every teacher sells subscriptions, collects money, and distributes the paper. Musical and dramatic groups are usually the responsibility of special teachers, although all classrooms may be interrupted as youngsters are excused from class for music lessons or to practice on the eve of a performance. Entire faculties may be assigned tasks at an athletic event from selling tickets and popcorn to supervising spectators. Sales of tickets to performances may be conducted through the classroom and the teacher may act as an accountant and treasurer and may even be placed in charge of a highly competitive sales contest. Serious questions could be raised about the time and effort required of teachers in the conduct of noninstructional programs in some schools.

The extreme emphasis on noninstructional aspects of the classroom is evident in contests that are conducted to determine the fifth-grade or district high school football or basketball champion, prize-winning speech and drama entries, and the top-rated school bands, orchestras, or choirs. Serious questions about the educational goals of activity programs for individual youngsters may be raised when one observes the large trophy cases lining school hallways or notes the scheduling of athletic contests at night in order to accommodate adult spectators.

consultation with laymen

Some schools have a local chapter of the Parent-Teachers Association, which is affiliated with the National Congress of Parents and Teachers. Others sponsor nonaffiliated parent-teacher organizations or parent-teacher-student groups. A PTA may meet monthly or bimonthly. Meetings may involve considerable effort by a teacher who is responsible for a program or by all teachers if a parent visitation is scheduled. Generally speaking, the demands placed on teachers by a local PTA are infrequent and minimal.

Scheduled parent conferences, which are required by some schools, are time-consuming for teachers. Parent conferences may take the place of report cards as a means of reporting a pupil's progress to the parents or to supplement the report card and establish a closer relationship between the teacher and the parents. The parent conference is a valuable communicative link between teacher and parent. Conferences, however, require considerable time and should be scheduled for at least one-half hour. Conferences may involve scheduling problems, particularly for working parents. It is difficult to arrange to meet with parents who do not share middle-class values toward education, who remember with distaste their own school days, or who expect to find the conference an unhappy experience. Preparing, scheduling, and conducting conferences constitute a major undertaking for a teacher. Some schools ease the problems by dismissing school to provide time for conferences.

A few teachers, on their own initiative or as a matter of school policy, make a practice of meeting and talking with parents in the home. While this requires more organization and greater effort and time on the part of the teacher, it does provide opportunities to observe in the home and to gather more information about a youngster and his environment. Activities of this nature provide teachers with much information and many valuable insights about youngsters, but actual involvement with parents is limited by the time and energy available to a teacher.

There are occasions when a teacher may consult with nonschool specialists. A dentist or physician may be consulted for dental or medical advice and an ophthalmologist or optometrist may be sought for aid in sight problems. Police, probation officers, a lawyer, or a court may aid with legal matters. Other problems may require the assistance of welfare or social workers or a clergyman. It is a formidable task for a teacher to become acquainted with all the possibilities for referral and consultative assistance. Each consultation, moreover, requires particular interest, determination, time, and energy.

teacher evaluation

An important but little discussed aspect of teaching beyond the instructional role is self-evaluation by every teacher. An individual's self-evaluation may lead to escape from the schoolhouse into the kitchen or selling or independent merchandising. It may lead from the classroom into administration or academic specialist positions or to college supervision or teaching. Or it may lead a young teacher to make a positive and determined commitment to spend his career in the classroom and to increase his knowledge and improve his teaching techniques.

The evaluation of teaching has been a haphazard process in which evidence is elusive and judgments are highly suspect as personalized expressions of opinion. For some teachers, evidence is compiled from the professional judgment of colleagues and supervisors, the opinions of parents, reactions of students, and the results of standardized testing programs. For others, their largely subjective judgments reflect their own confidence in their knowledge of subject matter and competence in teaching. Those with problems may take refuge in such arguments as the absence of sympathy and support from parents, lack of understanding and backing of administrators, and an inability of pupils to respond because of lack of motivation or low intelligence.

New techniques for the evaluation of teaching have been developed in teacher education programs and will find their place in the ordinary classroom. Most prominent among the techniques for evaluating teaching is the interaction analysis developed by Ned A. Flanders. The Flanders technique provides for classification and tabulation of classroom interaction at intervals of three seconds. Broad categories of interaction are identified as teacher talk, student talk, and silence. Teacher talk is further classified as indirect and direct influence. Under indirect influence are (1) accepts feeling, (2) praises or encourages, (3) accepts or uses ideas of student, and (4) asks questions. Direct influence includes (5) lecturing, (6) giving directions, and (7) criticizing or justifying authority. Under student talk are listed (8) student talk—response and (9) student talk—initiation. The last category is (10) silence or confusion. Interaction is tallied by category numbers for about twenty minutes and then is recorded on a ten-point matrix. Analysis of the matrix shows whether teacher talk or student talk predominated in the classroom and the nature of the dominance.

A teacher may tape record a lesson and analyze it later using the Flanders technique, or one teacher can observe another in the classroom and analyze the interaction. Video-tape machines are used in teacher education programs. They are often used in micro-teaching procedures for both audio and visual recording of short teaching situations. Video-taping a teacher in the classroom will permit him to analyze his own teaching techniques and mannerisms as well as the interaction during the lesson.

These self-evaluation techniques are used voluntarily by teachers. In some schools, however, evaluation of teachers is assigned to administrators and sometimes is required of the faculty. Formal evaluation may be used to determine whether to rehire a teacher, grant him tenure, or award him a merit pay increase. In formal self-evaluation the teacher may judge his teaching effectiveness, classroom management, interpersonal relations, professional growth, and community activities. Formal self-evaluation is not demanding or time-consuming, but teachers may consider it to be a threatening and unpleasant task when it is related to matters of employment and salary and allied to formal evaluation by others. Some schools require that each teacher complete a self-evaluation form which is then filled out by an administrator. A conference may follow to discuss instances of agreement and disagreement.

conclusion

The importance of noninstructional facets of teaching cannot be ignored. In the state of New York, for example, a complicated attendance register has been ruled to be a legal instrument. New York courts have affirmed the right of a school board to dismiss a teacher who refused to submit advance lesson plans to the school administration. Less may be known about the learning that takes place in a classroom than whether the teacher is a strict disciplinarian, is steadfast in standing hall duty, or is a keeper of exact records.

Unfortunately it is necessary for the teacher to undertake his noninstructional roles as seriously as he does his teaching function. Educators should be spending more time and energy in increasing the effectiveness of classroom instruction and the efficiency of learning. Two means of reducing the peripheral or noninstructional tasks of the teacher are to hire teacher aides, who may be assigned routine matters and clerical duties, and to utilize team-teaching techniques. Commendable as these procedures may be, a more realistic approach for many schools is to closely examine the peripheral and noninstructional activities in which teachers engage and to eliminate those not relevant to effective teaching.

Perhaps because noninstructional roles are less exciting and because there is a wide variety of practices and expectations from state to state or school system to school system or even from principal to principal, there is less material available in this area than in others. Administrative relationships are treated in texts written for the preparation of administrators. Among such references are Percy E. Burrup, *Modern High School Administration* (New York: Harper & Row, 1962), and Claude W. Fawcett, *School Personnel Administration* (New York: Macmillan, 1964), or books of readings incorporating a wide variety of problems and viewpoints, such as Robert E. Wilson's (ed.) *Educational Administration* (Columbus, Ohio: Merrill, 1966). In some states, legal aspects of teaching are a matter of concern in books such as Lee O. Garber, Robert L. Drury, and Roger M. Shaw's *The Law and the Teacher in Ohio* (Danville, Ill.: Interstate, 1966).

The guidance role of the teacher in the elementary school is discussed in Roy D. Willey, *Guidance in Elementary Education,* rev. ed. (New York: Harper & Row, 1966). A more general treatment is found in Bruce Shertzer and Shelley C. Stone, *Fundamentals of Guidance* (Boston: Houghton Mifflin, 1966). Among the journals in the field of guidance that may be of interest are the *Personnel and Guidance Journal* and *Journal of Counseling Psychology.* Less technical articles may be found in the National Education Association publication, *Today's Education,* and in *American Education* and the various state education journals.

Students who are interested in the role of extracurricular activities in the school could reflect in an analytical and critical manner on the extracurricular program in their own high schools. What were the purposes of the program? How much time and effort was required of teachers? Were they given extra pay or extra time for these activities? What were the feelings and reactions of youngsters concerning extracurricular programs? What were the expectations, feelings, and reactions of parents?

A student of teaching should attend a PTA meeting and, through observation of the behavior of the participants, attempt to determine the motives of those present and the effect of the meeting. He ought to answer the questions: Was the meeting useful? How could it have been improved? Was the effort worthwhile to parents and teachers? Why? Conferences with parents are often the subject of articles in educational journals, particularly those conferences that are a means of reporting pupil progress to parents. Simulated conferences may be useful in preparing teachers to meet with parents.

Teachers may be aided in analyzing their own behavior and proficiency by referring to Ray H. Simpson's *Teacher Self-Evaluation* (New York: Macmillan, 1966). The Flanders technique is described in Ned A. Flanders, *Teacher Influence, Pupil Attitudes, and Achievement* (Washington, D.C.: Government Printing Office, 1965), and a modification of the technique is the subject of Edmund J. Amidon and Elizabeth Hunter in *Improving Teaching: The Analysis of Classroom Verbal Interaction* (New York: Holt, Rinehart, and Winston, 1966). Articles on microteaching may be found through the *Education Index*.

The most useful way to become acquainted with the teacher's noninstructional role is to visit with a teacher, observe other-than-teaching activities, and ask for a detailing of the full scope of clerical, organizing, and maintaining activities. Particular note should be made of duties that are required of all teachers, those peculiar to a school, and others unique to a teacher, subject, or class.

additional references

Corsini, Raymond J., and Daniel D. Howard. *Critical Incidents in Teaching.* Englewood Cliffs, N.J.: Prentice-Hall, 1964.

Heald, James E., and Samuel A. Moore, II. *The Teacher and Administrative Relationships in School Systems.* New York: Macmillan, 1968.

Hodgkinson, Harold L. *Educational Decisions: A Casebook.* Englewood Cliffs, N.J.: Prentice-Hall, 1963.

Hughes, James M. *Human Relations in Educational Organizations.* New York: Harper & Brothers, 1957.

Hurlburd, David. *This Happened in Pasadena.* New York: Macmillan, 1951.

Kushel, Gerald. *Discord in Teacher-Counselor Relations: Cases from the Teacher's View.* Englewood Cliffs, N.J.: Prentice-Hall, 1967.

Savage, William W. *Interpersonal and Group Relations in Educational Administration.* Glenview, Ill.: Scott, Foresman, 1968.

11

facilitators of instruction

It is an oversimplification to propose that the success of an educational system depends solely upon the energy, ability, and dedication of classroom teachers. One cannot ignore the role that support by others plays in the success of instruction. Public schools require strong and sustained public support, and private schools depend upon religious or lay groups for their purposes and sustenance. School boards set policies that facilitate or inhibit instruction. Major administrators structure morale, detail instructional and noninstructional duties, provide access to physical properties, and distribute instructional materials, while administrative assistants provide counseling and assistance in personal relations with youngsters and in the use of instructional techniques. The noninstructional staff provides essential services to the classroom teacher.

public support

Much is said among educators about the need for public support of the public schools and an important task of any school staff is to facilitate good public relations. Larger school systems employ public relations experts to conduct an organized information and propaganda program directed toward the public. A school staff relies upon public support in school bond issue elections, and extensive and intensive campaigns are sometimes organized in classrooms, by schools, or through parent-teacher associations to systematically ensure support at the polls.

The concept of "a public" as a unified entity representing society is a myth. Only in the private school is there an approach to the unity of "a public" and many private school educators will testify that such cohesiveness is more apparent than real. In the midst of what was interpreted as unification of an inner-city ghetto Thomas K. Minter reported: "When Board of Education officials ask who speaks for the parents, they are distressed to find so many shades of opinion among those who answer. It is not realistic to expect a ghetto community to speak with a united voice."[1] The ghetto is certainly not unique in this regard. It would be difficult to find a community where there is an individual who speaks for every member of the community in regard to school affairs.

Yet reality is ignored when it is assumed that the quality of education in a school does not represent the consensus that evolves from a general philosophical position shared by a community or that is imposed on a community. Public support of education is interpreted by school board members who, as any other publicly elected officials, may act on the basis that their own beliefs and values are representative of those of the community or who may seek information and guidance from groups or individuals in the electorate and thus will accommodate their personal inclinations. There are many organized groups that have a special interest in the schools. Taxpayer groups, for instance, exert a strong influence to hold down school taxes. They oppose bond issues and increased taxes and seek to reduce existing school expenditures. For these groups the level of taxation may seem to be more important than the level of educational achievement. Groups like the American Legion or Daughters of the American Revolution may exert pressures to include or exclude subject matters in the curriculum. Religious and antireligious groups may demand increased or decreased moral-religious experiences for youngsters. Assorted groups may make other demands on the schools.

Individuals as well as groups may also exert strong influences on the school and its program. A single powerful property owner in a community may have more to say about school finances than an organized taxpayer group. A self-appointed censor may force curricular change or deletion of certain instructional materials. Even a single pupil may cause a crisis in the life of an individual teacher.[2]

It may be true that it is easier to be basically negative

[1] Thomas K. Minter, *Intermediate School 201, Manhattan: Center of Controversy* (Cambridge, Mass.: Graduate School of Education, Harvard University, 1967), p. 18.

[2] See Maurice McNeill with Richard Cohen, "How My Town Saved Me from a White Girl's Lie," *Ladies' Home Journal,* 85 (March 1968), 81, 140–144.

toward a specific issue than to be broadly supportive of a general philosophical position. There is less of a tendency to sustain effort in support of a relatively unspecified program whose execution may be delegated to professionals. Continuously active groups that might be labeled "pro-educational" seem to be difficult to organize and perpetuate. Most of the groups that tend to be critical of the schools are organized about some other common purpose. Concern for the schools, then, is one aspect of a broader program of action.

parents

"The public" is composed of individuals, among whom the strongest potential supporters of an educational program are parents of youngsters in school. A parent's appraisal of a school and a teacher is quite naturally centered about the success of his youngster in school and his perception of the child's abilities and educational future. Parents see their children as extensions of themselves; thus parental reactions to the experiences of their youngsters may be emotional rather than rational. A parent's information about events in school comes from conversations with youngsters and from the parent's own experiences with teachers or from attending meetings at school. Even the most sophisticated public relations program cannot be expected to counteract parental personal experiences or the vicarious experiences a parent derives through his youngsters.

Many teachers look on parent visitation or conferences with fear and trepidation. Many parents face meeting with teachers equally unsure of themselves. The parent-teacher confrontation may be an emotionally loaded situation when the teacher's concern is to defend his interaction with a youngster and a parent views problems affecting the child in the classroom as threats to an extension of his own ego. Interaction between teachers and parents is facilitated when they meet to discuss common matters other than the resolution of a crisis in the classroom. A helpful practice is parent visitation scheduled early in the school year, if not prior to school or as school starts. If an exchange between a teacher and a parent has brought about understanding by each of the expectations of the other and an opportunity to get acquainted in a relaxed situation, conferences to resolve problems may be arranged more easily, be conducted in a healthier atmosphere, and be more productive. Preschool conferences may inform parents of classroom procedures and expectations. Prior information may permit parents to recognize problems as early as the teacher or before a teacher is aware of increasing difficulties.

Just as the teacher must accept individual differences among the youngsters in a class, so should he be able to recognize, allow for, and accept differences in the parents of his youngsters. There are differences in attitude toward children, school, and education. The teacher adjusts his reactions to the needs of youngsters; he accepts each as an individual. Similarly the teacher should accept each parent as an individual—the reluctant, resistant, and antagonistic parent as well as the eager, cooperative, and friendly one. It is not easy for some teachers to meet many parents, but it is essential if every youngster is to be served effectively in the classroom.

In some school systems school social workers serve as full-time intermediaries between homes and classrooms. The social worker may be effective in the resolution of serious problems because he is a full-time, trained person. Other school systems provide time for teachers to visit the homes of pupils with the opportunity to gain information about the parents, home, and neighborhood. In other communities teachers are hired to conduct the local school census. They are able to become acquainted with the community in general, if not with the parents of their own pupils.

Excessive or inappropriate demands are made on the schools. Teachers may be expected to compensate for parental inability to acquaint their youngsters with proper behavior or desirable moral standards or religious values. A school may be expected to guarantee college entrance and success to every youngster, victory in every athletic contest, and a harmless outcome to every meeting between the sexes. Some teachers are faced with the impossible situation of having to deal with simultaneous parental complaints about too little and too much homework, too permissive and too restrictive classroom discipline, or expectations that teachers provide for individual needs while maintaining group standards.

The public consensus that is expressed in school elections and school board actions results in well-financed and adequately supported schools or in impoverished programs, inadequate school buildings, salary schedules that may recruit lesser-qualified teacher personnel and lead to continued strife between teachers and the school administration, and failure to provide sufficient learning experiences and materials. It is a pathetic irony that schools which serve youngsters who have the most severe personal, social, and educational problems usually have the least financial resources for the support of education. Inner-city schools, for example, represent areas with absentee property ownership, a professional and merchant group that may choose to live in the suburbs, a low-income resident population, and an unrepresentative and frequently machine-controlled political structure. Public support of public education often is not apportioned according to need.

Financial support of the schools is not the only evidence of public attitudes and actions, even if it is the most tangible. In some respects psychological support may be as essential as financial backing. While psychological support may not substitute for those benefits that may be purchased, lack of psychological support may render a superior plant and resources somewhat irrelevant. A community expresses psychological support through pride of school buildings and an expectation that they are kept up-to-date, confidence in a school board and administration, approval of the educational program, and belief in the competence and integrity of the teachers. A tragic example of the failure of psychological support to follow financial support is the confused story of Intermediate School 201, New York City's first windowless, air-conditioned school building.[3] This school became the center of controversy between the immediate community and the school board. Racial issues complicated the struggle over control of the school. Perhaps a more bizarre situation occurred when a Michigan community constructed an expensive new high school and then let it stand empty for a year while controversy raged about initiating and financing an instructional program.

the school board

The school board plays a major role in the facilitation of instruction. School boards serve the classroom best when they recognize that the single legitimate purpose of the school is the education of youngsters. To this end the school board has a fourfold responsibility: to represent the interests of the public, to set school policy to implement public interests, to provide local financing for the schools, and to employ a school staff. The most significant action of a school board that facilitates instruction is employing a competent staff, which is then given

[3] Minter, *Intermediate School 201.*

authority and responsibility for conducting a satisfactory educational program. There are many school boards that observe appropriate responsibilities and relationships, but there are others that fail to do so. Reports of news media, court records, and published investigations by professional organizations document many cases of abuse of authority while other serious instances may remain unreported. A random selection of newspaper headlines points out some of the issues: "Claim School Board Prejudged Teacher," "Teacher Bias Laid to School Board," "School Election Divides Teaneck," and "Streetsboro Teachers End Strike as Board Gives In." The seriousness with which election to a school board may be pursued is evidenced by this head to a full-page ad: "Your June 11 Vote Will Help Decide—Will Fear or Freedom Rule Our Schools?"

Criticism of school boards and proposals to increase their effectiveness are old and apparently honorable educational pastimes in the United States. Criticism has come from educational leaders such as James E. Allen, Jr., respected former New York State Commissioner of Education, who was reported to have warned his state's school boards that they faced increased centralization of power to the state government unless they met educational problems more effectively. The so-called Bundy Report offered a plan to decentralize school control as a resolution to the problems of governing New York City schools. The report proposed establishing from thirty to sixty largely autonomous community school districts in the city. The proposal was supported by U.S. Commissioner of Education Harold Howe, II, and opposed by two groups that are usually found at odds with each other, the New York City Board of Education and the United Federation of Teachers. An initial experiment in local community control in the city experienced severe difficulties and became a center of controversy.

While the Bundy plan is one alternative to centralized school control in large cities and another may be direct state control over the schools, there are some educators who suggest as their alternative to the traditional structure the assertion of greater teacher participation in educational decision making. The possibilities of using the power that became available to teachers through the collective-bargaining process may alter the entire policy- and decision-making procedure. The kind of responsibilities delegated to teachers may be determined by the final results of a serious and destructive struggle of teacher power against the existing system. As some picture it, the assumption of control by teachers would represent a dispersal or decentralization of some functions to be carried out in each individual school. A faculty would thus participate in making major decisions for itself.

school administration

A public school is administered, placing responsibility for its operation somewhere between governance and management. The school is basically framed in an authoritarian mold, yet it depends for its success on the willing contributions of a group of independently minded specialists. The effective administrator treads a narrow path between leading and following, telling and suggesting, and granting authority and demanding accountability. He cannot raise a school above the potential of its teachers, nor can he force them beyond the potential of a community.

THE SUPERINTENDENT The school superintendent is in the most strategic position to facilitate instruction. This is because his efforts involve direction of others and do not necessitate a personal involvement that is limited by his time and energy. The compromised position of the superintendent frequently restricts his actions. A superintendent who is inclined to expand teaching opportunities may not be free to do so. Many school boards are anxious to hire as their agent a superintendent who will be able to satisfy the board and also gain the confidence of the teaching staff. A school board may demand satisfaction in terms of a quiescent public, a minimal budget, a well-disciplined student population, cooperative teachers, and a high level of instruction. Expectations are listed roughly in order of priority, although what happens in the schools or in a community might lead to slight adjustments in the order. Control of school board priorities is demanding enough of a superintendent, but his task may become unmanageable if it is complicated by organized teachers who attack the status quo, school board members who interfere in the daily routine of the classroom, or outside critics who wage war against the school.

A public that remains inactive in school matters is a rare phenomenon. A lack of interest in the schools may suggest more concern for other priorities, problems in the availability of funds for schools, or the socioeconomic level of the pupils who attend the school. A major task for the superintendent, then, is continual involvement in matters of public relations, from hearing the complaint of an individual parent to participation in community affairs and civic organizations. He may be expected to be an active member of the community and a periodic speaker to local groups. Except for the larger cities, where an extended circle of contacts demands more of his time, the local superintendent is expected to make an appearance at each PTA meeting, class play, concert, and athletic event.

Attending to public relations erodes a superintendent's time and energy, but financial restrictions may compromise his relations with the staff. If buses for field trips are too expensive and tattered texts are to be used for another year and instructional materials come too little and too late, the level of instruction and morale of the teaching staff suffer. If instruction is restricted and morale problems prevail, pupils may become restive and insurgent.

Within the framework of priorities that determine his success, the superintendent is generally free to make some decisions that determine the success of the enterprise. His recruitment of staff is of crucial importance, especially the selection of school principals, although every appointment is an important decision. The budget is a factor in staff recruitment, for in a situation where there may be wide variations in salary from district to district and from one state to another, the superintendent whose district has the lowest salary schedule may experience difficulties in recruiting staff. A wise principal or teacher may willingly sign a contract for a somewhat lesser salary when there are other compensating factors, such as a satisfactory teaching environment with excellent staff relationships and abundant opportunities for successful teaching and learning. It is also frequently true that a school system which offers low salaries to teachers is also employing lesser-salaried administrators (with whatever implications that may have). Such schools may be unable to replace inadequate buildings and usually do not provide sufficient teaching materials and assistance to teachers.

Ideally a superintendent of schools should be first an educational leader and then, if there is time, a business manager and public relations expert, but the realities of the situation seldom permit this emphasis for long. Many chief school administrators are selected on the basis of their business acumen. Some schools that have had difficulties in gaining public approval of bond issues will hire a superintendent primarily on the basis of his previous success in public relations programs that have led to success at the polls. Parallels are often drawn between school administration and the conduct of private business. The major failure of the analogy, however, is that the first concern of a business enterprise is to make a profit while the primary concern for a school system is to effect learning. The one requires a business (i.e., financial) expert, the other a knowledgeable and skillful educator. Nevertheless, the here and now of financing new construction, maintenance and improvement of the existing physical plant, negotiating salaries, running a bus system and a food business, and purchase of supplies from alphabet letters to zoological specimens seldom releases a superintendent from the business of running a school system so that he may supervise the ways in which learning takes place.

Most school superintendents started their professional careers as classroom teachers. They chose to study for a masters degree in school administration and entered administrative work at the principal or assistant principal level. The trend in state certification of school superintendents is toward a minimum of two years of graduate study. If ambitious, a superintendent may move progressively into the superintendencies of increasingly larger school districts or he may move up the administrative ladder within a single large district. The superintendency is often a well-paid position, which is one of the reasons many men move into school administration, but it carries the risks of uncertain tenure, because tenure is dependent on the success with which a superintendent may serve the school board and with which he conducts the manifold and complex aspects of the position.

A large school system may have a number of administrative assistants and assistant superintendents for instruction, business affairs, plant maintenance, personnel, or public relations. Some large systems are divided into subordinate districts under the direction of district superintendents. An array of subordinates distributes responsibilities and extends the executive functions for the chief administrative officer but it may result in the establishment of a large, powerful, and unwieldy bureaucracy.

THE PRINCIPAL The principal is the key figure in the school hierarchy, although his influence centers about the daily affairs of an individual school rather than broad policy concerns or general financial matters. The principal may have little to say about the adequacy of his school building or the funds available for plant maintenance or instructional supplies. The pay of his teachers is tied to a system-wide salary schedule; therefore, his opportunities to increase a teacher's financial position are limited to the granting of merit-pay awards, assignment to extra-paid duties or summer school instruction, or appointment or recommendation for appointment to a departmental chairmanship. Some principals are delegated a major responsibility in the hiring of new staff or the granting of tenure to experienced teachers. Others may make recommendations about their staff to superiors and some have little to say about its composition.

Extreme perceptions of the principalship were demonstrated in two best-selling books: One principal was completely isolated and the other was persistently interfering in the classroom.[4] Many principals operate in the moderate range as visible and helpful leaders and aids to their teachers. The major characteristic of a successful principal is his ability to relate to other people, for only if he can work with teachers can he lead them in the common endeavor. At the same time, an expertise in human relations must be accompanied by the necessary experience and information to provide expertise in the teaching process. The principal is not more expert than every teacher of every grade and subject, but he must certainly know general principles of curriculum construction and the teaching and learning processes.

The principal evaluates and facilitates instruction directly as he engages in supervision of the classroom. Supervision is resented by some teachers and may be ridiculed as "snoopervision." Yet there is no substitute for supervision in any productive endeavor as a means of determining the efficiency of the total process and the effectiveness of individual production units. The teaching faculty ought to plan a curriculum that will lead youngsters through a systematic and cohesive series of learning experiences, and the principal as a supervisor must both know the plans and observe their realization. He is the responsible agent to guarantee that society's educational objectives are realized in the classroom. If the school administration is to fulfill its obligation to ensure the quality of instruction and

[4] Bel Kaufman, *Up the Down Staircase* (Englewood Cliffs, N.J.: Prentice-Hall, 1964) and Jonathan Kozol, *Death at an Early Age* (Boston: Houghton Mifflin, 1967).

instructors, it must find free and frequent access to the classroom.

Unfortunately, there are few schools where supervision is conducted properly. In some schools supervision takes on the trappings of vindictive prying. In many schools it is conducted in a formal, ritualistic fashion, with the teacher and principal acting out a simulated supervision. The basic relationship is structured by an implicit agreement in which the principal respects the privacy of the teacher behind the closed classroom door as long as the teacher maintains a situation free from problem youngsters or problem parents. Failure to establish a satisfactory supervisory procedure makes the screening of teaching staff especially difficult. Decisions to retain or dismiss a teacher may then depend on hearsay and speculation rather than solid evidence.

Principals begin their educational careers as teachers. They elect to leave the classroom and pursue a masters degree in educational administration in order to receive state certification to qualify for employment as a school principal. Classroom teaching experience is usually a requirement for the principalship. A principal may seek advancement by moving from smaller to larger schools or to those considered more desirable at an increasingly higher salary, or he may move into a superintendency. Some successful principals are noted for their efficient organization of a school, while others move to better positions on the basis of their records as curriculum innovators.

THE COORDINATOR Many school systems employ elementary coordinators or supervisors who are responsible for the educational program in the elementary schools. The coordinator may have administrative responsibility over the principals or he may be placed in a cooperative relationship with them. In some systems the coordinator has a primary role in teacher recruitment and supervision. Other coordinators or supervisors may be employed in the school system by the central office as subject matter specialists who provide assistance to classroom instruction. They may engage in visitation of and consultation with individual teachers, be responsible for curriculum design and the preparation of teaching materials and evaluation procedures, and may plan and conduct workshops or other in-service programs. There may be audio-visual, library, or personnel services coordinators. States have certification requirements for supervisory personnel. Sometimes, for lack of a more appropriate title, a school system may identify as a subject matter "coordinator" or "specialist" a teacher who is assigned responsibilities for teaching subjects like art or music or physical education in more than one school.

instructional assistance

A teacher is an expert who presents as evidence of his expertise the record of a four-year educational program. Yet, like other experts (legal, medical, and commercial), he relies on the assistance of specialists who have concentrated on particular aspects of his broader responsibilities. In seeking assistance in the area of instruction, the teacher will gain invaluable assistance from those in school personnel services, from librarians, audio-visual and health specialists, and from secretarial or clerical and custodial personnel.

THE GUIDANCE COUNSELOR Pupil personnel services are helpful in facilitating classroom instruction. A school counselor should be available to every teacher at every level of instruction. Up to now guidance programs have been oriented toward secondary schools, a practice that would seem to be concentration on the wrong age levels. There should be, rather, consideration for the early identification, diagnosis, and treatment of psychological, emotional, and learning problems. But the guidance movement had a vocational emphasis at its inception, and occupational information or training and college placement have continued to be important aspects of the counseling program. Only as increased concern is shown for early treatment of problems that interfere with learning in the elementary school years will there be an acceleration of pupil personnel services into the lower grades.

State certification of counselors generally requires a masters degree with study in guidance procedures, psychology, testing techniques, vocational information, and supervised practice in counseling. Teaching and nonschool job experience may be required.

While guidance programs provide vocational and further educational advisement to secondary school pupils, youngsters of all grade levels may benefit from personal, social, or educational counseling. In addition, the counselor is able to provide teachers with information about their students—their abilities and achievements, home and family situations, and emotional, psychological, and health conditions. The guidance office garners much information about youngsters through administration of tests and questionnaires and it is the logical center for collecting and recording other information.

Many schools establish a procedure in which new youngsters enrolling in the school are directed first to the counselor who will administer the appropriate tests and collect the necessary information. Counselors should be able to work with minor personal problems of youngsters and make appropriate referrals for treatment of severe problems. The role of disciplinarian, however, undermines the status of the counselor; instead, the guidance office should work with teachers and administrators in solving school behavioral problems. Counselors ought to be valuable consultants in the identification and treatment of learning problems and may be consulted on questions of grade placement or grouping assignments.

THE SCHOOL PSYCHOLOGIST Whereas every counselor should be able to administer and interpret standardized group tests and in some cases is qualified to administer individual tests, the school psychologist administers individual or group ability or diagnostic tests and works with children who have severe problems. Although every school should have at least one counselor, the school psychologist will serve several schools. In contrast to the counselor who is concerned with all youngsters, the school psychologist concentrates on the exceptional youngster: the retarded or slow learner, the gifted, and the physically and emotionally or psychologically handicapped. The psychologist works with many problem youngsters and may refer serious cases to a psychiatrist who accepts school referrals. The psychologist is called upon to identify emotional and psychological problems. He recommends youngsters for placement in classes for the gifted or retarded. He may also supervise special classes for exceptional youngsters or work closely with teachers whose classes include children with serious problems.

SPECIAL TEACHERS, ATTENDANCE OFFICERS, AND SOCIAL WORKERS The classroom teacher may consider among his most helpful colleagues the special teachers who remove from his classes the mentally retarded youngster, the emotionally disturbed, the seriously crippled, or the sight- or hearing-handicapped. He is aware of the aid rendered by remedial specialists who seek through part-time instruction to bring the reading, arithmetic, or speech skills of youngsters up to expectations or to assist children in removing deficiencies in school achievement. Visiting teachers go into the community to instruct homebound youngsters, who may also be served through educational television or two-way telephone instruction from the classroom. Others who serve the schools in the community include attendance officers, whose task is to enforce the state's compulsory education laws, and school social workers. The social worker works with teachers, youngsters, and parents in attempting to alleviate or resolve school problems. His task is similar to that of the counselor, but his efforts are directed toward those problems that are centered in the home. States may have established requirements for certification of special and visiting teachers and school social workers.

THE SCHOOL LIBRARIAN Books are important learning tools and the school library is an essential resource for instruction and an adjunct to the classroom. Most secondary schools have a library, but most elementary schools do not, even though attitudes toward books and the habit of visiting the library ought to be developed early in school. The school librarian should ensure that effective use is made of the school library. Of course, a librarian may find it difficult to maintain an adequate and up-to-date library collection if an inadequate budget is provided for library acquisitions. An important service rendered by some librarians is to assemble books on a specific subject for a teacher to use in the classroom. The librarian is also a valuable assistant to a teacher in the instruction of study skills; they may even teach units on library usage to classes. In some schools individual youngsters serve as library assistants and may be organized into a library club.

Practices established in schools can reduce the effectiveness of a school library. The unfortunate use of the library as a refuge from the boredom or tyranny of a study hall may build negative associations toward libraries among a student body. Lack of sufficient staff may result in a library that is not available to pupils during periods of the school day. Some schools issue cards that are punched when a pupil visits the library; one school, for example, limited students to two punches a week. School librarians may discourage youngsters from using the library by the cross and unsympathetic way they enforce rigid and unrealistic rules controlling pupil behavior and library usage. In addition, school librarians may be continually behind in cataloging and shelving acquisitions. Not only are pupils denied use of the books, but also much library work and study space is thus taken up with piles of delivered but unprocessed volumes.

Many school library problems might be solved if youngsters learned library usage and skills early in their school experience. Other difficulties might be alleviated by employment of properly educated librarians. Remaining concerns may be responsive to the efforts of teachers who recognize the importance of adequate libraries that are properly used. Bookmobile visits to school or taking a class to a public library are not effective substitute experiences for youngsters in schools that do not have a library, but they are far more satisfactory than no library experiences at all.

THE AUDIO-VISUAL COORDINATOR Many schools have an audio-visual coordinator, a position that may be a full assignment in a large school or a part-time responsibility of a teacher in a smaller school. Responsibility for the audio-visual program was a relatively simple task into the 1960s: It was concerned with scheduling films and arranging their showing and providing filmstrips, tape recordings, record players, and opaque projectors for use in the classroom. The rush season for the audio-visual coordinator was in late winter or early spring, when film orders were filed and filmstrips or other materials selected and requisitioned.

The floodgates for new instructional materials opened during the post-Sputnik panic, although there is little evidence to suggest that the international space race really had anything to do with the fact that technology finally took notice of the field of education. Perhaps an equal impetus was the challenge to the classroom status quo that was posed by educational television and programmed instruction. Rapid development of new techniques increased the scope of instructional tools for the classroom and the knowledge and skills needed by the local "expert." Reproducing and duplicating techniques, for instance, have been brought together by the copying machine; thus many tasks previously performed separately by the secretarial staff and audio-visual personnel are now done swiftly and conveniently on a single machine.

The audio-visual specialist has provided a wide range of instructional tools for the classroom. There should be very few classrooms that do not benefit from the extensive audio-visual techniques that are now available, even if there is a similarly small proportion that enjoys the full potential of what has been provided. But the average classroom is now offering a greater number of experiences, a wider variety of techniques, and more meaningful learning experiences than have been available to any previous group of students.

Expanse of the audio-visual tools and techniques has led to proposals that a more descriptive and functional label is "multimedia" techniques. Some instructional innovations, such as team teaching, have emphasized the preparation and use of classroom tools and devices, and one result of this emphasis is to store and produce devices and materials in the library, which is then expanded to house multimedia procedures and becomes a teaching materials center. The advantage of organizing procedures is that those things that ought to be done can be done. Excessive organization, however, tends to create operational bottlenecks that may be so suffocating and demanding that potential users prefer to struggle without the service. The most promising and exciting schoolhouse phenomenon has been the development of a fascinating array of tools and techniques for the classroom. Special graduate degree programs have been developed by many colleges for audio-visual or multimedia personnel and increased state certification requirements will develop in the pattern of other schoolhouse specialties.

SCHOOL HEALTH SERVICES The premise that healthy youngsters learn better is generally accepted. Thus the school nurse provides important assistance to the classroom in instructional services, makes information available to teachers, and consults with them. Nurses check the physical condition of youngsters and determine whether to send them home or admit them to school. They make routine hearing or sight examinations and, in cases of emergency, may screen for disease or infection. Treatment of youngsters in school by a nurse is usually restricted to emergency or first-aid measures.

The nurse should inform teachers about those youngsters with health problems or physical disabilities and advise them of the routine or emergency attention that may be required. Special concern is directed toward the identification of pupils who may have serious health problems, such as epilepsy or diabetes. Proper reactions to emergencies like epileptic seizures or insulin shock and the more common fainting or classroom and playground injuries should be explained to a teaching staff. First-aid demonstrations and practice should be a regular part of a school's in-service program.

In more routine matters, teachers should be acquainted with symptoms of childhood diseases and ought to be alerted when there are infections or contagious diseases or the threat of them present in the community. The teaching staff should be able to identify potential sight or hearing problems and the school nurse should inform teachers of cases of substantiated sight or hearing loss so that corrective measures may be taken in the classroom.

Every school should have a nurse on duty, but some schools employ nurses on a part-time basis only and others provide no health services at all. There are some school systems that include dental and/or medical treatment. Public health measures, such as the free distribution of polio vaccine, may also be conducted in the school. Some youngsters drink free or inexpensive milk and eat economical but nutritious lunches at school; children of families on welfare may be given free lunches. Some large city public schools have adopted a Scandinavian innovation that provides a free breakfast for poor children in the inner city. Teachers in those schools have commented on the improved reactions of pupils who previously had come to school without a substantial breakfast. School health services do pay dividends in improved learning and more effective teaching.

THE SUBSTITUTE TEACHER Unnoticed and underrated in the educational picture is the substitute teacher. The stereotype of the substitute is a bewildered individual who vainly tries to prevent extensive property damage and personal injury in a classroom during the absence of the regular teacher. Often little more is expected of a substitute than that pupils be kept occupied and out of trouble. The reaction of the other teachers and the school principal when a substitute is employed may be to ignore the substitute and his problems. The casualness with which the interests of the teacher who is absent, a class of youngsters, and the substitute teacher may all be ignored is an unfortunate circumstance. Team-teaching procedures may eliminate the crisis situation when a single teacher must be absent from the classroom. In addition, nearly every community includes among the housewives, professionals, and merchants many former teachers who could be available for short-term substitution in the classroom. However, most school systems do not exert the energy needed to compile an extensive substitute-teacher roster but are content to rely on volunteers.

The substitute teacher is more important than is generally

conceded by professional educators or the public. To be wisely and effectively used, the substitute must be granted necessary support and assistance. As a significant aid to the practicing teacher, he should be honored and recognized for the service he performs.

TEACHER AIDES Teacher aides have begun to come into use in the schools. Usually they are relatively untrained teacher assistants. Other terms used for teacher aides include "school volunteers," "paraprofessionals," and "auxiliary personnel." Teacher aides are included in many plans for team teaching but they were first used in the traditional classroom to handle clerical tasks and to relieve the teacher of many noninstructional responsibilities. Teacher aides do perform a wide variety of tasks in the schools, from monitoring halls, lunchrooms, playgrounds, and study halls to correcting compositions for an English class. Housewives often serve as part-time teacher aides and even off-duty firemen have been employed. State departments of education have now shown a concern for the qualifications of those approved for teacher aide duties in schools. The outlook is that certification of teacher aides will become accepted practice and training programs will be offered by an increasing number of colleges and universities.

THE SECRETARIAL AND CLERICAL STAFF Many experienced teachers recognize the extremely important role that may be performed by a school's secretarial and clerical staff. Whether or not the office force promptly prepares and runs off assignments, tests, or teaching aids; whether these tasks are done carefully and correctly; and whether a secretary or clerk responds to requests with a smile or a frown may determine how often a teacher seeks such aid or whether the teacher will prefer to spend his time awkwardly doing what others may do with ease.

Clerical services are of lesser importance in those schools that have set up teaching materials centers or that have available to teachers some of the new and efficient duplicating and copying devices that have been developed. The office personnel may be of assistance to a teacher as consultants and sources of invaluable information. Not only might they suggest that this is not the right morning to make a request of an administrator, but clerks may have important information about the community. Many veteran secretaries have witnessed a parade of teachers who have worked effectively in the community or who have encountered difficulties there, and they can suggest individuals or groups in the community who may be of assistance to classroom instruction. There is nothing mysterious about the way a teacher gains cooperation from a school office force. It requires nothing more or less than to exercise with secretaries and clerks those rules of interaction that prevail in the successful classroom: courtesy, patience, understanding, and a respectful attitude.

THE CUSTODIAN The unseen, unknown, and unsung hero in one fictionalized account of teaching in a large city school[5] is the custodian. He probably has many counterparts in real life. A custodian is charged with routine maintenance. His primary task is to clean the school. Many custodians attend to minor problems, such as a thermostat that requires adjusting or a broken window that needs replacing, although a large school system might employ carpenters, painters, plumbers, and other skilled craftsmen who would be responsible for all repairs and major maintenance. In the experience of many teachers, the custodian is far more than a janitor, for he is an instant zipper repairman or the volunteer builder of models and gadgets for the classroom. Many custodians are pleased to sand desks that snag clothing or fashion extra shelving from an inexhaustible supply of scrap lumber. The custodian's encyclopedic knowledge of a building may bring out useful castoffs from a remote storage space in the basement or will make available an item that lies unused by one teacher to another teacher who will use it. The custodian may respond readily to those who acknowledge his efforts and grant him respect, or he may remain hidden in the bowels of a school to the demanding snob.

conclusion

Learning is the sole purpose for the existence of a school, and the primary aid to learning is teaching. Learners and teachers are dependent on many others, who may inhibit or facilitate the process. The effective teacher understands and responds to the roles of the public, the school board, potential resources in the community, the administration and the specialists it employs, and the noninstructional staff. He makes use of those techniques of human interaction that will initiate confidence

[5] Kaufman, *Up the Down Staircase.*

rather than fear, acceptance rather than rejection, and an appreciation of common and long-range goals instead of selfish egocentrism and a concern only for an immediate and limited focus. As he seeks employment in a school, the sensitive and perceptive teacher first honestly and thoughtfully assesses his own strengths and weaknesses and his personal and professional needs and goals. He then seeks information about a prospective school system and its community to determine how well his purposes and personality will fit in with the uniqueness of the community. He is searching for a school where he may find success in teaching, for failure is not only a personal tragedy but it also means that youngsters have been deprived of learning experiences. The veteran teacher should be constantly reexamining himself and his actions, the actions of administrators and colleagues, and those of the public and the community to ascertain where are the points of strength and weakness that affect his classroom. He may alter his own behavior or exert an influence for more satisfactory attitudes on the part of his colleagues and the public.

on your own

The teacher-to-be should study the various individuals and groups that affect the role of the teacher and the activities of the school. Educational periodicals may discuss the teacher and the public, parents, administrators, and other school personnel. Surveys of vocational opportunities in education are not plentiful, but one useful reference is John A. Green, *Fields of Teaching and Educational Services* (New York: Harper & Row, 1966).

The best place for a student of education to begin analyzing local influences on the schools is in the community with which he is most conversant. If he can analyze a familiar community, then he should be able to proceed in strange situations. What kind of support, for instance, is given the public schools in your hometown? What is there about the socioeconomic level or political structure of the community that accounts for this level of support? How are community attitudes reflected in the school's physical plant, extent of curricular offerings, amount of instructional materials, and salaries paid to the public schoolteachers?

How is the school board or school committee selected in your community? What kind of persons are on the board? Why are they there? Are you able to identify the local power structure that runs your community and its schools? What are its major concerns in education?

Would you rate the administrators of the schools you attended as superior, average, or mediocre? On what do you base this judgment? What was the relationship between the school administration and pupils in the school? What do you think the relations were between the administration and the teaching staff? Provide examples to substantiate your opinions.

Recalling the schools you attended, describe the forms of assistance provided to teachers in student personnel services, subject matter specialists, library facilities, and health services. What was your opinion of the clerical and custodial staffs? Substantiate your opinions.

Having evaluated the schools you know in the light of your own experiences, describe the ideal community and school system in which you would prefer to teach. What are your chances to be employed in this type of a situation when your own background, ability, experiences, and special needs are considered? What would be the logical adjustments that should be made in your expectations or in the limits you have placed on the kind of community or school where you would seek employment?

The public and the schools are a continuing story as reported in the public media, particularly in news stories in the daily press and in popular periodicals. *Time* and *Newsweek* usually include a section on education. Case studies of public controversy centering on the schools are reported in David Hurlburd, *This Happened in Pasadena* (New York: Macmillan, 1951); Thomas K. Minter, *Intermediate School 201, Manhattan: Center of Controversy* (Cambridge, Mass.: Graduate School of Education, Harvard University, 1967); and Estelle Fuchs, *Pickets at the Gates: The Challenge of Civil Rights in Urban Schools* (New York: Free Press, 1966). A general discussion is included in V. T. Thayer and Martin Levit, *The Role of the School in American Society,* 2nd ed. (New York: Dodd, Mead, 1966).

A particular problem is the subject of Walter G. Hack's *Economic Dimensions of Public School Finance: Cases and Concepts* (New York: McGraw-Hill, 1967). The National Commission on Professional Rights and Responsibilities of the National Education Association publishes reports of investigations into school systems where serious problems have developed. An example of the commission's work is the report

Knoxville, Tennessee: When a City Government Fails to Give Full Support to Its Schools (Washington, D.C.: the Commission, 1967).

Those interested in school administration might consult Roald F. Campbell, John E. Corbally, and John A. Ramseyer, *Introduction to Educational Administration,* 3rd ed. (Boston: Allyn and Bacon, 1966); and the book of readings edited by Robert E. Wilson, *Educational Administration* (Columbus, Ohio: Merrill, 1966).

The relations of teachers to other school personnel is the subject of discussion in Dean L. Hummel and S. J. Bonham, Jr., *Pupil Personnel Services in Schools: Organization and Coordination* (Chicago: Rand McNally, 1968); Cecil H. Patterson, *The Counselor in the School* (New York: McGraw-Hill, 1967); Jack J. Delaney, *The School Librarian* (Hamden, Conn.: Shoe String Press, 1964); and Gertrude Noar, *Teacher Aides at Work* (Washington, D.C.: Commission on Teacher Education and Professional Standards, National Education Association, 1967).

additional references

Byrd, Oliver E. *School Health Administration.* Phila.: Saunders, 1964.

Byrne, Richard H. *The School Counselor.* Boston: Houghton Mifflin, 1963.

Dapper, Gloria, and Barbara Carter. *A Guide for School Board Members.* Chicago: Follett, 1966.

Detjen, Ervin Winfred, and Mary Ford Detjen. *Elementary School Guidance.* 2nd ed. New York: McGraw-Hill, 1963.

Fawcett, Claude W. *School Personnel Administration.* New York: Macmillan, 1964.

Gross, Neal. *Who Runs Our Schools?* New York: Wiley, 1958.

Haviland, Virginia. *Children's Literature: A Guide to Reference Sources.* Washington, D.C.: Government Printing Office, 1966.

Huck, Charlotte S., and Doris Young Kuhn. *Children's Literature in the Elementary School.* 2nd ed. New York: Holt, Rinehart and Winston, 1968.

Janowitz, Gayle. *Helping Hands: Volunteer Work in Education.* New York: Harper & Row, 1966.

Koerner, James D. *Who Controls American Education—A Guide for Laymen.* Boston: Beacon Press, 1968.

Lane, Willard R., Ronald G. Corwin, and William G. Monohan. *Foundations of Educational Administration.* New York: Macmillan, 1967.

Ohlsen, Merle M. *Guidance Services in the Modern School.* New York: Harcourt, Brace & World, 1964.

Pois, Joseph. *The School Board Crisis: A Chicago Case Study.* Chicago: Aldine, 1964.
Wiles, Kimball. *Supervision for Better Schools.* Englewood Cliffs, N.J.: Prentice-Hall, 1967.

12

philosophy and theory

Philosophy is frequently a frightening word to school people. Certainly one of the most demanding intellectual activities is that philosophy which is a highly specialized scholarly pursuit of the meaning of life and of man, of the purposes of individual, social, political, scientific, and religious concerns, and of the ways in which the perception, definition, and significance of life are interpreted. Historically, philosophizing has been reserved for exalted thinkers. Although the scholar may scoff at the thought, philosophy as a system of principles or beliefs is the prerogative of every individual who possesses some kind of a philosophical base, even though that base may be disorganized or contradictory.

philosophy and theory in society

Philosophies may mold societies; they have led to the creation and the destruction of civilizations. In a philosophical promise enslaved men have seen themselves made free, the poor have seen wealth, and the guilt-ridden have seen their own redemption.

Theories have directed the form and style of life. Pursuit of theories have led men to confront the dangers of the unknown from mysterious natives on a strange shore to the vast emptiness of space. They have led men to find new uses for nature. Thundering water, for instance, has electrified cities and discarded minerals have unlocked the means to previously unimagined power.

basic philosophical positions

The dominant philosophy determines how a social order shall be organized, what the purposes of that organization shall be, and what relations with other societies should be established. One major difference in philosophical beliefs has to do with the nature of man—whether he is basically good or evil. A society that considers man basically good tends to grant the individual greater freedom with which to exercise his goodness, is inclined to judge a man innocent until proved guilty, and exalts the equality of persons and the rights of the individual. A society that describes man as basically evil seeks a high degree of control over the individual through the family, in the practice of religion, or through governance of the state. Without engaging in a complete discussion of the philosophical positions concerned, a few illustrations may clarify the importance a philosophical assumption exercises upon the people who are under the influence of that philosophy.

In the modern world basic differences in describing the nature of man are expressed in the structuring of totalitarian or democratic societies. In the communist world, for example, the capitalist system is said to have corrupted man, who has become both a product of exploitation and an exploiter of his fellow-man. It is therefore the duty of the state to rigidly control the citizen until he evolves out of the selfish pattern and learns to live free of exploitation in a perfect society. In addition, because other societies are exploitative in nature and because they seek to destroy communism, communists must war against these capitalistic and imperialistic groups.

The modern noncommunist totalitarian society conceives of man as too ignorant or too weak to participate in the process of governing himself. The major enemy is identified as the threat of communism to overthrow the existing social and economic order. The near-extinct absolute and hereditary monarchy presupposes that some mysterious power, which may be described as a gift of divine origin, has granted to a family the right and duty to manage the lives of its subjects. In a theocratic society supreme knowledge and power rest in the church, which derives its authority from divine sources. Thus in a totalitarian society wisdom rests in an individual or in a small group; it is never acknowledged to rest in the mass of a population.

A democratic society credits each individual with the right and ability to make many decisions for himself and to participate to a greater or lesser extent in making the major decisions for his neighbors. The state serves rather than controls its citizens; it often acts as a buffer for minority groups against the tyranny of the majority. The degree of freedom in a society may be measured by the acceptance of nonconformity in such matters as religion, customs, language, dress, and even political beliefs. While defending themselves against totalitarian enemies, democracies tend to depend upon less aggressive, more reasonable, and more optimistic measures than overt or covert aggression. Believing in the inherent good of man, the democrat expects that the citizen in a dictatorship will eventually and inevitably assert his rights and gain his freedom. Wisdom in the democratic society rests with dialogue and the arriving at a consensus by the people.

the evolution of a philosophy

The evolution of a philosophy is not a mysterious process. Built upon the traditions and culture of the past, a philosophy is oriented toward an understanding of the present and aimed toward adaptation to the future. In the leisurely world that endured through the eighteenth century, changes required to meet nature and adapt to a human environment came about slowly. Those principles and beliefs that served as the prevailing philosophies were challenged slowly when they were challenged at all and tended to assume an exaggerated status of perpetual truth. As changes were accelerated through scientific advances and the development of nation-states, attempts to restructure beliefs to accommodate to and explain change suffered from the lack of extended exposure and persistent repetition, which a leisurely evolution had permitted through the centuries. The later philosophies have all lacked the aura of truth of the ancient; today a philosophy becomes outmoded and discarded before it may be understood or tested.

In the developing United States the dominant and traditional philosophy was able to withstand most of the pressure from the myriad of cultures that were represented by the waves of immigrants that flooded the country, for an "Americanization" process reduced differences and absorbed the newcomers into the established mold. An evident instance of the elimination of one philosophy in a conflict was the experience of the Mormons, who migrated to Utah to establish a separate society only to be eventually recaptured into the greater society. In this instance the majority enforced its position in this philosophical conflict as a condition for the admission of the state of Utah into the Union. The clash of philosophies that has occurred in recent history has been with groups in our urban ghettos. These economic and ethnic groups had become isolated and insulated from the dominant pattern. The role that tradition has played in molding the present provides a base upon which a philosophy must be structured.

An important influence to a developing philosophy is that some explanations or theories that were once described in rational terms are now verified in scientific terms and have thus become excluded from the metaphysical clash. While it might seem that this consequence would reduce the range of the philosophical field of action, one may recognize the increasing complexity of human problems that are not yet subject to scientific analysis. Some of these problems have become as great a threat to the survival of man as some frightening scientific advances. Included among these increasingly difficult questions are the purposes, structure, and function of the educational system.

derivation of a theory

The description of an existing order or a proposal for a new one requires a systematic structuring from philosophy to theory to practice. Accepting a philosophical position leads to the selection of theories that support it. There is a multiplicity of theories about anything, including some that are true or false, weak or strong. No theory is pure and unaffected by other factors. Even scientific theories do not stand in full truth when applied in practice. Theories describing the effect of gravitational forces on freely falling bodies, for example, are modified in practice by friction, winds, and earth rotation. The carefully structured space program finds theories accommodated by the application of various corrections during orbital flights. Practical demonstrations of theoretical inaccuracies led to changes in astronaut activity in a weightless state.

The particular philosophy that is applied to solve problems or discover meanings leads to the development of theories that explain how to reach specific objectives. Theories are general principles that seek to explain phenomena. They are derived from plausible explanations or empirical data. Theories tend to originate from within a philosophical framework as reasonable explanations when scientific evidence is lacking. Thus questions of the relation between man and god or man and nature led to theories that the earth was flat and that natural disasters were punishment visited upon man by the gods. As scientific data changed the known shape of the world and the source of earthquakes, those theories became divorced from philosophy and became philosophically neutral. Atoms are split and satellites orbited in the same fashion under any system of philosophical doctrine.

While a philosophy is all-encompassing in its attempt to meet the broad needs of man and is scarcely subject to verification in its grand form, a theory is directed toward a specific problem and is subject to experimentation and testing. Nonscientific theory may be executed and evaluated; it is interpreted subjectively and is supported by beliefs and opinions; but this process has obvious weaknesses.

The alternative to rational or scientifically derived theory is no theory at all. Conversely, to attempt to operate without a theory is an impossible situation. The narrow view that does not tolerate any theory not supported by scientific evidence ignores the fact that even objectively derived theory may have been the result of a concern first demonstrated by intelligent guess and the statement of a rational theory. Any thinking individual fills in the nonverified gaps in his perception with the best substitute within his repertory. A logical explanation provides an acceptable alternative when a systematically documented theory is not available.

role of the philosopher in building a philosophy

In building a philosophy the philosopher formulates a defensible construction of the present, incorporating his interpretation of the influences of the past. He must either accept or reject the ancient premises. He identifies major problems, describes their nature, and proposes means for their solution. His major contribution is to suggest the new structure of the future that is to replace the present. This new structure may be phrased in general terms or in detailed theories. If he is to build a system that is relevant and meaningful to those who are to come to know and accept it, the philosopher cannot be aloof from his civilization; he must be immersed in it. A philosopher who is imprisoned in an ivory tower may search his own soul or engage in linguistic gymnastics; out of touch with the world, however, he cannot meet it or its problems.

The role of the philosopher may be compared to that of the scientist. Both men construct theories out of their total information. Unlike the scientist, however, the philosopher's source of information is internal. He evolves his theory from the sum of his own perceptions, while the scientist relies upon verifiable evidence. Yet if the philosopher's theory lacks scientific evidence, it cannot be assumed that the theory is false. It may stand as a viable theory until replaced by scientific evidence or by a theory graced with superior logic or until the times and needs have changed and the original problem no longer exists in a form that is appropriate to the theory.

philosophy and theory in education

Most schools consider the stating of a philosophical position an important undertaking. The ever-present teachers' handbook, for example, commonly includes a statement of the school's philosophy, and it may appear to emphasize paragraphs that read pleasantly rather than descriptions of the true principles which the school staff reflects in practice. Similarly, the learning theories accepted by the teachers may be unrelated to activity in the classrooms. The discrepancy is less obvious, however, because a statement of the theoretical position is seldom published.

the importance of a basic philosophical position to the schools

Only indirectly do the schools mold the society. They play an important role in the attitudes that are formed and the verbal skills and competencies acquired by future citizens. What the school does to, for, or with youngsters is dictated by how the school perceives its task and the model of the youngster it seeks to mold. Perceptions and models involve ideas (principles) and are the reflection of a philosophical position.

Children in school may divide numbers in the same manner, yet the purpose of the school, the presence or lack of indoctrination, the degree and kind of responsibilities of the teacher, the structure of administration, the organization of nonacademic activities of youngsters, and instruction or absence of it in religious principles or Marxist ideology are dictated by the governing philosophy. Theories are structured about school administration, curriculum construction, the nonacademic responsibilities of the school, and the role of the public, administrator, teacher, and pupil. Theories describe what is happening, what has happened, or what should happen. Theory leads from philosophy directly to practice.

Because the beliefs that are held relative to the nature and purposes of god, man, nature, society, and government dictate what the school should be and how the educational process ought to take place, philosophy in and of education is extremely important in the life of a society and the career of a teacher. As the primary means by which society seeks to perpetuate itself, the school is central in interpreting the needs of society and in fulfilling them.

a democratic school philosophy

A democratic society by its nature permits a wide range of beliefs and practices by its citizenry, and its schools are bound to be caught up in a conflict of philosophies. While the school is open to the influences of diverse philosophical positions, it must serve the beliefs held by the larger society. In a democracy the school must operate upon a philosophy that promotes the worth of the individual and respects the majority and minority needs, aspirations, dreams, and realities. A pluralistic society requires a cohesive philosophy to maintain pluralism. The school is a central agency in promoting this philosophy.

Where does the classroom teacher fit into this matter of philosophy? Certainly all faculty members are not expected to become philosophers for the schools, with a responsibility to interpret the aims of the greater society and derive theories of structure, curriculum, and learning. However it is the teacher's task to understand the relationship between philosophy and theory so that he may execute theory into practice and the grand social objectives may be realized. Thus if the society accepts respect for the individual as an expression of its philosophy, then the classroom teacher fosters mutual respect by demonstrating acceptance of every youngster in his classroom. Respect for all is mutually extended by members of the class through the way a teacher exerts control over the situation. If freedom of expression and free inquiry are objectives to be achieved, the teacher avoids imposing his opinions on youngsters and allows free discussion in the classroom. The distinction between freedom with responsibility and license with irresponsibility becomes a limiting framework for approved or disapproved behavior. If the aim of a democracy is to educate all youngsters to their capacity, a teacher does not bend his efforts to the class elite at the expense of casting aside the slow learner. He does not force advanced pupils to sit by in idleness while he conducts drills for slower-learning pupils. He does not bore both extremes by catering to the average pupil but strives to meet the needs of all pupils: slow, average, and accelerated.

The teacher is in a peculiarly pivotal spot as a major symbol of authority and is the primary contact for many youngsters with a representative of the social order. If the teacher rejects them, the youngsters will feel that they are rejected by the social order. If the teacher is sympathetic to them, they will feel that the society has demonstrated interest in them. Thus the teacher is an implementer of the greater philosophy. He is an active element in the execution of theory.

The role of philosophy in the classroom becomes a personal affair to teachers and youngsters. The classroom is more than a center for learning, although learning is its major purpose. There are many peripheral activities that are not dictated by the needs of a democratic society and a teacher is permitted a wide latitude in conducting the affairs of the classroom. Therefore, in a democracy where differences are to be encouraged and permitted, a teacher's personal philosophy is probably the greatest influence on the eventual practice that evolves in the classroom.

Lacking the control and the supervision that a totalitarian structure provides, the American teacher may nevertheless actually be operating contrary to the democratic philosophy. Imagine, for example, a student-run meeting in which the chairman bangs his fist against the lectern growling, "And this meeting is going to be conducted in a democratic manner!" An instructor may reject the purposes outlined by society and impose his own contrary beliefs. If he is not aware of the true nature of the principles upon which he operates, a teacher may unwittingly contradict the greater social and philosophical principles that he believes he is upholding. As a very minimum, he should know how his practice is relating to a theory and a philosophy.

Perhaps the most serious charge against philosophy and theory is that they do not conform to reality. There are some who complain about a conflict between theory and practice in education. Teacher education programs are often said to propose theory that is remote from reality. A common criticism is that proposed methods or techniques are not effective in practice. Committee procedures, for example, are alleged to sound fine in the college classroom but lead to mayhem in the schoolroom. In some instances the criticism may be justified, but the charge may be a reflection of differences in frames of reference. Indeed, the educationist reflects a broad experience in teaching and acquaintance with a wide variety of schools, communities, youngsters, teachers, and administrators. A student or an onlooker whose judgments are based on a limited background may not accept facts or observations that do not conform to his own experiences. Those who attended highly authoritarian schools, for example, may dismiss the possibility that youngsters can learn in a permissive atmosphere. In addition, the graduate of a middle-class suburban school may refuse to concede the possibility that the study of an ancient civilization is considered completely irrelevant by a ghetto youngster in the center city. The student in education who relies on his own background to evaluate theories about teaching and learning is sheltered from reality by the limits of his experience. The system he accepts as valid may be the most absolute, the simplest, and the farthest from reality.

theory into practice in the classroom

In trying to systematize the art of teaching, demands for the undistorted application of theories in education to practice are ridiculous when they are not required of the most exacting operating sciences. Theory in the human realm is as important as it is in the physical sciences; but as in the sciences, application of theory about human behavior requires preciseness in the way it is carried into practice. Certainly the necessary corrections must be made to meet the problems caused by "human friction."

Practical application of theory in the classroom requires that the theory be logical or substantiated and painstakingly and correctly put into practice. Only by following a theory exactly may it be tested to ascertain its validity. If a school or a classroom is to become an educational laboratory for the purpose of testing a theory, a precision comparable to that observed in a scientific laboratory is required. The difficulty of controlling human factors in educational experimentation does not mean that theories cannot be tested, but it does suggest that it is more difficult to accept research findings with confidence.

Education does suffer from false theories as well as misapplication of theory. Faculty psychology theories have long been discarded but the senseless rote memory they propounded is still common practice in many classrooms. Sometimes ineffectiveness of classroom teaching methods is attributed more readily to incorrect application by the teacher rather than to basic faults in the theory. Core curriculum theories, for instance, suffer more from teachers who conduct block-time instruction exactly as they would under divided subject scheduling than from theoretical faults. Programmed instruction and educational television find resistance from teachers or administrators who do not understand or accept the techniques or who are too insecure to vary their sterile methods of teaching.

Teachers develop their own theories, their own explanations of known phenomena. The boiler room or teachers' lounge is a common forum for the enunciation of grass-roots theorizing: "The reason John Doe doesn't learn is because he has come under the influence of that gang from Elm Street," or "Elmer Smith is such a behavioral problem because his father is too busy making money and his mother is too busy spending it." A generous amount of hypothesizing is mixed with this theorizing: "If we flunked a few more of these kids they would change their attitudes." When these explanations are mere speculation or gossip or idle chatter, there is little impact on the classroom process. However, serious consequences may result from simplistic explanations that become the basis for a teacher's behavior and his means of operation.

John Dewey was correct in stating: "There is no inherent opposition between theory and practice; the former enlarges, releases and gives significance to the latter; while practice supplies theory with its materials and with the test and check to make it sincere and vital."[1] Insistence on the belief that there is conflict between theory and practice serves to immobilize education. It forces the school into an archaic and irrelevant position in a world of change and denies the opportunity to test theory so that that which is true may be separated from that which is false. Human problems have become more complex as a result of the technological revolution and they continue to become more serious despite the possibility that technology could or should be solving some problems that men have been unable to resolve. As social problems grow in their complexity, educational problems become more important to society and more demanding of those who are responsible for the schools. New social concerns for education are reflected in

[1] John Dewey, "Individuality and Experience," *Journal of the Barnes Foundation*, 2 (1926), as reported in Ralph B. Winn, *John Dewey: Dictionary of Education* (New York: Philosophical Library, 1959), p. 135.

the ever-growing concern for the quality of instruction, more persistent demands for its improvement, and the instability that results from the high rate of teacher turnover. Philosophies determine what the grand objectives are; theories determine how they will be achieved. To the extent that theories are not practiced, philosophies are not implemented.

base of current philosophy

A comprehensive examination of the various American educational philosophical positions is beyond the scope of this presentation. However, it is deemed advisable to consider the roots of the philosophical present with a particular emphasis on the role of the progressive education movement, which was the most important philosophical force planning an encouraging educational change in the twentieth century.

evolution of progressive education

Progressive education evolved out of the pragmatic philosophy of John Dewey. Growing out of a traditional heritage, pragmatism responded to the serious problems arising from industrialization and urbanization. In the area of educational philosophy, Dewey acknowledged the influence of Jean Jacques Rousseau, Johann Heinrich Pestalozzi, Friedrich Froebel, and Johann Friedrich Herbart. Spadework in the ideas of these European pioneers had been introduced in the United States by Edward A. Sheldon at the Oswego (N. Y.) Normal School, who popularized the "object method" of teaching, by the Charles Peirce inquiry into pragmatism, by G. Stanley Hall's psychological studies, and by Francis Wayland Parker's practice school, among others. Dewey also spoke of his debt to the American philosopher William James. It was John Dewey, however, who united the fragmented ideas, furnished philosophical purposes for reform of the schools, marked out a direction for the new education, and popularized these ideas through an active lecturing, publishing, and teaching career that spanned more than half a century.

At the turn of the century the educational world was ready for a Dewey to push the schools into a pivotal role in social development. There was a need to resolve social problems by emphasis on group processes. This need was also evidenced in the expansion of the right to vote, the growth of the labor movement, and the rise of professional organizations, such as the National Education Association and the American Federation of Teachers. As individual effort became lost in an expanding technology and the growth of the cities, it was necessary to develop within the individual the skills to govern himself and his society. Schools had to be moved from the irrelevance of a retreat to the academic clouds into a curriculum designed to prepare the individual for the realities of the world. Rather than perform only peripheral responsibilities of a meager elementary schooling for the vast majority and a stilted advanced course of study for the few, the school was to become the means by which everyone would adjust to a new, dynamic, ordered, and orderly society.

successes and failures in implementing the new philosophy

Serious efforts to implement the progressive educational philosophy were initiated and continued even into the decline of the progressive era. There were some outstanding triumphs among these efforts, some moderate successes, and a burden of failures. Among the results were those successes which exerted influence beyond the schools into the greater society. The most profound change was the successful attempt to bring the great bulk of youth into the basic educational system while extending the mass education movement past the high school into the colleges and universities. The curriculum was expanded and the most significant extension of the school program was the inclusion of terminal and vocational studies into a previously limited concern for college preparation. A selective education became comprehensive and highly organized extracurricular activities were added to the academic studies.

The vocational education movement gained wide popularity with the assistance of federally financed programs, but it has still failed to keep pace with technological developments. The division of the school structure after the first six years to separate the early adolescent into the junior high school gained wide acceptance, but the junior high school has been challenged by critics who complain that it does not meet the problems it was to have resolved. Attempts to democratize the schools by incorporating diverse elements into common classrooms have failed as the society has become racially and economically segregated through housing practices and the growth of private schools. Efforts to involve youngsters in democratic practices in the schools have not made significant progress. Instructional innovations, such as the core curriculum, have not fulfilled the ambitions of their proponents. Newer methodologies, including educational television and programmed instruction, have not revolutionized instruction; instead, their inclusion into the school program has been belabored and relatively ineffective.

Progressive education and the pragmatic philosophy have not been evaluated adequately because there was never a full-fledged trial in the schools in which potentials could be tested and the merits or defects identified with some degree of confidence. Lack of adequate leadership was a crucial factor in the failure to provide a realistic assessment of progressivism. Even Dewey was unable to control his own movement and felt compelled to speak out periodically against the excesses and misinterpretations of some of his followers. The decentralized nature of education makes it difficult or impossible for leadership to be effective in the profession, although as a short-lived approach to an effective expression of national leadership the remarkable tenure of Francis Keppel as the U.S. Commissioner of Education should be cited.

A significant factor in the reluctance of teachers to abandon old processes for new is their feeling of insecurity about their relations with children, parents, administrators, school boards, and the public. At one time the insecurity of teachers was due to a general lack of preparation for teaching. Then, when the education of teachers was extended, teacher insecurity reflected the increasingly difficult learning problems of mass education as well as a general instability in the profession. The result has been the conflict between teachers and administrators and school boards. The scope of this insecurity by teachers has been borne out by the disturbing rates of teacher shortage and turnover.

The lesson of progressive education demonstrated the potential and the limitations faced by the proponents of a philosophy in directing the development of an educational system. Modern schools have moved a great distance from those of the latter nineteenth century, and this was in large measure due to the initiative and goading of progressive education. At the same time, progressive philosophers failed to provide for an orderly transfer to a new order of philosophers seeking new directions for a changing world. A philosophy that was once considered radical had become moderate for the times or even outmoded, deficient, and stagnant. The triumphs of a philosophy in effecting educational change may demonstrate both a permanent and transient character, for some of the new developments that seem to be of the greatest importance at the time of change may be among the least significant in the longer term.

successors to progressive education

Among the hopeful successors to the progressive philosophers have been the reconstructionists under the leadership of Theodore Brameld. However, the net result of their effort has been an anxious waiting in the wings with never a call onto center stage. It is not likely that reconstructionism, with its emphasis on the school as the means through which the society shall be reformed, will take up the pragmatic cudgel. A central problem for the reconstructionist is the attempt to place the schools in a position of leadership in society when the schools are by their nature reactive to the demands of society. Lack of response to the reconstructionist offer is due to the lack of relevance of the philosophy rather than to conservatism or ignorance on the part of professional educators.

A more noteworthy successor to progressivism has been existentialism, which chose to break with the progressive ideals rather than to extend them. Where progressivism and reconstructionism exuded optimism, existentialism is pessimistic. Where the first two emphasized the role of society and the importance to the individual in becoming a part of the group, existentialism focuses on the uniqueness of the individual. Where progressivism and reconstructionism relied on social action to solve problems, existentialism proposes that the individual must rely on himself for the fulfillment of the future. Where the social-oriented proponents fought for a unity of their system, the individualists deplore the search for a system.

Dewey was the major spokesman for progressivism and Brameld for reconstructionism, but the existentialists do not have nor do they want or need a spokesman. They collect the existentialist writings of Sören Kierkegaard, Karl Jaspers, Jean Paul Sartre, and others. It would be contradictory for those who adopt as their keystone a belief in the irrationality of the world to deny that irrationality by proposing a rational system of their own. Finally, just as progressivism was a contradiction of its predecessors, existentialism contradicts the progressive theme.

In its appeal to the individual, existentialism has relevance to an education that must reorient its emphasis from that of the individual as a member of the group to recognition that the group is comprised of individuals. It even has some pertinence to the irrelevancy of an education that changes too slowly and clings too doggedly to curricular traditions.

conclusion

While it is important for the teacher to become knowledgeable about the greater philosophy directing the school, it is more essential that he recognize a responsibility to analyze, define, and organize his own beliefs as well as to understand, modify, and redirect his own set of principles to fulfill the grand purpose of the classroom. The teacher should not surrender his own philosophy to adopt uncritically that of someone else. Such subservience belongs in a totalitarian society. As a servant of society the teacher should support the basic philosophy by the manner in which he operates in the classroom. The American teacher has a responsibility to contribute significantly to the preparation of citizens for life in a democratic and technological society.

If a philosophy is to be meaningful, it must be consistent. If a set of operating principles are to be consistent, they must be understood. Therefore, a teacher should be asking and answering these vital questions: What are the essential components of man, god, and nature? For what purpose is man on earth? What should be the relations between men, man and nature, man and society, man and technology, and man and religion? What is the role of education to society, the individual, traditions of the past and hopes of the future? to church, state, social class, economic interest, and the family? What is the role of the teacher in fulfilling his own self? in meeting pupils, parents, administrators, taxpayers, and special interest groups? The answers that are formulated should be compared to the precepts that constitute the framework of the governing philosophy. Each belief should be weighed and evaluated.

The teacher who would have a well-formulated and consistent philosophy is a constant student of philosophy, the world, the great issues of the day, and the important questions confronting individual man. He contemplates the nature of the educational art, its new methodology, the findings of its research, and the subjects of conversation and debate among its artisans.

The teacher should not feel that these expectations are exorbitant or unrealistic. Every craftsman spends hours perfecting his craft and bringing himself up-to-date. The salesman attends regular meetings acquainting himself with the latest products and new techniques and technology. The accountant brushes up on accounting procedures to meet new tax requirements. The lawyer divides his time between studying new laws and the legal interpretations of the old. The physician ponders recent medical developments and the claims for new drug products. Thus as the individual meets his own personal changing world, he is reflecting on his old beliefs and changing some principles. He wrestles with internal conflicts and reframes his perception of himself, his role, and his place in the society. Every man is a student of philosophy. The teacher's task, however, is more generalized than are the responsibilities of many others. In addition, he is under greater pressure than most. There are certainly great demands on a teacher as a social agent in the formation of individuals and society.

on your own

The student of educational philosophy has a world to explore. Some of the great names come to mind: Aristotle, Plato, Locke, Rousseau, Emerson, Marx, Hegel, Kant, James, Dewey, Kierkegaard. Two prominent recent writers in education are Theodore Brameld and Israel Scheffler. Harsh criticism of the schools has been reflected in the writings of Arthur Bestor and Hyman Rickover, while writers like James B. Conant and Jerome Bruner have contributed reasonable and studied commentaries on education.

Examples of recent publications are S. J. Curtis and M. E. A. Boultwood, *A Short History of Educational Ideas* (London: University Tutorial Press, 1964); Philip H. Phenix (ed.), *Philosophies of Education* (New York: Wiley, 1961); and Ernest E. Bayles and Bruce L. Hood, *Growth of American Educational Thought and Practice* (New York: Harper & Row, 1966). Progressive education was analyzed by Lawrence A. Cremin in *The Transformation of the School: Progressivism in American Education, 1876–1957* (New York: Knopf, 1961) and has been the subject of discussion in educational journals, such as the article by Paul Nash, "The Strange Death of Progressive Education," *Educational Theory,* 14 (April 1964), 65–75, 82. Existentialism as it may apply to teaching is discussed in the collected writings edited by Maxine Greene, *Existential Encounters for Teachers* (New York: Random House, 1967).

Among the periodicals to be consulted for information on educational philosophy are *Studies in Philosophy and Education, Educational Theory* and journals such as *Harvard Educational Review, Teachers College Record, Educational Forum, Phi Delta Kappan, School and Society,* and *Educational Record.* Major bibliographical references are *Education Index* and *Social Sciences and Humanities Index.*

Theories of learning are described in John S. Brubacher (ed.), *Modern Philosophies and Education,* Fifty-fourth Yearbook of the National Society for the Study of Education (Chicago: University of Chicago Press, 1955). Curricular theory is discussed in Hilda Taba, *Curriculum Development: Theory and Practice* (New York: Harcourt, Brace & World, 1962). Edgar Dale in *Audio-Visual Methods in Teaching,* 2nd ed., (New York: Holt, Rinehart and Winston, 1955) is concerned with theory and use of instructional materials. Books on educational methods and child or adolescent development are concerned with theory. The specialized educational periodical literature also shows concern for theory, but the general, more popularly directed educational periodicals occasionally discuss theoretical matters.

To fathom one's own philosophy, an individual ought to bare his basic beliefs. The crucial questions should be listed on paper, where the facts may stand out. The answers, when compared with the basic principles of a democratic philosophy, will serve to delineate the individual's philosophical position, its consistencies and, of greatest importance, its contradictions. The philosophically sensitized teacher will measure classroom and schoolhouse procedures, outcomes, atmosphere, and human dynamics to determine the extent to which the greater objectives are being achieved and will seek ways to implement the grand philosophy.

One makes a philosophy alive by living it and by constantly assessing it, striving to perfect it, and pushing it to meet new demands faintly discernible in the future. One seeks to make a philosophy pertinent and significant and earthy by refusing to avoid it or relegate it to the ivory towers of academe.

Archambault, Reginald D. (ed.). *Dewey on Education: Appraisals with an Introduction.* New York: Random House, 1966.

Arnstine, Donald. *Philosophy of Education: Learning and Schooling.* New York: Harper & Row, 1967.

Brubacher, John S. *Modern Philosophies of Education.* 3rd ed. New York: McGraw-Hill, 1962.

Bruner, Jerome S., *Toward a Theory of Instruction.* New York: Norton, 1968.

Kneller, George F. *Introduction to the Philosophy of Education.* New York: Wiley, 1964.

Nash, Paul, Andreas M. Kazamias, and Henry Perkinson. *The Educated Man: Studies in the History of Educational Thought.* New York: Wiley, 1965.

Pai, Young, and Joseph T. Myers. *Philosophic Problems and Education.* Phila.: Lippincott, 1967.

Scheffler, Israel. *Conditions of Knowledge: An Introduction to Epistemology and Education.* Glenview, Ill.: Scott, Foresman, 1965.

——— (ed.). *Philosophy and Education: Modern Readings.* Boston: Allyn and Bacon, 1966.

13

teaching as a profession

In the first half of the twentieth century educators directed much attention and effort to the attainment of professional status for teachers. The importance of education was expressed by business, social, and political leaders who placed the responsibility for the success of a democratic political system, the proper functioning of complex commercial and industrial enterprises, and the solution of ever more threatening problems on the doorstep of the schoolhouse. The notion then circulated among teachers that they deserved the same prestige and reward that were the marks of professionals, and they looked upon medicine as the model for the building of teaching as a profession. While the money that a physician earned was mentioned as a proper goal for educators, the prestige granted to doctors and the resultant social and civil prerogatives and responsibilities were probably valued just as highly.

professional status

There is general agreement about the criteria that determine whether a vocation has achieved professional status. The first requirement is that the occupation perform a vital public service. The second requirement is that the professional have an extended and specialized education. The third is that the members of a profession should control admission into their select group. The fourth is that they should subscribe to a code of ethics, the observance of which is enforced by all members of the profession.

As educators viewed the situation, education had become a major and crucial public service by the turn of the century. At the same time, two-year normal schools were extending their programs, while some of the major universities had established departments or schools of education and were granting degrees in pedagogy. The path to professional recognition seemed to be relatively simple: a code of ethics remained to be adopted and enforced.

obstacles to achieving professional status

Failure to gain professional status may be traced in part to the fact that while the educational demands for teaching were increased, they merely kept pace with the extended education demanded for an increasing number of vocations. Moreover, in contrast to most other occupations, teaching has not been able to enforce the increased educational requirements. Many classrooms have been staffed with nonqualified persons under emergency certification provisions. In the decade 1955–1965, the number graduating from teacher education programs doubled, but the shortage of teachers each fall was an increasingly frustrating problem.

There were a number of reasons for the shortage of teachers. The postwar population explosion increased the number of pupils in school beyond the capacity to staff the classrooms. Intensification of urban problems shifted teaching in the city from high to low priority among those seeking positions and the cities experienced severe problems of recruiting teachers. The economy continued to prosper, permitting teachers with a low level of frustration to escape into other employment. A rising militancy among teachers, which was accompanied by teacher strikes or the application of sanctions against city school systems and states, contributed to the increased level of teacher turnover. In addition, qualified teachers were absorbed into the many new administrative, supervisory, and special teaching positions that were added to the school staff. Expanded college faculties and increased state and federal educational programs also drew personnel from the public schools.

One of the results of the teacher shortage was to nullify attempts to upgrade the educational requirements for teaching. An interesting contrast in this context may be made between medicine and teaching. Each has been in short supply in the period of burgeoning population. While the society unhappily struggles along without providing a substitute for adequate medical care, it solves the teaching problem by placing unqualified individuals in the classroom.

While there has been general acceptance of the need for the increased educational requirements for teaching, the status of teacher preparation programs has been challenged constantly. Some challengers have primarily been concerned with providing a ready supply of individuals for the classroom. They sometimes express the belief that anyone can teach. Other challengers are academicians who do not accept the legitimacy of professional programs for teachers. A group under continual harassment or the threat of it may react by an increased caution and conservatism, and this has been the response of some teacher educators to attacks upon them.

The matter of prestige in teacher education may also be reflected by students preparing to be teachers. In many instances the morale among students enrolled in elementary education programs is superior to their fellow students in secondary education. The elementary teacher-in-preparation is more certain about teaching as a career than some secondary education majors who are seeking job security in the knowledge that they may teach if other vocational preferences do not materialize or who feel that receiving a teaching certificate is preferable to earning a liberal arts degree without a specific vocational orientation. Each year a higher proportion of graduates from elementary education actually enter a classroom than do the graduates from secondary education.

Teachers generally have not been as enthusiastic about gaining professional status as their leaders. Most teachers would support the contention that teaching should provide higher financial rewards, although there may be teaching wives, single persons, or those with an especially strong dedication to teaching who do not place as much emphasis on an increase in teacher pay. There may be many more educators who do not believe that professional status is necessary or desirable, and still others who are not willing to accept the responsibilities that go along with professional status. Teachers, for example, resist the suggestion that they should be responsible for judging the actions of colleagues and they experience difficulty in accepting the idea that they could ever be placed in a position to bring charges of malpractice against another teacher or to hear such charges and pass judgment on them. They prefer to continue the traditions that have established the sanctity of a teacher's classroom and have placed supervision in the realm of administration. Moreover, teachers who look on the classroom as temporary employment rather than as a career and those who appear in the classroom without the minimum requirements of teaching would not be expected to show much interest in or support for the professionalization of teaching.

Interest in professional status by administrators was evidenced in the early 1960s when it was proposed that a separate profession be established for educational administration. To the extent that an educational profession of classroom teachers would undermine the traditional structure of school authority, however, administrators are inclined to be less than enthusiastic. Administrative support would readily be extended toward an increasing prestige for the classroom teacher, for example, for that would reflect positively on administrators. But those administrators who picture their role as being parallel to that of a business manager would resent the proposition that teachers should engage in policing of the profession. Many of these same administrators would object to the idea of the professional expressing his expertise through a greater participation in policy formation and execution. Some administrators would also experience difficulty in making the adjustment from the traditional pattern that has evolved in school administration to a situation similar to that of the hospital administrator who must cooperate with professionals in the formation of policy.

The public has not been concerned about the professional status of teachers. Local public representatives, the school boards, could be expected to resist the strengthening of the position of teachers and their assumption of additional responsibilities in the determination of policies and the operation of the schools. Yet despite the potential political power of teachers, state legislators, too, have not felt compelled to alter the status quo to grant additional prerogatives to teachers. Apparently the public and its representatives do not recognize a need for granting professional status to teachers, nor do they feel the pressures to do so.

the outlook for the future

However the future of teaching shall evolve, it will in large part be determined by the influence that teachers exert through their organizations. It might be expected that the eventual result of the exercise of teacher power will be a compromise between what the most optimistic teachers would propose and what those who prefer the status quo would demand. It is conceivable that professional status could evolve as readily from educational associations as from teacher unions. It is probable that one or the other will eventually become dominant and represent all teachers, and it is possible that circumstances could lead to a merger of the two groups.

Professional status would seem to be a worthy goal for teachers. It is an unrealistic expectation that professional status would automatically guarantee a high level of income. However, it should increase the qualifications of those who teach and reduce the rate of turnover in the classroom. It ought to provide opportunities for teachers to protect themselves and their classrooms against those encroachments that interfere with efficient teaching and learning. But if there is an increase in teacher effectiveness and greater stability within the ranks of teachers, then there should be less resistance to increased remuneration for teachers. The degree of commitment and the kind of activities that are required of teachers to gain professional status would necessitate a greater competence in the use of power and a more responsible leadership of the group. This would constitute a revolution within education. Whether this will come about depends largely on the effectiveness of the programs and activities of teacher organizations.

teacher organizations

The first type of teacher organization was the local association. The earliest is believed to have been the Society of Associated Teachers of New York City, which was established in 1794. Five years later the School Association of the County of Middlesex was organized in Connecticut. The first state associations were established in Rhode Island and New York in 1845. Many of the early teacher education textbooks were not concerned with the question of professionalism, and the exceptions that were, such as David P. Page's *Theory and Practice of Teaching* (1847),[1] mentioned teacher associations only in passing.

[1] David P. Page, *Theory and Practice of Teaching: or, the Motives and Methods of Good School-Keeping* (Syracuse, N.Y.: Hall and Dickson, 1847), 285–286.

Edgar B. Wesley in *NEA: The First Hundred Years*[2] reported four previous attempts to found a national organization of teachers before the National Teachers' Association was organized at a Philadelphia meeting in 1857. Membership was initially limited to men, although women could be elected as honorary members. Officers were elected and biennial meetings were scheduled. In 1870 the National Teachers' Association was combined with the American Normal School Association and the National Association of School Superintendents into the National Educational Association, which became the National Education Association in 1906. In the same year two departments were established, one for higher education and the other for elementary education.

The association grew in membership and added a number of departments. It supported (and at times implied that it should be credited with) increased national interest in education and expanding federal programs, from the Morrill Act and establishment of the Bureau of Education (later the U.S. Office of Education) to agricultural and vocational subsidies to federal interventions in schools in the 1960s. Not until 1921 was the *Journal of the National Education Association* first published. In 1946 it became the *NEA Journal* and in 1968, *Today's Education.*

The National Education Association mounted a largely ineffective lobby in Congress. Political leadership seemed to be most successful in establishing a cabinet post in a shared department with health and welfare interests, in supporting judicial decisions in matters of racial segregation in the schools, and in providing federal aid to education after a twenty-year struggle. A significant contribution to these changes was rendered by the research activities of the NEA and the proceedings and publications of many of its departments. In 1968 the membership of the National Education Association passed the one-million mark. The organization had begun to exercise more strength in supporting the growing militancy of teachers, and it began to impose sanctions against some states for failure to meet educational problems. The significance of this action was not in the effectiveness of sanctions but in the fact that they had been imposed. The NEA ordered the consolidation of racially segregated state affiliates

[2] Edgar B. Wesley, *NEA: The First Hundred Years* (New York: Harper & Row, 1957).

and proposed that NEA departments should require membership of at least departmental officers in the NEA, if not the entire departmental membership.

state and local associations

For over one hundred years the power of educational associations was exercised by local or state associations and departments of the National Education Association. Local and state associations varied widely in strength and a willingness to exercise their power. The pattern in Southern states was the establishment of two separate, racially segregated state associations. In some states the direction of the state organization was securely in the control of school administrators. In many cases teachers were coerced into joining local, state, and national associations, with school systems that boasted 100 percent membership duly noted in the appropriate journals. Before the enactment of district-wide salary schedules and state tenure laws, a teacher who refused to join an association or who engaged in unionizing activities might be penalized by a reduction of salary in the next year's teaching contract or by not being rehired.

Much effort was expended by state associations before and after World War II toward legislative action to increase certification requirements for teaching. Some state associations supported the development of two-year normal schools into four-year teachers' colleges. Associations also worked for the establishment of state retirement systems for teachers. It was not until after World War II in a period of teacher shortage, however, that educational associations came out of the shadow of administrative domination and teachers were able to substitute a uniform salary schedule for the process of bargaining individually for their pay. This was also the period when many states adopted tenure laws and some legislatures established and kept up-to-date state minimum salaries for public school teachers. However, unified teacher action was unable to prevent discriminatory laws from singling out teachers to sign loyalty oaths as a condition of employment in many states. Some groups unsuccessfully fought the enactment of legislation prohibiting strikes by teachers.

Most state associations now publish journals, which range from excellent to mediocre. They sponsor affiliate organizations for college students preparing to become teachers and also some worthy educational conferences and workshops.

Some provide legal services for teachers and funds to support legal actions in defense of teachers against unfair dismissal or other discriminatory actions. In addition, consultant and employment services for teachers are offered by some state associations. An increasing number of state associations are requiring unified dues of their members—the collection of local, state, and national dues in one lump sum.

the rise of unions

The most significant change in the National Education Association has been the increased militancy in furthering the interests of teachers as employees against state and local employers. This shift in policy, purpose, and action is directly attributable to unions for teachers. A court decision in 1961 provided for the granting of exclusive contract negotiation rights to the victor in a bargaining election held in New York City. The election was won by the unionized United Federation of Teachers. The UFT was an affiliate of the national American Federation of Teachers, which was in turn affiliated with organized labor, the American Federation of Labor–Congress of Industrial Organizations.

Although individual local teacher unions had been affiliated with the American Federation of Labor as early as 1902, when a San Antonio, Texas, group sought such recognition, the American Federation of Teachers was organized in 1916 in Chicago. The organization was prompted by a dispute over the right of Chicago teachers to belong to a union. At that time the AFT was supported by a few influential educators, among them John Dewey.

The growth of the AFT has been centered in the large cities. Accurate membership figures are difficult to accept from any of the competing groups, but the ratio of NEA to AFT members is about six- or eight-to-one. NEA membership includes teachers, administrators, and other noninstructional personnel. The AFT, on the other hand, emphasizes membership of classroom teachers and eliminates or restricts membership by other school staff. Furthermore, the AFT is not divided into subdivisions like the NEA, and its research activities have not been extensive, although it has published some excellent studies. The organization's journal, the *American Teacher,* was replaced by *Changing Education* in 1966.

AFT claims for the influence exerted by unionized teachers in advancing their interests seem to be as excessive and unrealistic as those of the NEA. However, it must be acknowledged that the AFT has changed the *modus operandi* of teacher organizations in their quest for answers to educational problems. One result is bargaining elections between teacher unions and associations, common in metropolitan areas. In addition, both types of organizations negotiate the conditions of employment with school boards. Unions engage in "collective bargaining," however, and associations participate in "professional negotiation." Until 1963 the AFT stated that it did not favor the strike as a weapon, even though it had resorted to striking and by then had made the strike an acceptable tool in practice. Strikes by teachers are illegal in some states, but schoolmen engage in coordinated "sick" or "professional study" days. Similarly, teachers have chosen to challenge directly the legal authority over the schools and have shown a willingness to ignore laws that would limit their actions.

Some teachers are concerned about the affiliation of teacher unions with organized labor. It is argued that teachers should not become identified with one sector of the economy, for they teach the children of all facets of society. The argument continues that teachers should not be placed in a position where they may be called on to support other unions in matters that do not concern teachers. The use of teacher strikes is rejected by some educators who propose that it is improper and unprofessional for teachers to go on strike whether or not laws have been passed prohibiting the strike. Countering arguments suggest that teachers in other countries have affiliated with labor unions without difficulties. The right to strike is said to be as necessary and proper for teachers in seeking solutions to their problems as for any other group.

professional activities

There are many opportunities for teachers to participate in professional activities. Those who show interest in organizational work and a willingness to expend the necessary time and effort are welcome additions to most faculties. Some teachers will have had valuable experience in college as members of student affiliates of the National Education Association or the American Federation of Teachers, as well as in other special college organizations for those preparing to teach. Many state organizations are divided geographically into districts or zones, which hold regular meetings to which all members are invited. In some cases the entire membership may be included in the regularly scheduled state meetings. Regional, state, or national meetings feature celebrated individuals as speakers. Teachers seldom congregate without having an opportunity to visit rooms filled with displays of the products of educational publishers and manufacturers of educational materials who are eager to take advantage of the occasion. The sponsoring educational organizations usually conduct their business at these meetings, and many teachers become active in these groups.

Professional activity need not be limited to teachers' associations or unions. Some of the divisions of the National Education Association provide opportunities for teachers to engage in activities that may be personally satisfying as well as educational. Every teacher who has joined the NEA, for instance, has been enrolled as a member of the Association of Classroom Teachers. Those who are interested in subject matter areas may join the American Association for Health, Physical Education and Recreation, the Music Teachers' National Conference, the National Council for the Social Studies, or similar groups in the areas of industrial arts, home economics, vocational education, art, journalism, mathematics, foreign languages, science, speech, and business. There are also departments for elementary and secondary school principals, teachers of exceptional children, audio-visual specialists, and others. Most departments publish journals or yearbooks, and some support excellent research projects and activities.

Efforts by the NEA to restructure relationships with the departments may result in some of the affiliated groups withdrawing from the parent organization to join any of a large number of other special teacher organizations. There is at least one organization for each teacher special interest group. There are many, varied groups through which teachers may cultivate their special concerns, including some with a special interest in educational philosophy or sociology, the teaching of reading, English, or religion, or the study of comparative education. Many groups publish journals, reports, or yearbooks. They hold periodic meetings and conduct workshops and conferences.

A review of an annual meeting of the National Council for the Social Studies is typical of most annual meetings. NCSS meetings are held in large cities throughout the country. In successive years the council met in Miami, Cleveland, Seattle, Washington, and Houston. The meetings are held during Thanksgiving week, with some participants arriving the previous weekend. Some business is transacted early in the week, but most of the group arrives on Wednesday or Thursday. Scenic tours are provided and there are visits to schools in the area. Some general meetings are scheduled for Wednesday afternoon, but the activity begins in earnest on Thursday morning when about 100 exhibits open and numerous discussions, lectures, or demonstrations are presented. Until Saturday afternoon participants ponder the state of the social studies, listen to suggestions for improving instruction, conduct the business of the organization, and visit the exhibits where they may be presented with gifts from apples to pencils or free textbooks for examination purposes, teaching materials, and sales catalogs. They watch demonstrations of the latest instructional gadgets and place orders for teaching materials.

By the time the teacher heads home from a national meeting of this kind he has participated in an intensive philosophical, theoretical, and practical reexamination of his craft. He has been exposed to the most exalted members and greatest minds of his group. He has had an opportunity to renew old acquaintances and gain new ones. The expense involved is often assumed or shared by a teacher's school system in the hope that some recognition of the community may result from professional activities and in the expectation that the teacher will profit from the experience in ways that will contribute to the affairs of the school and the instruction in the classroom.

honorary societies

Education, like many other endeavors, has honorary societies to which many teachers belong and through which they engage in professional activities. Three of the major honorary societies for teachers are Phi Delta Kappa, Kappa Delta Pi, and Pi Lambda Theta.

Phi Delta Kappa traces its founding to 1905, although the organization as it is now constituted dates from 1912. Membership is limited to men who meet requirements for graduate study and are considered to be potential leaders in education. The national organization publishes a newsletter and ten issues a year of the highly respectable *Phi Delta Kappan*. The organization has sponsored publication of Carter V. Good's *Dictionary of Education* and compilations of doctoral dissertations and research studies in education.

Kappa Delta Pi is open to both men and women in education whose scholastic rank is in the upper fifth of their institution. Founded in 1911, the society organized a Laureate Chapter in 1925 with a maximum of sixty members selected from the most distinguished educators in the nation. The organization's journal, *The Educational Forum,* dates from 1936, is published quarterly, and shares distinction as a quality publication with the *Phi Delta Kappan.* The society sponsors a Kappa Delta Pi lecture series and an annual fellowship in international education.

Pi Lambda Theta is open to women in education. Founded in 1910, the society publishes the quarterly journal, *Educational Horizons.* The society provides an annual *Education Book List,* which includes a continuing report on most of the books published in education and lists the outstanding books in the field. Books are listed by subject area. Educators find the publication very useful.

increasing competencies

With the fantastic increase in knowledge and the continuing development of new teaching techniques, it is necessary for teachers to continue to improve their subject matter background and instructional skills. Many schools engage in educational programs through which their faculties may seek to gain increased competence in selected areas of concern.

Some teachers participate in the in-service programs that are provided by a school system to increase the efficiency of its faculty. Large school districts may include the organizing and executing of in-service programs as one of the duties of supervisory or coordinating personnel. Smaller schools seldom have adequate staff for such purposes and arrange with colleges or universities to provide leadership and instruction for the in-service program. Opportunities to increase knowledge or improve skills may be required of teachers or provided for those who wish to participate. The arrangements may vary from a single lecture to the several meetings of a workshop or to a regular college-level course of ten or more lessons conducted after school once or twice a week. Some publishers sell packaged courses of study on the improvement of classroom instruction or on techniques of evaluation to the schools for use with in-service programs.

In-service programs may seem to be contemporary additions to school programs, but the procedure of improving teaching through lectures or group instruction has a long history. Teachers' institutes were initiated in the state of New

York in 1843, at about the same time that the first New York normal school was organized. In 1845 an attempt to provide state funds for institutes failed, but the money was voted two years later. In 1881 a permanent state organization was established to service teachers' institutes, with attendance made compulsory in 1885. The institutes were continued in New York until 1911.

Most institutes in New York were organized through county school superintendents. Both men and women teachers were in attendance at the sessions, which lasted as long as two weeks. The content of instruction at the institutes differed from the modern in-service program in the reading of Scriptures and prayers, but other aspects were comparable. Classes were conducted in organizing for instruction and the teaching of grammar, music, reading, geography, and science. Instruction at the institutes was provided by public officials, experienced teachers, and normal school or college instructors.

An infrequent but rewarding experience for teachers is the accreditation of a school. A properly conducted accreditation procedure provides an unusual opportunity to engage in a critical self-appraisal, an examination of what has been and what is, and the chance to dream about what may be. It permits a faculty to join in a common effort for improvement rather than to be concerned with individual problems. The expectation is that an accreditation process will be followed by efforts to correct deficiencies and meet the criticisms that were identified in the self-evaluation or the visitation report.

High schools and colleges are accredited by six regional agencies: the New England, Middle States (mid-Atlantic area), Southern, North Central (nineteen states in the center and near-west of the country), Western (the state of California), and Northwest associations. The accreditation associations have many critics, but the process seems to continue to gain in acceptance among schools and colleges throughout the nation. Procedures vary in the differing regions. Some state departments of education conduct separate evaluations of schools and others join in the accreditation with regional agencies. For instance, California's economy-minded legislature of 1966 terminated the state's role in a cooperative accreditation process with the Western Association.

In 1963 representatives of elementary school organizations in five central states organized the Association for the Evaluation of the Elementary School with the intention of adapting accreditation procedures to the lower school form. A series of accreditation procedures from kindergarten through graduate school could conceivably lead to an eventual standardizing of education on a national level. Like the proposal for a national assessment of the schools, the prospect should be an interesting and complex matter for study by educators.

The accreditation process includes four phases: application by the school for accreditation, self-study, evaluation by a visiting team of experts, and the decision by the agency involved whether or not to approve the institution and its program. Approval or accreditation certifies that an institution has a suitable physical plant, staff, and program; it grants a measure of approval to the graduates of the institution. Accreditation is sometimes required of institutions, particularly on the college and university level, to qualify for special programs or to be granted certain other privileges.

In the accreditation process faculty members follow detailed procedures to judge their institution and its programs. They write out a common philosophy, outline instructional objectives, and describe procedures. The self-evaluation is used as a guide by the visitation team, which spends several days in studying the institution and its program. The visitors report their findings to the accreditation agency and may confer with the institution to discuss the findings and to explain their recommendations for institutional self-study or improvement.

There is a ladder of advancement in teaching as in most other vocations. The common introduction to professional education is as a classroom teacher. To succeed in education is to become an acknowledged master teacher, to move into a position as departmental chairman, to become an administrator, or to teach on the college level. Master teacher status may be dependent on the local reputation of a teacher or it may be related to graduate study in teacher education or liberal arts programs. Administrative positions are related to the completion of a program in educational administration. The position of guidance counselor, subject matter coordinator, and principal or superintendent is dependent on the receipt of a masters degree. In some instances the school psychologist, school superintendent, or other specialist positions may require a six-year educational program leading to the certificate of advanced study. Completion of a program of study leading to the doctor of philosophy or doctor of education degree is an expectation for the professor in a college or university. The doctorate may also be the top preparatory degree for some superintendencies or other administrative positions.

The teacher who is interested in advancement in the field of education through graduate study must ascertain whether he qualifies for admission to the program offered by an institution of higher education. He needs to determine his long-range educational aspirations. Those who do not qualify for graduate study may increase their background and skills by attending college classes as special, nondegree students or they may engage in programs of self-study. It is still common practice for school boards to recognize efforts of teachers to improve their qualifications through foreign travel and certain kinds of summer activity or employment (archeological exploration or summer camp work, for example).

conclusion

Professionalism in education is a multifaceted subject. It is a matter of concern for all teachers who must decide what they should be and how their goals will be realized. The basic decision is left to the individual teacher, who has the option to join with colleagues to seek solutions to educational problems or to remain aloof. It is a matter for the individual to decide whether to increase his knowledge and improve his skills, to seek his future as a master teacher and to pursue additional studies to meet the requirements for other positions in education, or to find satisfaction as a classroom teacher.

on your own

The subject of teacher organization is a matter of interest to the future teacher. It may be of equal concern to the teacher in the classroom, although he may be influenced by the particular school in which he teaches. The teacher in an urban area, for instance, may find that union membership is accepted or expected. A teacher in a suburban or rural area may find union membership to be suspect and unusual. Whether a teacher joins a union, teacher association, or neither should be a matter of personal decision that is unrelated to community or school or peer expectations. The future teacher should decide how he will fulfill his professional responsibilities. He should find out which organizations are available to him in his school and what are their purposes and programs.

The student of teaching may become acquainted with professional activities through student affiliates of educational organizations, including the National Education Association or teacher unions. He should sit in on meetings of local organizations and occasionally may have an opportunity to attend a national meeting. The student-teaching experience should also include opportunities to observe local teachers as they function in their organizations. Students should peruse journals of educational organizations to determine the interests of the group and the kinds of activities in which they engage. Information about the American Federation of Teachers may be obtained from local affiliates or the national office. The *NEA Handbook* is published yearly and includes a comprehensive discussion of the National Education Association and its associated organizations, programs, and goals.

Each school should have an education library that includes books on professionalism which are useful references for teachers. A continuing standard reference is Myron Lieberman's *Education as a Profession* (Englewood Cliffs, N.J.: Prentice-Hall, 1956). T. M. Stinnett and Albert J. Huggett have authored *Professional Problems of Teachers,* 3rd ed. (New York: Macmillan, 1968). The National Society for the Study of Education included a discussion of professionalism in the Society's Sixty-first Yearbook, G. Lester Anderson (ed.), *Education for the Professions* (Chicago: University of Chicago Press, 1962).

additional references

Blackington, Frank H. III, and Robert S. Patterson. *School, Society and the Professional Educator.* New York: Holt, Rinehart and Winston, 1968.

Elam, Stanley, Myron Lieberman, and Michael Moskow (eds.). *Readings on Collective Negotiations in Public Education.* Chicago: Rand McNally, 1967.

Lieberman, Myron. *The Future of Public Education.* Chicago: University of Chicago Press, 1960.

———, and Michael Moskow. *Collective Negotiations for Teachers: An Approach to School Administration.* Chicago: Rand McNally, 1966.

Shils, Edward B., and C. Taylor Whittier. *Teachers, Administrators and Collective Bargaining.* New York: Crowell, 1968.

Stinnett, T. M. *Turmoil in Teaching.* New York: Macmillan, 1968.

———, Jack H. Kleinmann, and Martha L. Ware. *Professional Negotiation in Public Education.* New York: Macmillan, 1966.

Vollmer, Howard M., and Donald L. Mills. *Professionalization.* Englewood Cliffs, N.J.: Prentice-Hall, 1966.

14

Two futures concern those interested in American education. One is the very personal future of those who are preparing to become teachers or who are contemplating the possibility of teaching as a career. The other is the general future of education, which is important to teachers and to all others interested in the school. This final chapter will deal with these contrasting topics. The first topic is a very practical one and would be almost mundane if it were not raised so frequently by students who express great concerns about completing teacher education programs, securing positions, and initiating a career in the classroom. While it is essential that the nagging questions of students should be answered, the speculative, uncertain topic of the future development of the schools should also be met and aired. The future of teachers and prospective teachers reaches beyond a first day or a first year of school. It extends into a revolutionary era for the classroom.

the student-teaching experience

The student in education studies the general nature of education and the special problems and practices of his teaching area. He contemplates the physiology and psychology of youngsters and the philosophy, sociology, history, and economics of education. His concern for the role of teachers is expressed in a search for answers to questions of relationships with fellow teachers, administrators, school boards, parents, and the public. Techniques for conducting classroom routine and the means for meeting crises in the classroom are discussed. Teaching lessons are analyzed in planning lessons, selecting methods, and study of the process of guiding learning. Students observe classes in action and participate by teaching practice lessons, tutoring individuals, or working with small groups.

the future

Many students report that the student-teaching assignment was their most significant experience in the teacher education program. The usual prerequisites for student teaching include satisfactory completion of introductory courses in education and special methods classes. Some programs require physical or emotional screening or demonstrating competencies in speech and basic skills such as handwriting.

Many colleges provided teaching experiences in their own campus laboratory schools in the past, but growth of teacher education programs has led to reliance on the cooperation of public or private schools for placement of student teachers. Frequently colleges have little choice in the selection of the cooperating teachers to whom students are assigned, although it is a common requisite that the teacher have at least three years of teaching experience. Sometimes cooperating teachers are paid for their services, or they may be granted tuition credit for study at the institution.

Student teaching is organized on a full-time or half-day basis. It may extend for an academic quarter or a semester. Some colleges divide semesters into two experiences at different grade levels. Suggestions that an extended apprenticeship should replace the limited student-teaching experience have not been realized.

Colleges supervise students in their teaching assignments. The preferable arrangement is to assign methods instructors to supervise their own students. However, problems of the number of students involved, distances traveled, and arranging schedules of college instructors to include classroom instruction and off-campus supervision have resulted in the employment by many institutions of full-time student-teaching supervisors. Some colleges have established student-teaching centers, where an instructor is assigned to supervise students in the area. He often conducts seminars in which problems are discussed and where philosophy, theory, and practice are considered in the context of the classroom. Some supervisors who are assigned to distant student-teaching centers live in the communities. Difficulties may arise, of course, if the supervisor becomes isolated from the college and problems develop in communication.

Many students are confused about the relationships in the student-teaching experience. They often overemphasize the role of the principal and the college supervisor and underestimate that of the cooperating teacher. A student should be advised to consider his role as that of a visitor, to look on the cooperating teacher as the major figure in the experience, and to perceive the college supervisor as a major consultant but not a director of the cooperating teacher. Few principals become involved with student-teaching situations.

The value of a student-teaching experience depends primarily on the skill with which a student can operate in a complex interrelationship. The central interaction is that between the student teacher and the cooperating teacher. The student facilitates the process by working closely with the teacher, especially in the planning of instruction. In establishing relationships with the class, it is important that the student maintain procedures with youngsters and make demands of them that are compatible with those of the cooperating teacher. The student teacher should not imitate the cooperating teacher, but neither should a class of youngsters be placed in contradictory situations. Pupils must not be forced to adjust to radical changes in environment, practices, or expectations: They must not swing from restrictive to permissive situations or from excessive assignments to none at all.

A college student is free to engage in reasonable variations from established practice, for a profitable use of the student-teaching experience is to try out ideas about teaching. The student-teacher who is an innovator in the classroom is secure in the support and advice of an experienced teacher and in the knowledge that assistance is available if problems develop.

obtaining a position

In the completion of his college program, the student must decide whether to seek a teaching position. The four out of five elementary majors and three out of four secondary majors who actually teach after completing college (according to reports of the United States Office of Education) usually obtain their first position through their college placement bureau. Students may also employ private agencies, use services provided by state departments of education or state teachers' associations, or register with NEA-SEARCH, a computer-based placement service, which was established in 1967. Regardless of the placement agency used, students will be expected to provide information about themselves and to supply references concerning their qualifications and experiences. Some employing officers suggest that one of the more useful references in assessing the competencies of the college graduate applying for a teaching position is that of the cooperating teacher from the student-teaching experience. Other references concerning personal characteristics, along with college academic records and reports of nonacademic activities, are considered significant.

Because the first teaching position is of crucial importance to the attitudes and practices of a teacher and is a determining factor in teacher satisfaction, the graduating student should exercise special care and judgment in seeking and accepting employment. A careful search for a first teaching position should reduce the likelihood of a teacher later feeling the need to move from one school system to another in an attempt to find a satisfactory place from which to pursue further ambitions. The student must know himself to know where he wants to go and what he wants to do; thus the prospective teacher should evaluate his personality and the particular needs that might fit his personal characteristics. He ought to assess with as much objectivity as possible his competence in subject matter and methods of teaching. A teacher may be able to function with some socioeconomic groups better than others. Profound patience is essential to the teacher of slow-learning youngsters, for instance; less patience will not interfere with instruction of brighter youngsters.

The prospective teacher should have thought out his financial needs, geographical preference, and the size and type of community where he would choose to live. Many prospective teachers limit their places of potential employment. The necessity to locate near a university or the wish to live in a specific geographic area may restrict some choices. The limits of commuting distances may reduce the number of employment possibilities for a married woman whose residence is determined by her husband's job. Fewer options in selecting a teaching position require a more exact process of evaluation, for communities within a limited area may be relatively similar and the differences more subtle. The teacher who is moving to a new teaching position should increase to the highest level possible his chances for success in the new school.

The student should evaluate the community in which he is considering a teaching position. He ought to know its size, geographic setting, economic facts, available housing, political orientation, general philosophy, and the shopping, religious, medical, and cultural facilities and transportation services. Information about a community may be available through a local chamber of commerce. Some schools send information about their communities to prospective teachers.

Most schools require applicants to arrange for interviews at the school or with a representative who may visit colleges and universities to recruit teachers. When feasible, the applicant should visit the school and community. Informal listening and observing may provide more useful information than formal interviews. Spending half an hour in the teachers' lounge, for instance, is an excellent way to find out about interpersonal relations among teachers and their perceptions of the administration, youngsters, and the community. Observing youngsters on the playground and in the classroom provides information about the kind of children that attend the school and their attitudes toward learning. Lunching in the cafeteria and watching children in the halls are ways to evaluate administrative policies and student reactions to them. Visiting classrooms aids in determining how well instruction is supported with teaching materials. Waiting in the outer office affords an opportunity to observe the attitudes and work habits of the secretarial and clerical staff.

Other important information may be difficult to obtain. The philosophy, attitudes, and practices of the school board have an important impact on the teacher. It would be helpful to know the power structure that influences the school board and the motives and objectives of those in the controlling group. However, few teachers have extensive information about their school board and fewer know anything about the local power structure. When direct information is difficult to obtain, indirect information may be of some use. A significant bit of indirect information is the amount and kind of unpleasantness that has occurred in a school system. A prospective teacher should be asking what events have made news in the schools and the who, how, and why of the episodes.

Those entering teaching should contemplate their role in the evolving educational scene. Most teachers will have opportunities to influence the changing curriculum or the revolution in teaching methods either directly in their own classroom or indirectly by supporting positive change whenever the occasion may arise. Activity in educational organizations is one way of influencing change in general. Participation in school or school district committee work may aid in moving the local schools forward.

the first day of teaching

Many of those who expect to teach are concerned about their first day of teaching and what to do on that introduction to the classroom. The implication is that a happy beginning is important to successful pursuit of a teaching career. That may be an exaggeration of the importance of one day in the life of the teacher, but the posing of the question suggests a lack of confidence shared by many prospective teachers.

The most pertinent answer would be that there are no magic formulas and no simple recipes for a solution to the complex problems of teaching. There is no blueprint that guarantees success in the classroom. Success depends on many factors within a community, school system, group of youngsters, and a teacher. There are suggestions, however, that experienced teachers may offer to the schoolhouse novice.

The greatest assurance of success for the prospective teacher is that he be fully prepared for teaching. He must be competent in the subject matter that he is teaching. The elementary teacher must have a broad knowledge of many subjects; he can never be "one page ahead of the youngsters." The secondary teacher needs both broad general knowledge and profound competence in his area of expertise, for no subject forms an island of information isolated from all other topics. The teacher must also be expert in the methodology of teaching. He should have a wide variety of techniques at his disposal and he must know the equipment and materials that will be available to him in the coming school year.

The first day and the first week of school should be particularly well-planned, for the beginning teacher does not have the veteran teacher's experience on which to depend for instant response to unexpected problems. The teacher should be familiar with the previous achievement of youngsters. He ought to know both the level of achievement and the content of the studies. He should have studied available records for information about the experiences, abilities, and personal characteristics of his pupils.

The teacher should know the community socioeconomic characteristics and attitudes toward school in general and toward specific subjects or topics. He must know school policies and the expectations of administrators toward the processes and outcomes of the classroom. It might seem to be a matter of routine for a principal to brief his staff, and particularly new teachers, on administrative expectations and standard procedures at the start of a school year. There are many schools, however, where orientation of new teachers is done inadequately, if at all. A teacher must know how to meet emergency situations and when and how to contact the principal, nurse, or custodian. He should know what his noninstructional duties are. He ought to be especially concerned about fire-drill procedures. The legal rights, duties, responsibilities, and liabilities of the teachers, pupils, parents, and school should be understood.

It would be advisable for the beginning teacher to make a list of concerns to be checked. These should include: information required by the principal, nurse, or guidance office; whether money is to be collected, what it is for, how much is to be collected, accounting procedures, and where the teacher turns in the money; what teaching materials are to be bought by the pupils or issued to them and what records are to be kept; procedures to arrange for field trips or the use of audio-visual tools; and whether window shades and electric outlets are available.

Some teachers worry about a particular aspect of their relations to youngsters. How should students address them? Should it be Mr. Jones, Miss Smith, Coach, Teach, or Sam? Regardless of how a teacher is addressed, the necessary relationship must be one of mutual respect. Experience suggests that "Sam" or "Coach" has been a more respectful means of addressing some teachers than "Miss Smith" or "Mr. Jones" has been for others. Teachers can expect to have difficulty if they seek to reject the role of organizer and guide of instruction and the symbol of expertise and authority for the role of friend and confidant. If the teacher will accept his own role, the question of how he will be addressed will become the minor matter that it should be. For most teachers with most youngsters in most schools, the traditional Mr., Miss, or Mrs. is the preferable first form of address. Changes may be made later, if advisable.

There are things that the teacher should tell his pupils. They ought to know what the seating procedures will be, the instructional materials they will need, and the classroom routines, requirements, and expectations. Pupils need to know how discipline is to be handled in the class.

The first contacts between a class and a teacher provide opportunities for youngsters to test out the character of a teacher and for a teacher to come to know a group of youngsters. It is the time that teacher roles and pupil roles are defined. Youngsters will make preliminary judgments about a teacher: whether he is competent, reasonable, and understanding and whether he is able to organize the classroom and the instructional processes. Some judgments about the teacher will be a reflection of the assurance with which he meets matters of class organization and instruction. If the teacher has confidence in his own knowledge and teaching abilities, his assurance will be reflected in the attitudes that youngsters form about him.

future control of schools

While the teacher will be concerned with his own immediate problems, he will also play a role in the future development of schools. Teachers will participate in making important educational decisions, such as who will control the schools of the future. In the absence of evidence that there is a reduction in the abuse of power by school boards or by local individuals or groups, the movement of control over the schools from the localities to the states will continue. State influence will grow as additional instructional services are required of local school districts by state departments of education. The shift of power from local administrative units is related to matters of financing the schools. The cost of education will continue to rise and the local tax base will find increasing difficulty in meeting its gradually reduced share of the expenses. The state contribution may remain relatively constant as more federal funds are made available for education.

teacher, local, or state power?

The issue is no longer whether the traditional powers of community control will be reduced but where the power shall be centered. Proponents of teacher power would suggest that much policy formation and administrative decision should be exercised by the teaching staff of a school. Some local groups, including spokesmen for certain ghetto organizations, would have power over local schools bypass the traditional public representative, the school board, and rest in newly organized citizen councils. Some who speak in behalf of states' rights would add state control of federal funds distributed to the schools to the extension of control over local schools, and they would propose a resurrected power of nullification over federal intervention in school matters such as racial integration.

It is probable that none of these ambitions will be realized.

Teachers have not been able to use power effectively and have not convinced the public that power over the schools should be granted to teachers.

An important factor in the exercise of teacher power is the supply of teachers available for the schools. The available supply of teachers increases when a lowering of the birth rate results in a reduction in school population and during periods of economic recession. An important result of any large increase in the proportion of the working force that engages in teaching will be a commonality of the teacher in society and a resultant loss of prestige unless the increased numbers are drawn from the most talented segment of the population, an eventuality that automation might provide.

The long history of abuse of power at the local level and the tendency to personalize policy issues suggest that local control over schools will not work in many communities whether it is in the hands of elected school boards or less formally constituted neighborhood councils. Those who seek to extend state control over local school districts will be forced to recognize that the same logic they employ will deny them the right to exercise unfettered control over aid dispersed by the federal government.

Movement of power over the schools to the state governments may guarantee a general depersonalization of school problems, but it will not automatically improve educational leadership. Power and quality of leadership do not go hand in hand, as has been demonstrated in history. Many of the states will have to improve the quality of state leadership, the processes of selecting personnel for state departments of education, and the financial remuneration for state education officers. The problems that have haunted large educational systems are the stodginess, impersonality, and inefficiency of a bureaucracy. Irritating as these may be, they are easier to live with than the bitter, personal, vindictive, and persistent abuse that may develop at close range. Provisions may be established to bypass an unresponsive bureaucracy; it is more difficult to blunt intimate and direct confrontation.

the role of the federal government

If the direct power over the schools shall be exercised by the states, the greatest influence over education will come from the federal government. Because the problems faced by society as a whole are increasingly related to the various kinds of knowledge, competencies, and skills that have been assigned to the schools, the central government must exercise a greater role in the educational system. Vocational, agricultural, and home economics education were nationalized with dispatch under federal subsidy programs. Problems of racial integration of the schools were at best tortuously slow and at the worst retrogressive before intervention of the federal government. Similarly, the quality of education achieved in the schools will become an increasing concern of the national political structure.

A major objective of the federal government is to guarantee a minimum level of education throughout the nation. This will mean a raising of the educational level of the poorer states. The national administration may be expected to increase the redistributing of financial resources from those states with the most to those with the least. Whether the basic racial problems may be resolved through the schools is open to question, but there would seem to be little doubt that the schools will continue to be utilized as integrative media. It may be that one form of escapism for adults in the solution of adult problems is to expect resolution of the problems by someone else, in this instance schools and children.

The federal government will play a major role in another national problem, the disintegration of the city. In addition to reconstruction of the physical city, federal programs will seek solutions to human problems, including education. If the urban school power structure remains immobilized and tied to an unimaginative bureaucracy, the federal government may be forced to the alternative of establishing a separate school system. The Head Start program illustrated a partial disassociation from professional education. It was first administered through the Office of Economic Opportunity rather than the U.S. Office of Education. It was implemented locally by boards of education because such an arrangement facilitated access to physical facilities, but it could have been executed by other local agencies. The Upward Bound program was directed toward recruitment and preparation of disadvantaged high school youth for admission to college. It was administered by public or private colleges rather than the public schools. Future solutions to educational problems may also bypass the educational establishment.

Changes to be made in the inner-city schools may come about through local leadership, state action, or the imposition of federal power. Funds to support education will probably be shifted from suburban areas where school problems are minor to the inner city where problems are overwhelming. Priority for new schools and abundant teacher materials will be given to the inner city. The best qualified teachers will be recruited for the urban schools and they will receive the highest salaries. Their classes will number twenty-five, fifteen, or ten youngsters, with the size of the class determined by the number that can be taught effectively. The inner-city teacher will have access to a rich assortment of learning materials and techniques.

the role of the public

The role of the public is difficult to project. Public attitudes are learned and do change, but changes are made individually rather than collectively. The general consensus changes fairly rapidly under guidance of leadership in which the public has confidence or when the impact of a situation is remote. An excellent example of rapid change in public attitudes were those toward Japan, Germany, and the Soviet Union during and following World War II.

If the affairs of the schools become more remote, particularly if the financing of schools is channeled through the federal government and control over general policy is handled on the state level, public reaction to effective teaching and responsible leadership and followership among educators could lead to more favorable public attitudes and significantly increased public support for the schools. However, educators should depend on their own ingenuity, intelligence, and judicious use of power for change in the schools rather than wait for a revolution or evolution of public attitudes.

professional influence

Teacher influence will be exercised by professional organizations through political influence on the state and federal levels rather than dependence on use of power at the local level. Perhaps the least important issue is whether teacher unions or educational associations shall control teacher organization. Eventually teachers will be organized in groups that exclude those who are not classroom teachers.

The history of organized labor suggests that a period of militancy during which the right to exercise power is begrudgingly surrendered by management is followed by the opportunity to exercise a more reasonable use of power. In the case of the schools, the idea that teachers are employees who might resort to union techniques for self-protection or pursuit of their own selfish interests is accepted slowly, reluctantly, and painfully. Nowhere is the tradition of a master-servant relationship more firmly established than in public employment. Public employees are always vulnerable to the charge of unpatriotic actions or a callous disregard for the health, safety, or welfare of the society. It is easier to become aroused when a fire or police post is untended or a school unmanned than when a private enterprise is closed, regardless of the merits of the employees' complaints.

the teaching revolution

The role of the teacher must undergo profound changes, which will be concentrated in the classroom process rather than in matters of determining policy or administering the schools. The school calendar must be changed from an outmoded agrarian orientation to a schedule that will meet learning needs. The nine-month school should become a twelve-month school with recesses spaced to the rhythm that most adequately facilitates learning. While the motivation behind a change in schedule is to improve learning, the fact that inner-city youngsters no longer will be forced to spend an idle summer on the streets will be a significant additional benefit.

Another matter of scheduling in the school is anticipation of a reduction of the work week from forty hours per week to thirty-two or twenty. When the reduction in teaching hours comes about teachers will share classes during the week, either by dividing the schedule by days or by dividing each day. But even before this change is made, the privacy of a teacher and a class behind a closed door will be shattered by a pattern of cooperative teaching. Once the isolation of a single teacher has been abandoned for cooperative or team teaching, greater flexibility may be expressed in the size of classes and the length of instructional periods.

The adjustments to a new schedule and cooperative teaching are the least significant changes in the life of the future teacher. The real revolution in teaching will take place in the reorganization of the curriculum and the development of new teaching techniques. The methods revolution is well under way, although it is a sad commentary that use of new techniques, such as programmed instruction, may be more often found in industrial or military training programs than in the schools. Part of the responsibility for failure to use new instructional media is lack of finances. However, money may be exaggerated as an excuse for failure to do something in education. More valid reasons are ineffective leadership and lack of knowledge and skills in the new techniques by teachers. Teacher education curricula and in-service programs may provide knowledge and an opportunity to develop teaching skills, but there is no simple way to resolve the problem of unsatisfactory, irresponsible, or unresponsive leadership.

The real classroom revolution will come about through major revisions of the curriculum. Because some new teaching techniques are more adaptable to individual learning and other old and new techniques are suitable to group instruction, curricular revisors must reconsider the nature of learning and of subject matter. Individual learning techniques will be the major methods used in some subject areas. These aspects of the curriculum will be structured so that some youngsters may learn rapidly and advance quickly through their studies while others learn slowly. Thus each youngster in a class would be engaging in separate, individualized instruction. The nature of other learnings would continue in traditional group procedures. There may be subjects that will be shifted from formal instructional techniques to an informal exposure type of experience in which emphasis is placed on experiencing rather than learning. Serious consideration should be given to the cyclic nature of the present curriculum and to the possibility that learning which is progressively functional may be introduced earlier in school and need not be repeated later. The school experience will be lengthened and become more efficient. Only then will it be possible to learn all that is necessary to meet increasingly complex social and technological problems.

One of the confusing aspects of individualizing instruction is that it does not fit into traditional evaluation procedures. If group members are engaged in different levels of instruction because of differences in learning abilities, evaluating individuals against the group is neither appropriate nor possible. A satisfactory evaluative procedure to be used in the schools is measuring the individual's learning in terms of his own capabilities. One suitable procedure is the derivation of an individual's learning efficiency, which would be the ratio of measures of achievement to ability. The ideal would be to have every individual learning at 100 percent efficiency. Experience would have to evolve a reasonably satisfactory level, which might be from 50 to 75 percent. A thoughtful appraisal of the approximate learning efficiency of pupils in contemporary schools would suggest that the ordinary classroom is probably operating below 25 percent of learning efficiency, and that figure might be too high for many youngsters in many schools. A hopeful aspect of learning efficiency is that it would be a simple matter to program measures of learning efficiency into a computerized program of instruction.

To compare an individual's school achievement at any one time with that of other youngsters would be to consider learning efficiency rates and subject matter placement. One twelve-year-old might be operating at 85 percent of learning efficiency at the algebra stage of a mathematics program while his classmate in the next seat might be operating at 75 percent efficiency at the stage of multiplying two-digit numbers. A comparison of the two pupils would conclude that the first is learning well and is at an advanced level in the mathematics program. The second youngster is learning at a satisfactory pace but his academic achievement is at a relatively slow pace. When group measures are replaced by individual measures, there is no longer the granting of instant and effortless success to the brightest youngster in the class or the frustrating automatic failure that goes to the pupil with the least ability. Every youngster will be able to find success in school.

Changes in the school environment ease the task of the teacher. Carpeting reduces noise level. Air conditioning makes school in the summer possible and eliminates oppressive heat discomfort as a contributing factor to misbehavior. New building materials, including plastics, will permit less expensive school construction and the replacement of schools as they become outdated. A school is no longer satisfactory when it cannot adjust to changing teaching methods and new demands on the physical environment. Educational campuses and schools that are part of self-contained housing and commercial buildings will be built. Their use will be justified or found undesirable not through conjecture but in practice.

Reduction of the legal work week and accompanying guarantees against individuals working at two twenty-hour-a-week jobs will result in a recreational and leisure-time revolution. The schoolbuilding will be used after school hours for recreational purposes, including extensive adult education programs. A large labor force will staff the recreation industry. The schools will only house recreational activities; educators will not staff them. One probable result of increased recreational programs will be the elimination of the conflict between extra-curricular or athletic and academic programs as the recreation establishment absorbs the nonacademic activities. The year-round school will afford opportunities for joint camping-educational projects, which will take children, particularly those from the urban areas, into rural camps for two weeks or a month every year. The schools will work with the public recreation industry in practical application of camping and recreation instruction instead of taking over the program.

conclusion

The future of the prospective teacher is a matter of established practice in satisfying state certification requirements and completing college degree programs. The options available in selecting a position and planning a teaching career are not subject to radical change in the future. Chance may play a role in the success and satisfaction a teacher experiences in the classroom, but the conscious choices made are of greater importance. In selecting a teaching position the teacher should emphasize those factors that are related to the school or nature of the position.

There is nothing to support speculation about the future of teaching, however. Most who have sought to look into the future have been judged as excessive and wild dreamers at that moment and proved to have been limited and conservative in the test of time. Speculation does not predict the future, but it creates an awareness of changing needs, desires, and practices. It aids individuals in acceptance of change and makes progress possible or perhaps desirable.

Schools that are pertinent and worthy are not created to perpetuate the past but should move society out of the past, through the present, and into the future. Education and teaching are exciting because they face the future through the very real minds and bodies of evolving personalities. The true reward of the teacher is not in a well-executed lesson or the wiping of a tear but in meeting former pupils as adults who have been successful in resolving the challenges they have faced. The future belongs to those who dream as they labor and, hopefully, most of all to those who labor and dream in the classroom.

on your own

Students in teacher education programs should know exactly the requirements for satisfaction of college and state certification requirements. They ought to become familiar with teacher placement agencies and know the geographic location and size and character of the community and school system where they wish to teach.

In seeking to plan the grand changes ahead in education, students should become acquainted with some of the major statements that propose a model for society and the schools. One of the most significant statements is John W. Gardner's *Excellence: Can We Be Equal and Excellent Too?* (New York: Harper & Row, 1961). Projections of the future may be found in the category "Future" in *Readers' Guide to Periodical Literature, Education Index,* and *Social Sciences and Humanities Index.* As the twenty-first century approaches, greater numbers of conferences, books, and periodical articles will seek to plan and project the future.

Prospective teachers should become acquainted with innovations in teaching, including new teaching tools as well as changes in organization of the schools for instruction. Consideration should be given to the new roles that may be demanded of the teacher, especially as a member of an instructional team.

The process of change may be purposeful or accidental. Although planned, purposeful change is most desirable, change is not always guided and controlled. Those interested in the process of reform might consult *Education for All American Youth* (Washington, D.C.: Educational Policies Commission, National Education Association, 1944), which provided an excellent guide for change after World War II. A study of the changes that took place will demonstrate how well-laid plans may be brushed aside in the realities of technological and political progress. A useful exercise would seek to determine why the planned changes did not come about and what differences there would have been if the dreams of *Education for All Amer-*

ican Youth had been realized. Try to answer the question, "What does this suggest for future school change?"

additional references

Benson, Charles S. *The Cheerful Prospect: A Statement on the Future of American Education.* Boston: Houghton Mifflin, 1963.

Bushnell, Don D., and Dwight W. Allen (eds.). *The Computer in American Education.* New York: Wiley, 1967.

Elam, Stanley, and William P. McLure (eds.). *Educational Requirements for the 1970's.* New York: Praeger, 1967.

Frazier, Alexander (ed.). *The New Elementary School.* Washington, D.C.: National Education Association, 1968.

Goodlad, John I. (ed.). *The Changing American School.* Sixty-fifth Yearbook of the National Society for the Study of Education, Part II. Chicago: University of Chicago Press, 1966.

Hirsch, Werner Z., *et al. Inventing Education for the Future.* San Francisco: Chandler, 1967.

Massialas, Byron G., and Jack Zevin. *Creative Encounters in the Classroom.* New York: Wiley, 1967.

Miller, Richard I. *Perspectives on Educational Change.* New York: Appleton-Century-Crofts, 1967.

National Advisory Commission on Civil Disorders. *Report of the National Advisory Commission on Civil Disorders.* Washington, D.C.: Government Printing Office, 1968, pp. 236–252.

National Commission on Teacher Education and Professional Standards. *The Real World of the Beginning Teacher.* Washington, D.C.: National Education Association, 1965.

Watson, Goodwin (ed.). *Change in School Systems.* Washington, D.C.: National Training Laboratories, National Education Association, 1967.

Wrenn, C. Gilbert. *The Counselor in the Changing World.* Washington, D.C.: American Personnel and Guidance Association, 1962.

bibliography

A Bibliography: Selected Reading on Programed Learning. Albany, N.Y.: The State Department of Education, 1963.

Abraham, Willard. **Common Sense About Gifted Children.** New York: Harper & Row, 1958.

———. **Time for Teaching.** New York: Harper & Row,1964.

Ahmann, J. Stanley, and Marvin D. Glock. **Evaluating Pupil Growth.** 3rd ed. Boston: Allyn and Bacon, 1967.

Alberty, Harold B., and Elsie J. Alberty. **Reorganizing the High-School Curriculum.** 3rd ed. New York: Macmillan, 1962.

Alexander, William M., Vynce A. Hines, *et al.* **Independent Study in Secondary Schools.** New York: Holt, Rinehart and Winston, 1968.

Allison, Mary L. (ed.). **New Educational Materials: Pre-Kindergarten Through Grade Twelve.** New York: Citation, 1967.

Alpren, Morton. **The Subject Curriculum: Grades K–12.** Columbus, Ohio: Merrill, 1967.

American Council on Industrial Arts Teacher Education. **Approaches and Procedures in Industrial Arts.** Fourteenth Yearbook. New York: McKnight, 1965.

Amidon, Edmund J., and Ned A. Flanders. **The Role of the Teacher in the Classroom: A Manual for Understanding and Improving Teachers' Classroom Behavior.** Minneapolis: Paul J. Amidon Associates, 1963.

———, and Elizabeth Hunter. **Improving Teaching: The Analysis of Classroom Verbal Interaction.** New York: Holt, Rinehart and Winston, 1966.

Anastasi, Anne (ed.). **Testing Problems in Perspective.** Washington, D.C.: American Council on Education, 1966.

Anderson, G. Lester (ed.). **Education for the Professions.** Sixty-first Yearbook, National Society for the Study of Education. Chicago: University of Chicago Press, 1962.

Anderson, Margaret. **Children of the South.** New York: Farrar, 1966.

Archambault, Reginald D. (ed.). **Dewey on Education: Appraisals with an Introduction.** New York: Random House, 1966.

Arnold, Martin. "P.S. 178: Study in Disrepair," **The New York Times,** February 28, 1968.

Arnstine, Donald. **Philosophy of Education: Learning and Schooling.** New York: Harper & Row, 1967.

Ashton-Warner, Sylvia. **Teacher.** New York: Simon and Schuster, 1963.

Association for Supervision and Curriculum Development. **Individualizing Instruction.** Washington, D.C.: the Association, National Education Association, 1964.

Ausubel, David P. **The Psychology of Meaningful Verbal Learning.** New York: Grune & Stratton, 1963.

Bailyn, Bernard. **Education in the Forming of American Society.** Chapel Hill, University of North Carolina Press, 1960.

Baldwin, Alfred L. **The Theories of Child Development.** New York: Wiley, 1967.

Bang, Mary A., and Lois V. Johnson. **Classroom Group Behavior: Group Dynamics in Education.** New York: Macmillan, 1964.

Barbe, Walter B. (ed.). **Psychology and Education of the Gifted: Selected Readings.** New York: Appleton-Century-Crofts, 1965.

Bayles, Ernest E., and Bruce L. Hood. **Growth of American Educational Thought and Practice.** New York: Harper & Row, 1966.

Beggs, David W., III, and Edward G. Buffie (eds.). **Nongraded Schools in Action.** Bloomington: Indiana University Press, 1967.

Benson, Charles S. **The Cheerful Prospect: A Statement on the Future of American Education.** Boston: Houghton Mifflin, 1963.

Bernstein, Abraham. **The Education of Urban Populations.** New York: Random House, 1967.

Best, John H., and Robert T. Sidwell (eds.). **The American Legacy of Learning: Readings in the History of Education.** Phila.: Lippincott, 1967.

Biddle, Bruce J., and William J. Ellena (eds.). **Contemporary Research on Teacher Effectiveness.** New York: Holt, Rinehart and Winston, 1964.

Bingham, Caleb (ed.). **The Columbian Orator.** Boston: J. H. A. Frost, 1828.

Biological Sciences Curriculum Study. **Biology Teachers' Handbook.** New York: Wiley, 1963.

Black, Hillel. **The American Schoolbook.** New York: Morrow, 1967.

Blackington, Frank H. III, and Robert S. Patterson. **School, Society and the Professional Educator.** New York: Holt, Rinehart and Winston, 1968.

Blair, Medill, and Richard G. Woodward. **Team Teaching in Action.** Boston: Houghton Mifflin, 1964.

Bloom, Benjamin S. (ed.). **Taxonomy of Educational Objectives, Handbook I: Cognitive Domain.** New York: McKay, 1956.

Bolmeier, Edward C. **The School in the Legal Structure.** Cincinnati: W. H. Anderson, 1968.

Bond, Guy L., and Eva Bond Wagner. **Teaching the Child to Read.** 4th ed. New York: Macmillan, 1966.

Bouwsma, Ward D., Clyde G. Corle, and Davis F. Clemson. **Basic Mathematics for Elementary Teachers.** New York: Ronald, 1967.

Breckenridge, Marian E., and E. Lee Vincent. **Child Development; Physical and Psychological Growth Through Adolescence.** 5th ed. Phila.: Saunders, 1965.

Brown, B. Frank. **The Ungraded High School.** Englewood Cliffs, N.J.: Prentice-Hall, 1963.

Brown, Claude. **Manchild in the Promised Land.** New York: Macmillan, 1965.

Brown, James W., Richard B. Lewis, and Fred F. Harcleroad. **A-V Instruction: Materials and Methods.** 2nd ed. New York: McGraw-Hill, 1964.

Brubacher, John S. (ed.). **Modern Philosophies and Education.** Fifty-fourth Yearbook of the National Society for the Study of Education. Chicago: University of Chicago Press, 1955.

———. **Modern Philosophies of Education.** 3rd ed. New York: McGraw-Hill, 1962.

Bruner, Jerome S. **The Process of Education.** New York: Vintage Books, 1960.

———. **Toward a Theory of Instruction.** New York: Norton, 1968.

Bugelski, B. R. **The Psychology of Learning Applied to Teaching.** Indianapolis: Bobbs-Merrill, 1964.

Burrup, Percy E. **Modern High School Administration.** New York: Harper & Row, 1962.

Burton, William H. **The Guidance of Learning Activities.** 3rd ed. New York: Appleton-Century-Crofts, 1962.

———, Roland B. Kimball, and Richard L. Wing. **Education for Effective Thinking.** New York: Appleton-Century-Crofts, 1960.

Bushnell, Don D., and Dwight W. Allen (eds.). **The Computer in American Education.** New York: Wiley, 1967.

Byrd, Oliver E. **School Health Administration.** Phila.: Saunders, 1964.

Byrne, Richard H. **The School Counselor.** Boston: Houghton Mifflin, 1963.

Campbell, Roald F., John E. Corbally, and John A. Ramseyer. **Introduction to Educational Administration.** 3rd ed. Boston: Allyn and Bacon, 1966.

Cantor, Nathaniel F. **The Teaching-Learning Process.** New York: Dryden Press, 1953.

Chall, Jeanne S. **Learning to Read: The Great Debate.** New York: McGraw-Hill, 1967.

Chemical Education Material Study. **Chemistry: An Experimental Science.** San Francisco: Freeman, 1963.

Clark, Kenneth B. **Dark Ghetto: Dilemmas of Social Power.** New York: Harper & Row, 1965.

Coleman, James S. **Adolescents and the Schools.** New York: Basic Books, 1965.

Colman, John E. **The Master Teachers and the Art of Teaching.** New York: Pitman, 1967.

Combs, Arthur W. **Perceiving, Behaving, Becoming.** Washington, D.C.: Association for Supervision and Curriculum Development, National Education Association, 1962.

Conant, James B. **The Comprehensive High School: A Second Report to Interested Persons.** New York: McGraw-Hill, 1967.

———. **The Education of American Teachers.** New York: McGraw-Hill, 1963.

———. **Slums and Suburbs.** New York: McGraw-Hill, 1961.

Cornfield, Ruth R. **Foreign Language Instruction, Dimensions and Horizons.** New York: Appleton-Century-Crofts, 1966.

Corsini, Raymond J., and Daniel D. Howard. **Critical Incidents in Teaching.** Englewood Cliffs, N.J.: Prentice-Hall, 1964.

Crank, Doris H., and Floyd L. Crank (eds.). **New Perspectives in Education for Business.** Yearbook of the National Business Education Association. Washington, D.C.: the Association, National Education Association, 1963.

Cremin, Lawrence A. **The Transformation of the School: Progressivism in American Education, 1876–1957.** New York: Knopf, 1961.

Crosby, Muriel. **Curriculum Development for Elementary Schools in a Changing Society.** Boston: Heath, 1964.

Crow, Lester D., and Alice Crow. **Mental Hygiene for Teachers.** New York: Macmillan, 1963.

———. **The Student Teacher in the Secondary School.** New York: McKay, 1964.

Cruickshank, William M., and G. Orville Johnson (eds.). **Education of Exceptional Children and Youth.** Englewood Cliffs, N.J.: Prentice-Hall, 1967.

Curtis, S. J., and M. E. A. Boultwood. **A Short History of Educational Ideas.** London: University Tutorial Press, 1964.

Dale, Edgar. **Audio-Visual Methods in Teaching.** 2nd ed. New York: Holt, Rinehart and Winston, 1965.

Dapper, Gloria, and Barbara Carter. **A Guide for School Board Members.** Chicago: Follett, 1966.

De Cecco, John P. **The Psychology of Learning and Instruction: Educational Psychology.** Englewood Cliffs, N.J.: Prentice-Hall, 1968.

Deciding What to Teach. Washington, D.C.: National Education Association, 1963.

DeKieffer, Robert E. **Audiovisual Instruction.** New York: The Center for Applied Research in Education, 1965.

Delaney, Jack J. **The School Librarian.** Hamden, Conn.: Shoe String Press, 1964.

Denemark, George W. "The Teacher and His Staff," **NEA Journal,** 55 (December 1966), 17.

Dentler, Robert A., Bernard Mackler, and Mary E. Warschauer (eds.). **The Urban R's: Race Relations as the Problem in Urban Education.** New York: Praeger, 1967.

Detjen, Ervin Winfred, and Mary Ford Detjen. **Elementary School Guidance.** 2nd ed. New York: McGraw-Hill, 1963.

Dewey, John. **Democracy and Education.** New York: Macmillan, 1916.

Diamond, Robert M. **A Guide to Instructional Television.** New York: McGraw-Hill, 1964.

Douvan, Elizabeth, and Joseph Adelson. **The Adolescent Experience.** New York: Wiley, 1966.

Drake, William E. **Intellectual Foundations of Modern Education.** Columbus, Ohio: Merrill, 1967.

Dufay, Frank R. **Ungrading the Elementary School.** West Nyack, N.Y.: Parker, 1966.

Dunn, Joan. **Retreat from Learning.** New York: McKay, 1955.

Dunn, Lloyd M. (ed.). **Exceptional Children in the Schools.** New York: Holt, Rinehart and Winston, 1963.

Ecroyd, Donald H. **Speech in the Classroom.** Englewood Cliffs, N.J.: Prentice-Hall, 1960.

Education for All American Youth. Washington, D.C.: Educational Policies Commission, National Education Association, 1944.

Elam, Stanley (ed.). **Improving Teacher Education in the United States.** Bloomington, Ind.: Phi Delta Kappa, 1967.

———, and William P. McLure (eds.). **Educational Requirements for the 1970's.** New York: Praeger, 1967.

———, Myron Lieberman, and Michael Moskow (eds.). **Readings on Collective Negotiations in Public Education.** Chicago: Rand McNally, 1967.

Erdman, Robert L. **Educable Retarded Children in Elementary Schools.** Washington, D.C.: Council for Exceptional Children, National Education Association, 1965.

Erickson, Carlton W. H. **Fundamentals of Teaching with Audiovisual Technology.** New York: Macmillan, 1965.

Faunce, Roland C., and Nelson L. Bossing. **Developing the Core Curriculum.** 2nd ed. Englewood Cliffs, N.J.: Prentice-Hall, 1958.

Fawcett, Claude W. **School Personnel Administration.** New York: Macmillan, 1964.

Fenton, Edwin. **Teaching the New Social Studies in Secondary Schools: An Inductive Approach.** New York: Holt, Rinehart and Winston, 1966.

Flanders, Ned A. "Intent, Action and Feedback: A Preparation for Teaching," **The Journal of Teacher Education,** 14 (September 1963), 251–260.

———. **Teacher Influence, Pupil Attitudes, and Achievement.** Washington, D.C.: Government Printing Office, 1965.

Fleming, Robert S. (ed.). **Curriculum for Today's Boys and Girls.** Columbus, Ohio: Merrill, 1963.

Ford, G. W., and Lawrence Pugno (eds.). **The Structure of Knowledge and the Curriculum.** Chicago: Rand McNally, 1964.

Francis, W. Nelson. **The English Language: An Introduction.** New York: Norton, 1965.

Frazier, Alexander (ed.). **The New Elementary School.** Washington, D.C.: National Education Association, 1968.

Fuchs, Estelle. **Pickets at the Gates: The Challenge of Civil Rights in Urban Schools.** New York: Free Press, 1966.

Full, Harold (ed.). **Controversy in American Education.** New York: Macmillan, 1967.

Gallagher, James J., Mary Jane Aschner, and William Jenne. **Productive Thinking of Gifted Children in Classroom Interaction.** Research Monograph B5. Washington, D.C.: Council for Exceptional Children, National Education Association, 1967.

Gans, Roma. **Common Sense in Teaching Reading.** Indianapolis: Bobbs-Merrill, 1963.

Garber, Lee O., Robert L. Drury, and Roger M. Shaw. **The Law and the Teacher in Ohio.** Danville, Ill.: Interstate, 1966.

Gardner, John W. **Excellence: Can We Be Equal and Excellent Too?** New York: Harper & Row, 1961.

Gittell, Marilyn, and T. Edward Hollander. **Six Urban School Districts.** New York: Praeger, 1968.

Glaser, Robert (ed.). **Teaching Machines and Programed Learning, II; Data and Directions.** Washington, D.C.: Department of Audiovisual Instruction, National Education Association, 1965.

Good, Carter V. **Dictionary of Education.** New York: McGraw-Hill, 1959.

———. **Introduction to Educational Research: Methodology of Design in the Behavioral and Social Sciences.** 2nd. ed. New York: Appleton-Century-Crofts, 1963.

Goodlad, John I. (ed.). **The Changing American School.** Sixty-fifth Yearbook of the National Society for the Study of Education, Part II. Chicago: University of Chicago Press, 1966.

———, John F. O'Toole, Jr., and Louise L. Tyler. **Computers and Information Systems in Education.** New York: Harcourt, Brace & World, 1966.

Goodman, Paul. **Growing Up Absurd: Problems of Youth in the Organized System.** New York: Random House, 1960.

Graham, Grace. **The Public School in the American Community.** New York: Harper & Row, 1963.

Grambs, Jean D. **Intergroup Education: Methods and Materials.** Englewood Cliffs, N.J.: Prentice-Hall, 1968.

Green, John A. **Fields of Teaching and Educational Services.** New York: Harper & Row, 1966.

———. **Teacher-Made Tests.** New York: Harper & Row, 1963.

Greene, Mary Frances, and Orletta Ryan. **The Schoolchildren: Growing Up in the Slums.** New York: Pantheon, 1965.

Greene, Maxine. **Existential Encounters for Teachers.** New York: Random House, 1967.

Grooms, M. Ann. **Perspective on the Middle School.** Columbus, Ohio: Merrill, 1967.

Gross, Neal. **Who Runs Our Schools?** New York: Wiley, 1958.

Hack, Walter G. **Economic Dimensions of Public School Finance: Cases and Concepts.** New York: McGraw-Hill, 1967.

Harrington, Michael. **The Other America: Poverty in the United States.** New York: Macmillan, 1962.

Hatcher, Hazel M., and Mildred E. Andrews. **The Teaching of Home Economics.** Boston: Houghton Mifflin, 1963.

Havighurst, Robert J. **Education in Metropolitan Areas.** Boston: Allyn and Bacon, 1966.

Haviland, Virginia. **Children's Literature: A Guide to Reference Sources.** Washington, D.C.: Government Printing Office, 1966.

Heald, James E., and Samuel A. Moore, II. **The Teacher and Administrative Relationships in School Systems.** New York: Macmillan, 1968.
Heller, R. L. (ed.). **Geology and Earth Science Sourcebook.** American Geological Institute. New York: Holt, Rinehart and Winston, 1962.
Hentoff, Nat. **Our Children Are Dying.** New York: Viking, 1966.
Highet, Gilbert. **The Art of Teaching.** New York: Vintage Books, 1959.
Hilgard, Ernest R. (ed.). **Theories of Learning and Instruction.** Sixty-third Yearbook of the National Society for the Study of Education. Chicago: University of Chicago Press, 1964.
Hirsch, Werner Z., *et al.* ***Inventing Education for the Future.*** San Francisco: Chandler, 1967.
Hocking, Elton. **Language Laboratory and Language Learning.** 2nd ed. Monograph #2. Washington, D.C.: Department of Audiovisual Instruction, National Education Association, 1967.
Hodgkinson, Harold L. **Education, Interaction, and Social Change.** Englewood Cliffs, N.J.: Prentice-Hall, 1967.
———. **Educational Decisions: A Casebook.** Englewood Cliffs, N.J.: Prentice-Hall, 1963.
Holt, John. **How Children Fail.** New York: Pitman, 1964.
———. **How Children Learn.** New York: Pitman, 1967.
Huck, Charlotte S., and Doris Young Kuhn. **Children's Literature in the Elementary School.** 2nd ed. New York: Holt, Rinehart and Winston, 1968.
Huebner, Dwayne (ed.). **A Reassessment of the Curriculum.** New York: Teachers College, Columbia University, 1964.
Hughes, J. L. **Programed Instruction for Schools and Industry.** Chicago: Science Research Associates, 1962.
Hughes, James M. **Human Relations in Educational Organizations.** New York: Harper & Brothers, 1957.
Hummel, Dean L., and S. J. Bonham, Jr. **Pupil Personnel Services in Schools: Organization and Coordination.** Chicago: Rand McNally, 1968.
Hunter, Evan. **Blackboard Jungle.** New York: Simon and Schuster, 1954.
Hurlburd, David. **This Happened in Pasadena.** New York: Macmillan, 1951.
Hyman, Ronald T. **Teaching: Vantage Points for Study.** Phila.: Lippincott, 1968.
Inlow, Gail. **The Emergent in Curriculum.** New York: Wiley, 1966.
Janowitz, Gayle. **Helping Hands: Volunteer Work in Education.** New York: Harper & Row, 1966.
Jarolimek, John. **Social Studies in Elementary Education.** New York: Macmillan, 1967.
Jarvis, Oscar T., and Lutian R. Wootton. **The Transitional Elementary School and Its Curriculum.** Dubuque, Iowa: Brown, 1966.
Jersild, Arthur T. **When Teachers Face Themselves.** 2nd ed. New York: Teachers College, Columbia University, 1957.
Joyce, Bruce R., and Berj Hartootunian. **The Structure of Teaching.** Chicago: Science Research Associates, 1967.
Kaufman, Bel. **Up the Down Staircase.** Englewood Cliffs, N.J.: Prentice-Hall, 1964.
Kaufman, Irving. **Art and Education in Contemporary Culture.** New York: Macmillan, 1966.
Keach, Everett T. **Elementary School Student Teaching: A Casebook.** New York: Wiley, 1966.
Kemp, Jerrold E. **Planning and Producing Audiovisual Materials.** San Francisco: Chandler, 1963.
Keppel, Francis. **The Necessary Revolution in American Education.** New York: Harper & Row, 1966.
Kieth, Lowell, Paul Blake, and Sidney Tiedt. **Contemporary Curriculum in the Elementary School.** New York: Harper & Row, 1968.

King, Arthur R., and John A. Brownell. **The Curriculum and the Disciplines of Knowledge, A Theory of Curriculum Practice.** New York: Wiley, 1966.

Kinney, Lucien B. **Certification in Education.** Englewood Cliffs, N.J.: Prentice-Hall, 1964.

Kirk, Samuel A. **Educating Exceptional Children.** Boston: Houghton Mifflin, 1962.

Kneller, George F. **Introduction to the Philosophy of Education.** New York: Wiley, 1964.

Koerner, James D. **The Miseducation of American Teachers.** Boston: Houghton Mifflin, 1963.

———. **Who Controls American Education—A Guide for Laymen.** Boston: Beacon Press, 1968.

Kohl, Herbert. **36 Children.** New York: New American Library, 1967.

Kowall, Bonnie C. **Perspectives in Music Education.** Source Book III. Washington, D.C.: Music Educators National Conference, National Education Association, 1966.

Kozol, Jonathan. **Death at an Early Age.** Boston: Houghton Mifflin, 1967.

Krathwohl, David, Benjamin S. Bloom, and Bertram B. Masia. **Taxonomy of Educational Objectives, Handbook II: Affective Domain.** New York: McKay, 1964.

Krug, Edward A. **The Shaping of the American High School.** New York: Harper & Row, 1964.

Kushel, Gerald. **Discord in Teacher-Counselor Relations: Cases from the Teacher's View.** Englewood Cliffs, N.J.: Prentice-Hall, 1967.

Landreth, Catherine. **Early Childhood Behavior and Learning.** New York: Knopf, 1967.

Lane, Willard R., Ronald G. Corwin, and William G. Monohan. **Foundations of Educational Administration.** New York: Macmillan, 1967.

Lange, Phil C. (ed.). **Programed Instruction.** Sixty-sixth Yearbook of the National Society for the Study of Education, Part II. Chicago: University of Chicago Press, 1967.

Lee, Gordon C. **Education and Democratic Ideals.** New York: Harcourt, Brace & World, 1965.

Lieberman, Myron. **The Future of Public Education.** Chicago: University of Chicago Press, 1960.

———. **Education as a Profession.** Englewood Cliffs, N.J.: Prentice-Hall, 1956.

———, and Michael Moskow. **Collective Negotiations for Teachers: An Approach to School Administration.** Chicago: Rand McNally, 1966.

Lifton, Walter M. **Working with Groups: Group Process and Individual Growth.** 2nd ed. New York: Wiley, 1966.

Lindgren, Henry C. **Educational Psychology in the Classroom.** 3rd ed. New York: Wiley, 1967.

Lindvall, C. M. **Measuring Pupil Achievement and Aptitude.** New York: Harcourt, Brace & World, 1967.

Long, Nicholas J., William C. Morse, and Ruth G. Newman (eds.). **Conflict in the Classroom: The Education of Emotionally Disturbed Children.** Belmont, Calif.: Wadsworth, 1965.

McGeoch, Dorothy M. **Learning to Teach in Urban Schools.** New York: Teacher's College Press, Columbia University, 1965.

McNeill, Maurice with Richard Cohen. "How My Town Saved Me from a White Girl's Lie," **Ladies' Home Journal,** 85 (March 1968), 81, 140–144.

Maritain, Jacques. **Education at the Crossroads.** New Haven, Conn.: Yale University Press, 1960.

Massialas, Byron G., and Jack Zevin. **Creative Encounters in the Classroom.** New York: Wiley, 1967.

Mayerson, Charlotte Leon (ed.). **Two Blocks Apart.** New York: Holt, Rinehart and Winston, 1965.

Medley, Donald M. "Experiences with the OScAR Technique," **The Journal of Teacher Education,** 14 (September 1963), 267–273.

Melton, Arthur W. (ed.). **Categories of Human Learning.** New York: Academic Press, 1964.

Meyer, Adolphe E. **An Educational History of the American People.** 2nd ed. New York: McGraw-Hill, 1967.

Michaelis, John U., Ruth H. Grossman, and Lloyd F. Scott. **New Designs for the Elementary School Curriculum.** New York: McGraw-Hill, 1967.

Miller, Harry L. (ed.). **Education for the Disadvantaged.** New York: Free Press, 1967.

Miller, Richard I. **Perspectives on Educational Change.** New York: Appleton-Century-Crofts, 1967.

Minter, Thomas K. **Intermediate School 201, Manhattan: Center of Controversy.** Cambridge, Mass.: Graduate School of Education, Harvard University, 1967.

Montessori, Maria. **The Montessori Method.** New York: Stokes, 1912.

NEA Handbook. Washington, D.C.: National Education Association, 1969.

Nash, Paul. **Models of Man: Explorations in the Western Educational Tradition.** New York: Wiley, 1968.

———. "The Strange Death of Progressive Education," **Educational Theory,** 14 (April 1964), 65–75, 82.

———, Andreas M. Kazamias, and Henry Perkinson. **The Educated Man: Studies in the History of Educational Thought.** New York: Wiley, 1965.

National Advisory Commission on Civil Disorders. **Report of the National Advisory Commission on Civil Disorders.** Washington, D.C.: Government Printing Office, 1968, pp. 236–252.

National Commission on Professional Rights and Responsibilities. **Knoxville, Tennessee: When A City Government Fails to Give Full Support to Its Schools.** Washington, D.C.: the Commission, National Education Association, 1967.

National Commission on Teacher Education and Professional Standards. **The Real World of the Beginning Teacher.** Washington, D.C.: National Education Association, 1965.

Neill, A. S. **Summerhill: A Radical Approach to Child Rearing.** New York: Hart, 1960.

Nixon, John E., and Ann E. Jewett. **Physical Education Curriculum.** New York: Ronald, 1964.

Noar, Gertrude. "Nature of Human Relations in the Classroom," **North Central Association Quarterly,** 39 (Fall 1964), 196–199.

———. **Teacher Aides at Work.** Washington, D.C.: Commission on Teacher Education and Professional Standards, National Education Association, 1967.

Nordstrom, Carl, Edgar Z. Friedenberg, and Hilary A. Gold. **Society's Children: A Study of Ressentiment in Secondary School Education.** New York: Random House, 1967.

Norton, John K. (ed.). **Dimensions in School Finance.** Washington, D.C.: Committee on Educational Finance, National Education Association, 1966.

Ohlsen, Merle M. **Guidance Services in the Modern School.** New York: Harcourt, Brace & World, 1964.

Page, David P. **Theory and Practice of Teaching: or, the Motives and Methods of Good School-Keeping.** Syracuse, N.Y.: Hall and Dickson, 1847.

Pai, Young, and Joseph T. Myers. **Philosophic Problems and Education.** Phila.: Lippincott, 1967.

Patterson, Cecil H. **The Counselor in the School.** New York: McGraw-Hill, 1967.

Perkinson, Henry J. **The Imperfect Panacea: American Faith in Education, 1865–1965.** New York: Random House, 1968.

Perrodin, Alex F. **The Student Teacher's Reader.** Chicago: Rand McNally, 1966.

Peterson, Dorothy G. **The Elementary School Teacher.** New York: Appleton-Century-Crofts, 1964.

Peterson, John A., and Joseph Hashisaki. **Theory of Arithmetic.** 2nd ed. New York: Wiley, 1967.

Phenix, Philip H. (ed.). **Philosophies of Education.** New York: Wiley, 1961.

Physical Science Study Committee. **Physics.** 2nd ed. Boston: Heath, 1965.

Pois, Joseph. **The School Board Crisis: A Chicago Case Study.** Chicago: Aldine, 1964.

Public Affairs Committee. **How Good Are Our Colleges?** New York: Public Affairs Pamphlet, No. 26, 1938.

Read, Katherine H. **The Nursery School: A Human Relationship Laboratory.** Phila.: Saunders, 1966.

Riessman, Frank. **The Culturally Deprived Child.** New York: Harper & Row, 1962.

Rippa, S. Alexander. **Education in a Free Society: An American History.** New York: McKay, 1967.

Roberts, Joan I. (ed.). **School Children in the Urban Slum: Readings in Social Science Research.** New York: Free Press, 1968.

Rosenthal, Robert, and Lenore Jacobson. **Pygmalion in the Classroom.** New York: Holt, Rinehart and Winston, 1968.

Rossi, Peter H., and Bruce J. Biddle (eds.). **The New Media and Education.** Garden City, N.Y.: Doubleday, 1967.

Ryans, David G. **Characteristics of Teachers.** Washington, D.C.: American Council on Education, National Education Association, 1960.

Saettler, Paul. **A History of Instructional Technology.** New York: McGraw-Hill, 1968.

Savage, William W. **Interpersonal and Group Relations in Educational Administration.** Glenview, Ill.: Scott, Foresman, 1968.

Sax, Gilbert. **Empirical Foundations of Educational Research.** Englewood Cliffs, N.J.: Prentice-Hall, 1968.

Scheffler, Israel. **Conditions of Knowledge: An Introduction to Epistemology and Education.** Glenview, Ill.: Scott, Foresman, 1965.

——— (ed.). **Philosophy and Education: Modern Readings.** Boston: Allyn and Bacon, 1966.

Selakovich, Daniel. **The Schools and American Society.** Waltham, Mass.: Blaisdell, 1967.

Sexton, Patricia. **Education and Income: Inequalities of Opportunity in Our Public Schools.** New York: Viking, 1961.

———. **Spanish Harlem: Anatomy of Poverty.** New York: Harper & Row, 1965.

Shaplin, Judson T., and Henry F. Olds, Jr. (eds.). **Team Teaching.** New York: Harper & Row, 1964.

Shertzer, Bruce, and Shelley C. Stone. **Fundamentals of Guidance.** Boston: Houghton Mifflin, 1966.

Shils, Edward B., and C. Taylor Whittier. **Teachers, Administrators and Collective Bargaining.** New York: Crowell, 1968.

Shulman, Lee S., and Evan R. Keislar (eds.). **Learning by Discovery.** Chicago: Rand McNally, 1966.

Shuster, George N. **Catholic Education in a Changing World.** New York: Holt, Rinehart and Winston, 1967.

Sigel, Irving E., and Frank H. Hooper. **Logical Thinking in Children: Research Based on Piaget's Theory.** New York: Holt, Rinehart, and Winston, 1968.

Simpson, Ray H. **Teacher Self-Evaluation.** New York: Macmillan, 1966.

Skinner, B. F. "The Science of Learning and the Art of Teaching," **Harvard Educational Review,** 24 (Spring 1954), 86–97.

———. **The Technology of Teaching.** New York: Appleton-Century-Crofts, 1968.
Smith, B. Othanel, William O. Stanley, and J. Harlan Shores. **Fundamentals of Curriculum Development.** Rev. ed. New York: Harcourt, Brace & World, 1957.
Smith, Bob. **They Closed Their Schools: Prince Edward County, Virginia, 1951–64.** Chapel Hill: University of North Carolina Press, 1965.
Smith, Karl U., and Margaret Foltz Smith. **Cybernetic Principles of Learning and Educational Design.** New York: Holt, Rinehart and Winston, 1966.
Smith, Louis M., and William Geoffrey. **The Complexities of an Urban Classroom: An Analysis Toward a General Theory of Teaching.** New York: Holt, Rinehart and Winston, 1968.
Spache, George D. **Good Reading for Poor Readers.** Rev. ed. New York: Garrard, 1964.
Stevenson, Harold W. (ed.). **Child Psychology.** Sixty-Second Yearbook of the National Society for the Study of Education, Part I. Chicago: University of Chicago Press, 1963.
Stinnett, T. M. **A Manual on Certification Requirements for School Personnel in the United States.** Washington, D.C.: National Commission on Teacher Education and Professional Standards, National Education Association, 1967.
———. **Turmoil in Teaching.** New York: Macmillan, 1968.
———, and Albert J. Huggett. **Professional Problems of Teachers.** 3rd ed. New York: Macmillan, 1968.
———, Jack H. Kleinmann, and Martha L. Ware. **Professional Negotiation in Public Education.** New York: Macmillan, 1966.
Strom, Robert D. **Teaching in the Slum School.** Columbus, Ohio: Merrill, 1965.
Taba, Hilda. **Curriculum Development: Theory and Practice.** New York: Harcourt, Brace & World, 1962.
———, and Deborah Elkins. **Teaching Strategies for the Culturally Disadvantaged.** Chicago: Rand McNally, 1966.
Terman, Louis, *et al.* **Genetic Studies of Genius.** 5 vols. Stanford, Calif.: Stanford University Press, 1925–1959.
Thayer, V. T., and Martin Levit. **The Role of the School in American Society.** 2nd ed. New York: Dodd, Mead, 1966.
Thomas, George, and Joseph Crescimbeni. **Individualizing Instruction in the Elementary School.** New York: Random House, 1967.
Torrance, E. Paul. **Guiding Creative Talent.** Englewood Cliffs, N.J.: Prentice-Hall, 1962.
Travers, Robert M. W. **Essentials of Learning.** New York: Macmillan, 1967.
Tyack, David B. (ed.). **Turning Points in American Educational History.** Waltham, Mass.: Blaisdell, 1967.
Ulich, Robert. **Education in Western Culture.** New York: Harcourt, Brace & World, 1965.
———. **History of Educational Thought.** New York: American Book, 1950.
Van Til, William, Gordon F. Vars, and John H. Lounsbury. **Modern Education for the Junior High School Years.** 2nd ed. Indianapolis: Bobbs-Merrill, 1967.
Vidick, Arthur J., and Joseph Bensman. **Small Town in Mass Society.** Princeton, N.J.: Princeton University Press, 1958.
Vollmer, Howard M., and Donald L. Mills. **Professionalization.** Englewood Cliffs, N.J.: Prentice-Hall, 1966.
Watson, Goodwin (ed.). **Change in School Systems.** Washington, D.C.: National Training Laboratories, National Education Association, 1967.
Webster, Staten W. (ed.). **The Disadvantaged Learner: Knowing, Understanding, Educating.** San Francisco: Chandler, 1966.

Wesley, Edgar B. **NEA: The First Hundred Years.** New York: Harper & Row, 1957.
Whitehead, Alfred North. **The Aims of Education and Other Essays.** New York: Free Press, 1967.
Wiles, Kimball. **Supervision for Better Schools.** Englewood Cliffs, N.J.: Prentice-Hall, 1967.
Willey, Roy D. **Guidance in Elementary Education.** Rev. ed. New York: Harper & Row, 1966.
Wilson, Robert E. (ed.). **Educational Administration.** Columbus, Ohio: Merrill, 1966.
Winn, Ralph B. **John Dewey: Dictionary of Education.** New York: Philosophical Library, 1959.
Wrenn, C. Gilbert. **The Counselor in the Changing World.** Washington, D.C.: American Personnel and Guidance Association, 1962.
Yamamoto, Kaoru. **Creative Thinking and Peer Conformity in Fifth-Grade Children.** Kent, Ohio: Kent State University, 1965.
Yates, Alfred (ed.). **Grouping in Education.** New York: Wiley, 1966.

index

index

about the author

John F. Ohles, Associate Professor of Secondary Education at Kent State University, received a B.S.Ed. and an M.A. from the University of Minnesota and an Ed.D. from the State University of New York at Buffalo. He has held positions as a high school teacher and guidance counselor as well as professor of education at various universities. In addition to holding membership in national, state, and local professional organizations and in professional and academic honorary societies, Professor Ohles has been a member of accreditation teams for the North Central Association of Schools and Colleges. He has been a prolific writer and has contributed various articles on educational psychology, educational programs in Denmark, and the world of the teacher to journals such as *School and Society, The Journal of Teacher Education, The Clearing House, Education,* and the *Peabody Journal of Education.*